Microsoft

Microsoft
Word 2013 Plain & Simple

Jay Freedman

Published with the authorization of Microsoft Corporation by:
O'Reilly Media, Inc.
1005 Gravenstein Highway North
Sebastopol, California 95472

ISBN: 978-0-7356-6938-3

2 3 4 5 6 7 8 9 10 QG 8 7 6 5 4 3

Printed and bound in the United States of America.

Microsoft Press books are available through booksellers and distributors worldwide. If you need support related to this book, email Microsoft Press Book Support at mspinput@microsoft.com. Please tell us what you think of this book at http://www.microsoft.com/learning/booksurvey.

Microsoft and the trademarks listed at *http://www.microsoft.com/about/legal/en/us/IntellectualProperty/Trademarks/EN-US.aspx* are trademarks of the Microsoft group of companies. All other marks are property of their respective owners.

The example companies, organizations, products, domain names, email addresses, logos, people, places, and events depicted herein are fictitious. No association with any real company, organization, product, domain name, email address, logo, person, place, or event is intended or should be inferred.

This book expresses the author's views and opinions. The information contained in this book is provided without any express, statutory, or implied warranties. Neither the authors, O'Reilly Media, Inc., Microsoft Corporation, nor its resellers, or distributors will be held liable for any damages caused or alleged to be caused either directly or indirectly by this book.

Acquisitions Editor: Kenyon Brown
Developmental Editor: Kathryn Duggan
Production Editor: Kristen Borg
Editorial Production: Peter Amirault
Technical Reviewer: Kristen Merritt
Copyeditor: Bob Russell
Indexers: Fred Brown and Bob Pfahler
Cover Design: Twist Creative • Seattle
Cover Composition: Zyg Group, LLC
Illustrator: S4Carlisle Publishing Services

[2013-05-03]

To Andi, my bashert.

Contents

Acknowledgments xv

1   About this book. **1**

What do you want to do? 2

A quick overview 3

A few assumptions 6

Adapting task procedures for touchscreens. .7

A final word 8

2   Introducing Word 2013 . . . . **9**

What's new in Word 2013 10

Starting the Word program 12

Exploring the ribbon 14

Using the Quick Access Toolbar 16

Switching views. 17

Using built-in keyboard shortcuts 18

Opening documents 20

Editing a PDF document 22

Getting information about a document 23

Saving documents 24

Exporting a document to other file types 26

Recovering lost work 28

Using the Read Mode 30

Managing your online accounts. 32

Printing a document 34

Finding help in Word. 36

Finding help on the Internet. 37

3 Creating and revising documents **39**

Starting a new document 40

Selecting text. 42

Inserting and overtyping text. 44

Copying and moving Items. 45

Managing the Office clipboard 48

Undoing mistaken actions. 49

Navigating a document in the Navigation pane. 50

Navigating by using the search feature 51

Replacing existing text. 54

Using wildcard find and replace. 56

Organizing topics 59

Inserting built-in building blocks. 61

Creating your own building blocks 62

Managing building blocks. 64

4 Correcting and improving the text **67**

Correcting a spelling or grammar error 68

Running a manual spelling or grammar check 70

Marking text to ignore spelling 71

Adding common misspellings to AutoCorrect. 72

Using AutoCorrect entries as shortcuts. 74

Setting AutoFormat options. 76

Getting definitions and synonyms. 79

Counting words. 82

Finding a translation 83

Changing the proofing language of text 86

5 Formatting text for best appearance. **89**

Formatting with styles. 90

Creating and modifying styles 94

Using the Styles pane. 100

Changing the character formatting of text 103

Applying highlighting 105

Using the Format Painter. 106

Changing paragraph alignment and indents. 107

Changing line and paragraph spacing 110

Controlling line and page breaks. 113

Adding borders and shading 116

Building a bulleted or numbered list. 120

Changing the bullets or numbering 121

Changing numbering values. 126

Using multilevel numbered headings 128

Revealing existing formatting. 132

6 **Building impressive documents. 135**

Inserting a section break. 136

Inserting headers and footers 138

Choosing page size and margins. 140

Changing the page orientation 144

Changing the number of columns. 148

Applying a border around a page. 151

Inserting a cover page. 154

Working with the Normal template. 156

Finding and downloading templates. 159

Customizing an existing template 161

Designing a template. 165

Basing a new document on a custom template 168

Designing a template for two-sided printing 170

Using themes and style sets 173

7 **Making layouts with tables and text boxes 179**

Inserting tab stops on the ruler 180

Inserting a simple table. 181

Copying an Excel table into Word 183

Converting text to a table and back again. 184

Setting tab atops in table cells. 186

Adding and deleting rows and columns. 187

Resizing rows and columns. 188

Setting table alignment. 189

Setting table text wrapping 190

Merging and splitting cells. 191

Setting cell alignment and direction. 192

Repeating header rows 193

Using table styles for uniform appearance. 194

Inserting text boxes 196

Linking a chain of text boxes 198

8   Managing data in documents **199**

Using the Field dialog box 200

Inserting fields from the keyboard 202

Toggling field codes and updating fields. 203

Controlling field formatting by using switches 205

Inserting Page and Date fields by using shortcuts 210

Using bookmarks 211

Inserting hyperlinks 212

Repeating information by using cross-references. 216

Inserting content controls. 217

Grouping content controls for a form. 222

Using document properties 223

Sorting a list. 225

9 Formatting reports and formal documents **227**

Making a different first page header or different odd
and even pages header 228

Unlinking a header 232

Extracting text for a header or footer from body text 234

Inserting a watermark 237

Adding footnotes and endnotes 241

Generating a table of contents 243

Updating a table of contents 248

Modifying table of contents styles 249

Using multiple tables of contents 252

Indexing a document 255

Using multiple indexes 258

Making tables of tables and tables of figures 262

Creating a bibliography 264

10 Making pictures work for you **269**

Choosing illustration types 270

Inserting a picture from your computer 274

Inserting an online picture 276

Inserting online video 278

Inserting a screenshot 280

Positioning pictures on the page 282

Resizing a picture 284

Cropping a picture 286

Replacing a picture. 288

Changing the appearance of a picture 290

Removing the background from a picture. 293

Applying special effects. 295

Setting a transparent color 296

11 Adding your own artwork **297**

Inserting a shape 298

Changing the appearance of a shape 300

Building charts to display data. 304

Creating SmartArt diagrams. 308

Adding WordArt effects 312

12 Mailing paper or pixels **315**

Printing a single envelope. 316

Printing multiple copies of an envelope 320

Changing envelope address formatting 323

Creating mailing labels and business cards 326

Sending a document by email 332

Starting a mail merge 334

Choosing the recipients. 337

Adding merge fields. 341

Adding information with rules 343

Finishing the merge 346

13   Reviewing documents **349**

Adding comments 350

Showing and hiding comments 352

Tracking changes 353

Showing and hiding tracked changes 354

Setting options for Track Changes. 356

Accepting and rejecting changes. 358

Comparing reviewed versions 359

Merging reviewed versions. 361

14   Sharing and coauthoring in Word **363**

Exploring Word Web App. 364

Sharing with SkyDrive 370

Working with coauthors 372

Talking to your coauthors 374

Blogging with Word. 375

Presenting a document online 378

15   Ensuring privacy and security **381**

Viewing the Word 2013 Trust Center 382

Changing which files open in Protected View. 383

Adding trusted locations and trusted publishers 387

Setting privacy options 390

Using the Document Inspector 392

Protecting a document by using a password. 394

Restricting editing and formatting 397

Marking a document as read-only or final. 400

Adding a digital signature. 403

16 Installing and using Apps for Office **405**

Adding an app from the Office Store 406

Using an app in a document. 410

17 Customizing Word. **413**

Customizing the screen. 414

Customizing the keyboard 417

Customizing the Quick Access Toolbar. 421

Creating a custom tab or group on the ribbon. 423

Adding tools to a custom group 426

Setting general options. 428

Controlling what is displayed and printed 429

Setting spelling and grammar options 430

Changing the default file format for saving documents 434

Working with advanced options 436

Managing styles 442

Recording macros. 444

Index. 447

About the author 457

Acknowledgments

Every book is the product of many hands, and I thank each person who has helped to create this one. Even if I don't know your name, please know that I'm grateful for your efforts.

Special thanks go to Senior Editor Kenyon Brown of O'Reilly Media for asking me to write Microsoft Word 2013 Plain & Simple. His early guidance and encouragement were invaluable.

Developmental Editor Kathi Duggan made hundreds of excellent suggestions that greatly improved the logical flow of the manuscript, and Technical Reviewer Kristen Merritt played an important role in keeping me on the right path. The three of us make quite a team!

Thanks to Senior Production Editor Kristen Borg and copyeditor Bob Russell, who polished my language and helped me to adhere to Microsoft Press standards. We've given Word's Track Changes feature a good workout!

I've answered thousands of questions about Microsoft Word over nearly twenty years in Internet newsgroups and forums. To every one of you who asked those questions, thank you for the inspiration to learn about the mysteries of Word. I also thank all of the Microsoft Office development team members with whom I've had many fruitful discussions, especially Stuart Stuple, Tristan Davis, and Jonathan Bailor.

Most of all, I thank my wife, Andi Freedman, who thought I had retired months ago. Soon...

About this book

1

Microsoft Office 2013 is like a room full of tool boxes; it's an enormous resource for doing many kinds of jobs that involve information. When you start a project, you should know which box to reach for and what tools it contains. Sometimes you'll need more than one tool—or even more than one tool box—to complete your work.

One of the biggest tool boxes in Office 2013 is Microsoft Word 2013. As a word processor, it's mainly for writing and formatting text, but it doesn't stop there—its tools help you with pictures, videos, charts, and graphs. Although its traditional role is printing paper documents, it can produce webpages, blogs, email, and other kinds of output meant to be read online. There are tools for sharing documents with others as well for working with several people on the same document simultaneously.

The aim of this book is to show you how to choose the right tool in Word 2013 for the job at hand, and how to use each tool quickly and efficiently.

In this section:

- What do you want to do?
- A quick overview
- A few assumptions
- Adapting task procedures for touchscreens
- A final word

What do you want to do?

Among the millions of people who use Word every day, there are beginners and experts, users at home and at school, and in businesses small and large. The work we do, the sources of our information, and the formats of our documents are unimaginably varied.

If you're creating a shopping list, a memo, a court pleading, or a novel, your main interest will likely be in Word's text tools. You might need the ability to write a draft; to reorganize and revise, and to check spelling and grammar; to show the document to others for review, and to act on their suggestions; and to make the document available in one or many formats.

Maybe you design magazine articles, advertisements, newsletters, or posters—documents that depend on illustrations, complex layouts, and eye-catching formatting to give them impact. In addition to Word's text tools, you'll be using its graphics capabilities, building tables to control layout, and working with its special text effects.

Business documents often have unique requirements. They might need to conform to your organization's formatting standards, which should be contained in templates with well-designed styles. They might draw information from spreadsheets or databases through tools such as fields or mail merge. Portions of documents might be used to create other documents. Instruction manuals and policy statements could have very long lives and be revised many times, so you need a way to mark up these documents to show the changes made from one version to the next.

A quick overview

Whatever you're doing in Word 2013, that job is composed of a series of small tasks. This book shows you—step by step, with pictures and simple instructions—how to do each task. When you need to know what to click or type, just look up the task in the table of contents or the index and go to that page. You can jump directly to any task to find the instructions you need for the job you're doing at the time.

Many tasks are accompanied by a *Tip* or *Try This* reader aid that provides a little extra information. Where necessary, you will see a *Caution* to help you avoid mistakes. Because the results of some tasks depend on how you've done other tasks, occasionally there's a *See Also* reference to point to another page.

Although the individual tasks are independent, there is an overall organization to the book, and being aware of it will help you to locate the right page quickly. Each section contains related tasks, roughly in order of increasing complexity.

Section 2 begins with a description of the newest features and enhancements in Word 2013, which will be of interest if you've used an earlier version of Office. The rest of the section shows you how to carry out tasks that you'll do in almost every kind of document: opening, viewing, saving, and printing. It also introduces the new integration of Word 2013 with your Microsoft Account and with online services for storing and sharing your documents. When you need more information than this book can provide, use the Help resources listed at the end of the section.

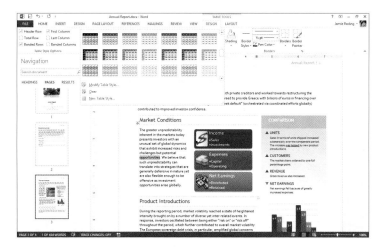

Section 3 guides you through creating new documents, editing text, navigating through your document, outlining and reorganizing topics, and inserting building blocks to reuse content.

Section 4 contains tasks to help you correct and improve your text by checking spelling and grammar, and making the best use of the automatic corrections and formatting features offered by Word. Several tools that are near and dear to the hearts of writers are also covered here, including the dictionary and thesaurus, the word counter, and automated translation to other languages.

Section 5 is about the many formatting tools that Word makes available. Styles are of great importance in Word, so you'll learn how to use, modify, and create them. This section also covers formatting applied directly to parts of the text.

You'll find instructions for setting up lists, managing headers and footers, and revealing the formatting of existing text.

Section 6 describes how to design pages that give your documents more impact. You'll learn how to customize an existing template or create one of your own, and how to change the overall look of a document with just a few mouse clicks.

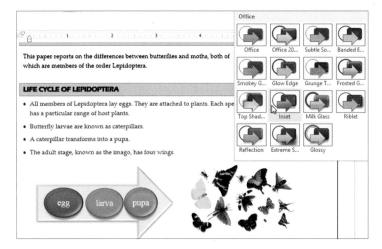

Section 7 describes tables, a feature in Word that has many uses, from simple alignment of columns of text to the creation of complex page layouts. The section closes with tasks for using text boxes.

Section 8 provides you with instructions on how to use the tools in Word 2013 for managing data: hyperlinks, cross references, fields, content controls, and document properties.

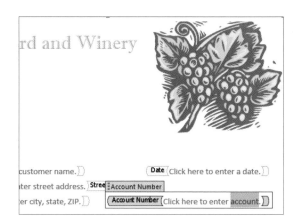

Section 9 is about tools that you might use in longer, more formal documents such as reports. The tasks deal with headers and footers, watermarks, footnotes, tables of contents, indexes, and bibliographies.

Section 10 focuses on pictures and illustrations that come from outside Word. This includes searching for them, inserting them, positioning them in the document, and using tools to edit and enhance them.

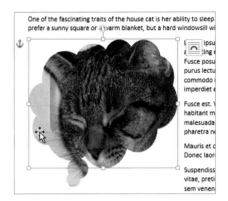

Section 11 shows you how to create artwork directly within a Word document by using the drawing tools, charts, SmartArt diagrams, and WordArt effects.

Section 12 brings together tasks for mailing documents, either printed on paper or sent electronically. Topics include printing envelopes and labels, sending a document by email as an attachment to a message, and the wonders of mail merge.

Section 13 discusses how to mark up a document for review, with comments and tracked changes, and how to compare and combine reviewed copies of a document.

Section 14 is about sharing documents online and collaborating with other Word users on the same document simultaneously. This section also includes tasks for writing blog posts in Word and for hosting an online presentation of your Word document.

Section 15 describes the tools that Word 2013 provides for preventing malware attacks, for avoiding the release of personal information, and for restricting the ability of a document's recipients to make unauthorized changes.

Section 16 covers an exciting new feature of Office 2013 called *Apps for Office*. These web-based programs can interact with your documents to provide up-to-the-minute information, dictionary definitions, fax service, and more.

Section 17 describes some of the ways in which you can customize Word 2013 to fit how you work by controlling what appears on the ribbon and the Quick Access Toolbar, how keyboard shortcuts work, and how Word saves, checks spelling, and more.

A few assumptions

My assumption is that you have at least some experience with Microsoft Windows and possibly some experience with a word processor, either an earlier version of Word or another program. I'm not going to explain fundamentals such as how to use a keyboard and mouse, or how to find a folder on your disk. If the last version of Office you used was 2003 or earlier, however, the ribbon-based interface that was introduced with Office 2007 might seem foreign until you get used to it. If that's the case, you should use the training materials at *office.microsoft.com/en-us/word-help/make-the-switch-to-word-2013-RZ102925062.aspx* to find out where your favorite menu items have gone.

I've also made the assumption that you already have Word 2013 installed on your computer, either as a stand-alone program or as part of Office 2013. If you don't have the other Office programs, a small group of the tasks in this book won't apply, but everything else will be the same. If you haven't installed Office 2013 yet, there are several ways you can get it. In addition to the traditional CD-based package, there is an Internet delivery method that will automatically keep you up to date with the latest patches. Internet delivery is standard for Microsoft Office 365, a subscription plan that accommodates installation on multiple devices.

To install and run Office 2013, you need either Windows 7 or Windows 8. Except for a minor change in the way you start the Word program (described in Section 2), Word 2013 runs identically in both versions of Windows.

To use some of the best new features in Word 2013, you'll need to sign up for a free Microsoft Account, if you don't already have one. Just use your web browser to go to *www. live.com* and click Sign Up Now link. The account gives you access to storage space on SkyDrive, with the ability to share and coauthor with other Word users. You can also open and edit your documents on SkyDrive from any computer, wherever you happen to be—provided, of course, that you have access to the Internet.

The display in Word 2013, especially on the ribbon, changes with the width of the program's window and with the resolution of the screen. As you make the window narrower or the resolution lower, the ribbon first makes some of the buttons smaller, then removes some of the labels, and finally collapses entire groups to a single button. The screenshots in this book were captured at a resolution of 1280×800 pixels, with the Word window maximized. If your computer has different settings, you might not see quite the same display as shown in the screenshots.

Adapting task procedures for touchscreens

In this book, I provide instructions based on traditional keyboard and mouse input methods. If you're using Word on a touch-enabled device, you might be giving commands by tapping with your finger or with a stylus. If so, substitute a tapping action any time I instruct you to click a user interface element. Also note that when I tell you to enter information in Word, you can do so by typing on a keyboard, tapping in the entry field under discussion to display and use the onscreen keyboard, or even speaking aloud, depending on how your computer is set up and your personal preferences.

A final word

I hope you find this book helpful. When I wrote it, I had these goals in mind:

- To provide clear instructions for using Word
- To steer you to things you can do in Word that you didn't know you could do
- To make you a confident Word user

Good luck in your adventures with Word!

Introducing Word 2013

2

In this section:

- What's new in Word 2013
- Starting the Word program
- Exploring the ribbon and Quick Access Toolbar
- Switching views
- Using built-in keyboard shortcuts
- Opening documents
- Editing a PDF document
- Saving documents
- Exporting to other file formats
- Using the Read Mode
- Managing your online accounts
- Printing a document
- Finding help

In designing Word 2013, Microsoft focused on streamlining the user experience by removing or reducing distractions. This section begins with a brief description of the changes the new version brings and a pictorial tour of the Word window.

The rest of the section brings you up to speed on the basic operations of the word processor: opening, editing, saving, and printing documents. Along the way, you'll learn a few new capabilities, such as opening Adobe Portable Document Format (PDF) documents, operating in Read Mode, and connecting to online accounts. Finally, there's a task for finding answers to questions that don't fit into this book by using either the Help feature built into Word or online sources.

What's new in Word 2013

If you've used Word 2010, much of Word 2013 will feel familiar. Most of the commands on the ribbon are in the same places, and many of the dialog boxes haven't changed. A major focus of this version is on making the process of reading and editing documents smoother, with fewer diversions. The icons are simpler, and everything outside the document itself is less attention-grabbing. Of course, there are also new features and new ways of using older features.

When you need to read a document rather than edit it, the new Read Mode is a clean, distraction-free environment. It automatically adapts the width of its columns to the size of your display, which is great if you're using a tablet. You can quickly zoom in on pictures, charts, and tables, or display comments.

If you're working in Print Layout view in a long document, you can easily collapse or expand a heading along with everything within it. This new feature lets you hide unwanted detail until you're ready to see it, without having to switch to Outline view. You can also collapse the ribbon completely, hiding both the command buttons and the tabs.

When you work with tracked changes in a reviewed document, the new Simple Markup view reduces the clutter and makes it easier for you concentrate on specific changes and comments.

If you log on to Office with a Microsoft Account, your list of recently used documents is stored in the cloud. No matter what computer you use to log on, that information is available. The cloud also remembers the last page you were reading when you closed each online document and offers to pick up where you left off. Opening and saving documents on SkyDrive or SharePoint is seamless, and you can integrate Office with other online services.

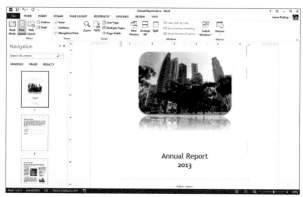

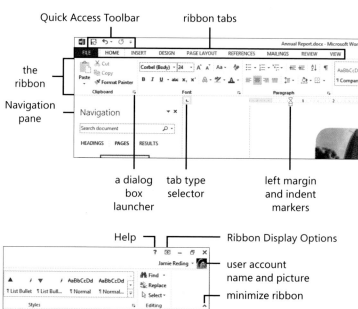

Quick Access Toolbar — ribbon tabs

the ribbon

Navigation pane

a dialog box launcher — tab type selector — left margin and indent markers

Help — Ribbon Display Options

user account name and picture

minimize ribbon

horizontal ruler

right margin marker

The online integration of Office 2013 also improves your ability to share documents and to collaborate with other authors on the same document, either separately or at the same time. You can contact the others directly from within Word via email, instant messenger, or phone.

Word 2013 can open most PDF documents so that you can edit or reformat the contents and save the result as a Word document or back to PDF, among other formats.

You can embed online videos right in your documents and watch them within Word. Also, you can insert online pictures directly into documents without having to save them to your computer first.

As you drag pictures and tables in a document, the text around them instantly reflows, giving you better control over the final position. Alignment guides automatically appear to help you line up images with the page margins and text paragraphs on the page.

This version also updates the free online Word Web App to align it with Word 2013 on the desktop.

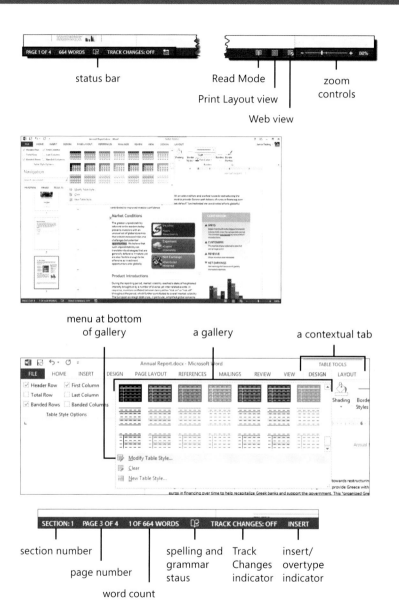

status bar

Read Mode

zoom controls

Print Layout view

Web view

menu at bottom of gallery

a gallery

a contextual tab

a collapsed comment

selected text

table's Move box

section number

page number

word count

spelling and grammar staus

Track Changes indicator

insert/ overtype indicator

Starting the Word program

Sometimes, you'll want to start the Word program with a blank document that you'll just need to fill in. At other times, you might want Word to start with a document that already exists in a file so that you can read it or make changes to it.

Both Windows 7 and Windows 8 make extensive use of *shortcuts*, which are icons that point to files. Some shortcuts point to programs and others point to documents. In Windows 7, shortcuts to programs are usually on the Start menu, but you can also place them on the desktop, pin them to the taskbar, or both. In Windows 8, you'll find a *tile* for each of the Microsoft Office programs on the Start screen, and you can also create

shortcuts to the programs on the desktop or the desktop's taskbar.

If you start Word without instructing it as to what document to open, it creates a blank document for you.

To start Word with an existing document, you usually open the File Explorer and double-click the icon of the document itself. When you have a document that you open frequently, it's useful to make a shortcut to the document and place the shortcut on the desktop or the taskbar.

Use the Word shortcut in Windows 7

1 Click the Start menu.

2 Click All Programs.

3 Scroll to the Microsoft Office 2013 folder and expand it.

4 Click Word 2013.

Use the Word shortcut in Windows 8

1 Click the Start box.

2 Click the tile for Word 2013.

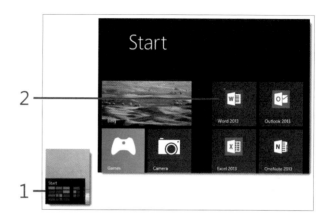

Use a document's icon

1 Start the file manager (called Windows Explorer in Windows 7 and File Explorer in Windows 8).

2 Go to the folder that contains the document that you want to use.

3 Double-click the document's icon.

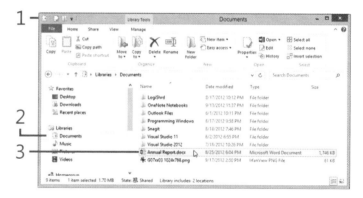

TRY THIS Create a desktop shortcut to a document: Right-click the icon of a document you use frequently. In the options menu that appears, point to Send To and click Desktop (Create Shortcut). Double-click the document shortcut to start Word.

Exploring the ribbon

The ribbon is the broad swath of tabs and command buttons that occupies the top of the Word window. As you click each of the tabs, the ribbon displays the items in that category. Some buttons invoke commands that take effect immediately when you click them, whereas others open a *gallery* of items from which you can choose.

When you select certain kinds of objects in a document—for example, a header, a picture, or a table—the ribbon displays a *contextual tab* that contains commands specific to that type of object. The contextual tab stays visible only as long as the object remains selected.

Find common commands

1 Click each of the tabs in turn.

2 Point to each command button on the displayed ribbon and read the name and short description of the command in the ToolTip that appears.

3 If the command button shows a downward-pointing triangular arrow (also referred to as a down-arrow), click the arrow to view its associated gallery.

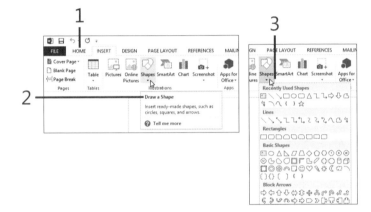

TRY THIS To get more space for the document, you can collapse the ribbon to just the row of tabs. Double-click any tab to minimize the ribbon; do the same to expand it once again. Single-click a tab on the minimized ribbon to open that tab. The ribbon automatically minimizes again when you click a command button.

TIP Many galleries end with one or more menu items, which you should explore, as well.

Use a contextual tab

1 Click the Insert tab.

2 In the Header & Footer group, click Header.

3 At the bottom of the gallery, click Edit Header.

4 Explore the Header & Footer Tools | Design contextual tab, which appears only while the cursor is in the header or footer pane.

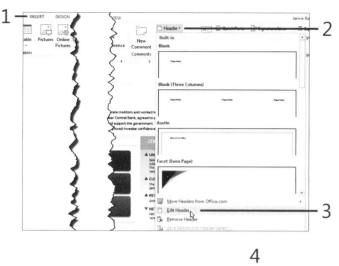

Hide the ribbon

1 In the upper-right corner of the Word window, click the Ribbon Display Options icon.

2 Click the Auto-Hide ribbon item.

3 If you want to display the ribbon to use just a few commands, in the upper-right corner, click the three dots.

When you click in the document text, the ribbon automatically hides again.

4 If you want to show the entire ribbon all the time or to show just the tabs, click the Ribbon Display Options icon again and click the option that you want.

cursor in header

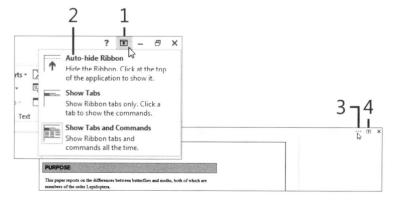

> **SEE ALSO** For information about putting your favorite tools in more convenient locations on the ribbon, see "Creating a custom tab or group on the ribbon" on page 423 and "Adding tools to a custom group" on page 426.

Using the Quick Access Toolbar

The Quick Access Toolbar is an easily customized place to put command buttons that you use frequently. You don't have to select a tab first, because buttons on the Quick Access Toolbar are always visible. With just a couple of clicks you can add or delete buttons on the toolbar, so you can use it to gather the commands for a special task and remove them when they are no longer needed.

The first time you use Word, the Quick Access Toolbar appears above the ribbon. At this point, it holds just a few buttons. To make it more easily accessible, you can move it below the ribbon.

Add a command to the toolbar

1 On the ribbon, right-click a command button or a group title.

2 Click Add To Quick Access Toolbar.

Remove a command from the toolbar

1 On the Quick Access Toolbar, right-click a command button.

2 Click Remove From Quick Access Toolbar.

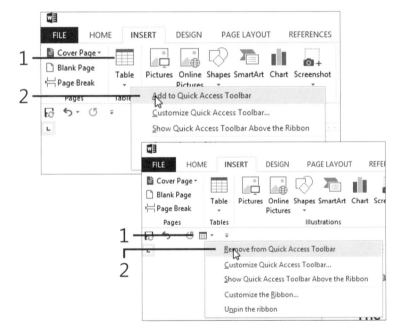

TRY THIS Click the down-arrow at the right end of the Quick Access Toolbar. Select or clear the listed commands and click Show Below Ribbon.

SEE ALSO For information about adding commands that don't appear on the ribbon and adding commands for specific documents, see "Customizing the Quick Access Toolbar" on page 421.

Switching views

Word 2013 offers many ways to look at your document. The default view is Print Layout, in which you can see how the document will look on paper. Web Layout view shows the document as a webpage, without the conventional page breaks of a printed document. In Outline view, the headings form an outline. You can expand or collapse each section and reorganize topics by dragging them to new positions.

Read Mode is optimized for reading the text in documents on your screen. Objects such as pictures, tables, and comments become smaller or collapse to icons, although you can double-click them to view them at full size.

Use the View tab on the ribbon

1 Open a document that contains an assortment of headings that use the built-in styles.

2 On the View tab, in the Views group, click Outline.

3 Click Web Layout.

4 Click Read Mode.

5 To return to the most recently used view, in the View menu, click Edit Document.

2

1

3

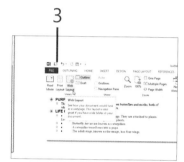

4

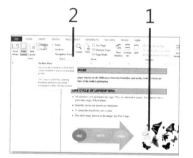

5

TRY THIS   In Print Layout view, move the cursor onto a heading paragraph. When a triangle appears in the left margin, click it to collapse or expand the text and lower-level headings under it, similar to the behavior of the Outline view.

TIP   You can reach the Read Mode, Print Layout, and Web views by clicking the buttons on the status bar, located to the left of the zoom controls.

Using built-in keyboard shortcuts

With all the command buttons on the ribbon and those that you can add to the Quick Access Toolbar, it's tempting to reach for the mouse for almost every action you can do in Word. However, for those folks who more often use a keyboard and mouse to input a lot of text, it's much quicker to use keyboard shortcuts.

Word 2013 has two separate sets of shortcuts: one set reflects the names of the command buttons on the ribbon, whereas the other set—also used by older versions of Word—covers more commands and is customizable.

Use keyboard shortcuts

1 Press and release the Alt key to display *keytips*.

Keytips are letters and numbers that represent the ribbon tabs and the buttons on the Quick Access Toolbar. Press the letter for the tab that you want, and more keytips appear for the commands on that tab.

2 Press the letter or letters for the command that you want.

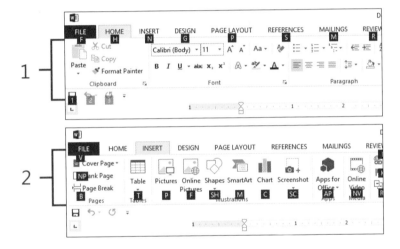

Keyboard shortcuts for common commands

Command	Keyboard shortcut
Open a document	Ctrl+O
Save a document	Ctrl+S
Close a document but leave Word running	Ctrl+W
Copy the selection	Ctrl+C
Cut the selection	Ctrl+X
Paste the clipboard contents	Ctrl+V
Hide or show the ribbon	Ctrl+F1
Apply bold direct formatting	Ctrl+B
Apply italic direct formatting	Ctrl+I
Apply single underline direct formatting	Ctrl+U
Left-align a paragraph	Ctrl+L
Center-align a paragraph	Ctrl+E
Right-align a paragraph	Ctrl+R
Undo the last command	Ctrl+Z
Redo the last command	Ctrl+Y
Apply the Normal style	Ctrl+Shift+N
Print the document	Ctrl+P
Open the Help box	F1

TIP This table lists just a few of the more common built-in shortcuts. To learn about other shortcuts that you might find useful, press F1 (to display the Help box) and open the article "Keyboard Shortcuts for Microsoft Word."

SEE ALSO For information about assigning your own keyboard shortcuts, see "Customizing the keyboard" on page 417.

Opening documents

When you click the File tab, Word displays *the Backstage view*. The Backstage view is a set of pages containing information and commands that deal with the document or the program as a whole, such as opening, saving, and printing documents; managing accounts; and setting options that affect the entire program.

While the Word program is running, you can open more than one document at the same time. Each document has its own

icon on the taskbar, which makes it simple to switch from one document to another (or you can use the Switch Windows button on the View tab). You can also easily copy text and graphics from one document to another.

If you've connected your Office suite to your Microsoft Account, you can open documents stored on SkyDrive as if they were on a local disk. If you have access to a SharePoint Server, you can use it for storage in the same way.

Open a document from the Backstage view

1 On the ribbon, click File and then click Open.

2 If the document you want is in the Recent Documents list, click its name or icon to open the document immediately. Otherwise, continue with steps 3 to 7.

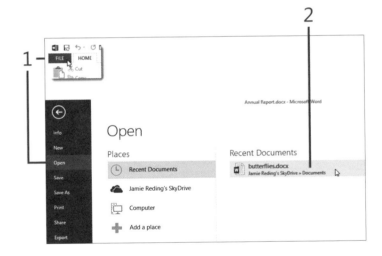

TIP Word 2013 can open many kinds of document files. Besides the default .docx format, you can select many others, including Word 97–2003 (.doc), Word template (.dotx, .dotm, and .dot), rich text format (.rtf), plain text (.txt), and OpenDocument Text (.odt) files.

3 If the file you want to open isn't in the Recent Documents list, click either Computer or your SkyDrive account.

4 Click Browse.

5 Navigate to the proper folder.

6 Select the document that you want.

7 Click Open.

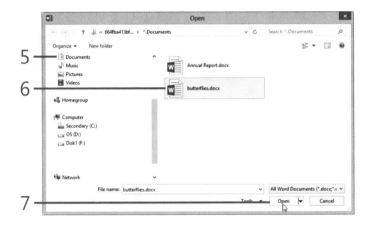

> **✓ TIP** If the document you open was created in a previous version of Word, the title bar of the Word window displays [Compatibility Mode] after the document's file name. When that happens, some of the new features of Word 2013 are disabled to preserve compatibility with the older version. To bring the document up to the 2013 format, click File, Info, and then Convert.

Editing a PDF document

In Word 2013, you can open a PDF file, get the text and pictures from it, and display it as an editable document. That's convenient when you need to reuse material that is available only in the normally uneditable PDF form.

Open a PDF file in Word

1 Click File and then click Open.

2 Click Computer or your SkyDrive account and then click Browse.

3 Click the file-type drop-down list.

4 Click PDF Files (*.pdf).

5 Select the document that you want and then click Open.

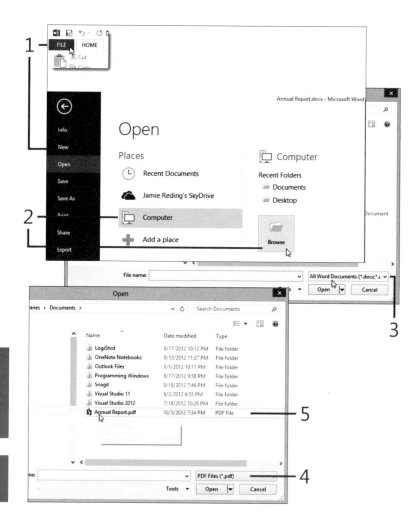

 TIP If the document content appears but isn't editable, the PDF file contains a picture of the text instead of the text itself. Word can't convert pictures to text (this a process called Optical Character Recognition or OCR), but Microsoft OneNote might be able to do that for you.

 TIP After you edit the document, you can save it as either a Word document file or a PDF file.

Getting information about a document

A Word file contains information about how the document was created and modified as well as optional data that can help you find the file later. You can see this information on the Info page of the Backstage view. You can add or change text in some of the document's properties, such as the Subject and Tags entries.

Other properties, such as the document's time and date of creation, are readable but not editable.

Use the Info page

1 Click File and then click Info.

2 Click the Show All Properties link.

3 Move the cursor over each property value. When the cursor is over an editable property, the cursor changes from an arrow to an I-beam and a box appears around the property's value. Click the box to activate it for input.

4 Enter text in an editable property.

5 Save the document.

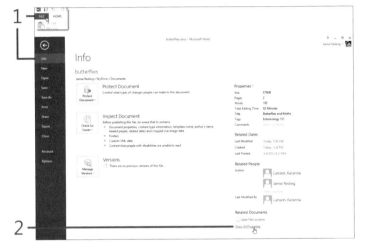

> **TIP** You can use the properties Subject, Categories, and Tags in the search box in File Explorer to locate files with specific values. For example, searching for **tags:biography** finds all documents that have a Tags property containing the word "biography."

Saving documents

Before you save a document for the first time, it exists only in the computer's memory and has a fake file name of **Document** followed by a number. When you do save the document for the first time, Word 2013 displays the Save As dialog box in which you can choose the folder and file name you want.

If you edit an existing document and save it in the same folder and with the same file name as before, it will replace whatever was previously in the file. To keep both the old version and the new version, you have to either give the new version a unique name or choose a different folder, or both.

Save a document for the first time

1 On the Quick Access Toolbar, click the Save button.

2 Under Places, click a location such as Computer or your SkyDrive account.

3 Click the folder you want if it appears in the Recent Folders list or click Browse to locate another folder.

4 Type the file name that you want.

5 Click Save.

> **TIP** The complete file path can be up to 260 characters long, including the drive letter, all the folders and subfolders, the file's name and extension, and the backslashes between the parts. Be aware that you can't use any of the following characters in a file name: \ / ? : * " > < |

> **TIP** After the first time you save the document, no dialog box will appear when you click Save. You might see a progress indicator in the status bar for a brief moment. It's an excellent idea to press Ctrl+S every time you stop to think about what to write next so that you won't accidentally lose the work you've already done.

Save a new version

1 Click File and then click Save As.

The Save As dialog box opens.

2 Choose a different folder from the current folder if you want to keep the same file name or choose the current folder if you plan to use a different file name.

3 Change the file name if you selected the current folder.

4 Click Save.

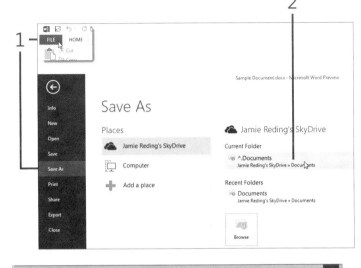

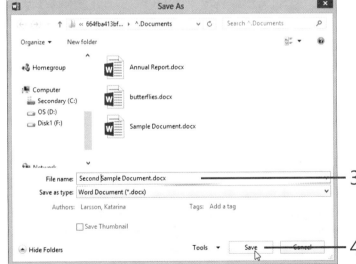

🔍 **SEE ALSO** For information about retrieving an unsaved document that you accidentally closed, see "Recovering lost work" on page 28.

Exporting a document to other file types

With Word 2013, you can save documents in many different formats beyond the default (.docx). In particular, you can save a document in the .doc format used by versions from Word 97 through Word 2003.

If you plan to send copies to other people who don't need to edit them, the Portable Document Format (PDF) is a good choice, because almost every computer has a viewer for it. The XML Paper Specification (XPS) has a similar purpose. Although support for XPS isn't as widespread as that of PDF, all Windows 7 and Windows 8 computers can view it.

Export to PDF or XPS format

1 Click File and then click Export.

2 Click Create PDF/XPS.

The Publish As PDF OR XPS dialog box opens.

3 Select the folder in which you want to save the exported file.

4 Accept the suggested name or enter a new name for the exported file.

5 If you want to save the file as something other than what's shown in Save As Type, select the desired file type from the drop-down list.

6 Change the options as needed.

7 Click Publish.

> **TIP** Click the Options button to open a dialog box in which you can choose which pages to include, whether to include markup, and whether to protect the exported PDF file with a password.

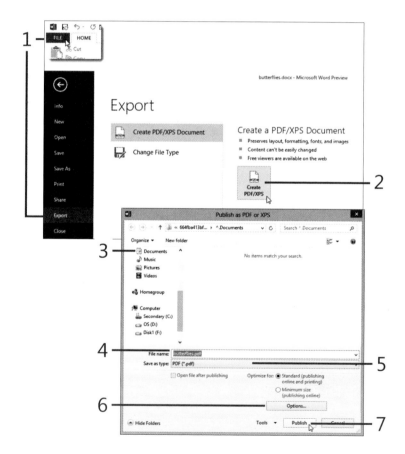

Change the file type

1 Click File and then click Save As.

The Save As dialog box opens.

2 Click the location, such as Computer or your SkyDrive, and click the desired folder or click Browse to choose a different folder.

3 Accept the suggested name or enter a new name for the file.

4 Click the Save As Type drop-down list and select the file type you want.

5 Click Save.

6 If the file type you choose doesn't support all of the Word features used in the document, respond to the Compatibility Checker dialog box or the warning message.

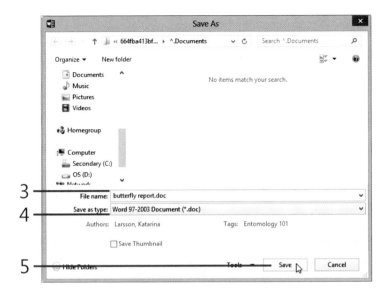

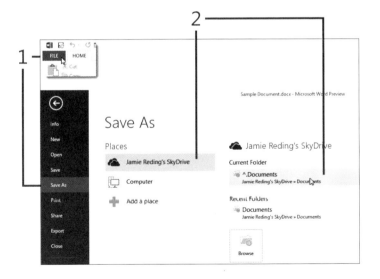

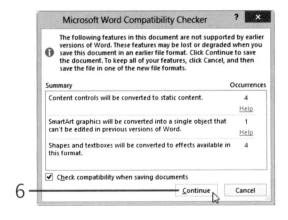

Recovering lost work

Have you ever suffered a power failure while you were working on a document, or accidentally clicked No instead of Yes when prompted to save your document while closing it? The good news is that with Word 2013, you can almost always get your work back!

Word has an AutoRecover feature that saves your document in the background at regular intervals. If your computer shuts down or crashes while Word is open, the automatically saved document is available when you restart Word. If you shut down Word normally, the AutoRecover file is deleted.

There's another option to help you avoid losing work. If you close a document that has changed, and you choose not to save it, Word saves a copy of the file. If you realize you made a mistake, even weeks later, you can open the file.

Configure AutoRecover

1 Click File and then click Options.

   The Word Options dialog box opens.

2 Click Save.

3 Select the Save AutoRecover Information and the Keep The Last Autosaved Version check boxes.

4 Set the AutoRecover interval to a time short enough that you probably wouldn't mind having to redo that much work. The default is 10 minutes, but you might want a shorter interval.

5 Click OK.

> ⚠️ **CAUTION** If you close an unsaved document before the first AutoRecover interval ends, there won't be any autosaved file. That's a good reason to set a short interval.

Open unsaved documents

1 Click File and then click Info.

2 Click Manage Versions and click Recover Unsaved Documents.

The open dialog box appears.

3 Double-click the autosaved file that you want.

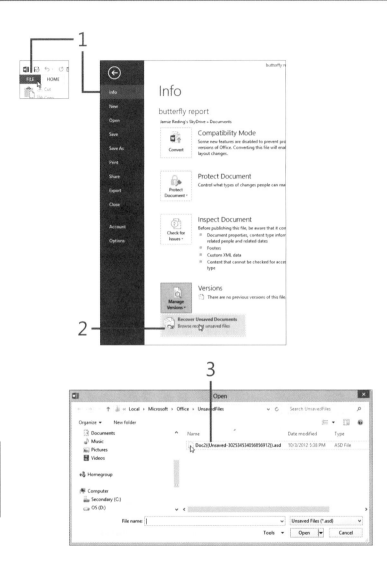

TIP On the Advanced page of Options, there is a separate option to store the previously saved copy of the document each time you save again. The saved copy is renamed as Backup of <*your filename*> with an extension of .wbk.

Using the Read Mode

The Read Mode in Word 2013 is more than just another view. It reformats the text into two or more columns, makes some pictures and tables smaller, hides the editing tools, and makes any markup less visible. This lets you focus on the text while you're reading, but you can expand any item when you need to.

Navigate in Read Mode

1 If the document is not already in Read Mode, on the View menu, in the Views group, click Read Mode.

2 Click the screen-change icon at the right or left edge of the screen to "page" or move by one screenful.

3 On the View menu, click Navigation Pane.

The pane works the same way as in other views.

4 On the View menu, click Edit Document to return to the most recent view (or click the Print Layout icon on the status bar, or press Esc).

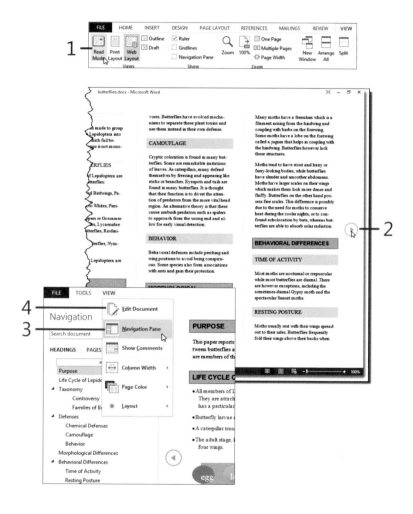

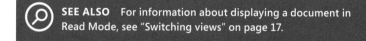

> **SEE ALSO** For information about displaying a document in Read Mode, see "Switching views" on page 17.

Expand objects

1 Double-click a picture or table in Read Mode.

2 Click the arrow icon to expand the object further, or click outside the object to return to the normal display.

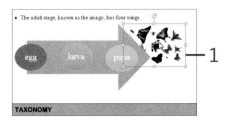

Managing your online accounts

When you install Office 2013, it prompts you to attach either a Microsoft Account or an account for your work or school. When you do that, the Office applications let you open and save documents in your SkyDrive space or SharePoint Server. They also give you access to the other services for that account, including file sharing, email, and roaming of Office settings. You can add connections to other social networks, including Facebook,

LinkedIn, and Twitter. If you have two or more accounts—for instance, one at home and one at work—you can attach both of them and switch between them at any time.

If your computer runs Windows 7, you can use Office 2013 without attaching a Microsoft Account. If you run Windows 8, Office 2013 automatically attaches your Windows logon account.

Sign in to a user account

1 Click File and then click Account.

2 If there is no account attached to Office 2013, and if you already have an account, click Sign In and then proceed to step 5.

3 Click either the Microsoft Account item or the Organization Or School item.

4 If Word is already logged on to an account but you want to use a different account, click the Switch Account link.

5 Enter the email address and password for the account that you want to use.

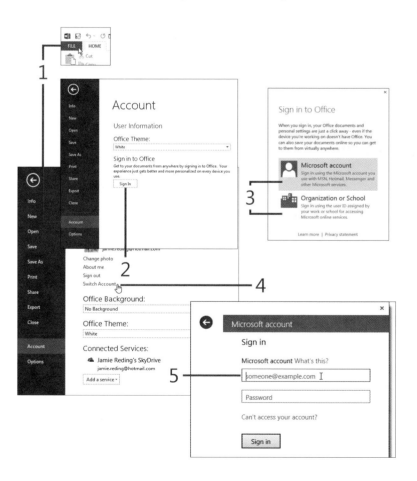

Connect to online services

1 Click File and then click Account.

2 Click the Add A Service button.

3 Point to one of the categories and click the service that you want to add.

4 Click the Connect button to open your web browser to a page on the selected service on which you can authorize access to your account on the selected service.

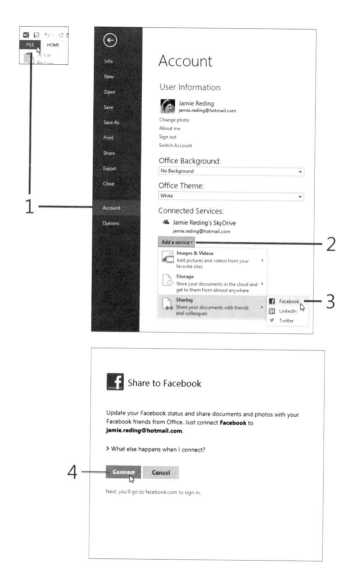

Printing a document

In the early days of word processing, the final stage of almost every document was printing on paper. Although electronic distribution has become far more important for many documents, printing is still a major function of Word 2013.

The Print page in the Backstage view has many settings that affect what will be printed. Here you can select the printer, which pages to print, how many pages to print on each sheet, and more. Some settings, including orientation, page size, and margins, can be set here or on the Page Layout tab on the ribbon.

You might sometimes want to print a document as a folded booklet. Word can automatically reorder the pages so they print in the proper places. Although it can take several steps to get it right, you can do it!

Choose a printer

1 Click File and then click Print.

2 If you want to use a different printer than the one selected, click the Printer box and choose from the drop-down list.

3 If necessary, click Printer Properties and select settings there.

   The printer driver software for the current printer creates the Printer Properties dialog box, so the dialog boxes supplied by various manufacturers are different.

Print part of a document

1 To print specific pages, enter their page numbers in the Pages text box. You can specify individual pages by separating them with commas, as in **1,3,4,8**. You can request a group of pages by entering the first and last page numbers separated by a dash, as in **12-15**. You can also combine these methods, as in **1,3,12-15**.

> **TIP** If the document has multiple sections in which page numbering is restarted, you must combine the page number and the section number, as in **p1s3-p4s3** to print pages 1 through 4 in section 3.

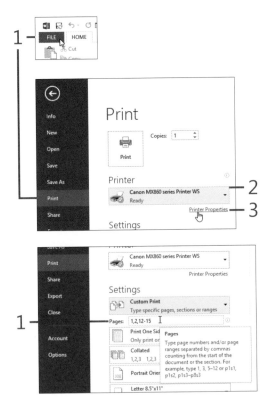

Print a booklet

1 On the Page Layout tab, in the Page Setup group, click Margins and then click Custom Margins at the bottom of the gallery.

2 Click the Multiple Pages drop-down list and choose Book Fold.

3 If the document is large, you should print it in small groups to make them easier to fold and bind. Click the Sheets Per Booklet drop-down list and choose a value such as 4 or 8.

4 Click OK.

5 Click File and then click Print.

6 If Print One Sided is selected, change it to Print On Both Sides.

7 If the document is in Portrait orientation, the Book Fold setting changes the printer orientation to Landscape and turns the page images to read correctly. Don't change this setting.

8 Click Print.

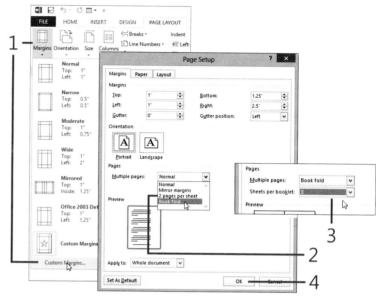

> ⚠️ **CAUTION** Before you print many sheets, output a test print to determine whether the printer orients the page on the back of the sheet correctly. If not, use the Printer Properties dialog box to change the duplex printing from short-edge binding to long-edge binding, or vice versa.

> 🔍 **SEE ALSO** For information about setting page size and orientation, see "Choosing page size and margins" on page 140 and "Changing the page orientation" on page 144.

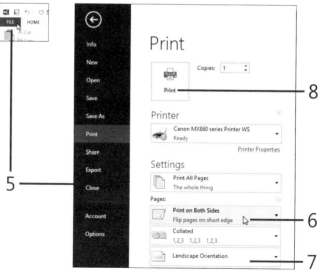

Finding help in Word

Microsoft Office 2013 installs an extensive Help system along with the software itself that you can use for assistance even if you're not connected to the Internet. When you are connected, you can access the Office Online help, which is both larger and more up-to-date.

Use the Help feature in Word

1 Press F1 or click the question mark in the title bar of the Word window or any dialog box.

2 If the word OFFLINE appears in the Help dialog box while you're connected to the Internet, click the arrow and choose Word Help from Office.com.

3 Click one of the listed topics or enter a word or phrase in the Search Help box and then click the magnifying-glass icon.

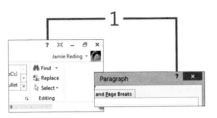

Finding help on the Internet

The Internet is a resource far larger than any help file on your computer. You can find tutorials, answer sites, forums, and templates to help you with almost anything that you want to do in Word 2013.

- In your browser, use a web search engine to look for information about Word 2013.

- Visit a site such as *http://answers.microsoft.com* and search for questions and answers about a topic.

- Visit *http://office.microsoft.com* and click Templates in the navigation bar. Look for templates suitable for the task you want to do.

Creating and revising documents

3

Are you ready to write something new? Whether it's a novel, a shopping list, a short memo, or a long report, you'll probably start with an empty page. In this section, you'll learn how to open a new Microsoft Word 2013 document and begin entering text. You'll also learn how to revise your text, including moving elements around and replacing one word or phrase with another.

Additionally, you'll often find that there are bits of text that can be used over and over. Word can store those pieces as building blocks. Then, you can easily insert them where they're needed.

In this section:

- Starting a new document
- Selecting text
- Inserting and overtyping text
- Copying and moving text
- Managing the Office clipboard
- Undoing mistaken actions
- Navigating a document
- Finding and replacing text
- Using wildcard find and replace
- Organizing topics
- Inserting and creating building blocks
- Managing building blocks

Starting a new document

When you start Word 2013 from the program's shortcut, it opens with a new blank document already in place. That document is based on a special template named Normal.dotm. You can think of a template as an empty "container" document that has many styles and formats already defined, such as page size, fonts, text sizes, heading styles, colors, and so on. When you start with a template, all you really need to do is "pour" your text into the document by typing or pasting it from other sources. When Word is already running, you can create more documents based on Normal.dotm or based on any other template.

When a document is *based on* a template, it inherits that template's styles and any text that is in the template. Changes you make in the document don't change anything in the template unless you take special steps to make that happen.

Enter text in a new blank document

1 Start Word from its shortcut or from a document's shortcut.

2 If an existing document is open, create a new blank document by clicking File to open the Backstage view. Next, select New and then click Blank Document.

3 On the Home tab, in the Paragraph group, click Show/Hide ¶.

This makes nonprinting characters and symbols such as spaces, paragraph marks, and tabs visible in your document. If you no longer need to see these marks, click the same tool again to remove the characters from view.

4 Type some text.

Press the Enter key only at the end of a paragraph, not at the end of each line. Word automatically moves text to the next line when necessary.

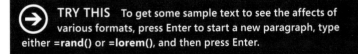

TRY THIS To get some sample text to see the affects of various formats, press Enter to start a new paragraph, type either =rand() or =lorem(), and then press Enter.

3   4

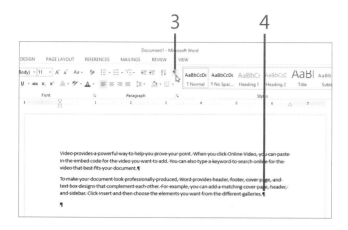

Start with a template

1 Click File to display the Backstage view and then click New.

This page of the Backstage view shows some templates that are stored on your computer as well as others that are supplied online from Office.com.

2 Browse through these templates and click one that you want to use such as Invoice or Student Report. If none of the visible templates are appropriate for the document you want to create, in the Search Online Templates box, type a word or phrase and press Enter.

3 When the template's preview appears, click Create.

SEE ALSO For more information about starting Word, see "Starting the Word program" on page 12. For more information about the content of a new blank document, see "Working with the Normal template" on page 156.

SEE ALSO For more information about getting or creating more templates, see "Finding and downloading templates" on page 159 and "Designing a template" on page 165.

Selecting text

Many things you do in Word 2013 require you to select the text that you want to manipulate. That's true for copying text, formatting text, replacing text with different words, applying styles, and so on. Because selecting is so fundamental, Word offers several ways to do it. You can use the method that best suits your needs and with which you're most comfortable.

Select text by using the mouse

1 To select a small amount of text, click and hold the mouse button at the beginning of the text that you want to select, drag to the end of the text, and then release the mouse button.

2 To select more than one screenful of text, click and release the mouse button at the beginning of the text to be selected. Use the vertical scroll bar (or the mouse's scroll wheel, if it has one) to move through the document. While holding down the Shift key, click the mouse button at the end of the text to be selected.

3 To select a single word, double-click anywhere in the word.

4 To select a sentence, hold down the Ctrl key while you click anywhere in the sentence.

5 To select a line, move the mouse cursor into the left margin next to the line and click there.

6 To select a paragraph, move the mouse cursor into the left margin next to the paragraph and double-click there.

7 To select everything in the main body of the document (not including headers, footers, footnotes, and endnotes), on the Home tab, in the Editing group, click Select and then click Select All.

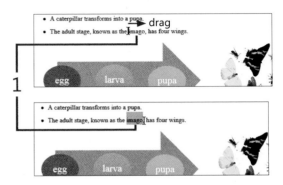

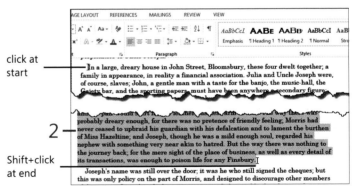

TIP   To deselect any selection, just click once anywhere in the document.

TRY THIS   Select some text. Then, hold down the Ctrl key while you select some text elsewhere on the page. This "non-contiguous selection" can be used to apply the same formatting to multiple places all at once, without affecting everything in between.

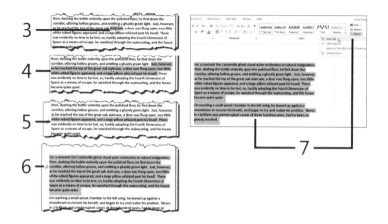

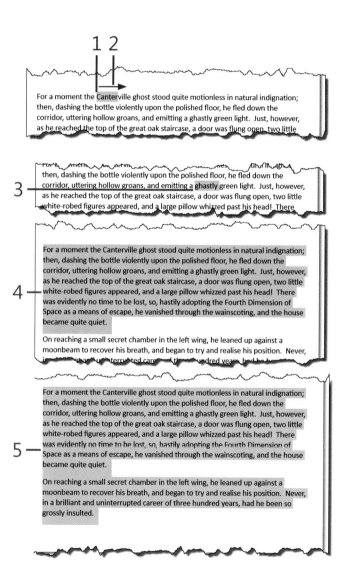

Select by using the keyboard

1 Using the mouse or arrow keys, place the text cursor at the beginning of the text to be selected.

2 Hold down the Shift key while you use the arrow keys to move to the end of the desired selection.

3 To select a word, hold down both the Ctrl and Shift keys while pressing the left or right arrow key.

4 To select a paragraph, hold down both the Ctrl and Shift keys while pressing the up or down arrow key.

5 To select everything in the main body of the document (not including headers, footers, footnotes, or endnotes), press Ctrl+A.

> **TRY THIS** The F8 key turns on Extend Mode. Press F8 once and move the cursor with the mouse or arrow keys, and Word will select continuously until you press Esc. Press F8 twice to select the current word, a third time to select the current sentence, a fourth time to select the current paragraph, and a fifth time to select the entire main document.

Inserting and overtyping text

When you place the text cursor within existing text and start to type, you usually want the new text to push the old text to the right or down. Word calls this *Insert mode*. If you want to have each new character replace the next existing character, you can use *Overtype mode*. You can easily switch between the two modes.

Switch between Insert and Overtype

1 Right-click the status bar.

2 In the options menu that opens, click Overtype.

  A check mark appears next to it.

3 On the status bar, see whether the indicator displays Insert or Overtype.

4 Press the Insert key or click the indicator in the status bar to toggle back and forth between Insert mode and Overtype mode.

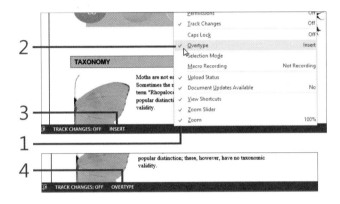

> ✓ **TIP** If pressing the Insert key doesn't change the mode, click File, choose Options, click Advanced, and then select the Use The Insert Key To Control Overtype Mode check box. Click OK to save the change.

Copying and moving Items

You might need to copy a piece of text, a picture, or other item and repeat it in various places within the same document, in a different document, or even in a different Microsoft Office program. Or, you might want to remove (*cut*) the item from its original location and paste it elsewhere.

Windows provides a virtual area for the temporary storage of an item that you copy or cut that's called the *clipboard*. You can paste an item that's on the clipboard into many other locations. Be aware that the Windows clipboard stores only one item at a time; if you copy or cut anything else, the previous content is

overwritten by the new content. Office provides a separate clipboard that can hold up to 24 items, but its contents are available only to Office programs.

When you paste text into Word 2013 from either the Windows clipboard or the Office clipboard, you can choose how to format it. Further, if the item on the clipboard is a picture, chart, Microsoft Excel worksheet, or anything other than text, you can control how the pasted copy behaves by using the Paste Special command.

Copy or cut an item

1 Select the item that you want to copy or cut.

2 On the Home tab, in the Clipboard group, click either Copy (shortcut, Ctrl+C) or Cut (shortcut, Ctrl+X).

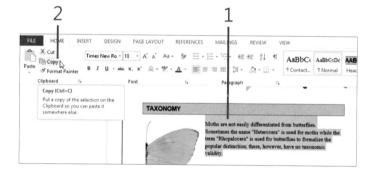

Paste an item

1 Click in the same document—or another document—at the desired location.

2 On the Home tab, in the Clipboard group, click the Paste button (shortcut, Ctrl+V).

3 If you need to change the appearance of the pasted text, click the Paste Options button next to the pasted text and choose one of the following options:

• Keep Source Formatting to apply only the formatting of the text as it was copied.

• Merge Formatting to combine the formatting of the source and the destination. For example, if the source was italic and the destination is bold, Merge Formatting makes the pasted text both italic and bold.

• Keep Text Only to discard the source formatting and apply only the formatting that has been applied at the destination.

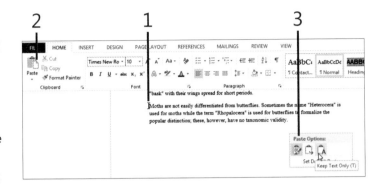

Use Paste Special

1 In Excel, enter some sample data in a worksheet and copy the data to the clipboard.

2 In your Word document, click where you want the copied Excel data to appear.

3 Click the down-arrow at the bottom of the Paste button and click Paste Special.

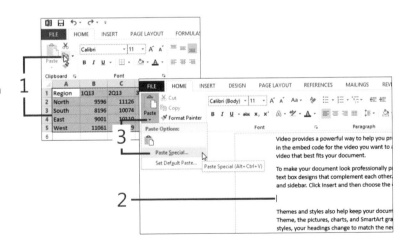

4 Click Paste Link, select Microsoft Excel Worksheet Object, and then click OK.

5 Right-click the table. In the shortcut menu that opens, point to Linked Worksheet Object, and then click Edit Link to go back to the worksheet in Excel.

6 Change some of the data in Excel.

Observe that the changes you make in Excel automatically appear in the linked table in Word.

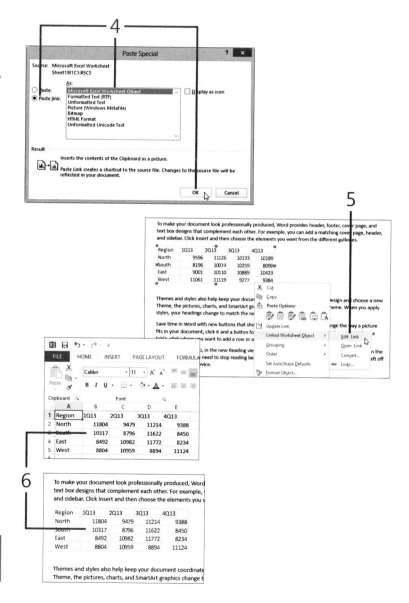

 TIP The list of formats offered in the Paste Special dialog box varies, depending on what type of object is in the clipboard.

Managing the Office clipboard

Unlike the Windows clipboard, the Office clipboard can collect up to 24 items that you copy or cut. If you exceed 24 items, the oldest item in the clipboard is discarded, replaced by the item that you just copied or cut. You can paste one or more of those items in any order, or paste all of them at once.

Paste from the Office clipboard

1 On the Home tab, in the Clipboard group, click the dialog box launcher (the small arrow icon in the lower-right corner).

2 In the Clipboard pane, click the down-arrow next to any item and the click Paste to paste the item into the document.

3 You can click Paste All to paste all the items in the clipboard at the current selection in the document.

4 You can click the down-arrow next to any single item and click Delete to remove that item from the clipboard, or click Clear All to remove all the items at once.

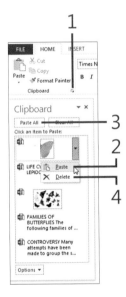

TIP The items are shown in the Clipboard pane with the most recent one at the top. When you click Paste All, the items are pasted into the document in the order in which they were collected, with the most recent one at the bottom.

TIP To control where and when the Clipboard pane appears, click the Options button at the bottom of the Clipboard pane.

Undoing mistaken actions

It can't be prevented—people make mistakes. When that happens in a document, though, Word 2013 can often restore your document to its previous condition. The Undo feature also lets you try out editing or formatting, and if you don't like the result, you can simply go back and try something else.

Word remembers the actions you take, and you can see them on the Undo button's drop-down list. You can then click one of the items in the list to undo that action and all the actions done after that one.

Undo one or more actions

1 Type some words in your document or change the formatting of some text.

2 On the Quick Access Toolbar, click the Undo button (or press Ctrl+Z).

3 Perform several different actions, such as adding text, applying a style from the gallery on the Home tab, and then deleting some text.

4 On the Quick Access Toolbar, click the down-arrow next to the Undo button.

5 In the drop-down list that appears, click an item, which highlights and undoes that action and all the items above it.

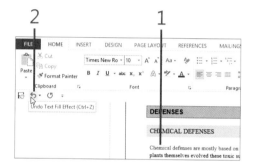

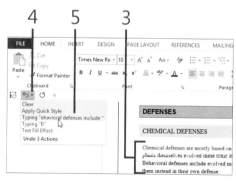

 TIP If you save a document with incorrect contents and immediately realize the mistake, use the entire Undo list to restore the document's original contents and then save it again. If you've already closed the document, though, Word's list of actions on the Undo button has been erased; in that case, you will need to have a backup copy of the original file.

TIP The Redo button (also on the Quick Access Toolbar) repeats the most recent action.

Navigating a document in the Navigation pane

Whenever your document grows longer than a few pages, locating specific places within it becomes more difficult. In Word 2013 you can find what you're looking for by using the Navigation pane.

This pane includes a search box and three tabs—one each for Headings, Pages, and Results—that offer different ways of locating text, graphics, tables, and other objects. Click any of the items in the pane to move the cursor to the corresponding location in the document.

Use the headings list

1 If the Navigation pane isn't visible, click the View tab, and then in the Show group, select the Navigation Pane check box.

2 Open a document that contains headings and text.

3 Click a heading in the list on the Headings tab of the Navigation pane to jump to that heading's location.

Use thumbnails

1 In the Navigation pane, click the Pages tab.

2 Click the thumbnail picture of any page to jump to the beginning of that page.

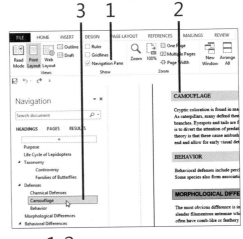

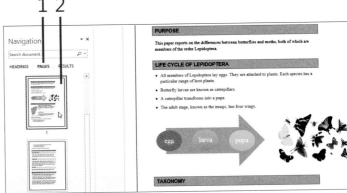

> **TIP** The items shown on the Headings tab of the Navigation pane can include text that doesn't have a heading style applied to it. To remove an item from the list, right-click that text in the document, and then in the options menu that appears, click Paragraph and set the Outline Level to Body Text.

Navigating by using the search feature

Often, the quickest way to get to a particular place in your document is to search for a word or phrase that you know is there. The Navigation pane's search box lets you do that with a minimum of effort.

Sometimes you need to look for something more complicated than a word or phrase. For example, you might want only occurrences of a phrase with specific capitalization, or both the singular and plural forms of a word. You can even search for a person's name when you know what it sounds like but not how it's spelled. These abilities and more are available in the Advanced Find dialog box.

Use search results

1 In the Navigation pane, click the Results tab.

2 Click in the search box.

3 Type the word or phrase that you want to find.

   As you type each letter, Word refines the results to only those that match the contents of the search box.

4 Click one of the results to jump to the corresponding location in the document.

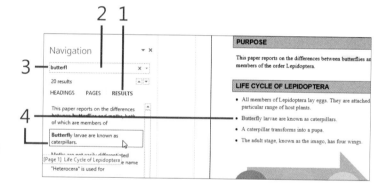

TIP If one occurrence of the word or phrase is already visible in the document, select it and press Ctrl+F. The selected text appears immediately in the search box, and all occurrences are shown in the Results tab.

TIP Click the Headings tab in the Navigation pane to see which headings contain the found text; or, click the Pages tab to see the locations in the thumbnails.

TRY THIS Instead of searching for text, click the down-arrow at the right end of the search box and choose Graphics, Tables, Equations, Footnotes/Endnotes, or Comments to find items of those types. Click the up-arrow or down-arrow buttons that appear below the search box to move through the results.

Use the Advanced Find dialog

1 On the Home tab, in the Editing group, click Find and then click Advanced Find.

The Find And Replace dialog box opens.

2 If the dialog box isn't expanded, click the More button.

3 In the Search Options section, select one or more check boxes to change the way Word will execute the search.

If you want to find only text that has specific formatting, click Format, and then in the drop-down list that appears, click one of the items. You can specify more than one kind of formatting if necessary, such as Paragraph formatting and Highlighting.

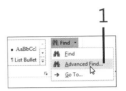

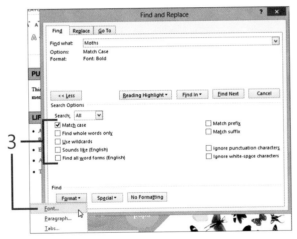

4 If you need to search for items that you can't type from the keyboard, such as a section break or a paragraph mark, click Special and select the desired item from the drop-down list that appears.

5 Click the Find Next button to move the cursor from one occurrence to the next.

6 If you want to choose which part of the document to look in, such as the main document or the headers and footers, click the Find In button and choose the name of the desired part in the drop-down list. Word selects all the occurrences in that part.

7 Click Reading Highlight to apply a yellow highlight to all occurrences, which makes them easy to see as you scroll through the document.

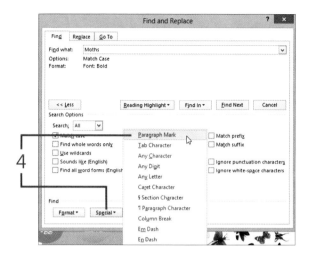

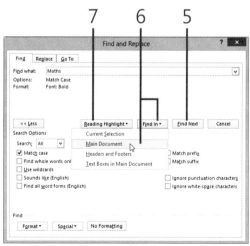

TRY THIS While the cursor is in the Find What box, press Ctrl+B once to search for occurrences of the search term that are bold. Press Ctrl+B again to search for occurrences that are not bold, and a third time to search for all occurrences. The same method works with Ctrl+I for italic and Ctrl+U for underline.

TIP If there's a foreign character in the text that you'd like to find and you know of an occurrence of that character elsewhere in the document, copy it to the clipboard and paste it (Ctrl+V) into the search box.

Replacing existing text

The Replace feature is one of the most powerful capabilities of Word 2013. You can make a simple replacement of one word or phrase with another, and you can also change the formatting, the style, or the case of text—or all of those together.

Replace text

1 On the Home tab, in the Editing group, click Replace (shortcut, Ctrl+H).

   The Find And Replace dialog box opens.

2 Type or paste the text to be replaced in the Find What box.

3 Type or paste the replacement text in the Replace With box.

4 Click Find Next to go to the next occurrence. Click Replace if you want to change that occurrence, or click Find Next again to leave it unchanged and go to the next occurrence.

5 If you want to change all the occurrences at once, click Replace All.

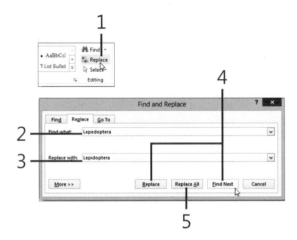

Replace formatting

1 In your document, select a few words and change the font color to red.

2 On the Home tab, in the Editing group, click Replace (shortcut, Ctrl+H).

   The Find And Replace dialog box opens.

3 If the Find And Replace dialog box isn't expanded, click More.

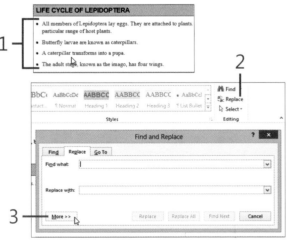

> **TIP** To limit the replacements to occurrences with specific capitalization, to whole words, or to other special circumstances, click More and select the desired search options.

4 Click in the Find What box, but leave it empty.

5 Click Format and then click Font.

6 In the Font Color gallery, select red and click OK.

7 Click in the Replace With box, but leave it empty.

8 Click Format and then click Font.

9 In the Font Style list, click Bold Italic and then click OK.

10 Click Replace All to style all red text as bold italic.

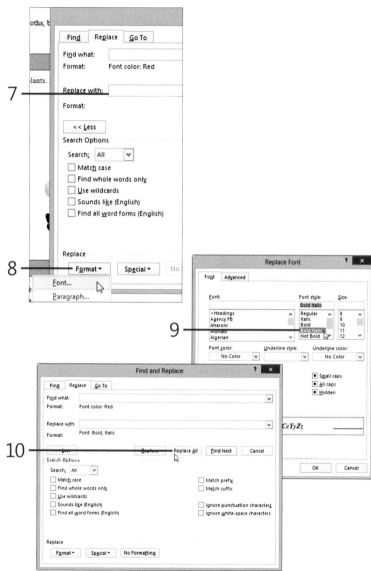

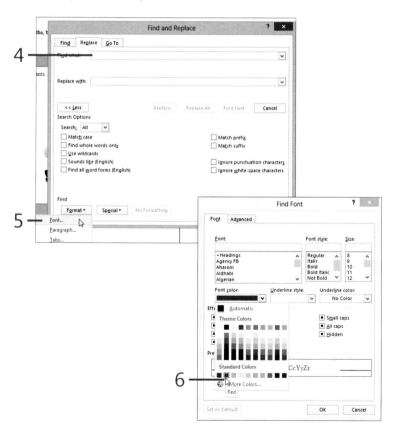

Using wildcard find and replace

Another option available to you when you're searching for something is to use a *wildcard*. This is a character or expression that represents a type of character or a range of characters in your text instead of specifying the exact characters themselves. For example, in simple searches, you can use wildcards such as ^? to instruct Word 2013 to search for any single character, or ^# to have it look for any single digit. These simple wildcards are listed under the Special button in the Advanced Find dialog box.

The Find And Replace dialog box also has an option labeled Use Wildcards that enables a more complicated set of wildcards. With this option, you can find and replace text in your document that can't be handled efficiently in any other way. As an example, if you have a list of people's names in "last-name, first-name" order, a wildcard replacement can reorder each name as "first-name last-name".

The wildcard feature uses a set of characters with special meanings to define the search.

Use wildcards in a Find expression

1 In a new blank document, type **=rand(5,1)** and press Enter to create sample text.

2 Copy one of the paragraphs and paste a copy immediately after the original so that there are two identical paragraphs together. (In real life, you might have sorted a list, resulting in multiple copies of the same item.)

3 On the Home tab, in the Editing group, click Find and then click Advanced Find.

The Find And Replace dialog box opens.

4 Click More and select the Use Wildcards check box.

5 Click in the Find What box and type **(*^13)\1**. This expression instructs Word to find any occurrence of two consecutive identical paragraphs.

6 Click Find Next.

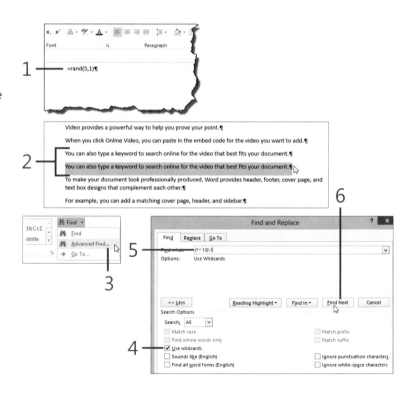

Meanings of wildcards for advanced searches

Wildcard	Meaning	Example
?	Any single character	h?t matches hat, hit, and hot, but does not match hart or hint
*	Any number of characters (including zero)	h*t matches hat, hit, and hot, and also matches ht (inside height or weight), hart, hint, and halftone
@	Any number of repetitions of the preceding character (including zero)	$1@. matches $1., $11., and $111. but does not match $121.
^13	A paragraph mark (ASCII 13)	.^13 matches a period at the end of a sentence, followed by a paragraph mark (¶).
< >	The start and end of a word, respectively	<ful matches fully and fuller, but not artful eight> matches height and weight but not eighth
[ ]	Any character from a sequence or range of characters inside the brackets	h[ai]t matches hat and hit, but does not match hot or hut [A-Z] matches any single uppercase letter, and [a-z] matches any single lowercase letter. [A-Za-z] matches any letter.
[!]	Any character except those in the sequence or range of characters following the exclamation mark	h[!ou]t matches hat and hit as well as h1T and h%t, but does not match hot or hut
( )	Divide the search expression into pieces that can be referenced in a replacement expression	(Soumya) (Singhi) matches Soumya Singhi, where each name can be referenced individually
\1, \2, and so on	Refer to the first, second, ... piece in the matched text	After finding (Soumya) (Singhi), the sequence \2, \1 in a replacement expression produces Singhi, Soumya

Use wildcards in a Replace expression

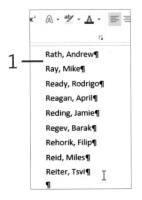

1. In a new blank document, type a list of names in "last-name, first-name" order, without middle names or initials, one per paragraph.

2. On the Home tab, click Replace.

   The Find And Replace dialog box opens.

3. Click More and select the Use Wildcards check box.

4. In the Find What box, type **(<*>), (<*>)(^13)**, including a space after the comma.

5. In the Replace With box, type **\2 \1\3**, including a space after the 2.

6. Click the Replace All button. The names are reordered as "first-name last-name."

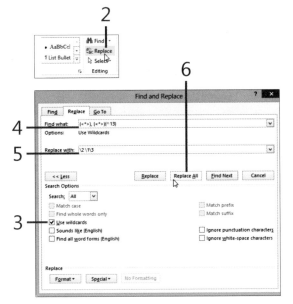

SEE ALSO For more information about using wildcards, see "Finding and replacing characters using wildcards" at www.word.mvps.org/FAQs/General/UsingWildcards.htm.

Organizing topics

An important part of writing is organizing your thoughts into a coherent structure. Word 2013 gives you several ways to see and change the order of headings and subheadings, including the Outline view and the Navigation pane. In addition, Word 2013 introduces a new feature for collapsing and expanding headings in Print Layout view, just as you can in Outline view.

When you collapse the headings and then move a heading to a new position, all the text and subheadings contained within that heading also move. If you delete a heading that has been collapsed, everything it contains is also deleted.

Collapse and expand headings

1 Open a document that contains headings and text.

2 If the display isn't already in Print Layout view, on the View tab, in the Views group, click Print Layout.

3 Point to a heading.

4 Click the triangle in the left margin next to the heading to collapse the content.

5 To expand the content under the heading, click the triangle again.

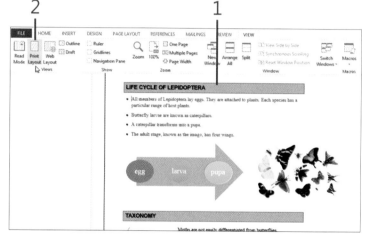

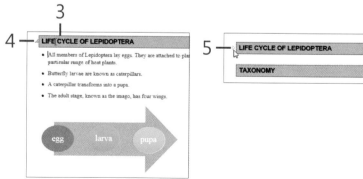

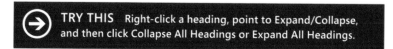

TRY THIS   Right-click a heading, point to Expand/Collapse, and then click Collapse All Headings or Expand All Headings.

Organize in Outline view or in the Navigation pane

1 If the Navigation pane isn't visible, on the View tab, in the Show group, select the Navigation Pane check box.

2 Open a document that contains headings and text.

3 On the View tab, in the Views group, click Outline.

4 Double-click the plus sign next to any heading to collapse it or expand it.

5 Drag a heading to another location in the document, using its plus sign as a handle.

6 On the Outlining contextual tab, in the Outline Tools group, use the arrows to promote a paragraph (make it a higher-level heading) or demote a paragraph (make it a lower-level heading).

7 Click Close Outline View.

8 In the Navigation pane, on the Headings tab, click the triangle to the left of a heading to collapse or expand it.

This affects only the display in the Navigation pane.

9 Drag a heading in the Navigation pane to a new location.

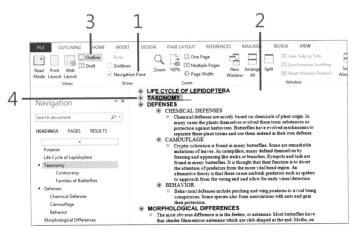

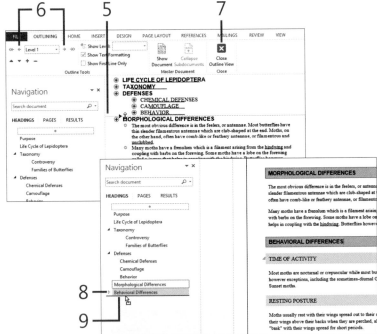

Inserting built-in building blocks

Word 2013 offers building blocks, which are predesigned, reusable items that you can insert into any document. The set of built-in building blocks includes cover pages, headers and footers, tables, text boxes, page numbers, equations, and watermarks. Each type of building block can be displayed in a gallery, in which you simply click an item to insert it in the document.

Select a building block from a gallery

1 On the Insert tab, in the Pages group, click Cover Page.

2 In the Cover Page gallery, click one of the previews.

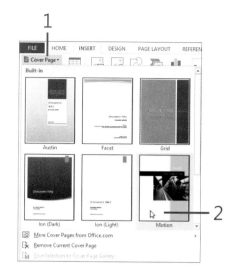

TIP If you don't like the cover page that's inserted, click Undo and try a different one.

Creating your own building blocks

As you work in Word 2013, you might find yourself using the same text or picture in more than a few different documents. You can save yourself some typing by turning that item into a building block.

There is no practical limit on the kind or size of items that you can store; save an entire table, several pages of text, a picture, a specialized watermark—the choice is yours.

Create and save a building block

1 Right-click in the header area and then click Edit Header.

2 Type some text in the header, such as your name. Tab to the center of the header and press Alt+Shift+P to enter a page number.

3 Select the entire paragraph, but not the paragraph mark at the end.

4 On the Header & Footer Tools tab, in the Header & Footer group, click Header.

5 At the bottom of the Header gallery, click Save Selection To Header Gallery.

6 Type a name for the new building block.

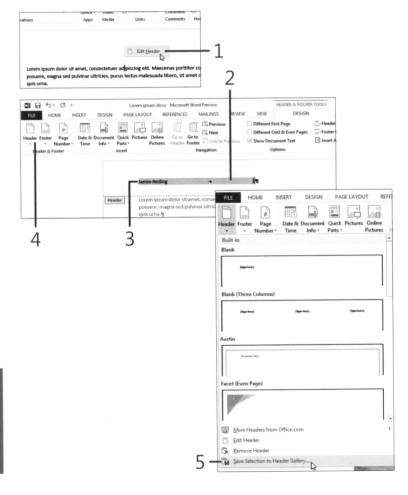

> ✓ **TIP** If you don't exclude the paragraph mark at the end of the text, the paragraph mark becomes part of the building block, too. If, for example, you insert that building block in a header that already contains a paragraph mark, the header will then contain two paragraph marks. That would make the header's height one line greater than desired.

7 Leave the Gallery drop-down list set to Headers.

8 Open the Category drop-down list and click Create New Category.

The gallery is divided into sections, one for each category, and you should make a new section for your custom building blocks.

9 In the Create New Category dialog box, type a name for a new category and click OK.

10 From the Save In drop-down list, choose the template in which to store the new building block.

11 Leave the Options set to Insert Content Only.

12 Click OK.

Managing building blocks

As you work in Word 2013, you might accumulate many custom building blocks in addition to the several dozen that are built in and many more that are available at Office.com. To manage this growing collection, Word provides a Building Blocks Organizer.

In the Organizer, you can see which building blocks are available, see how they're assigned to galleries, categories, and templates, and look at a preview. You can edit a building block's properties—for example, you can change its category or move it to a different template. You can also delete the selected building block from its template, or you can insert the building block into your document.

Use the Building Block Organizer

1 On the Insert tab, in the Text group, click Quick Parts and click Building Blocks Organizer.

   The Building Blocks Organizer dialog box opens.

2 Click a building block in the Building Blocks list.

3 Click Edit Properties.

   The Modify Building Blocks dialog box opens.

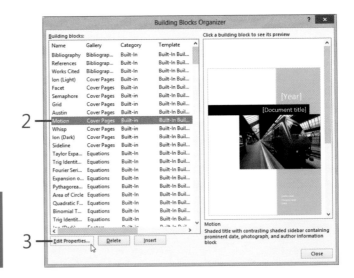

> ✓ **TIP** If you change the template named in the Save In drop-down list, the entry is moved from one template to another, resulting in changes in both templates. When you shut down Word, you'll be prompted to save the change in each template.

4 In the Modify Building Block dialog box, change the building block properties as desired and then click OK. Click the Yes button in the confirmation prompt dialog box to redefine the building block entry.

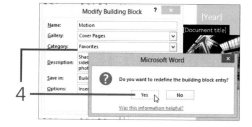

TIP **TIP** Word's built-in building blocks are stored in your profile in the *Built-In Building Blocks.dotx* file (%AppData% \Microsoft\ Document Building Blocks\1033\15\Built-In Building Blocks.dotx). You can save other templates in that folder, and Word will use any building blocks you create in those templates.

TIP When you save a building block, you must choose from a limited list of templates in the Save In dialog box. The templates Normal.dotm and Built-In Building Blocks.dotx are always available in the Save In list. If the current document is based on a template other than Normal.dotm, that template will also be in the Save In list.

Correcting and improving the text

4

Preventing or correcting any spelling and grammar errors is an important factor in effective writing. Microsoft Word 2013 has several tools to help you review and revise your text, including automatic correction of common typing mistakes, a spelling dictionary that can even suggest when you might have used the wrong word, and a grammar checker that helps you to express your thoughts clearly.

With Word's language tools you can translate your documents into many languages, or translate documents you receive from others so that you can read them. In Microsoft Office 2013, for the first time, the dictionaries and other proofing tools for many languages are available from the Microsoft website as free downloads.

In this section:

- Correcting a spelling or grammar error
- Running a manual spelling check
- Marking text to ignore spelling
- Adding common misspellings to AutoCorrect
- Using AutoCorrect entries as shortcuts
- Removing AutoCorrect entries
- Setting AutoFormat options
- Getting definitions and synonyms
- Counting words
- Finding a translation
- Changing the proofing language

Correcting a spelling or grammar error

No one types perfectly all the time. With that in mind, the spelling checker in Word 2013 can continuously compare your words to its dictionaries to detect typographical errors. In addition to its main dictionary, you can specify that Word use one or more custom dictionaries to which you can add your own words. The grammar checker can examine your text with a set of rules that can assist toward improving your writing.

When a word doesn't match anything in either the built-in dictionary or your custom dictionary, Word identifies it by using a red wavy underline, sometimes called a *squiggle*. The word might be a misspelling, or it could be a name or a word from a specialized field. If it is an error, you can easily correct it. However, if the word is correctly spelled but unrecognized, you can add it to your custom dictionary so that it won't be flagged again.

Word also tries to identify words that are spelled correctly but aren't appropriate for the context in which they're used. These *contextual errors* are usually words that sound alike such as *there*, *their*, and *they're*. The program highlights these words by using blue squiggle underlines.

The grammar checker also uses a blue squiggle to point out text that violates certain rules. These kinds of errors include incomplete sentences, subject-verb disagreement, and incorrect capitalization and punctuation. You can also choose to have the grammar checker examine style issues such as passive sentences and very long sentences.

Select a suggested correction

1 Right-click a word that is marked with a red or blue squiggle.

   A shortcut menu appears, in which you can find solutions to the problem.

2 If one or more suggestions appear at the top of the shortcut menu, click the one that corrects the error, or manually correct the text.

3 If the item at the top of the shortcut menu is *(No Spelling Suggestions)* or a grammar rule that includes *(Consider Revising)*, manually correct the text.

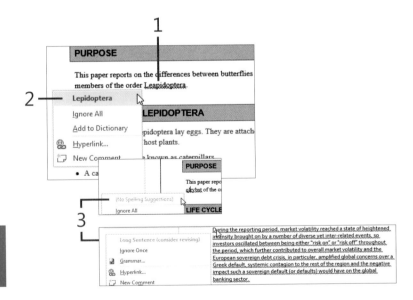

> ✓ **TIP** Previous versions of Word marked grammar errors with green squiggles. In Word 2013, they are marked with blue squiggles.

Add a word to the custom dictionary

1 Right-click a word that is marked with a red or blue squiggle.

2 In the shortcut menu that appears, click Add To Dictionary.

✓ **TIP** Yet another use of blue squiggles is to mark formatting inconsistency, which occurs when you apply direct formatting that matches an available style. For example, if you apply italic direct formatting to some text, Word suggests that you should apply the style named Emphasis, instead.

⚠ **CAUTION** Like most computer programs that deal with natural language, Word's grammar checker can misinterpret your text. It might indicate an error where there is none, and it might miss errors. You must use your judgment when reviewing your writing.

✓ **TIP** You can load several custom dictionaries simultaneously so that the spelling checker can match words in any of them. However, you can use only one of these dictionaries as the *default* custom dictionary for a particular language. When you click Add To Dictionary, the selected word goes into the default custom dictionary for its language.

🔍 **SEE ALSO** For information about choosing how the spelling and grammar checkers work, see "Setting spelling and grammar options" on page 430.

Running a manual spelling or grammar check

You might want not to see squiggles in the document while you're concentrating on typing, preferring instead to check all the text in one pass when you're ready. At any time you can choose to run a manual check of spelling and grammar.

Use the spelling and grammar panes

1 On the Review tab, in the Proofing group, click Spelling & Grammar (shortcut, F7).

   The Spelling pane appears along the side of the document work area.

2 Each time the Spelling pane identifies a word as incorrect, you can click a replacement in the list that appears and click either Change or Change All. If the word is spelled correctly, click either Ignore or Ignore All. If you want to enter it in your custom dictionary, click Add.

3 For each grammar error, read the suggestion and examples to help you decide how to reword the text.

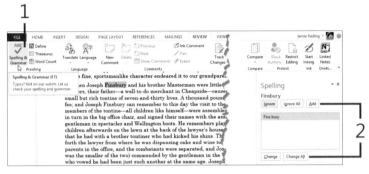

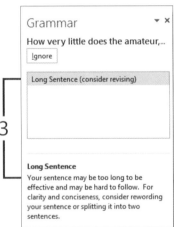

> ✓ **TIP**   Click any squiggle in the text to display that error in the Spelling pane or the Grammar pane.

> 🔍 **SEE ALSO**   For information about disabling the continuous spelling and grammar checker, see "Setting spelling and grammar options" on page 430.

Marking text to ignore spelling

When you see a red squiggle under a name or other word that you know is correctly spelled, you might not want to add it to your custom dictionary. Instead, you can just mark it so that the spelling checker will ignore it in the current document. Later, you can turn off the Ignore option and recheck the document.

Ignore a spelling error

1 Right-click a word marked with a red squiggle.

2 Click Ignore All to mark every occurrence of that word in the entire document.

Recheck the document

1 Click File to display the Backstage view and then click Options.

2 Click Proofing.

3 Click Recheck Document.

4 In the confirmation box that asks whether you want to continue with the recheck, click Yes, and then in the Options dialog box, click OK.

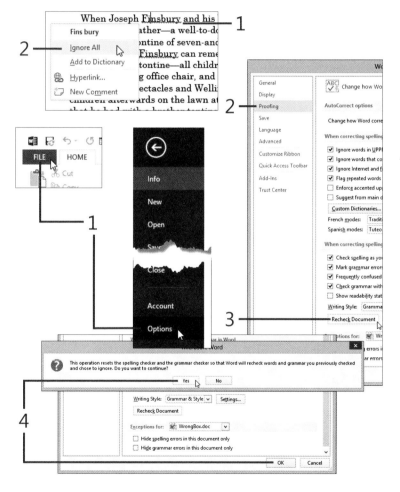

> **TIP** On the Review tab, in the Proofing group, you can click Spelling & Grammar to open the Spelling pane, in which you can click Ignore to mark a single occurrence of a word, or click Ignore All to mark all occurrences of the same word in the document.

> **SEE ALSO** For information about ignoring spelling in a large area of text or for all text formatted with a particular style, see "Mark text for no proofing" on page 88.

Adding common misspellings to AutoCorrect

The AutoCorrect feature of Word 2013 instantly replaces common misspellings with the corrected spelling. The feature compares each word you type to a list of known errors. If it finds a match, it substitutes the corresponding replacement text. When you install Office 2013, you start with a list of nearly a thousand AutoCorrect entries. You can add your own corrections to that list.

By default, AutoCorrect tries to match a misspelled word to a word in the main dictionary that the spelling checker uses, and it makes the correction if there is only one suggestion for the replacement. You can disable this feature if you prefer not to use it.

Add a spelling correction to AutoCorrect

1 Select a misspelled word.

2 Click the Backstage view and then click Options.

The Word Options dialog box opens.

3 Click Proofing and then click AutoCorrect Options.

4 The misspelled word you selected automatically appears under the Replace label.

5 Type the desired replacement text under the With label.

6 Click Add.

7 Click OK.

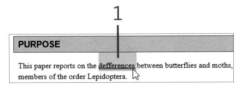

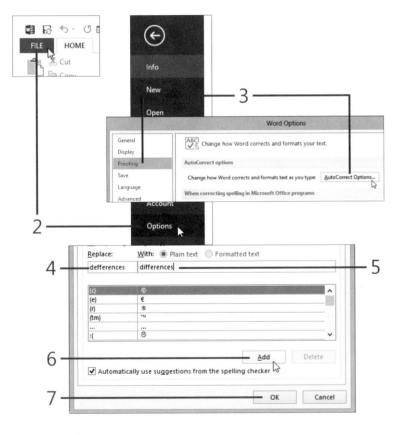

TIP The AutoCorrect substitution occurs in a document when you type a space or punctuation after the characters that Word recognizes.

Set AutoCorrect options

1 Click File to display the Backstage view and then click Options.

2 Click Proofing and then click AutoCorrect Options.

3 Select or clear the check boxes in the top half of the dialog box to set how AutoCorrect should treat capitalization errors.

4 If you don't want AutoCorrect to use suggestions from the main spelling dictionary, clear this check box.

5 Click Exceptions if you want to specify situations that AutoCorrect should ignore.

6 If you want to prevent AutoCorrect from capitalizing a word that you type after a specific abbreviation, on the First Letter tab in the AutoCorrect Exceptions dialog box, type the abbreviation in the Don't Capitalize After box and then click Add.

7 If you want to prevent AutoCorrect from correcting a word that contains mixed uppercase and lowercase letters, on the Initial Caps tab in the AutoCorrect Exceptions dialog box, type the word in the Don't Correct text box and then click Add.

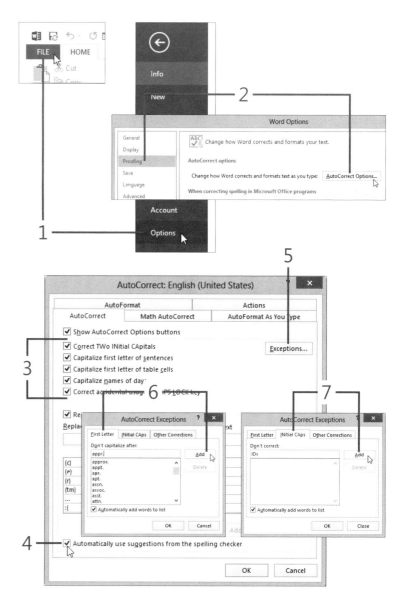

> **TIP** If you leave the check box selected for Show AutoCorrect Options Buttons, you can point to the beginning of text that AutoCorrect replaced. Word displays a small AutoCorrect Options button. Click that button to display options for reversing the replacement. Alternatively, click the Undo button or press Ctrl+Z.

> **TIP** You can select an entry in the AutoCorrect Options dialog box and click Delete to remove the entry from the list.

> **TIP** Keep the Automatically Add Words To List option selected. When you edit a document and you click Undo (or press Ctrl+Z) to remove an unwanted AutoCorrect change, Word adds the unwanted change to the exceptions list.

Using AutoCorrect entries as shortcuts

Although it's useful to have many spelling errors corrected automatically, the AutoCorrect feature can do more. Similar to Building Block entries, the replacement part of an AutoCorrect entry can hold nearly anything that you can put into a document, including formatted text, graphics, tables, and text boxes. Unlike a building block, however, an AutoCorrect entry's replacement appears in the document as soon as you type the entry—there's no need to press Enter or F3 afterward.

The AutoCorrect list contains both plain text replacements and formatted replacements. The plain text entries operate in most of the Office 2013 applications, but the formatted entries work only in Word.

Build a custom AutoCorrect entry

1   Type the desired replacement text in a document and apply a style or direct formatting to it if needed. You can also include other objects such as pictures or tables. Select the entire replacement.

2   Click File to display the Backstage View and then click Options.

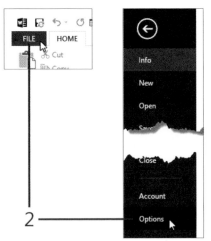

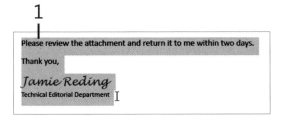

3 Click Proofing and then click AutoCorrect Options.

The AutoCorrect Options dialog box opens.

4 The replacement automatically appears in the text box under the With label, and the Formatted Text option is activated unless the replacement contains only plain text.

5 In the text box under the Replace label, type the characters that Word will recognize as the "name" of the entry.

6 Click Add.

7 Click OK.

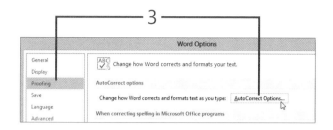

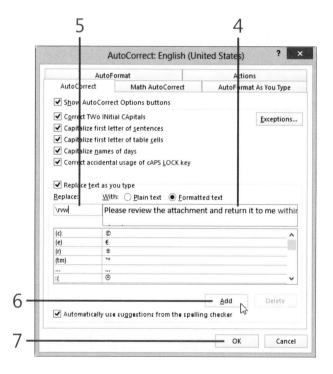

✓ **TIP** To make your custom entries easier to remember and to avoid inserting an entry by mistake, begin the entry's name with an uncommon character such as a backslash (\) or a hash (#).

Setting AutoFormat options

Word 2013 has the ability to apply some formatting to your text automatically. You might find that this is very helpful. However, if you don't understand why the changes occur, and how to control them or undo them, it can be very frustrating and your document can become an unsightly mess.

There are two separate parts of the AutoFormat feature. The part called AutoFormat does nothing until you start it with a manual command; it applies all of its rules in one pass. The part called AutoFormat As You Type applies its rules one by one, as soon as you type something the feature recognizes. The parts are controlled on separate pages of options in the AutoCorrect Options dialog box.

Explore the AutoFormat As You Type options

1 Click the Backstage view and then click Options.

The Word Options dialog box opens.

2 Click Proofing and then click AutoCorrect Options.

The AutoCorrect Options dialog box opens.

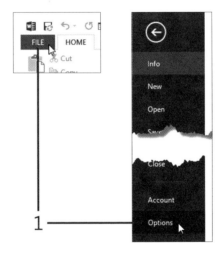

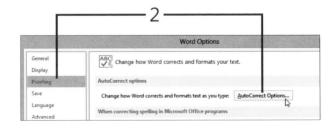

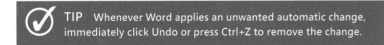

TIP Whenever Word applies an unwanted automatic change, immediately click Undo or press Ctrl+Z to remove the change.

3 Click the AutoFormat As You Type tab.

4 The options in the Replace As You Type section control the replacement of specific characters (such as quotes and fractions) and character formatting (such as Internet addresses). You'll probably want to keep the options in this group selected, once you know what they do.

5 The options in the Apply As You Type section change the text's paragraph style according to what you type. These options can cause unwanted changes and might be more annoying than helpful. The option to apply border lines causes trouble for many users because it applies a bottom border to the paragraph *before* the one in which you're typing. It's likely that you will rarely use the other options in this group, so you can usually clear their check boxes.

6 You should clear the options in the Automatically As You Type section because they often make unwanted changes in the document.

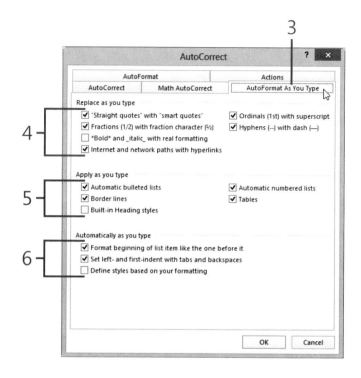

TIP To read full descriptions of the options in the dialog box, press F1 and search for the topic *Undo or Turn Off Automatic Formatting.*

Perform a manual AutoFormat

1 Click File to display the Backstage view and then click Options.

The Word Options dialog box opens.

2 Click Proofing and then click AutoCorrect Options.

The AutoCorrect Options dialog box opens.

3 Click the AutoFormat tab and set the options as you prefer.

Most of these options are the same as those for AutoFormat As You Type.

4 Click OK.

5 Press Ctrl+Alt+K, the keyboard shortcut for the AutoFormat Now command.

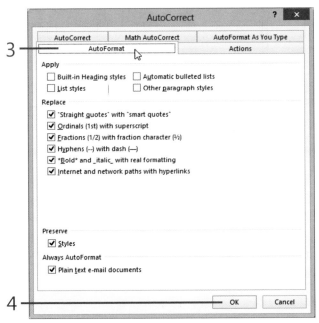

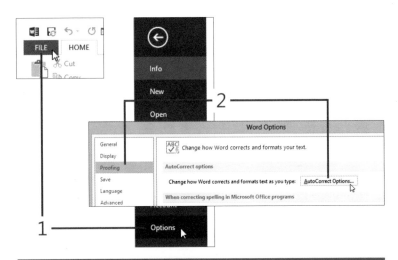

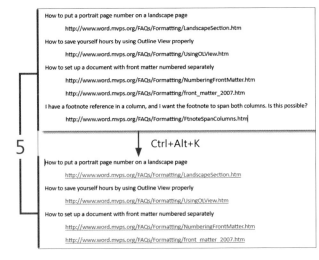

SEE ALSO   For information about adding a button to the Quick Access Toolbar to run the AutoFormat Now command, see "Customizing the Quick Access Toolbar" on page 421.

Getting definitions and synonyms

When you want to know the meaning of a word or phrase, or you want to view a list of synonyms, you don't have to leave your document; Word 2013 gives you direct access to dictionaries, a thesaurus, web search, and other research sources.

Get a definition from Encarta Dictionary

1 Hold down the Alt key while you click the word that you need defined.

2 If Encarta Dictionary isn't the current source shown in the Research pane, click the arrow and select Encarta Dictionary from the drop-down list.

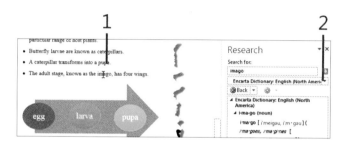

Get a definition from another dictionary

1 Select the word that you need defined.

2 On the Review tab, in the Proofing group, click Define.

3 If you haven't previously used the Define feature, select a dictionary from the list and click Download.

4 Read the definition in the dictionary's pane.

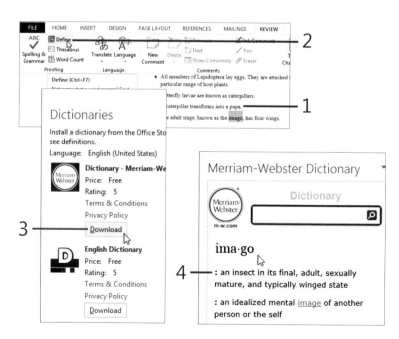

> **✓ TIP** The dictionaries offered in the pane are Apps for Office. For more information about these apps, see "Adding an app from the Office Store" on page 406.

Get a synonym on the shortcut menu

1 Right-click the word for which you want synonyms.

2 Point to Synonyms.

3 If you prefer one of the synonyms, click it to replace the original word in the document.

4 If there are no synonyms in the list, click Thesaurus to search for a synonym in the online thesaurus.

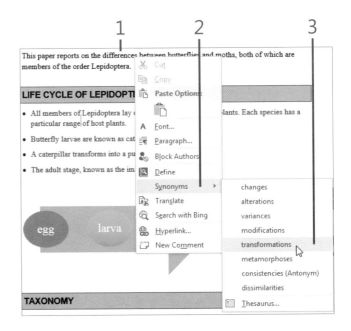

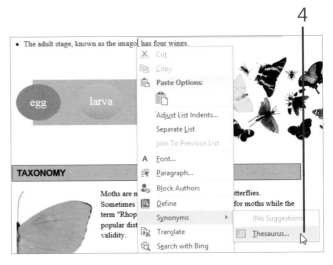

Get a synonym from the Thesaurus

1 Click the word for which you want synonyms.

2 On the Review tab, in the Proofing group, click Thesaurus .

3 If you want to replace the selected word in the document with one of the synonyms in the Thesaurus pane, click the down-arrow next to the synonym and then click Insert. Or you can choose Copy to put the synonym on the clipboard for future use.

4 If none of the synonyms in the list are useful, you can click one of the words that seems closest to your preference to refresh the list with synonyms of that word.

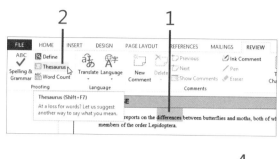

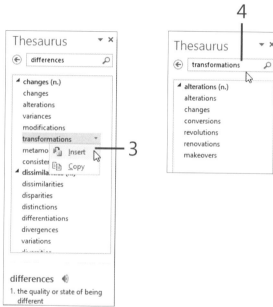

Counting words

In academic reports, news articles, and many other applications, it's important to know how many words you've typed in a document. Word 2013 can show a continuous tally in the status bar, and it presents more extensive information in a dialog box.

Show the word count on the status bar

1   If the word count doesn't already appear in the left part of the status bar, right-click the status bar.

The Customize Status Bar pop-up window appears.

2   Click Word Count to place a check mark next to it.

3   Click in the document to dismiss the pop-up window.

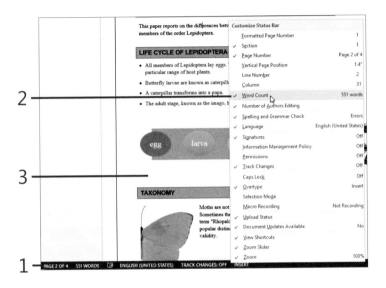

Open the word count dialog box

1   On the Review tab, in the Proofing group, click Word Count.

2   You can choose whether the count includes only the text in the main body of the document or whether it also includes text boxes, footnotes, and endnotes. Select or clear the check box at the bottom of the list, as preferred.

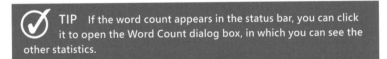

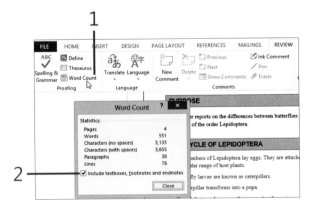

> **TIP**   If the word count appears in the status bar, you can click it to open the Word Count dialog box, in which you can see the other statistics.

Finding a translation

If you exchange files with friends or coworkers who speak another language, you might find the translation tools that Word offers to be useful. You can get the translation of selected text in the Research pane, in your web browser, or in the Mini Translator that pops up next to the selection. You can even request a translation of the entire document.

Choose translation languages

1 On the Review tab, in the Language group, click Translate and then click Choose Translation Language.

The Translation Language Options dialog box opens.

2 Select the language that you want the Mini Translator to use.

3 Select the source and destination languages that you want the Research pane and the web-based translator to use.

You can change these choices when the Research pane or the web-page appears.

4 If Microsoft makes available updates to the translation feature, the New Translation Services link appears. Click it to download the updates.

5 Click OK.

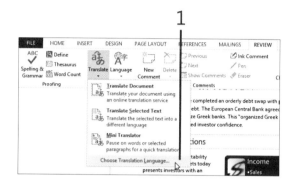

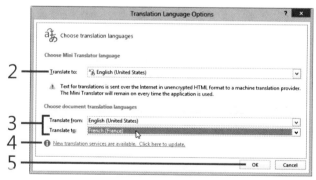

Translate selected text

1   Select the text that you want translated.

2   On the Review tab, in the Language group, click Translate and then click Translate Selected Text.

3   Click Insert to replace the selected text with the translation from the Research pane.

4   If you want to see a translation into another language, click the down-arrow for the To drop-down list and select the desired language.

5   If you want to translate the entire document, click the down-arrow next to Translate The Whole Document. In the confirmation box that opens, click Send. The translation appears in your default web browser.

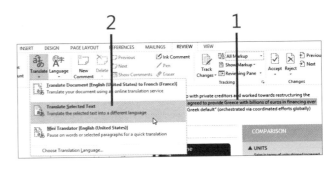

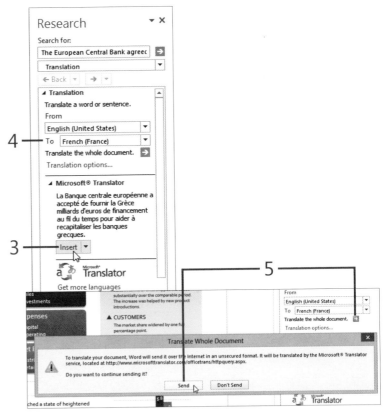

> ✓ **TIP**   To translate the entire document without displaying the Research pane, on the Review tab, in the Language group, click Translate and then click Translate Document.

Use the Mini Translator

1 On the Review tab, in the Language group, click Translate. Click Mini Translator to turn it on, if it isn't already turned on.

2 Select the text that you want translated.

3 Hold the cursor over the selected text until the Mini Translator appears.

4 Click Expand to open the Research pane for more information about the translation.

5 Click Copy to copy the contents of the Mini Translator to the clipboard.

6 Click Play to hear the translation spoken aloud.

For this feature to work, you must install a text-to-speech engine for the language that you want to use.

7 Click Help to read more about translation features.

8 If Microsoft makes available updates to the translation feature, the Update Services icon appears. Click it to download the updates.

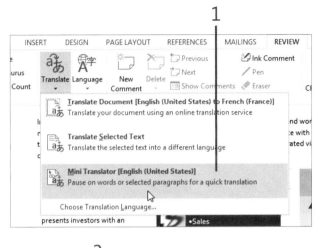

SEE ALSO For information about installing text-to-speech engines, search the Word Help for the topic "Using the Speak feature with Multilingual TTS."

Changing the proofing language of text

Word 2013 can check the spelling and grammar of many different languages, even within a single document. The proofing language of any part of the text is a formatting attribute, similar to bold or italic, and you can change it as needed.

Each language version of Office 2013 includes proofing tools—dictionaries for spelling and hyphenation, a thesaurus, and rules for grammar—for a set of companion languages. For example, when you install the English version of Office 2013, it includes proofing tools for Spanish and French as well as English. You can download free proofing tool packages for additional languages from the Microsoft Office website as you need them.

For some purposes you might want to prevent spelling and grammar checking of some parts of your document. For example, programming code contains many words that don't occur in Word's dictionary. Instead of setting the spelling checker to ignore each word individually, you can mark the whole passage so that it won't be checked.

Set the proofing language

1 Select the text for which you want to set the proofing language.

2 On the Review tab, in the Language group, click the Language button and then click Set Proofing Language.

   The Language dialog box opens.

3 Click the language that you want to use to check the spelling in the selection.

4 If you want to change the proofing language for all future new documents based on the Normal.dotm template, click Set As Default.

5 Click OK.

> ⚠ **CAUTION** If you often see red squiggles under words that are correctly spelled, it's possible that Word has automatically changed the proofing language of those words. To prevent unwanted language changes, in the Language dialog box, clear the Detect Language Automatically check box.

Download a proofing package

1 Set the proofing language for some text to the desired language.

2 If the Missing Proofing Tools banner appears below the ribbon, click Download. Then, skip steps 3 and 4, and resume at step 5.

3 If the Missing Proofing Tools banner doesn't appear, on the Review tab, in the Language group, click Language and then click Language Preferences.

4 In the Choose Editing Languages section, locate the desired language. If the notation Installed doesn't appear for that language, click the Not Installed link.

5 Your default browser opens to a webpage at Office.com. Select the language that you want and click Download.

6 Run the downloaded installer program.

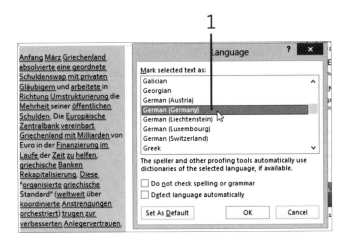

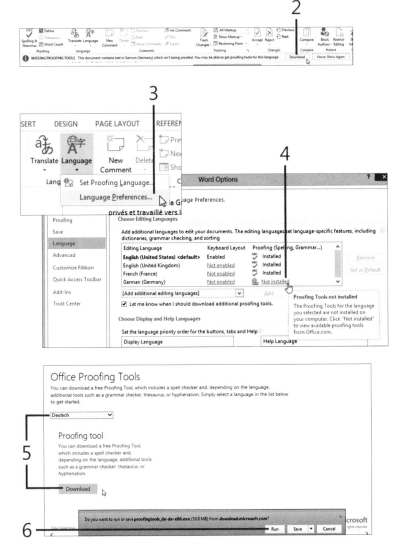

Mark text for no proofing

1 Select the text for which you want to prevent proofing.

2 On the Review tab, in the Language group, click the Language button and then click Set Proofing Language.

The Language dialog box opens.

3 Select the Do Not Check Spelling Or Grammar check box and click OK.

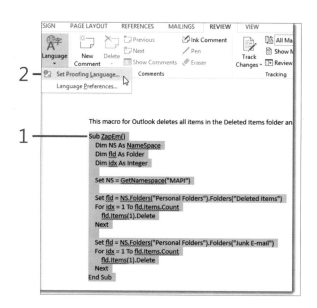

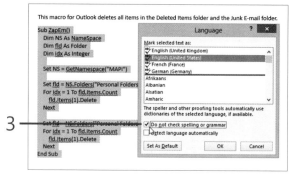

> **TRY THIS** You can add the setting for Do Not Check Spelling Or Grammar to the definition of a style. In the Modify Style dialog box, click Format, and then in the drop-down list that appears, click Language. Select the Do Not Check Spelling Or Grammar check box and click OK.

> **SEE ALSO** For information about marking individual words to ignore spelling, see "Marking text to ignore spelling" on page 71.

Formatting text for best appearance

5

You might use Microsoft Word 2013 to write a report, create a cookbook, or compose a letter. No matter what document you're working on, though, the appearance of your text is nearly as important as its content in getting your point across.

In this section you'll learn to use styles, which are collections of formats that can be applied in groups. You'll also find out how to apply direct formatting to selected text in addition to its style.

Lists of items are very common in Word documents. If the order of the items in a list is important, you can automatically number them. If all the items are equally important, you can format the list items as a bullet list using the standard solid-black dot or other shapes of your choosing.

When you modify an existing document, especially one that you didn't create yourself, you need to know what styles and direct formatting are responsible for the appearance of each part of the text. Word 2013 has tools to assist you in getting the job done.

In this section:

- Formatting with styles
- Creating and modifying styles
- Using the Styles pane
- Changing character formatting
- Applying highlighting
- Using the Format Painter
- Changing paragraph formatting
- Adding borders and shading
- Building a bulleted or numbered list
- Using multilevel numbered headings
- Revealing existing formatting

Formatting with styles

In Word 2013, most of the properties that determine the appearance of your text are divided into *character formats* and *paragraph formats*. Among the character formats are font name, font size, bold, italic, and underline. The character format commands are on the Home tab, in the Font group. The paragraph formats include line spacing, the spacing before and after paragraphs, alignment, and indents. The paragraph format commands are also on the Home tab, but in the Paragraph group.

A *style* is a collection of formats that are applied all at once. There are several kinds of styles:

- A *paragraph style* formats at least one whole paragraph. It includes both font formats and paragraph formats.

- A *character style* can format as little as a single character. It includes only character formats. You can add a character style to selected text, and it will overwrite the character formats defined by the text's paragraph style.

- A *linked style* acts like a paragraph style—setting both character formats and paragraph formats—if you apply it to an entire paragraph. It acts like a character style—setting only character formats—if you select less than an entire paragraph before you apply the style.

- A *table style* applies only to tables. It includes some character and paragraph formats plus borders and shading of cells, rows, and columns.

Every paragraph has some paragraph style. If you haven't applied any other style to a paragraph, by default, it has the Normal style. When you apply a style to part of your document, that text is formatted with all the settings defined in the style. If you change the definition of the style, all the parts of the document with that style change at once. It is in this way that styles can make formatting your document quicker, while also making the appearance of elements in your document consistent and easy to change.

Recognize kinds of styles

1 On the Home tab, in the lower-right corner of the Styles group, click the dialog box launcher (the small arrow icon).

You can also press Ctrl+Alt+Shift+S as a shortcut.

2 If the Styles pane contains only a few styles, click the Options link at the bottom of the pane. Otherwise, proceed to step 6.

3 In the Style Pane Options dialog box, in the Select Styles To Show drop-down list, select All Styles.

4 In the Select How List Is Sorted drop-down list, select Alphabetical.

5 Click OK.

6 Examine the symbols on the right side of the Styles pane. These symbols identify paragraph styles (¶), character styles (**a**), and linked styles (¶a).

7 To see the table styles, you need to first insert a table in a document. On the Insert tab, in the Tables group, click Table and then click one of the squares in the gallery that opens. On the Table Tools | Design contextual tab, examine the Table Styles gallery.

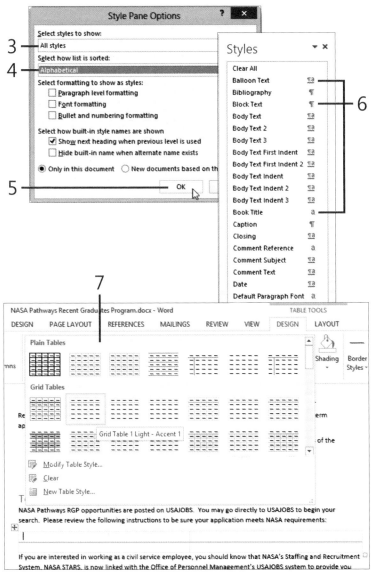

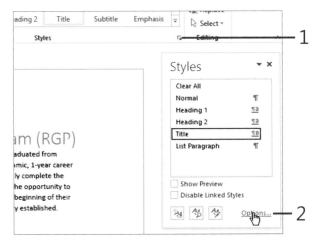

Apply a paragraph style from the Styles gallery

1 Click in the paragraph to which you want to apply a different paragraph style.

2 On the Home tab, in the Styles group gallery, point to the desired paragraph style or linked style and look at the live preview in the selected paragraph. When the live preview displays the format that you like, click the desired style in the gallery to apply it to the selected text.

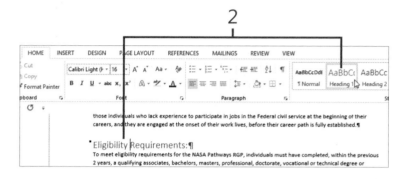

<table>
<tr><td>⚠️</td><td>CAUTION If the desired style is a linked style and you want to apply only its character formats, when you select the text, be sure not to include the paragraph mark (¶) as part of the selection. Otherwise, the linked style will be applied like a paragraph style.</td></tr>
</table>

⚠️ CAUTION If the desired style is a linked style and you want to apply only its character formats, when you select the text, be sure not to include the paragraph mark (¶) as part of the selection. Otherwise, the linked style will be applied like a paragraph style.

➔ TRY THIS You can also apply a style that isn't in the Styles gallery. On the Home tab, in the Styles group, click the dialog box launcher to open the Styles pane. There, you can click the name of the style you want.

Apply a character style from the Styles gallery

1 Select the part of a paragraph for which you want to change the character format.

2 On the Home tab, in the Styles group gallery, point to the desired paragraph style or linked style and look at the live preview in the selected text. When the live preview displays the format that you like, click the desired style in the gallery to apply it to the selected text.

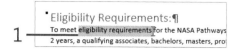

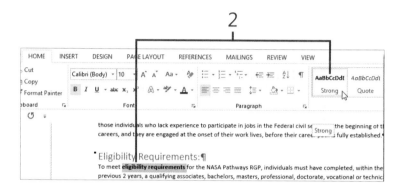

🔍 **SEE ALSO** For information about assigning a keyboard shortcut to apply a style, see "Customizing the keyboard" on page 417.

➔ **TRY THIS** Press Ctrl+Shift+S to open the Apply Styles dialog box. Click an item in the Style Name list, or just start typing the style name until the desired style appears in the list. Click the Apply button to apply the style to the text at the current selection.

Creating and modifying styles

Word 2013 includes dozens of built-in styles to format many kinds of text, but you might want something different. If you can't find what you'd like among the built-in styles, you can modify the formatting of any of those styles, or you can build your own styles to suit your needs.

When you create or modify a character style, you can specify any of the font formats—font name and size, color, bold, italic, and so forth. You can also set the proofing language, define borders and shading, and add text effects such as a shadow or an outline around the letters.

When you create or modify a paragraph style or a linked style, you can specify the same formats that are available for a character style, plus the paragraph formats: outline level, alignment and indentation, line spacing, tab stops, numbering, and more.

In Word 2013, you can also modify an existing style or create a new style by formatting some text with the desired appearance and then assigning a name to the style. This procedure uses the selected text as the basis upon which to define the style. If you need more control over all the formats in the style, you can use a dialog box, instead.

Each time you create or change a style by using a dialog box, you can choose whether to store the result only in the current document or in the template on which the document is based. If the document is based on the Normal.dotm template, the new or changed style will appear in new, blank documents.

Modify an existing style by example

1   Change the formatting of some text in your document so that it has the appearance you want for the modified style. Select the changed text.

2   If the style you want to modify is shown in the Styles group gallery on the Home tab, right-click it and then click Update *style name* To Match Selection (where *style name* is the actual name of the style of the text you're modifying).

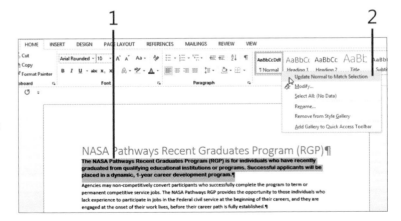

3 If the style you want to modify is not shown in the Styles group gallery, click the Styles group dialog box launcher (shortcut, Ctrl+Alt+Shift+S). Then, right-click the desired style and click Update *style name* To Match Selection.

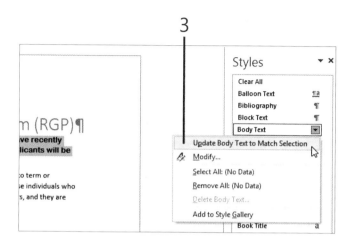

> ✓ **TIP**   Any style you modify by example will be stored only in the current document. It won't affect the document's template. If you want to store the style in the document's template, use the Modify Style dialog box, as described below.

Modify an existing style by using a dialog box

1 If the style you want to modify is shown in the Styles group gallery on the Home tab, right-click it and then click Modify.

2 If the style you want to modify is not shown in the Styles group gallery, click the dialog box launcher in the Styles group (shortcut, Ctrl+Alt+Shift+S). Then, right-click the desired style and click Modify.

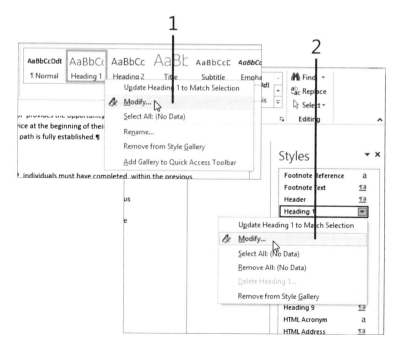

3 The group of items in the Formatting section represent the most commonly changed font and paragraph formats. (If the selected style is a character style, the paragraph formats are disabled.) Change any of the settings in this group to your preferences.

4 By default, the Only In This Document option is selected. If you want your changes to be saved in the document's template, click the New Documents Based On This Template option.

5 If you want to change any formats that aren't in the group of items in the Formatting section, click the Format button and then, in the drop-down list that appears, click an item.

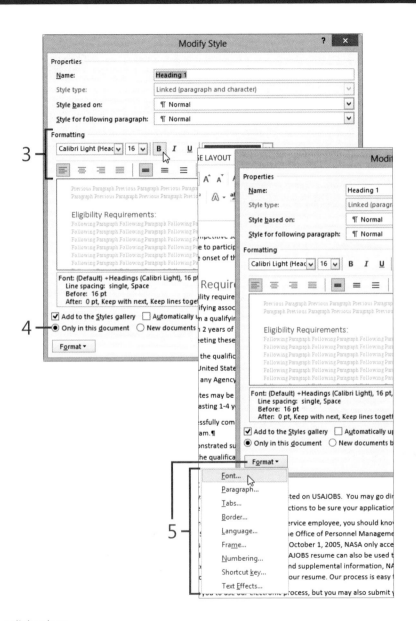

6 Change the desired formats in the dialog box—for example, the Font dialog box—and click OK. Repeat steps 5 and 6 to change other formats for the same style.

7 After you complete all the desired changes in the style's definition (which are shown in the preview along with the style's description), click OK.

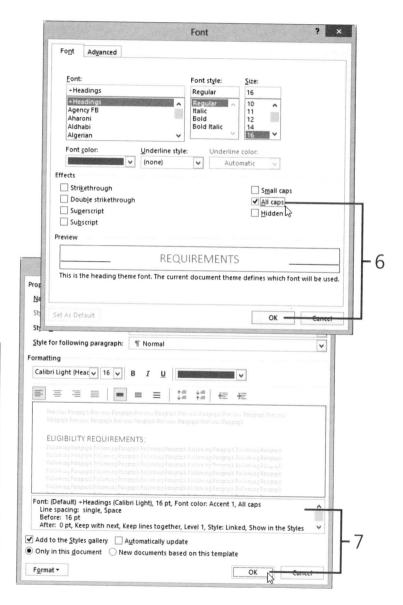

> ⚠️ **CAUTION**   Do not select the check box for the Automatically Update option. When you select that option for a style, any formatting change you make in a paragraph with that style is automatically saved to the style's definition. The change then appears in all other paragraphs of the document that have the same style, which probably is not what you intended. If you select that check box by accident or it has been selected in a document you received from someone else, follow the procedure in *word.mvps.org/FAQs/Formatting/WholeDocumentReformatted.htm*.

> ✓ **TIP**   If you choose to save the modified style in the document's template, you'll be prompted to save the template. If you want to keep the change in the template, you must click the Yes button in the prompt dialog box.

Create a new style by example

1 Change the formatting of some text in your document so that it has the appearance you want for the new style. Select the changed text.

2 Expand the Styles group gallery on the Home tab, and click the Create A Style item at the bottom of the gallery.

3 In the Create New Style From Formatting dialog box, type a name for the new style and click OK. The new style automatically appears in the Styles gallery.

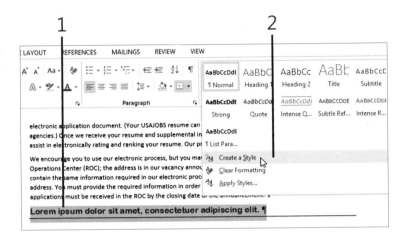

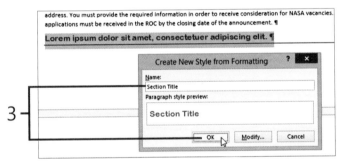

Create a new style by using a dialog box

1 On the Home tab, in the Styles group, click the dialog box launcher (shortcut, Ctrl+Alt+Shift+S).

2 Click the New Style button.

3 In the Create New Style From Formatting dialog box, enter a name for the new style.

4 In the Style Based On list, select the existing style that most closely resembles the desired appearance of the new style.

Any formats that you don't change in the new style will be inherited from the style in the Style Based On box.

5 In the Style For Following Paragraph list, select a style.

This style will automatically be applied to the next paragraph when you press Enter at the end of a paragraph that uses the new style. For example, a style for a heading element typically specifies Normal as the style for the paragraph that follows it.

6 Set the character formats and paragraph formats of the style.

7 If you want your changes to be saved in the document's template, click the New Documents Based On This Template option.

8 After you complete all the desired changes in the style's definition (which are shown in the preview along with the style's description), click OK.

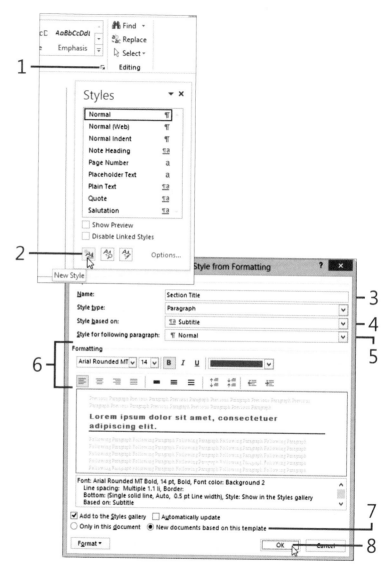

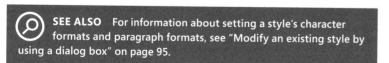

SEE ALSO For information about setting a style's character formats and paragraph formats, see "Modify an existing style by using a dialog box" on page 95.

Using the Styles pane

Usually, the quickest way to apply common styles in your document in Word 2013 is to click the Home tab and then, in the Styles group, click the style in the gallery. However, there are many styles that don't appear in the gallery. If you occasionally need to apply some of the less common styles or you want to examine their definitions, you need to use the Styles pane. To display the styles that you want or to control them, you might need to change some of the Styles pane options.

Set the Styles pane options

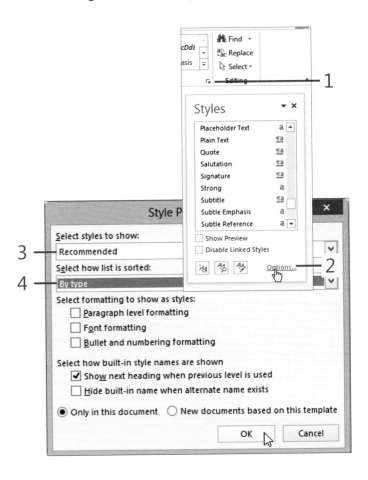

1 On the Home tab, in the Styles group, click the dialog box launcher (shortcut, Ctrl+Alt+Shift+S).

2 In the lower-right corner of the Styles pane, click the Options link.

3 In the Style Pane Options dialog box, in the Select Styles To Show drop-down list, click one of the following options, depending on what styles you want displayed:

- **Recommended** Limits the list in the Styles pane to a small set of styles that might be useful. You can change which styles are recommended (see "Managing styles" on page 442).

- **In Use** Limits the list to styles that are currently applied to some part of the current document.

- **In Current Document** Limits the list to styles that have ever been applied in the current document, whether or not they're applied now.

- **All Styles** Expands the list to all the styles in the document's template except for table styles, which appear only in the gallery on the Table Tools contextual tab.

4 In the Select How List Is Sorted drop-down list, click one of the following options, depending on how you want the style list sorted:

- **Alphabetical** Sorts the styles in the Styles pane alphabetically by name.

- **As Recommended**   Sorts the styles by the priority values assigned to them. You can change the priority values (see "Managing styles" on page 442).

- **Font**   Groups the styles by the name of the font (if any) specified in their definitions. Almost all built-in styles specify either +Body or +Heading, which are aliases for fonts defined by the current theme.

- **Based On**   Groups styles by the style on which they are based. Almost all built-in character styles are based on Default Paragraph Font, and almost all built-in paragraph styles and linked styles are based on Normal.

- **By Type**   Groups the styles as character styles, linked styles, and paragraph styles.

5 In the Select Formatting To Show As Styles section, select the check box for any type of direct formatting that you want the Styles pane to display as if it were a style.

6 In the Select How Built-In Style Names Are Shown section, select the check boxes if you want these behaviors:

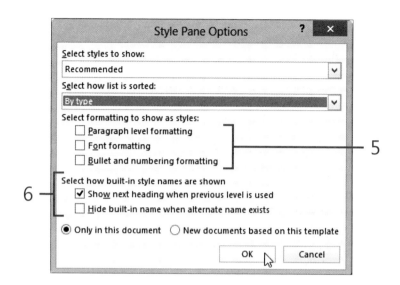

- **Show Next Heading When Previous Level Is Used**   When most of the heading styles are hidden, the Styles pane begins showing a heading style when you apply the style at the preceding level. For example, when you apply the Heading 2 style, the Styles pane makes the Heading 3 style visible.

- **Hide Built-In Name When Alternate Name Exists**   You can assign an alias to a built-in style by typing a comma and the alias name after the built-in name in the Name box in the Modify Style dialog box With this option, you can choose to have the Styles pane show only the alias and not the built-in name of the style.

7 If you want the set of options to be saved in the current document's template, click the New Documents Based On This Template option.

8 Click OK.

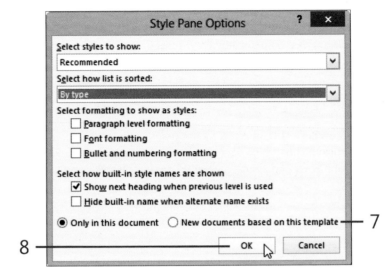

7

8

Select all text that has the same style

1 Right-click a style in the Styles pane and then, on the shortcut menu that appears, click Select All *number* Instance(s) (where *number* is the number of occurrences of that style that Word has found).

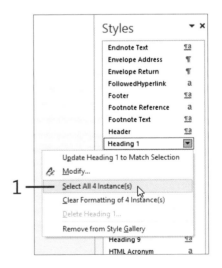

1

Changing the character formatting of text

Sometimes, you want to change the appearance of one small part of a document without having to find or create an appropriate style. Word 2013 makes it easy to apply direct formatting to selected text or to set the formatting and then start typing.

Format text by using ribbon buttons

1 Select the text to which you want to apply direct formatting.

2 On the Home tab, in the Font group, click the down-arrow on the Font box to display the drop-down list and then point to a font.

Look at the live preview in the selected text as you point to the names of different fonts. When you find the font that you want, click its name to apply it to the selected text.

3 Click the down-arrow on the Font Size box to display the drop-down list and click one of the numbers (in points) or type a number into the box. Press Enter to apply the size.

Look at the live preview in the selected text as you point to different sizes. You can also click the Increase Font Size or Decrease Font Size button to change the size of the selected text to the next larger or smaller number in the Font Size box.

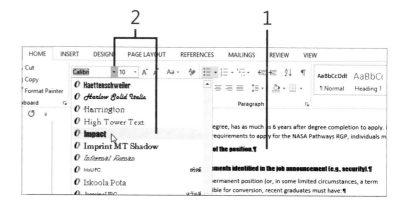

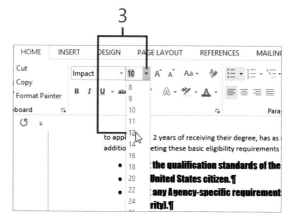

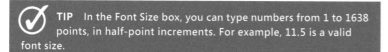

TIP In the Font Size box, you can type numbers from 1 to 1638 points, in half-point increments. For example, 11.5 is a valid font size.

4 Click the arrow on the Font Color button and point to one of the colors in the gallery.

Look at the live preview in the selected text as you point to different colors. The group of colors in the Theme Colors section changes when you select a different theme, but the group of colors in the Standard Colors section never changes.

5 Click any of the other buttons in the bottom row of the Font group to apply bold, italic, underline, strikethrough, subscript, or superscript settings as direct formatting.

6 Click the Change Case button and then, in the drop-down list that appears, click one of the items.

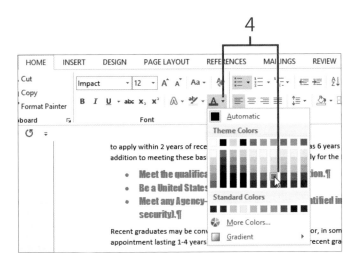

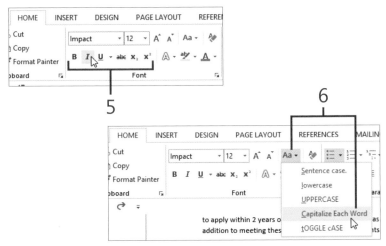

✓ **TIP** The font color named Automatic styles text as black when the background shading is white or a light color; if the background shading is a dark color, the text appears as white.

→ **TRY THIS** Select some text and keep the mouse cursor pointing to the selection or right-click the selection. The mini toolbar appears, in which you can access some of the same font formatting items as those on the Home tab.

🔍 **SEE ALSO** For information about using keyboard shortcuts to apply direct font formatting, see "Using built-in keyboard shortcuts" on page 18.

Applying highlighting

At some time or another, you have probably used a highlighter pen to emphasize printed text with a bright background color, perhaps as a study aid or to ensure that someone sees an important passage. Word 2013 has a tool that you can use in the same fashion to highlight text in your document with a range of colors.

Highlight some text

1 Select some text in your document.

2 On the Home tab, in the Font group, click the down-arrow on the Text Highlight Color button and then, in the gallery that opens, click the color that you want to use to highlight the selected text.

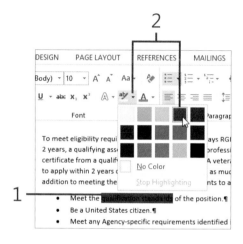

 TIP When you select a highlight color, it remains selected until you choose a different color, even when you shut down and restart Word. To use that color again, just click the main part of the Text Highlight Color button (not the down-arrow). To remove highlighting from text, select that text and choose No Color in the highlight color gallery.

 TIP You can search for highlighted text by using the Format button in the expanded Advanced Find dialog box.

Using the Format Painter

Often, you might find that you have text formatted exactly as you want it in one location, and you want to copy that formatting to text elsewhere in your document. To accomplish this, you can either create a style by example or use the Format Painter tool.

Format Painter acts like the Copy and Paste commands, but for format settings instead of words. The keyboard shortcuts for copying and pasting formatting (Ctrl+Shift+C and Ctrl+Shift+V) are similar to those for copying and pasting text (Ctrl+C and Ctrl+V).

Copy formatting to another location

1   On the Home tab, in the Paragraph group, click the Show/Hide ¶ button to display paragraph marks and other hidden formatting symbols.

2   Select the text that has the formatting you want to copy.

    If you want to copy only the character formatting, don't include a paragraph mark. If you want to copy only the paragraph formatting, select only the paragraph mark.

3   To copy the formatting, in the Clipboard group, either click the Format Painter tool or press Ctrl+Shift+C.

4   If you chose to copy the formatting with Format Painter, drag the special mouse cursor across the location where you want to apply the copied formatting. If you copied the formatting by pressing Ctrl+Shift+C, select the text to which you want to apply the settings and press Ctrl+Shift+V to paste the formatting.

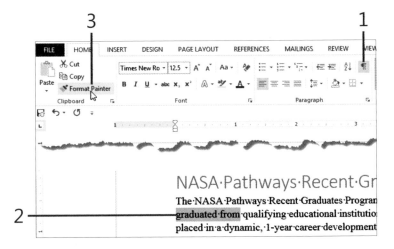

> ✓ **TIP**   If you want to repeat the same formatting in several places, double-click the Format Painter button to keep it turned on after its first use. Press Esc or click the Format Painter button again to turn it off. If you use the keyboard shortcuts, the copied formatting remains available until you copy some other formatting, and you can paste the same formatting as many times as you like.

Changing paragraph alignment and indents

In a Word 2013 document, you can align each paragraph at the left margin, the right margin, or both margins, or you can center each line between the margins. Most of the time, you'll use traditional left alignment. Titles and quotes are often centered.

In addition to the left or right alignment, you can indent the entire paragraph on one side or the other to make it stand out from the surrounding text. You can have the first line of the paragraph indented farther than the other lines, or you can keep the first line at the margin and indent all the other lines (which is called a *hanging indent*).

For quick adjustments to one or a few paragraphs, you can move the markers on the horizontal ruler. If you need more precise control of the indents, use the numeric settings in the Paragraph dialog box. Of course, the best practice for consistency throughout your document is to create or modify a paragraph style that you can apply wherever you need it.

Change alignment and indents on the ribbon and ruler

1 If the horizontal ruler isn't visible, on the View tab, in the Show group, select the Ruler check box.

2 Select the paragraphs that you want to format.

3 On the Home tab, in the Paragraph group, click one of the following alignment buttons (or use the corresponding shortcut), depending on how you want the selected text to be aligned:

- **Align Left (shortcut Ctrl+L)** Aligns the text at the left margin (or at the left indent if you set that). The right ends of the lines do not align (also called *ragged right*).

- **Center (shortcut Ctrl+E)** Centers the text between the left and right margins (or between the left and right indents).

- **Align Right (shortcut Ctrl+R)** Aligns the text at the right margin (or at the right indent). The left ends of the lines do not align (also called *ragged left*).

- **Justify (shortcut Ctrl+J)** Aligns the text at both the left and right margins or indents. To accomplish this, Word adjusts the width of the spaces between words, expanding or shrinking the spaces, as needed.

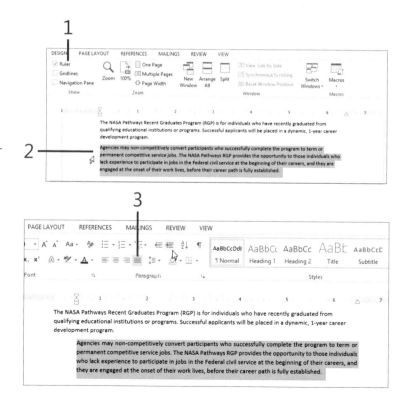

4 To move the left indent of the selected paragraphs in half-inch (1.27 cm) increments, in the Paragraph group, click either the Increase Indent or Decrease Indent button, as needed.

5 To move the left indent or right indent (or both) to any positions, drag the margin markers along the horizontal ruler.

6 To set a first-line indent or a hanging indent, drag one of the two sections of the left margin marker along the horizontal ruler.

The upper section sets the first-line indent; the lower section sets the hanging indent.

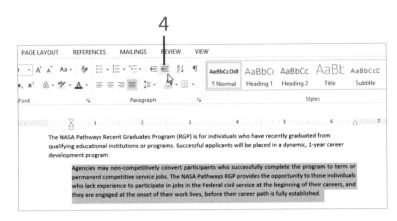

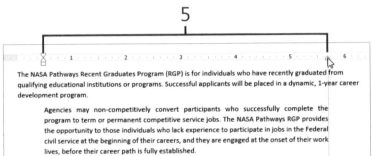

Top half: First-line indent
Bottom half: Hanging indent

> ⚠️ **CAUTION** If you use the shortcut Ctrl+E or Ctrl+J to change the alignment of selected paragraphs, be careful not to press the Shift key at the same time. The Ctrl+Shift+E shortcut activates the Track Changes feature. The Ctrl+Shift+J shortcut sets Distributed alignment, which is similar to Justified alignment except that the last line of the paragraph is also stretched to the right margin, no matter how short the line is.

> ✓ **TIP** In previous versions of Word, the Justify alignment always increased the widths of the spaces between words. In Word 2013, the widths of spaces may be either increased or decreased to get the best appearance. This usually results in better appearance, but be aware that it might change the line endings and page breaks in older documents that you convert to Word 2013 format.

Change alignment and indents in the Paragraph dialog box

1 Select the paragraphs that you want to format.

2 On the Home tab, in the Paragraph group, click the dialog box launcher.

3 In the Paragraph dialog box, in the Alignment drop-down list, select the paragraph alignment that you want.

4 In the Indentation section, enter the measurements that you want for the left and right indents.

5 If you want a first-line indent or a hanging indent, select the desired type of indent in the Special drop-down list and set the size of the indent in the By box.

6 Click OK.

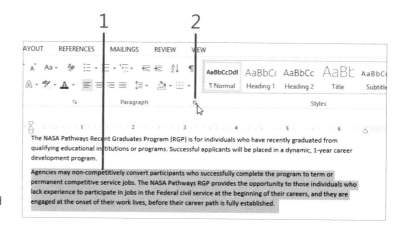

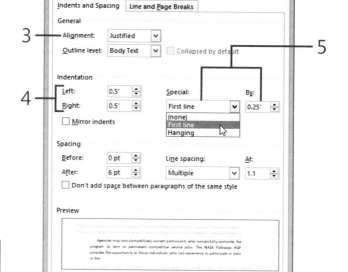

> **TRY THIS** You can set the left edge of selected paragraphs to the left of the page margin, which can be useful for major headings. To do this, in the Paragraph dialog box, enter a minus sign before the measurement in the Left Indent box.

Changing line and paragraph spacing

The distance between the lines within the paragraphs as well as between the paragraphs themselves is an important factor in the readability of your text. If the lines are crowded together vertically or spaced too far apart, readers might find it difficult to keep their eyes trained on the right line.

In the Normal style in Word 2013, the default spacing is 1.15 lines—that is, the distance between the *baselines* (the bottoms of the letters, as determined by the base of the letter "m")

within a paragraph is 15 percent larger than for single-spaced text. You might prefer to use single spacing for some kinds of text, and larger spacing for other kinds.

In text that has no first-line paragraph indents, added space between paragraphs is the only visual cue that signals the start of a new paragraph. In Word, you can set the amount of space to add both before and after each paragraph.

Change spacing between lines within a paragraph

1 Select the paragraphs that you want to format.

2 On the Home tab, in the Paragraph group, click the Line And Paragraph Spacing button.

3 If you see the line spacing you want in the list, click to apply it. Otherwise, continue to step 4.

4 If you want a line spacing that isn't in the list, click Line Spacing Options.

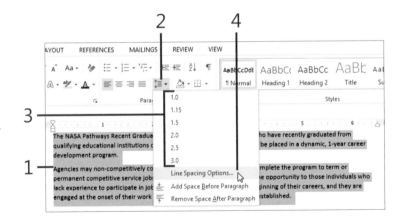

5 In the Paragraph dialog box, in the Line Spacing section, click the type of spacing that you want to apply to the selected text:

- **Single, 1.5 Lines, or Double** Sets the minimum distance between baselines to 1 line, 1.5 lines, or 2 lines. These are the same as the items 1.0, 1.5, and 2.0 in the list on the Line And Paragraph Spacing button.

- **At Least** Sets the minimum distance between baselines, using the number of points shown in the box in the At section. If you insert a large character or an inline graphic in the text, Word adds enough space above that line to show the entire object.

- **Exactly** Sets the exact distance between baselines, using the number of points shown in the box in the At section. If you insert a character or an inline graphic in the text that is taller than can fit in the space of a single line, Word displays only the bottom of the text or object.

- **Multiple** Lets you enter a multiple of the single-line spacing in the box in the At section, with up to two decimal places. For example, if you enter 2.3 in the At box, the distance between baselines is 2.3 times as large as for single-line spacing.

6 Click OK.

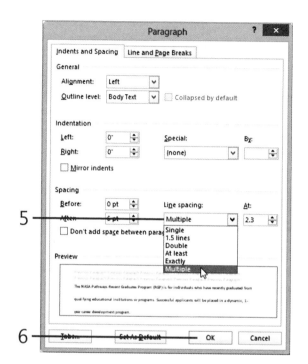

Change spacing between paragraphs

1 Select the paragraphs that you want to format.

2 On the Home tab, in the Paragraph group, click the dialog box launcher.

> ✔ **TIP** When one paragraph has some amount of added space after it, and the next paragraph has an amount of added space before it, Word uses only the larger of the two measurements; it does not add the two measurements together.

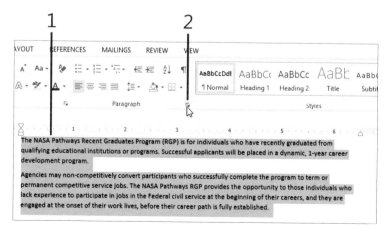

Changing line and paragraph spacing: Change spacing between paragraphs **111**

3 In the Paragraph dialog box, in the Spacing section, enter the amount of added space that you want before each selected paragraph in the Before box.

4 In the After box, enter the amount of added space that you want after each selected paragraph.

5 Click OK.

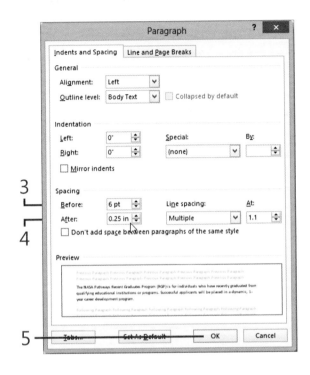

TRY THIS You can enter the measurements for the amount of space in any units by using the associated abbreviation: pt for points; in for inches; cm for centimeters; mm for millimeters; or li for lines. Word automatically converts your entry to the equivalent number of points (where 1 inch = 72 points) when you click OK, as you'll see if you reopen the dialog box.

CAUTION The Don't Add Space Between Paragraphs Of The Same Style option is useful mostly in the definitions of styles such as those used in numbered lists or bulleted lists. If you select the check box when you have selected some text but you aren't modifying a style, the option applies only to the selection, not to all paragraphs with the same style.

Controlling line and page breaks

As you insert text, pictures, and other items into your document, a part of the Word 2013 program called the *layout engine* continuously evaluates the positions of the text characters. As a line's content approaches the right margin, the layout engine decides whether the next word will fit on the same line or whether it needs to start a new line. As the text approaches the bottom margin, the layout engine decides whether to start a new page. You can change the rules that the layout engine uses to make these decisions by setting some options.

You usually want headings, table titles, and similar text to stay on the same page as the text that follows them. It's also good practice to avoid a single line from the end of a paragraph appearing at the top of a page (in printer's jargon, this is called a *widow*) or a single line from the beginning of a paragraph at the bottom of a page (called an *orphan*).

If you use automatic hyphenation in your document, you might want to prevent hyphenation in specific paragraphs or in certain styles.

You can control these layout actions by setting options in the definitions of paragraph styles, or by setting them one paragraph at a time.

Fix unwanted page breaks

1. Click in the paragraph that you want to format.
2. On the Home tab, in the Paragraph group, click the dialog box launcher to open the Paragraph dialog box.

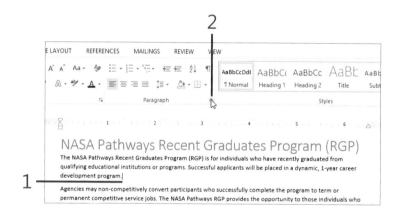

3 Click the Line And Page Breaks tab.

4 Select the check boxes for the options that you want:

- **Widow/Orphan Control**   If this option is not selected, the layout engine starts a new page when the next line won't fit on the current page. This might result in a single line from the beginning of a paragraph appearing at the bottom of the current page, or a single line from the end of a paragraph at the top of the next page. If this option is selected, Word moves at least one line of the paragraph to the next page. By default, this option is selected in the Normal style and all styles that are based on the Normal style.

- **Keep With Next**   If this option is not selected, an automatic page break is allowed to occur between the current paragraph and the next paragraph. If this option is selected, Word moves part or the entire current paragraph to the next page. By default, this option is selected in the built-in Heading styles.

- **Keep Lines Together**   If this option is not selected, an automatic page break is allowed to occur anywhere within the current paragraph. If this option is selected, Word moves the entire paragraph to the next page. By default, this option is selected in the built-in Heading styles.

- **Page Break Before**   Word inserts an automatic page break just before the beginning of the current paragraph.

5 Click OK.

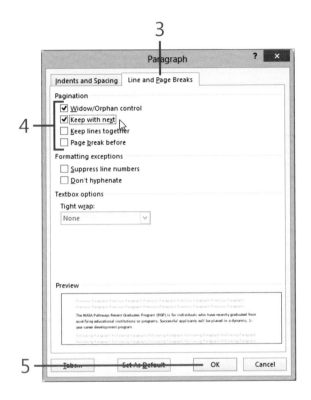

Prevent hyphenation

1 Click in the paragraph that you want to format.

2 On the Home tab, in the Paragraph group, click the dialog box launcher to open the Paragraph dialog box.

3 Click the Line And Page Breaks tab.

4 Select the Don't Hyphenate check box.

5 Click OK.

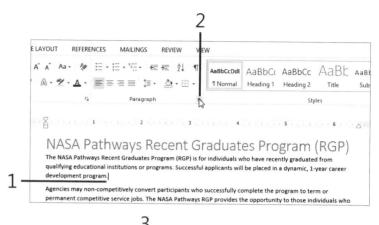

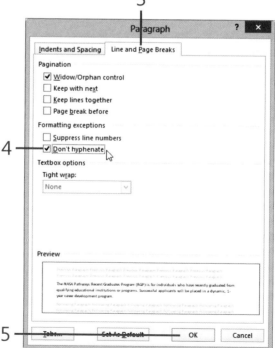

TRY THIS Good typesetting practice, especially in narrow, justified columns such as those in newspapers, requires that no more than three consecutive lines can end with hyphens. On the Page Layout tab, in the Page Setup group, click Hyphenation. In the drop-down list that appears, click Hyphenation Options. Select the Automatically Hyphenate Document check box. In the Limit Consecutive Hyphens To text box, enter the number 3.

Adding borders and shading

A color background shade behind a heading, a quote, or other important text serves to draw your readers' attention. Lines under headings and boxes around special text are other design elements in your toolbox. You can create these effects easily by using buttons on the ribbon. For more control, you can use the Borders And Shading dialog box.

Add borders and shading by using ribbon buttons

1 Select the paragraph or part of a paragraph that you want to format.

2 To add background shading, on the Home tab, in the Paragraph group, click the down-arrow on the Shading button.

3 In the shading colors gallery, point to the various color samples and watch the live preview in the selected text. If one of the colors is satisfactory, click it to apply the shading.

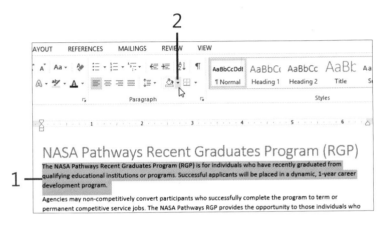

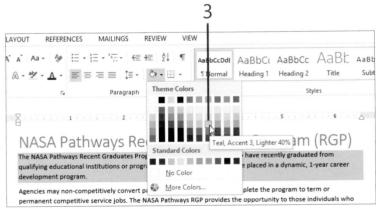

TRY THIS If you want a shading color that isn't one of the theme colors or standard colors in the gallery, click More Colors and use the color picker in the Colors dialog box.

4 To add a border, in the Paragraph group, on the Borders button, click the down-arrow to display a drop-down list of border options.

5 Point to the items in the drop-down list and watch the live preview in the selected text. If one of the borders is satisfactory, click it to apply the border.

6 If you want lines to border the paragraph on more than one side, but not a complete box border, you can repeat steps 4 and 5 and select the additional options that you want.

For example, if you want a border both above and below a paragraph, such as you might for a sidebar or a pull quote, apply the Top Border as just described and then go back and apply the Bottom Border in the same way.

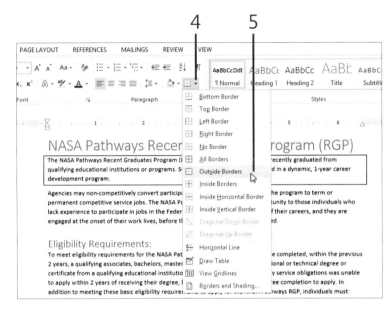

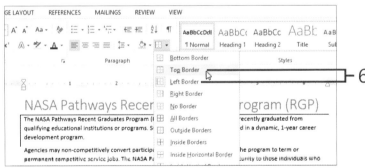

> **TIP** If you want to repeat the same shading or border as you used most recently, click the Shading button or the Borders button instead of the button's arrow. The icon on the button shows the most recent color or border.

> **TIP** If you select a word or sentence but less than a whole paragraph, you can only surround it with a complete box border, not individual lines.

Use the Borders And Shading dialog box

1 Select the paragraph or part of a paragraph that you want to format.

2 On the Home tab, in the Paragraph group, click the down-arrow on the Borders button and then, at the bottom of the drop-down list that appears, click Borders And Shading.

3 In the Borders And Shading dialog box, click the Borders tab.

4 In the Setting column, click an icon that represents the type of border that you want.

5 In the Style list, click the type of line that you want.

6 In the Color and Width drop-down lists, choose the desired color and line width.

7 If you want more than one side but not a complete box border, click the buttons around the preview to turn them off or on.

8 Click the Shading tab.

9 In the Fill box, select the desired color.

10 If you want, you can add a pattern of a second color by choosing a style other than Clear and then choosing a color.

11 Click OK.

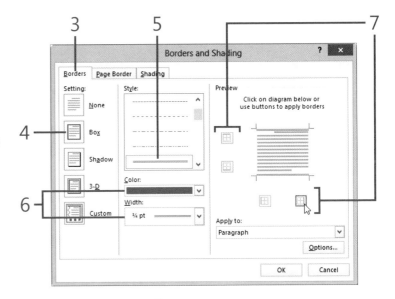

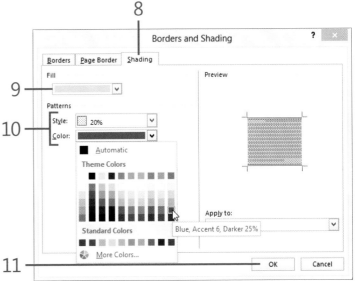

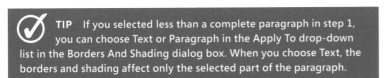

TIP If you selected less than a complete paragraph in step 1, you can choose Text or Paragraph in the Apply To drop-down list in the Borders And Shading dialog box. When you choose Text, the borders and shading affect only the selected part of the paragraph.

Adding borders and shading: Use the Borders And Shading dialog box   **119**

Building a bulleted or numbered list

You can use lists to break large topics into small, easily understood pieces. A numbered list is appropriate when you describe the steps in a procedure that should be done in a particular order. Also, a numbered list is a good format for placing similar items in priority order. A bulleted list can contain steps that can be done in any order, or items of equal priority.

When you start a bulleted or numbered list, Word 2013 applies the bullets or numbers automatically to each new item, and applies a hanging indent to the text of each item. If you move numbered paragraphs within the list, Word automatically renumbers them. You can restart the numbering to create a separate list, or include unnumbered paragraphs within the list.

Apply bullets or numbering

1 Click in the paragraph that will contain the first item of the list.

2 On the Home tab, in the Paragraph group, click the Bullets button to start a bulleted list or click the Numbering button to start a numbered list.

3 After you enter text for each item of the list, press Enter to start the next item.

4 When you've entered the last item of the list, press Enter twice to turn off the list tool.

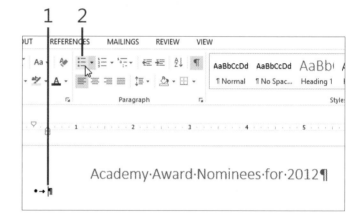

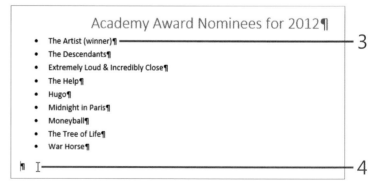

TRY THIS   Create a numbered list of three or four paragraphs. Select the last paragraph of the list and drag it to the beginning of the first paragraph of the list. Watch as Word renumbers the paragraphs to maintain the correct order.

Changing the bullets or numbering

The bullet that Word 2013 inserts by default is a solid-black circle. However, you can choose from several decorative bullets, use symbols from fancy fonts, or even use clip art or pictures.

In numbered lists, you can select Arabic or Roman numerals, or uppercase or lowercase letters. If the built-in assortment of formats doesn't suit your needs, you can define your own format.

Select from the Bullet Library

1 Click in the paragraph that will contain the first item of the list.

2 On the Home tab, in the Paragraph group, click the down-arrow on the Bullets button.

3 If you like one of the bullets in the Bullet Library gallery, click it to apply it to the entire list. Otherwise, continue to step 4.

4 If you prefer to use a symbol from a font, clip art, or a picture as a bullet, at the bottom of the gallery, click Define New Bullet.

5 In the Define New Bullet dialog box, if you want to use a symbol from a font, click Symbol.

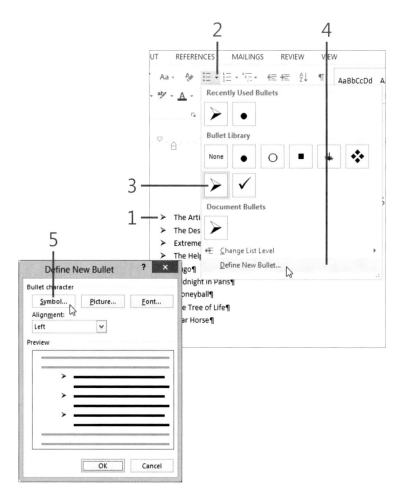

6 In the Symbol dialog box, choose a font in the Font drop-down list, click the desired symbol, and then click OK.

7 To use clip art or to use a picture from your computer or from the Internet, click Picture.

8 If you want a picture from your computer or from your SkyDrive account, click the corresponding item in the Insert Pictures dialog box.

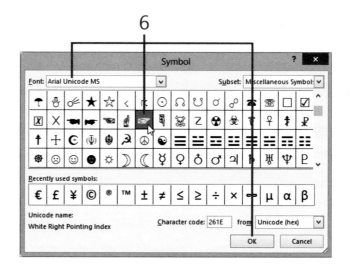

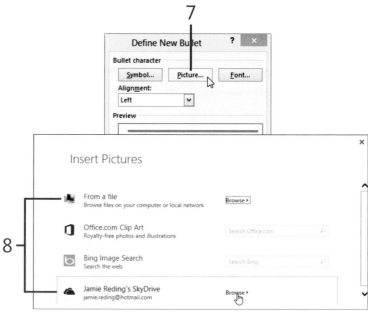

> **TIP** Word automatically chooses the Symbol font to display in the Symbol dialog box, but you can find many other symbols in fonts such as Wingdings and Webdings as well as in Arial Unicode MS and Lucida Sans Unicode.

> **TIP** To change the character formatting of a symbol, in the Define New Bullet dialog box, click the Font button and then, in the Font dialog box that opens, make any needed changes.

9 Navigate to the folder that contains the desired picture, click the picture, and then click Open (on SkyDrive, click Insert).

10 If you want clip art or a picture from the Internet, click Office.com Clip Art or Bing Image Search, enter a word or phrase to search for, and then press Enter.

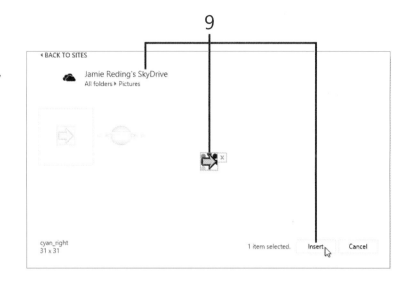

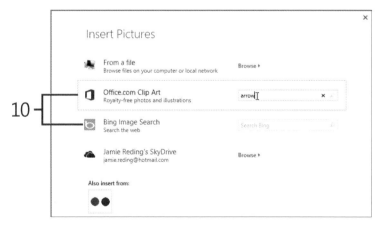

11 Click the desired clip art or picture and click Insert.

12 In the Define New Bullet dialog box, click OK.

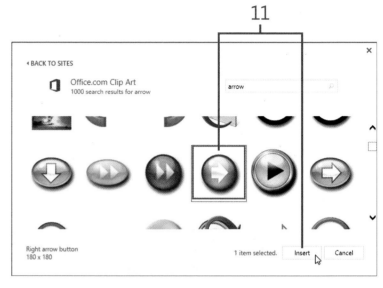

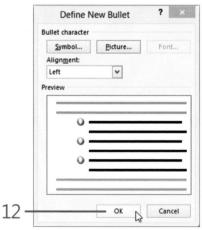

> ✓ **TIP** Because Word must resize your picture much smaller to make a bullet, it's best to choose a simple picture with a subject that fills the space.

> ✓ **TIP** When you create a new bullet, Word automatically adds it to the Bullet Library. If you don't plan to use a custom bullet again, you can remove it from the Library by right-clicking it and then, on the shortcut menu that appears, click Remove.

Select from the Numbering Library

1 Click in the paragraph that is to be the first item of the list.

2 On the Home tab, in the Paragraph group, click the down-arrow on the Numbering button.

3 If you like one of the numbering formats in the gallery, click it to apply it to the entire list. Otherwise, continue to step 4.

4 Click Define New Number Format.

5 In the Define New Number Format dialog box, in the Number Style drop-down list, select the desired kind of numbering.

6 If you want to apply different character formatting to the number or letter, click the Font button and select the font, size, color, or other formatting. Note that this formatting does not affect the text of the list items.

7 If you want to include static text (text that doesn't change) before or after the list item's number or letter, or if you want different punctuation, edit the text in the Number Format text box.

8 Click OK.

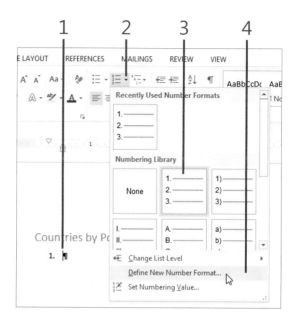

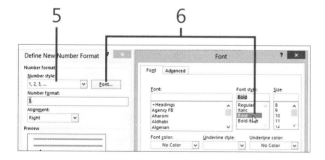

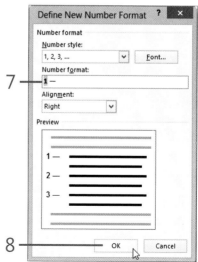

TIP When you create a new number format, Word automatically adds it to the Numbering Library. If you don't plan to use a custom format again, you can remove it from the Library by right-clicking it and then, on the shortcut menu that appears, click Remove.

Changing numbering values

You can mix numbered list paragraphs and unnumbered paragraphs in any order. You can format the unnumbered paragraphs with the same indent as the numbered paragraphs so that they act as a continuation of the preceding list item, or you can format them as ordinary non-list text.

Word 2013 also makes it possible for you to change the number of any numbered list paragraph. You have the option either to restart the numbering at 1 or to skip over some numbers and start at whatever number you need. When you change a paragraph's number, Word automatically renumbers all the paragraphs in the list that follow it.

Include unnumbered paragraphs in a list

1 Press Enter at the end of the numbered paragraph before the paragraph that will be unnumbered.

2 Click the Numbering button to turn it off.

3 Type one or more paragraphs of unnumbered text.

4 If you want to indent the unnumbered paragraphs so that they appear to be part of the list, select those paragraphs, on the Home tab, in the Styles group, click the dialog box launcher and apply the List Continue 2 style.

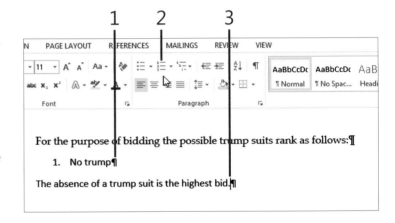

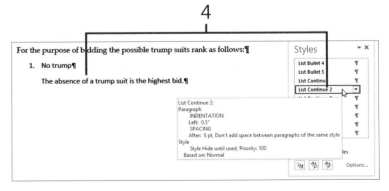

5 With the cursor in a new paragraph, click the Numbering button to turn it on again.

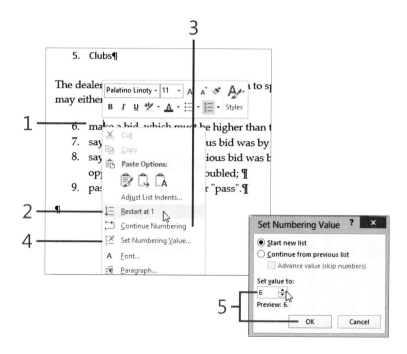

Restart numbering

1 Right-click in the numbered paragraph for which you want to restart numbering.

2 If you want the selected paragraph to start a new list, click Restart At 1.

3 If you previously restarted numbering but you now want the list to be continuous, click Continue Numbering.

4 If you want to skip one or more numbers in the list, click Set Numbering Value.

5 In the Set Value To spin box, type the desired value and click OK.

Using multilevel numbered headings

The Bullets tool and the Numbering tool on the Home tab are good enough for simple lists. But, when you need numbered headings at several levels, similar to an outline, you're going to want to use the multilevel list feature in Word 2013, instead.

Word automatically supplies the proper numbering whenever you apply one of the built-in heading styles.

Sometimes, the built-in list styles aren't quite what you want, but you can create a custom list style to suit your needs.

Use a multilevel list style

1 On the Home tab, in the Paragraph group, click the Multilevel List button.

2 In the List Library gallery, click one of the previews that show Heading style names.

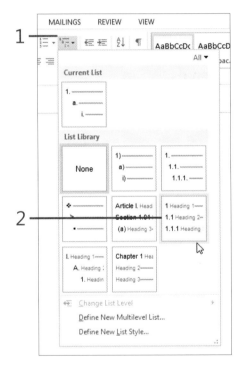

3 Apply the built-in Heading levels (Heading 1, Heading 2, and so on) to your text, as needed.

4 If you want to promote a heading (change it to the next higher level), in the Paragraph group, click the Decrease Indent button; to demote a heading, click the Increase Indent button.

5 You can drag a heading to a new location; Word will automatically renumber any affected headings.

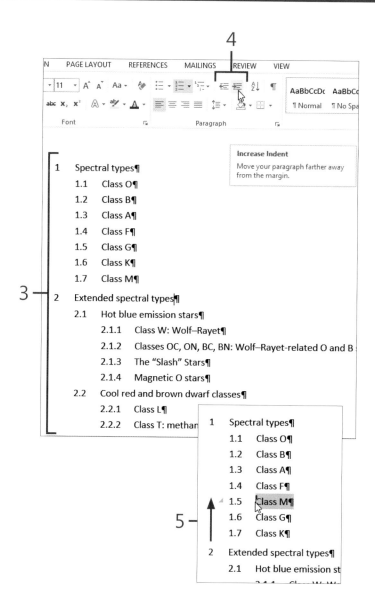

Customize a multilevel list style

1 On the Home tab, in the Paragraph group, click the Multilevel List button and then, in the gallery that opens, click the preview that is closest to the structure you want.

2 Click the Multilevel List button again. At the bottom of the gallery, click Define New Multilevel List.

3 In the Define New Multilevel List dialog box, if the More button is displayed, click it to expand the dialog box. (If the dialog box is already expanded, the button's label changes to Less.)

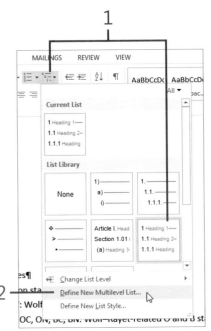

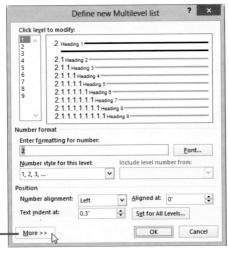

4 In the Click Level To Modify list, click the level that you want to change.

5 In the Enter Formatting For Number text box, add any text or punctuation that you want to include with the number. Delete any unwanted items.

6 If you want to apply different character formatting to the heading's number or letter, click the Font button and select the font, size, color, or other formatting. Note that this formatting does not affect the text of the headings.

7 In the Number Style For This Level drop-down list, select the format (number, letter, or other item) of the number itself.

8 Choose whether to apply the changes to the entire list or only to part of it. If the heading style assigned to the list level isn't correct, choose the desired style.

9 Click OK.

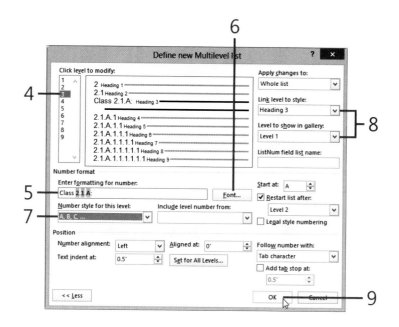

Revealing existing formatting

You might sometimes need to edit or reformat Word 2013 documents that you receive from someone else, or work with text that you copy and paste from other sources. If the formatting doesn't behave as you expect, it's important to find out what styles or direct formatting are responsible. One important tool for discovering formatting is simply to turn on nonprinting characters by clicking the Show/Hide ¶ button on the Home tab. Two other tools are the Reveal Formatting pane and the Style Inspector.

After you know why the text appears as it does, you should be able to remove any unwanted style or direct formatting to achieve the appearance that you want. Sometimes, it's easier to clear all the formatting so that the text has Normal style with no direct formatting, and then apply the style you need.

Use the Reveal Formatting pane

1 Press Shift+F1 to open the Reveal Formatting pane.

2 At the bottom of the pane, in the Options section, select both the Distinguish Style Source and the Show All Formatting Marks check boxes.

3 Click the document text for which you need to find the sources of the current format.

4 Examine the descriptions in the Reveal Formatting pane to determine which style or direct formatting is responsible for the text's appearance.

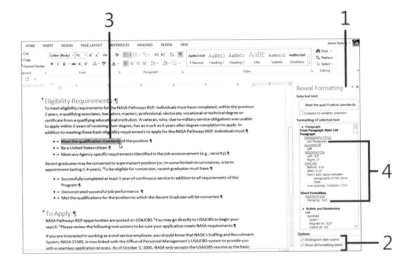

> ⚠️ **CAUTION** You can click any of the blue underlined links in the Reveal Formatting pane to open the corresponding dialog box for direct formatting. If the source of incorrect formatting is a style, you should modify the style's definition instead of applying direct formatting to override the style.

Use the Style Inspector

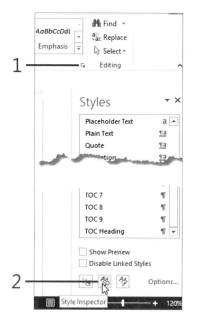

1 On the Home tab, in the Styles group, click the dialog box launcher (shortcut, Ctrl+Alt+Shift+S).

2 At the bottom of the Styles pane, click the Style Inspector button.

3 In the Style Inspector dialog box, click or select the document text for which you need to reveal the sources of the current format.

4 In the Paragraph Formatting section of the Style Inspector dialog box, read the name of the selection's paragraph style and any direct paragraph formatting that was applied there.

5 In the Text Level Formatting section, read the name of the selection's character style and any direct character formatting that was applied there.

6 To remove the paragraph style, character style, or direct formatting, you can click any of the four Clear buttons adjacent to each.

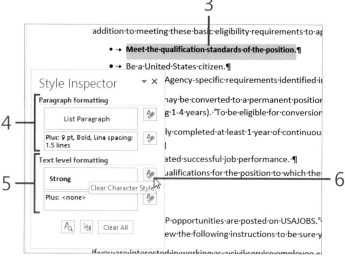

> **TIP** The Clear Character Style button in the Style Inspector dialog box is the only way to remove a character style from the selection without affecting any other formatting that was applied there.

> **TIP** If you select text that has more than one style or different kinds of direct formatting, one or more of the boxes in the Style Inspector will be blank. If this happens, select a smaller part of the text.

Building impressive documents

6

Although you'll find Microsoft Word 2013 useful for letters, memos, and other short tasks, the power of Word becomes obvious when you use it for longer and more complex documents that must make a good impression on your audience. Whether you write a newsletter, a report, or a marketing brochure, Word has the tools to help that document stand out.

You might create Word documents in which all of the pages have the same headers or footers, the same page measurements, and the same number of columns. In some documents, though, those formats need to change from one page to another. You'll learn how section breaks make that possible.

Some layouts should be repeated in many different documents, either to maintain a recognizable look within a series or to meet the requirements of a corporation, academic body, or other types of organizations. Word fills that need by using templates, which are files that save your styles, colors, and other tools. When you need a new document of a certain type, the template can supply everything you need to maintain a consistent look and feel to your documentation.

In this section:

- Inserting a section break
- Inserting headers and footers
- Choosing page size, margins, and orientation
- Changing the number of columns
- Applying a border around a page
- Inserting a cover page
- Working with the Normal template
- Finding and downloading templates
- Customizing or designing a template
- Basing a new document on a custom template
- Designing a template for two-sided printing
- Using themes and style sets

Inserting a section break

Within a Word 2013 document, you can change the margins, page orientation, page size, and number of columns. To separate any two regions of the document—called *sections*—where these characteristics differ, you must insert a section break.

You can decide whether you want each new section to begin on the same page as the preceding text or to start on a new page. You can also choose to force the new section to begin on an even page or an odd page: Word will automatically insert a blank page at the end of the preceding section, if necessary, to accommodate the page numbering.

Create a new section

1   Click in your document where you want the new section to begin.

2   On the Page Layout tab, in the Page Setup group, click Breaks and then, in the Section Breaks gallery that opens, click one of the four entries: Next Page, Continuous, Even Page, or Odd Page.

> ✓ **TIP**   To see section breaks in your document, on the Home tab, in the Paragraph group, click Show/Hide ¶. A section break appears as a double dotted line and displays the words Section Break and the type of the break.

> ✓ **TIP**   You can use the search box in the Navigation pane to find section breaks. First, click Show/Hide ¶ to render the breaks visible. Enter the code ^b in the search box and click the up or down arrow button in the pane to locate the previous or next section break.

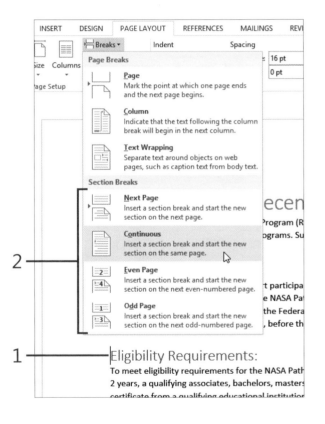

Change the section start type

1 Click in the section that you want to change.

2 On the Page Layout tab, in the Page Setup group, click the dialog box launcher (the small arrow icon in the lower-right corner).

3 In the Page Setup dialog box, click the Layout tab.

4 In the Section Start drop-down list, click the type of start that you want and then click OK.

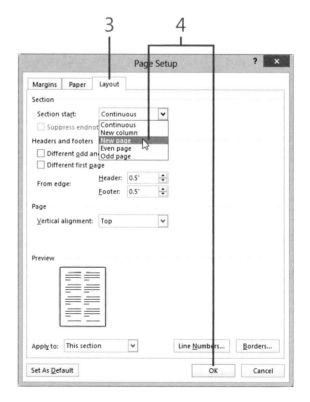

TIP If you insert a Continuous section break and then you change the orientation or the page size in the new section, Word automatically changes the section start type to Next Page.

Inserting headers and footers

In some documents, you might want certain identifying information to appear on every page, such as the page number, the document's title, your name, and/or the date. You can also include tables, graphics, and other kinds of items. Word 2013 reserves the header area at the top of the page and the footer area at the bottom of the page for this repeating information.

Word includes an assortment of built-in header and footer building blocks, many of them designed to coordinate with cover pages and other building blocks. If you want, you can add text to the building block you select, or replace it completely.

Insert a built-in header, footer, or page number

1 On the Insert tab, in the Header & Footer group, click one of the Header, Footer, or Page Number buttons to open the corresponding gallery.

2 Click one of the building blocks in the gallery.

3 If the building block includes places to enter text, type the required information.

4 On the Header & Footer Tools | Design contextual tab, click Close Header And Footer to return to the main text area.

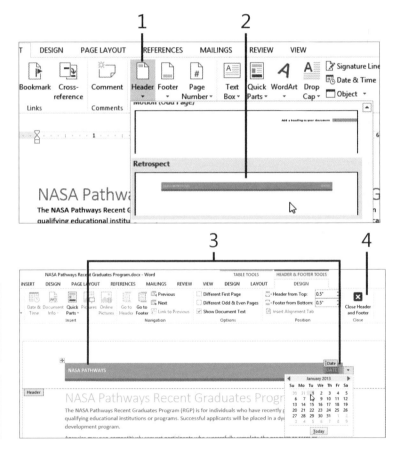

> **TIP** While you're working in the main text area of a document, the header and footer are automatically dimmed and you can't move the cursor into those areas. Similarly, while you're editing a header or footer, the main text area becomes dim.

> **TIP** When the cursor is in a header or footer, you can jump to the opposite area by clicking Go To Footer or Go To Header in the Navigation group on the Header & Footer Tools | Design tab.

Edit an existing header or footer

1 On the Home tab, in the Paragraph group, click the Show/Hide ¶ button.

2 Double-click the header or footer area to open it.

3 Position the cursor where you want to edit the text.

The default styles named Header and Footer include a center-aligned tab stop in the middle of the page and a right-aligned tab stop at the right margin, so you can press the Tab key to move to those positions.

4 Enter any additional text or fields that you want; delete any items that you don't want.

5 On the Header & Footer Tools | Design contextual tab, click Close Header And Footer to return to the main text area.

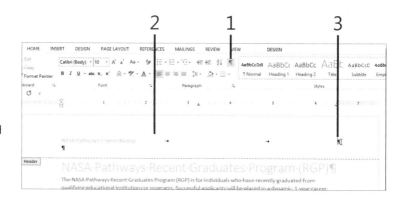

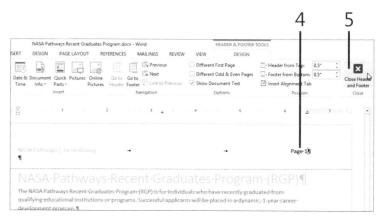

> ⚠ **CAUTION** If you insert a header building block and then insert a page number building block from the Top Of Page gallery in the Page Number button, the header building block is automatically removed. The same behavior occurs with a footer building block and the Bottom Of Page gallery on the Page Number button. To combine a header or footer building block and a page number in the same paragraph, use the Current Position gallery on the Page Number button, instead.

> → **TRY THIS** To change the page number that appears on the first page of a section (and to renumber all other pages in the section), on the Insert tab, in the Header & Footer group, click Page Number and then, at the bottom of the gallery that opens, click Format Page Numbers. In the Page Number Format dialog box, click the Start At option button and enter the number for the first page of the section.

> 🔍 **SEE ALSO** For information about making headers or footers different from those in the preceding section, see "Unlinking a header" on page 232.

Choosing page size and margins

Word 2013 offers many standard page sizes. The list of sizes you see in Word depends on which sizes are supported by the printer you select. If none of the entries in that list are right for your document, you can enter a custom size. Of course, you still must choose a size that your printer can handle.

Word also offers a selection of preset page margins as well as a way to set custom margins. Different types of documents often need different margins. A letter can use relatively wide margins, whereas a report might take smaller margins. A newsletter, magazine article, or book could be designed with a larger margin on one side of the page than on the other side to accommodate any binding.

Sometimes, you need different page sizes or margins in the same document. For example, you can include an envelope in a letter document (rather than maintaining two separate files). A section break is required to separate these two sections.

Choose a page size

1 If you want to apply a page size to part of your document that's different from the page size in the rest of the document, select that part.

2 On the Page Layout tab, in the Page Setup group, click Size.

3 If the size you want is one of the standard sizes in the Page Size gallery, and if you want to apply it to the whole document, click that item.

The sizes in the gallery are supplied by the printer driver. These sizes can differ from one brand or model of printer to another. If you don't see the size that you want, or if you selected text in step 1, continue to step 4.

4 At the bottom of the gallery, click More Paper Sizes.

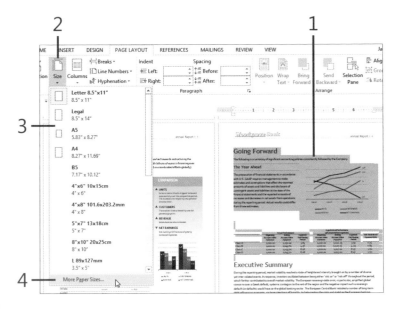

TIP If both the width and the height that you entered differ by 0.1 inch or less from the measurements of a standard size, the Paper Size text box shows the standard size. Otherwise, the Paper Size box shows Custom Size.

5 In the Page Setup dialog box, type the desired measurements in the Width and Height text boxes.

6 If you selected text in step 1, click the Apply To drop-down list and click Selected Text.

When you choose this option, a Next Page section break will be inserted automatically between the selected text and any unselected text that occurs before or after the selection.

7 If your printer has several ways to handle paper, you can choose the options in the Paper Source section for the first page and for the other pages.

The items in these lists are supplied by the printer driver, so they might differ from one brand or model of printer to another.

8 Click OK.

✓ **TIP** Word can't create a page larger than 22 inches (558.7 mm) in either direction, regardless of the maximum size the printer driver allows.

✓ **TIP** If you want all new blank documents based on the Normal.dotm template to start with the size you selected, click Set As Default. Then, click Yes when you are asked whether you want to change the default settings.

→ **TRY THIS** Instead of letting Word automatically insert Next Page section breaks before and after selected text, on the Page Layout tab, in the Page Setup group, click Breaks and insert the desired type of section breaks. Then, click in the section that you want to change and click the desired size in the Size gallery. For more information about section break types, see "Inserting a section break" on page 136.

Choose page margins

1 If you want to apply margins to part of your document that are different from the margins in the rest of the document, select that part.

2 On the Page Layout tab, in the Page Setup group, click Margins.

3 If the set of margins you want is one of the standard items in the Margins gallery, and if you want to apply it to the whole document, click that item. If you don't see the margins you want, or if you selected text in step 1, continue to step 4.

4 At the bottom of the gallery, click Custom Margins.

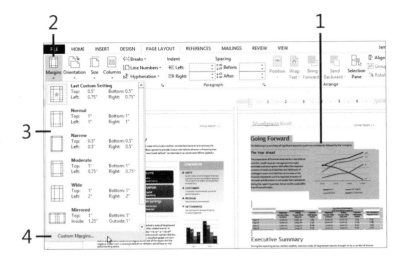

5 In the Page Setup dialog box, type the desired measurements in the Top, Bottom, Left, and Right text boxes.

If your design calls for an asymmetric layout, you can enter different values for Left and Right, or for Top and Bottom.

6 If your document will be printed on only one side of the page and then bound, you should add extra width to the left or top margin by entering a value in the Gutter text box and choosing an item in the Gutter Position drop-down list.

7 If you entered different left and right margins in step 5, and if you plan to print the document on both sides of the paper (duplex printing), click the Multiple Pages box and click Mirror Margins.

8 If you selected text in step 1, click the Apply To drop-down list and click Selected Text.

When you choose this option, a Next Page section break is inserted automatically between the selected text and any unselected text that occurs before or after the selection.

9 Click OK.

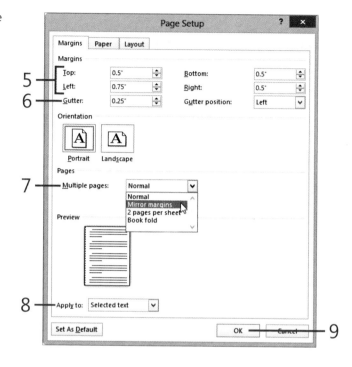

 SEE ALSO For more information about mirror margins, see "Designing a template for two-sided printing" on page 170.

TIP If you want to change the margins within a single page, on the Page Layout tab, in the Page Setup group, click Breaks and insert Continuous section breaks manually before you start this procedure. For information about inserting section breaks, see "Inserting a section break" on page 136.

Changing the page orientation

Although most documents use *portrait orientation* (in which the page height is greater than the width), tables and graphs sometimes require *landscape orientation* (the width is greater than the height) for a few pages. You can also print signs and posters with different orientations.

In a document that contains both portrait and landscape pages, you might want all the headers on both kinds of pages to appear in the same place and facing the same way. Word 2013 doesn't have an automatic way to do that, but this task explains how to make it happen.

Select an orientation

1 If you want to apply an orientation to part of your document that's different from the orientation of the rest of the document, insert section breaks before and after the part you want to change.

2 Click within the section that you want to change.

3 On the Page Layout tab, in the Page Setup group, click Orientation and then, in the drop-down list that appears, click Portrait or Landscape.

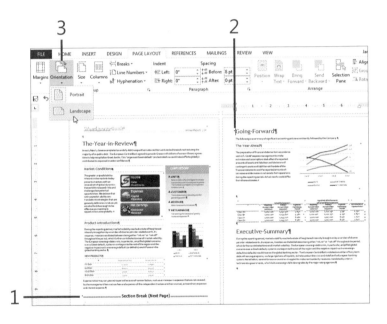

> ⚠️ **CAUTION** The choices on the Orientation button always apply to the entire document unless you insert section breaks first. For more information about inserting section breaks, see "Inserting a section break" on page 136.

> ✓ **TIP** When you print a document on both sides of the paper and that document contains both portrait and landscape pages, Word always rotates the landscape pages clockwise (to the right). You might be able to rotate the landscape pages counterclockwise by using a setting in the Printer Properties dialog box, depending on the printer driver for your specific printer. Alternatively, you can print the landscape pages separately by using the Manual Duplex setting on the Print tab of the Backstage view.

> ✓ **TIP** On the Print tab of the Backstage view, you can choose whether to print the document on one side of each sheet or on both sides. There are two choices for two-sided printing: flip the pages on the long edge, or on the short edge. Flipping on the long edge is appropriate for most documents, whereas flipping on the short edge is appropriate for documents that contain only landscape pages.

Create a portrait header on landscape pages

1 Double-click the header area of the section that contains landscape pages.

2 On the Header & Footer Tools | Design contextual tab, if the Link To Previous button in the Navigation group is turned on, click it to turn it off.

3 If a section containing portrait pages follows the landscape section, click its header and click Link To Previous to turn it off.

4 In the header of the landscape section, select the text of the header, and then on the Home tab, in the Clipboard group, click Cut (or press Ctrl+X).

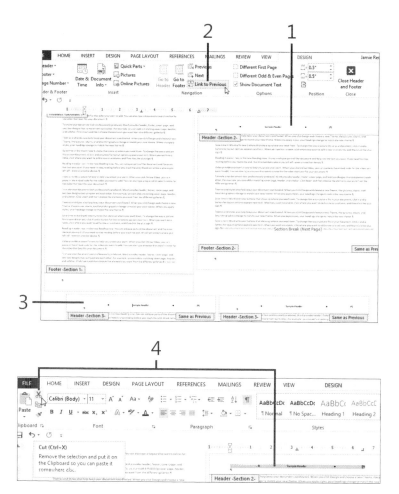

5 While the cursor is still in the header area of the landscape section, on the Insert tab, in the Text group, click Text Box and then, at the bottom of the gallery that opens, click Draw Text Box.

6 Drag the special cursor in the margin of the landscape page to create a text box in the relative location that matches the header text on the portrait pages.

7 With the cursor inside the text box, on the Home tab, in the Clipboard group, click Paste (or press Ctrl+V).

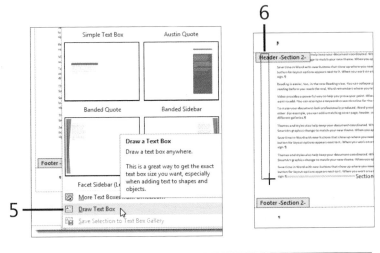

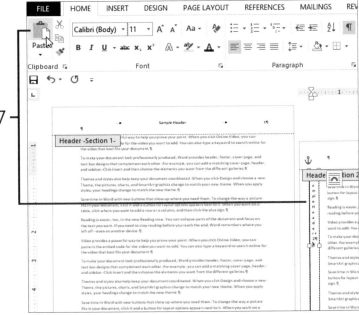

8 On the Drawing Tools | Format contextual tab, in the Text group, click Text Direction and then click the rotation option to pivot the content of the text box to face in the proper direction.

9 On the Drawing Tools | Format contextual tab, in the Shape Styles group, click Shape Outline and click No Outline to turn off the border for the text box.

10 On the Header & Footer Tools | Design contextual tab, click Close Header And Footer to return to the main text.

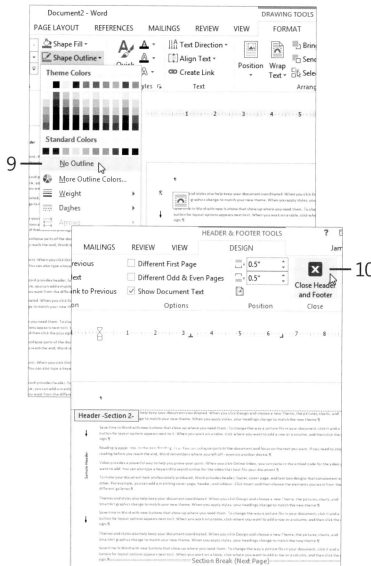

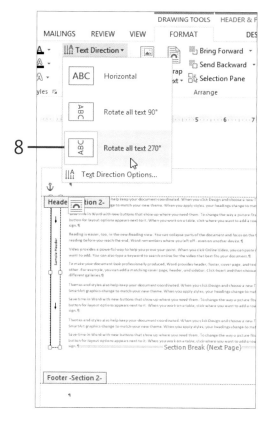

Changing the number of columns

Some documents contain long, unbroken blocks of text. If you use a common layout with a text width of more than 6 inches (15 cm), that text will be uninviting and hard to read. In newsletters, brochures, and similar documents, it's best to format the text in two or more narrower columns.

In Word 2013, you can create sections—on the same page or on different pages—with different numbers of columns. For example, you can place a heading in a one-column section, followed by body text in two or three columns.

Set up a multicolumn section

1 Select the text that you want to format into multiple columns.

2 On the Page Layout tab, in the Page Setup group, click Columns.

3 If you want to use one of the layouts shown in the Columns gallery, click it to apply it to the selected text. Otherwise, continue to step 4.

4 At the bottom of the gallery, click More Columns.

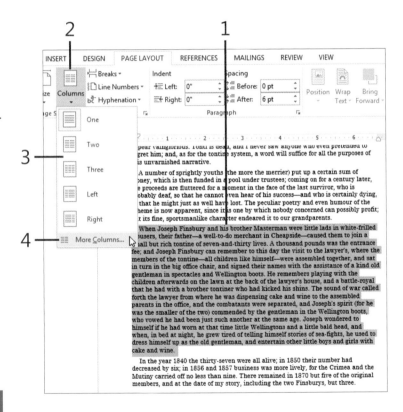

TIP If you want all the columns of a section to end at approximately the same height, insert a Continuous section break at the end of the last paragraph of the last column.

5 In the Columns dialog box, enter the number of columns that you want.

6 If you don't want all the columns to have the same width, clear the Equal Column Width check box. Then, type the measurements for the individual columns and the spaces between the columns.

7 If you want a divider line between the columns, select the Line Between check box.

8 In the Apply To drop-down list, ensure that Selected Text is showing.

9 Click OK.

> ✓ **TIP** As you enter one of the measurements and move to the next box, Word adjusts the other measurements to keep the total width of the columns and the space between them equal to the width between the page margins.

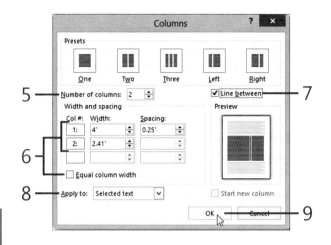

Span a heading across multiple columns

1 In the multicolumn text, press Enter to start a new paragraph. Type the heading and then apply a style and other formatting as needed. Select the heading paragraph.

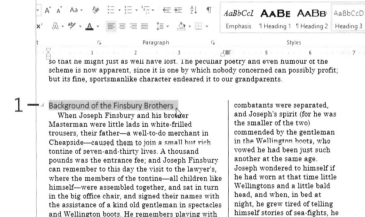

2 On the Page Layout tab, in the Page Setup group, click the Columns button. In the gallery that opens, click the option for One.

3 If you prefer, on the Home tab, in the Paragraph group, you can click Center (shortcut, Ctrl+E) to center the heading text on the page. You can also format the heading paragraph with shading or a border, which will extend across the page.

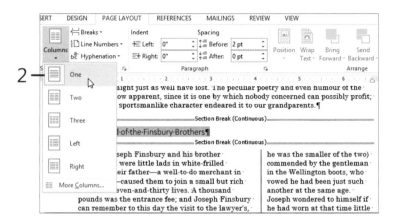

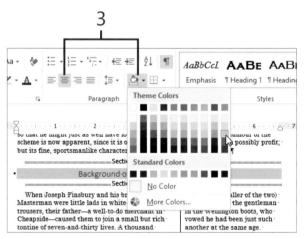

TIP When you select text and then change the number of columns, Word automatically inserts Continuous section breaks before and after the selection.

Applying a border around a page

For some letters or marketing brochures, your design might specify a line border around the pages. Word 2013 offers a number of design elements from which you can choose.

Less formal documents—party invitations, announcements, and the like—call for more lighthearted fare. Word provides art borders that include hearts and flowers, holiday themes, and elaborate designs.

Format a line border

1 On the Design tab, in the Page Background group, click Page Borders.

2 On the Page Border tab of the Borders And Shading dialog box, in the Setting column, click one of the buttons.

3 Choose a style, color, and width for the border.

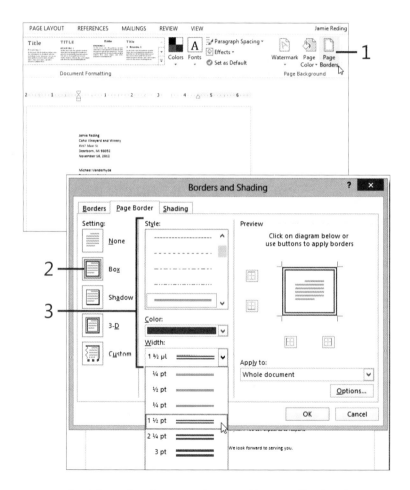

4 If you want a different style, color, or width for one or more of the page sides, first click one of those sides in the preview to remove it. Then, change the style, color, or width and click the same side in the preview to insert the new line.

5 If you want to limit the border to a particular section, in the Apply To drop-down list, choose the desired setting.

6 Click Options to set the distance of the border from the text or from the edge of the page.

If you choose to measure from the text, you can also specify whether to include the header and footer areas within the border.

7 Click OK.

 TIP The 3-D setting in the Borders And Shading dialog box produces the same result as the Box setting, unless you choose one of the line styles that isn't symmetric (for example, a thin line and a thick line).

TIP Some of the line styles offer a greater selection of widths than others.

Insert an art border

1 On the Design tab, in the Page Background group, click Page Borders.

2 On the Page Border tab of the Borders And Shading dialog box, in the Setting column, click the Box item.

3 In the Art box, click a selection to see it in the preview.

4 Choose a width (up to a maximum of 31 points) and a color, if the Color drop-down list is enabled.

5 If you want to limit the border to a particular section, change the Apply To drop-down list.

6 Click Options to set the distance of the border from the text or from the edge of the page.

If you choose to measure from the text, you can also specify whether to include the header and footer areas within the border.

7 Click OK.

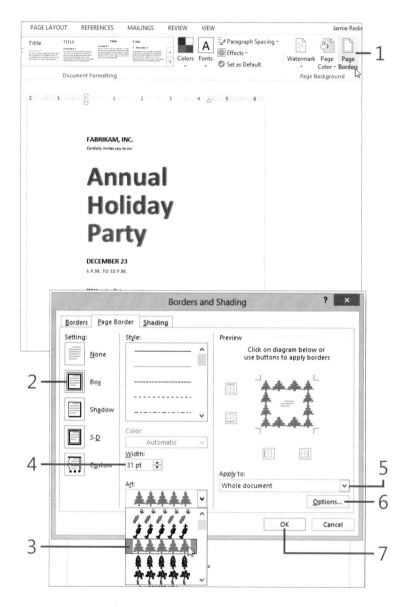

Inserting a cover page

Business and academic documents often need a cover page to help make a good first impression. The cover page might include your name or your company's name, a title and date, and other information. A logo, a tasteful design, or a striking photograph will draw attention to your work.

Word 2013 includes a selection of cover page designs as building blocks, and additional covers can be downloaded from Office.com. Many of these designs include content controls that automatically display or change the information shown on the Info page of the Backstage view.

Insert a built-in cover page

1. Switch to Print Layout view if you're not already using that view to display your document.

2. On the Insert tab, in the Pages group, click Cover Page, and then in the gallery that opens, click a thumbnail.

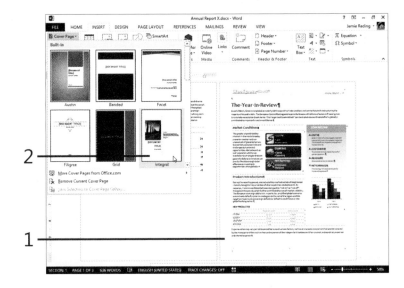

SEE ALSO For more information about content controls, see "Inserting content controls" on page 217.

3 Click each of the content controls on the cover page and enter the information that you want to appear on the page.

4 If you'd like, you can modify the cover page in any of the following ways:

- Click the Cover Page button and click a different thumbnail in the gallery, or at the bottom of the gallery, click Remove Current Cover Page.

- Click the Design tab, click Themes, and then select a different theme from the gallery. This changes the colors and fonts used throughout the document.

- If the cover page includes a picture, right-click the picture and click Change Picture. Then, select another picture from your computer or from an online source. You might also add a picture to a design that doesn't include one.

- If there's a content control that you don't want to use, right-click it and then, on the shortcut menu that appears, click Remove Content Control. If you want to add a content control, on the Home tab, in the Text group, click Quick Parts, point to Document Property, and then click the desired property name.

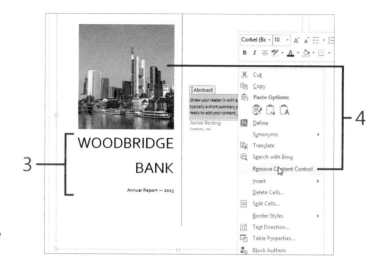

SEE ALSO For information about designing a template with a cover page for other people to use, see *www.shaunakelly.com/word/templates/front-cover-images-in-microsoft-word-report-templates.html*.

Working with the Normal template

Word 2013 uses templates—files saved with an extension of .dotx or .dotm—for several purposes. Some templates serve only as the basis for creating new documents. They might contain styles, text, building blocks, and macros that are present as soon as the new document appears on your screen. Other templates can supply macros and customized ribbon tabs or customized buttons on the Quick Access Toolbar, but they don't affect the text or styles that are available in new documents. These templates, which are any templates stored in the folder designated as your Word Startup folder, are called *global* because they're present with every document you open.

The template named Normal.dotm has a special status: it's both a global template and the basis for creating new documents. When you open Word by clicking the program's icon rather than clicking a specific document's icon, it starts with a document based on Normal.dotm. It also starts with any customizations you saved in Normal.dotm during previous sessions. When you click New in the Backstage view and then click Blank Document, that new document is based on Normal.dotm.

The Normal.dotm template must be stored in the folder that's designated as your User Templates folder. If you move the

Normal.dotm file to a different folder or change its name, it won't be recognized as the special template, and Word will create a new Normal.dotm in the User Templates folder. You can take advantage of this behavior to troubleshoot problems related to Normal.dotm, by temporarily moving or renaming the file.

Most changes that you might want to store in the Normal.dotm template can be saved without directly opening the file itself. Examples of these changes include the following:

- When you modify a style in a document based on Normal.dotm, you can select the New Documents Based On This Template option to modify the style in the template at the same time.

- When you change settings in the Font dialog box, the Paragraph dialog box, or the Page Setup dialog box, you can click the Set As Default button at the bottom of the dialog box.

- When you choose a theme on the Design tab, you can click Set As Default in the Document Formatting group.

> ⚠ **CAUTION** Although you can open and edit the Normal.dotm template like any other template, don't store any text in the main document area or the headers or footers of the Normal.dotm template. That text would appear in all new blank documents, and you would need to delete it from documents where it doesn't belong. Also, if you use the Labels feature on the Mailings tab to create labels or business cards, the presence of a header or footer inherited from Normal.dotm will cause the label text to print in the wrong locations.

Locate the User Templates folder

1 Click File to display the Backstage view and then click Options the Options tab.

2 In the Word Options dialog box, click the Advanced tab and then, at the right side of the dialog box, scroll to the bottom of the page. Click File Locations.

> **TIP** If macros are enabled in your Office 2013 installation, a quicker alternative for finding the User Templates folder is to open the macro editor (shortcut, Shift+F11), open the Immediate window (Ctrl+G), type the command **Print Options.DefaultFilePath (wdUserTemplatesPath)**, and then press Enter. The path appears on the next line.

3 In the File Locations dialog box, click the User Templates item and then click Modify.

4 In the Modify Location dialog box, read the path of the User Templates folder in the address box. If you want to be able to paste the path into the File Explorer, click the path in the address box to select it and then copy it by pressing Ctrl+C.

5 Click Cancel to avoid making any change in the path. Then, click Close in the File Locations dialog box and click Cancel in the Options dialog box.

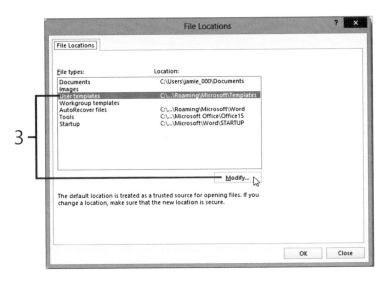

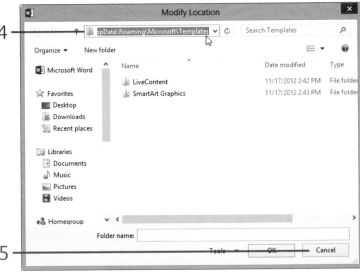

> ✓ **TIP** The User Templates location created by the Office 2013 installer is under the hidden AppData folder within your user profile. If you try to navigate to that location with the File Explorer, you won't see that folder unless you change the folder options of File Explorer to show hidden folders.

> ✓ **TIP** The first time you start Word after installing Office 2013, Normal.dotm might not exist yet. Instead, Word uses the default options and built-in styles stored in the program's code. When you exit from Word you might then be prompted to save Normal.dotm. If you upgraded to Office 2013 from a previous version, the customizations in the old Normal.dotm are preserved.

Finding and downloading templates

With a little searching on the Internet, you can find templates for almost any kind of document that you can imagine. You might be able to base documents on those templates directly, or you might need to modify them to suit your needs better.

Microsoft offers hundreds of templates for free download from the Office.com website, and you can search for them from the Backstage view in Word 2013.

Get templates from Office.com

1 Click File to display the Backstage view and then click the New tab.

2 Scroll through the Backstage view page to look at the thumbnails of some sample templates.

3 If you find a template that's suitable for your new document, click its thumbnail to open a preview dialog box. Then, click Create to download the template to your User Templates folder and create a document based on that template. Otherwise, continue to step 4.

> ⚠️ **CAUTION** When you download any files from the Internet, first be sure that you know and trust their source. Take extra care with templates, because they can contain virus-like programs written as macros. Do not store templates in a trusted folder (described on page 387) until you have opened them in Protected View and determined that they are safe to use.

4 Click in the search box and type a word or phrase that describes the kind of document that you want to create. Press Enter or click the magnifier icon.

5 Scroll through the thumbnails in the search results.

You can click one or more of the categories on the right side to reduce the number of thumbnails shown. If you find a template that's suitable for your new document, click its thumbnail to open a preview dialog box. Then, click Create to download the template to your User Templates folder and create a document based on that template.

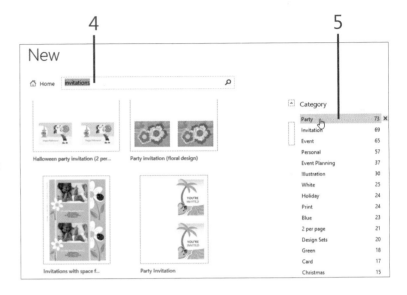

TIP When you see a thumbnail of a template that you might want to use again later, click the pushpin icon next to its name. That thumbnail will appear in the initial list on the New page of the Backstage view until you click the pushpin icon again to unpin it.

Customizing an existing template

When you use one of the standard templates in Word 2013 or when you receive a template from someone else, you might decide to change some of the styles. You could also add text, tables, form fields, and other content. Although you can make these changes in each new document that you base on the template, it's more efficient to customize the template just once.

If you want to modify the original template, use the Save command to store the changes in the same file. However, it's often preferable to use the Save As command to make a new file containing the changes, while leaving the original template unchanged.

Open a template for editing

1 Click File to display the Backstage view and then click the Open tab.

2 Click Computer and then click Browse.

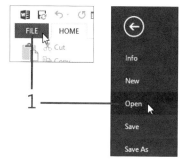

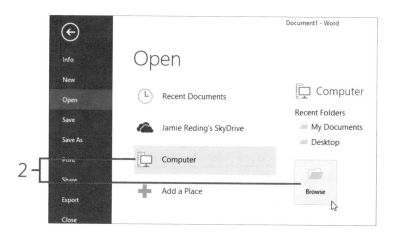

3 In the Open dialog box, click the file type drop-down list and click Word Templates (*.dotx).

4 Click in the address bar, type **%appdata%\Microsoft\Templates**, and then press the Enter key.

5 Click the template that you want to edit.

6 Click the Open button.

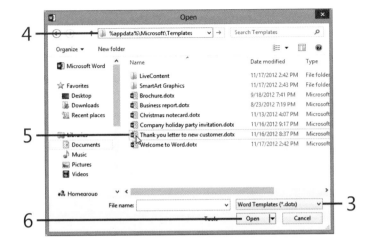

Modify and save the template

1 If you plan to save the modified template as a different file, keeping the original template unchanged, it's best to create the new file before you make any changes—that way, you won't accidentally save changes to the original location. Click File and then click the Save As tab.

2 Click Computer and click Browse.

3 In the Save As dialog box, ensure that the Save As Type drop-down list is set to Word Template (*.dotx). If the template contains macros, set it to Word Macro-Enabled Template (*.dotm). The Custom Office Templates folder is automatically selected.

4 In the File Name text box, enter a name for the new template's file.

5 Click the Save button.

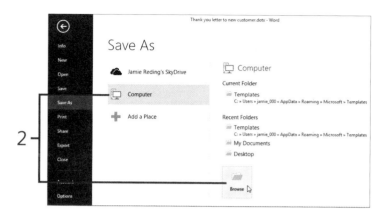

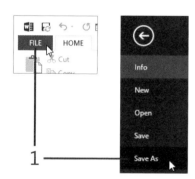

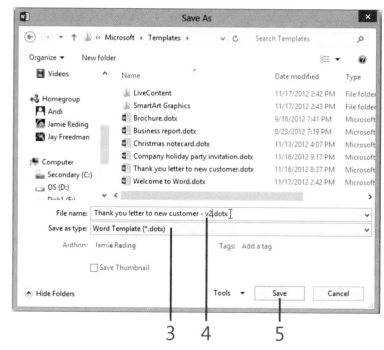

> ✓ **TIP** If you select the Save Thumbnail check box, you can see a preview of the template's contents on the New page of the Backstage view. However, many common templates don't have any visible text, so it isn't useful to enable a thumbnail for them.

> ✓ **TIP** When the Save As dialog box closes, ensure that you see the new file name in Word's title bar. You can also check that the folder path is correct by clicking File and then clicking Info. The file name and path appear below the Backstage view's page title.

6 Modify or add any text, graphics, styles, or other content in the new template.

As you work, you should frequently click the Save icon on the Quick Access Toolbar or press Ctrl+S.

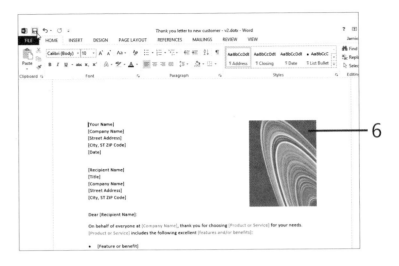

 SEE ALSO For information about modifying styles, see "Creating and modifying styles" on page 94.

 TRY THIS You can create a template by starting with a new or existing document instead of a template. Use the same steps as in this task to save the result as a template.

Designing a template

A template is like a cookie cutter; it's a tool for turning out lots of documents that have the same layout and appearance. The more thought and effort you put into designing your template, the less work you'll have to do when you use it to create documents.

Think about the purpose of the documents you'll create from the template, and the items that should be in those documents. Here are some useful guidelines:

- Documents that have different purposes should usually be based on different templates.

- Elements that are common to all the documents based on a single template should be included in that template.

- The places in which the documents differ should be represented in the template by placeholders such as bookmarks, form fields, and/or content controls.

- If the locations of certain items on the page should not change when the document is edited, use tables or text boxes to position those items.

- Consider using borders and shading in some styles to clarify the relationships of the document's parts, or to make important information stand out.

Create a new template

1 Click the File tab to display the Backstage view, click the New tab, and then click Blank Document.

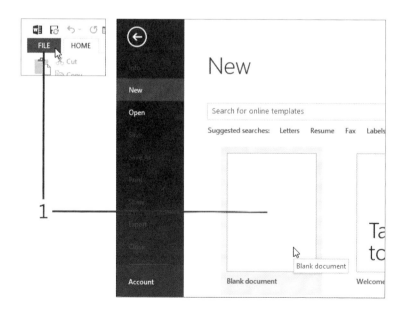

2 On the Quick Access Toolbar, Click the Save icon. Click Computer and then click Browse.

3 In the Save As dialog box, change the Save As Type box to Word Template (*.dotx), which automatically sets the path to the Custom Office Templates folder. Enter a file name and click Save.

4 Open the header or footer pane and insert any header or footer building blocks, text, and graphics that should repeat on every page.

5 If the template is intended as the base for documents such as invoices or letters, on the Header & Footer Tools | Design contextual tab, in the Options group, select the Different First Page check box and place a logo and/or address information in the first page header.

6 On the Header & Footer Tools | Design contextual tab, click Close Header And Footer.

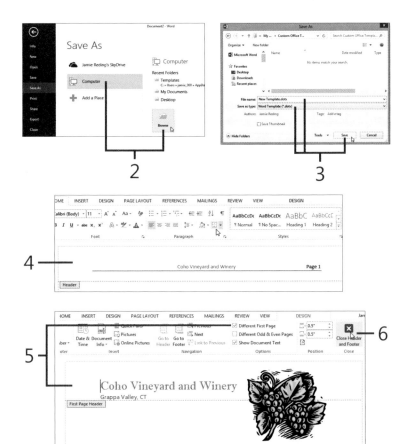

> **TIP** If you include a Date field in your template, that field will update to the current date every time you open a document based on the template. If you want each document to show the date that document was created, insert a CreateDate field in the template instead of a Date field. For more information about inserting fields, see "Using the Field dialog box" on page 200.

7 Enter any text and graphics that should be in the body of all documents based on this template. Save the template frequently as you work.

8 Insert a table to position items that must be aligned in rows or that must stay in fixed locations on the page. You can insert content controls or merge fields into the table's cells.

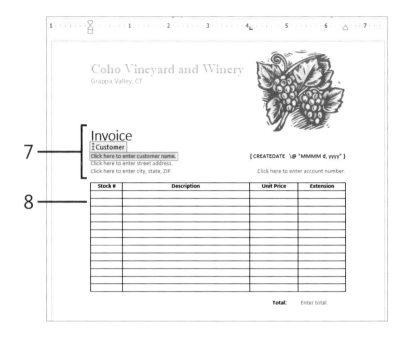

SEE ALSO   For more information about inserting content controls, see "Inserting content controls" on page 217. For more information about inserting merge fields, see "Adding merge fields" on page 341.

TIP   If you want to turn off all of a table's borders so that they won't print or show on screen, click in the table and press Ctrl+Alt+U. To see where the table's cells are, on the Table Tools | Layout contextual tab, in the Table group, click View Gridlines.

Basing a new document on a custom template

Word 2013 considers templates that you create by using the Save As command to be *custom templates*. By default, the program stores custom templates in the Custom Office Templates folder within your My Documents folder. If you've used previous versions of Word, which stored all templates in the User Templates folder, you'll recognize this as a significant change.

Before you create any custom templates, the New page of the Backstage view displays thumbnails for recently used templates, for files in the Templates folder on your computer, and for files that are available to download from Office.com.

If a path is specified for the optional Workgroup Templates location (see "Working with advanced options" on page 436), links for Featured and Shared appear on the New page. Click the Shared link to display the templates in the Workgroup Templates location. The Featured link returns the display to the original New page.

After you create your first custom template, the links change to Featured and Custom if you have specified a Workgroup Templates location, or Featured and Personal otherwise. Click the Custom or Personal link to display the custom templates as well as the Workgroup Templates location if it's specified.

Use a custom template

1 Click File to display the Backstage view and then click the New tab.

2 Click Custom or Personal.

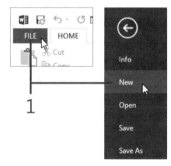

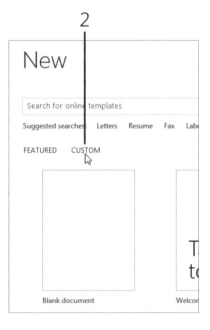

3 If both your Workgroup Templates location and the Custom Office Templates folder are visible, click Custom Office Templates. Otherwise, continue at step 4.

4 Click the custom template that you want to use to create a new document.

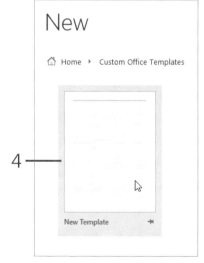

> **TIP** If you prefer to have the thumbnails for your custom templates on the Featured page of the New page in the Backstage view, you must save each custom template in the User Templates folder instead of the Custom Office Templates folder, or move each template after you save it.

Designing a template for two-sided printing

If documents based on your custom template will be printed on both sides of the paper (called *duplex* printing), there are a few additional design elements for you to consider.

First, you might want larger margins on one side of the page than on the other to allow for binding or three-hole punching or to leave space for notes. When the document is duplex printed, the wider and narrower margins should switch places on the front and back of the paper. Word 2013 does this automatically when you select the page layout option for Mirror Margins.

It's common in two-sided documents to place the page numbers at the margin opposite the binding edge so that the numbers can be seen without fully turning the pages. Also, the odd-numbered and even-numbered pages might have different information in their headers and footers—for example, the author's name on the even pages and the document's title on the odd pages. You can set up different odd and even headers and footers to meet both of these requirements.

Turn on mirror margins

1 On the Page Layout tab, in the Page Setup group, click Margins and then, at the bottom of the gallery that opens, click Custom Margins.

2 On the Margins tab of the Page Setup dialog box, in the Multiple Pages drop-down list, click Mirror Margins.

3 Enter different measurements for the Inside and Outside margins and, if desired, enter a measurement in the Gutter box.

4 Click OK.

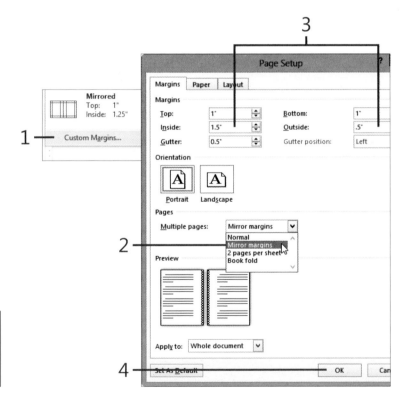

> **TIP** "Inside" refers to the binding edge of the paper, which is on the right for even-numbered pages and on the left for odd-numbered pages. The gutter measurement is always added to the inside margin when mirror margins are chosen.

Insert odd and even headers and footers

1 On the Home tab, in the Paragraph group, click Show/Hide ¶ to display nonprinting characters.

2 Your template must have at least two pages so that you can gain access to the even-page headers and footers. If your template currently consists of a single page, click at the end of the text and press Ctrl+Enter to insert a manual page break.

3 Double-click in the header area of the first page to open the header pane.

4 On the Header & Footer Tools | Design contextual tab, in the Options group, select the Different Odd & Even Pages check box.

5 Insert your choice of building block, page number, document property, or other text in the Odd Page header, the Odd Page footer, or both. When you insert a page number, place it at the right margin.

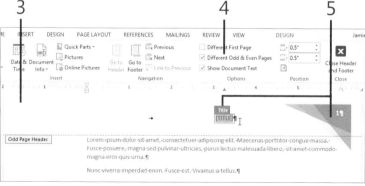

SEE ALSO For more information about inserting building blocks and page numbers, see "Inserting headers and footers" on page 138. For more information about inserting document properties, see "Using document properties" on page 223.

6 On the Header & Footer Tools | Design contextual tab, in the Navigation group, click the Next button to move the cursor to the Even Page Header.

7 Insert your choice of building block, page number, and other text in the Even Page Header, the Even Page Footer, or both. When you insert a page number, place it at the left margin.

8 On the Header & Footer Tools | Design contextual tab, click Close Header And Footer.

9 Select the page break at the end of the first page and press the Delete key. Save the template.

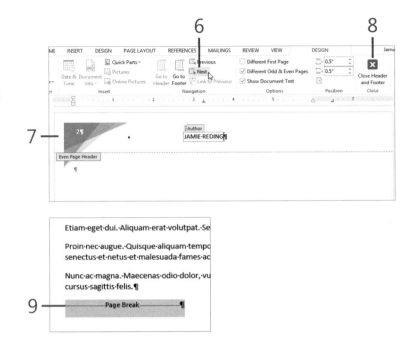

Using themes and style sets

Themes and style sets were introduced in Word 2007, and in Word 2013, they are gathered on the new Design tab on the ribbon. Together, these features let you change the overall appearance of your document quickly.

A *theme* is a collection of colors, fonts, and effects. By choosing a single theme in the Themes gallery on the Design tab, you apply the entire predefined collection to the document. In turn, the members of the collection are also collections of formats.

- A theme color collection is a set of 12 colors used for text, backgrounds, charts, shapes, and hyperlinks. Wherever you see a color gallery (such as the font color, background color, or shape fill color buttons), the section labeled Theme Colors is based on the current theme.

- A theme font collection consists of two fonts. One of the theme fonts is used by any style in which the font is specified as (Body), and the other theme font is used by any style in which the font is specified as (Headings). The two theme fonts can be different—for example, a serif font such as Cambria and a sans serif font such as Calibri—or they can be the same.

- A theme effect collection determines some of the look of shapes, charts, and SmartArt by adding shadows, outlines, gradients, and 3-D shading.

A *style set* is a collection of style definitions. For example, one style set might define the Normal style with a font size of 10 points, left-aligned; the Heading 1 style might be defined with a font size of 14 points, all caps, Accent 1 color, center-aligned, with a bottom paragraph border. Another style set could define Normal style with a font size of 11 points, justified; and the Heading 1 style with a font size of 16 points, the Accent 2 color, left-aligned, with no border. You can choose either appearance with a single click in the Style Sets gallery on the Design tab.

Select a built-in theme

1. On the Design tab, in the Document Formatting group, click Themes.

2. Point to thumbnails in the Themes gallery and watch the live preview in the document. When you see the appearance that you want, click the thumbnail to apply the theme.

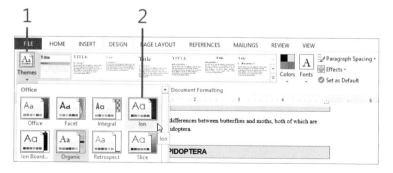

✓ **TIP** The Style Set gallery on the Design tab and the Styles gallery on the Home tab change to match the theme you select.

Modify a theme's fonts, colors, and effects

1 Open or create a document with a representative selection of headings, text, and graphics.

2 On the Design tab, in the Document Formatting group, click Themes and click the thumbnail of the theme that you want to change.

3 On the Design tab, in the Document Formatting group, click Colors and then, in the gallery that opens, point to the color samples in the gallery while watching the live preview in the document. If you see the appearance that you want, click the sample to change the theme color collection, and continue at step 7. Otherwise, continue at step 4.

4 If you don't see the specific colors you want, at the bottom of the gallery, click Customize Colors.

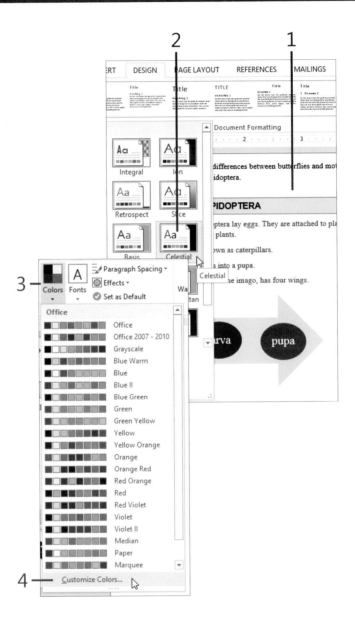

5 In the Create New Theme Colors dialog box, click each theme color button that you want to change and choose the desired color from the gallery.

6 Enter a name for the set of theme colors and click Save.

7 On the Design tab, in the Document Formatting group, click Fonts and point to the font samples in the gallery while watching the live preview in the document. If you see the appearance you want, click the sample to change the theme font collection and continue at step 10. Otherwise, continue at step 8.

8 If you don't see the specific fonts you want, at the bottom of the gallery, click Customize Fonts.

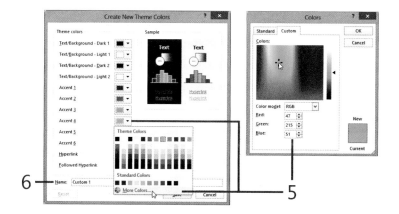

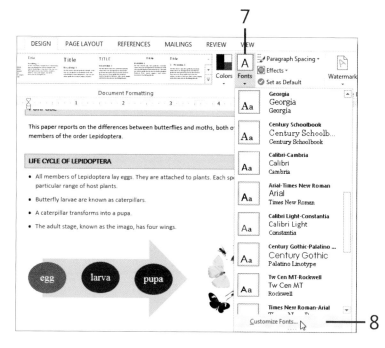

9 In the Create New Theme Fonts dialog box, select the fonts that you want in the drop-down lists for Heading Font and Body Font. Enter a name for the font collection and click Save.

10 On the Design tab, in the Document Formatting group, click Effects and point to the graphics samples in the gallery while watching the live preview in the document. If you see the appearance you want, click the sample to change the theme effect collection.

11 On the Design tab, in the Document Formatting group, click Themes, and then at the bottom of the gallery, click Save Current Theme. Enter a name for the new theme and click Save.

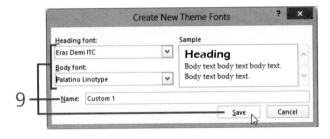

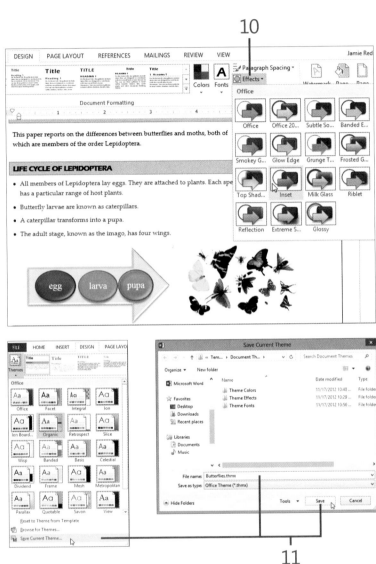

⚠ **CAUTION** If you apply fonts or colors in your document as direct formatting, or if you apply styles that use specific font names instead of (Body) or (Headings) in their font definitions, those parts of your document won't change when you apply a different theme.

Apply a style set

1 On the Design tab, in the gallery in the Document Formatting group, point to the thumbnails while watching the live preview in the document. If you see the appearance you want, click the thumbnail to apply the style set. Otherwise, continue at step 2.

2 If you want to change some of the styles in the style set, change the definitions of those styles in the current document. For each style that you want to change, right-click the name of the style in the Styles pane and click Modify. Make the desired changes in the Modify Style dialog box.

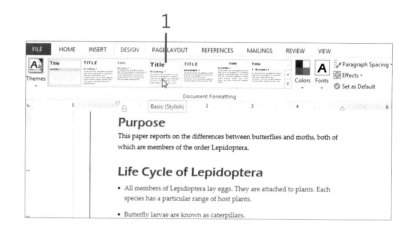

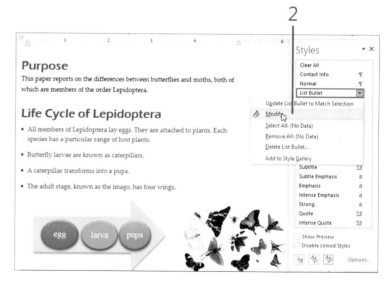

 SEE ALSO For more information about changing the definition of a style, see "Creating and modifying styles" on page 94.

3 On the Design tab, open the style set gallery and click Save As A New Style Set.

4 In the Save As New Style Set dialog box, enter a name for the new style set and click Save.

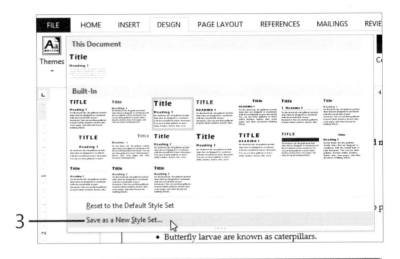

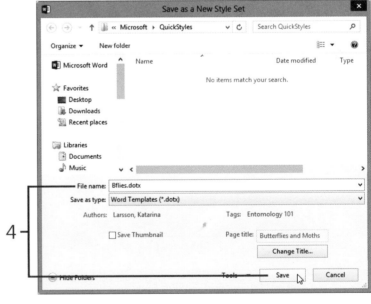

Making layouts with tables and text boxes

7

In many documents such as letters and contracts, the text starts at the left margin and just goes on until it reaches the right margin; then, it goes to the next line and does the same again. For other documents such as invoices, you need to line up text into two or more columns, with each set of related items on the same line. If you try to do that by typing spaces between the columns, the columns probably won't line up perfectly.

One way to solve this problem is to set a tab stop where you want each column to start, and press the Tab key to move from the end of one column to the beginning of the next column. This works well enough when each item fits on one line. However, if the items need to use two or more lines, or for precisely positioning pictures or other non-text objects, the preferred method is to insert a table. Word 2013 offers a wide array of tools for making tables, both plain and fancy.

When you want some text to stand out—similar to "pull quotes" used in magazine articles—you can insert a text box. Word provides an entire gallery of built-in text box designs, or you can draw and format a box to your taste.

In this section:

- Inserting tab stops on the ruler
- Inserting a simple table
- Pasting a table from Excel
- Converting text to a table and back again
- Setting tab stops in table cells
- Adding, deleting, and resizing rows and columns
- Setting table alignment and text wrapping
- Merging and splitting cells
- Setting cell alignment and direction
- Repeating heading rows
- Using table styles for uniform appearance
- Inserting and linking text boxes

Inserting tab stops on the ruler

Word 2013 automatically sets a tab stop every half inch (1.27 cm) from the left margin. Although that might be useful for a quick document that you'll print and discard, it's usually better to set a custom tab stop exactly where you need one.

Depending on where that stop is across the page, you only have to press the Tab key once to move to the desired tab stop instead of multiple times, a half inch at a time.

Set a custom tab stop

1 If the ruler isn't visible, on the View tab, in the Show group, select the Ruler check box.

2 Select the paragraphs in which you want to set tab stops.

3 Click the numbered part of the ruler at the desired position for a tab stop.

4 If the tab stop's position isn't correct, drag the tab stop marker to the left or right along the ruler, as needed.

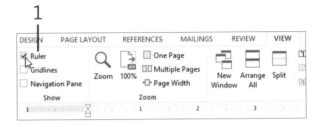

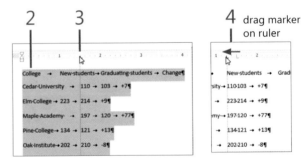

4 drag marker
   on ruler

> **TRY THIS** The usual kind of tab stop is left-aligned (that is, the left edge of text that follows the Tab character aligns there). Click the box at the left end of the ruler to change the alignment of the next tab stop that you insert. Click several times to select a center-aligned, right-aligned, decimal, or bar tab stop, or the first-line indent or the hanging (second and subsequent line) indent.

> **TRY THIS** Double-click the ruler to open the Tabs dialog box. Here you can change the locations of the default tab stops, set the leader (the repeated dots or lines that fill the space between columns), or clear all the tabs from the selected text.

> **TIP** If you want to use the same tab stop locations in many places, make the tab stops part of the definition of a paragraph style that you can apply wherever you need it.

> **SEE ALSO** For information about defining a style, see "Creating and modifying styles" on page 94.

Inserting a simple table

In Word 2013, a table is a special kind of object that's made up of *rows* and *columns*. The rectangle where a row and a column meet is a *cell*. Each cell can contain paragraphs of text, numbers, pictures—even another entire table.

Often it's easiest to insert the framework of an empty table and then start to fill its cells with text. Don't worry if you don't know

at first how many rows or columns you'll need, because they can be added or removed later.

The Quick Tables building block gallery includes a selection of common types of tables that you can drop into your document and then fill with your own text.

Use the Table button

1 On the Insert tab, in the Tables group, click Table.

2 In the display that opens beneath the Table button, move the cursor over the matrix of squares until it highlights the number of columns and rows you want.

3 Click the mouse.

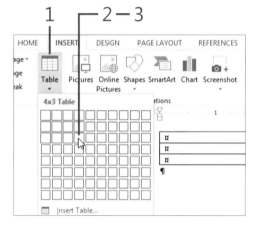

TIP   To insert a table with more than 8 rows or 10 columns by using a dialog box, click Table and then click Insert Table on the menu.

TRY THIS   Insert a table while the cursor is inside a cell of an existing table. This creates a *nested* table in the original table cell.

Insert a quick table

1 On the Insert tab, in the Tables group, click Table.

2 Point to Quick Tables and click one of the building blocks in the gallery.

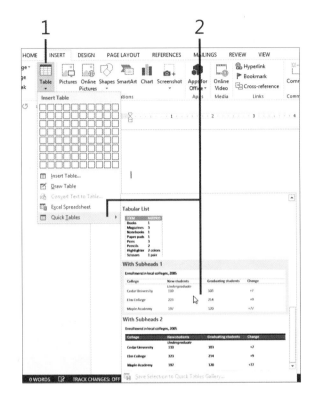

SEE ALSO For information about making a table larger or smaller, see "Adding and deleting rows and columns" on page 187.

Copying an Excel table into Word

Suppose that you're writing a report in Word 2013, and some of the supporting data that you would like to present is in a Microsoft Excel worksheet. No problem: you can simply copy the table in Excel and paste it into your Word document.

If you expect to change the data in the Excel worksheet, you can paste a *link* to the worksheet instead of plain text so that any changes made to the data also appear automatically in the Word document.

Paste a table from Excel

1 In Excel, select the part of a worksheet that contains the data for the table and copy it to the clipboard.

2 Click in the Word document at the point where you want the table to appear.

3 On the Home tab, in the Clipboard group, click Paste (shortcut, Ctrl+V) to insert the table from the clipboard.

4 If you want to link the Word document to the Excel worksheet, click the down-arrow for the Paste button and then click Paste Special.

5 Click Paste Link and choose Microsoft Excel Worksheet Object as the object type.

6 Click OK.

 SEE ALSO For more information about pasting a link to an Excel worksheet, see "Use Paste Special" on page 46.

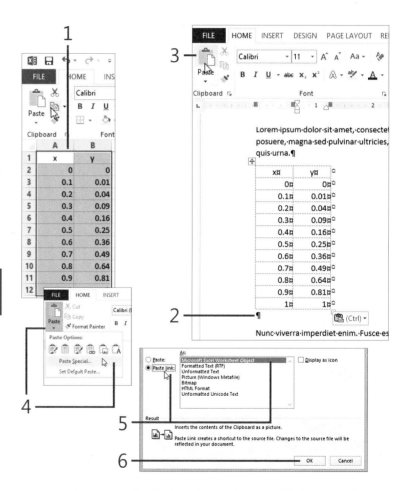

Converting text to a table and back again

Sometimes you receive text that's separated into columns by tabs or other unique characters, and you want instead to format it as a table. Fear not! You don't have to cut and paste many chunks of text into individual table cells—you can do the job with just a few clicks in Word 2013.

In other cases, you might have data in a table that must be changed to plain text. Again, Word makes quick work of the task.

Convert text to a table

1 Select the text that you want to convert.

2 On the Insert tab, click Table.

3 Click Convert Text To Table.

The Convert Text To Table dialog box opens.

4 Verify that the number of columns and rows shown in the dialog box is what you expect. If not, the wrong separator character might be selected at the bottom of the dialog box, or the text might contain the wrong number of separator characters in one or more lines. Correct these problems.

5 Click OK.

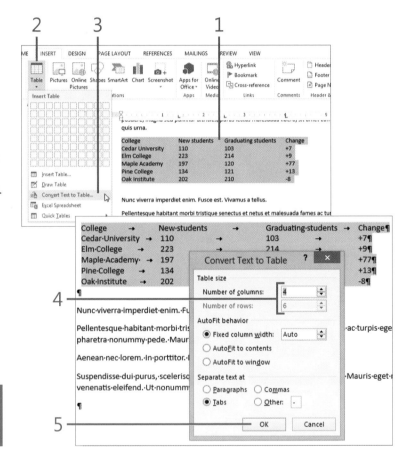

> **TIP** If the text doesn't appear in the correct cells of the table, click Undo on the Quick Access Toolbar, find and fix the cause of the problem, and then convert the text again.

Convert a table to text

1 Click anywhere in the table that you want to convert.

2 On the Layout tab under Table Tools, in the Data group, click Convert To Text.

The Convert Table To Text dialog box opens.

3 Click the separator character that you want Word to place in the text between the columns. A paragraph mark is always placed at the end of the text from each row of the table.

4 Click OK.

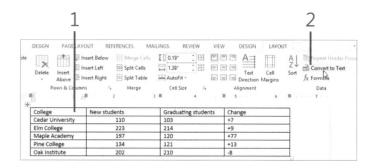

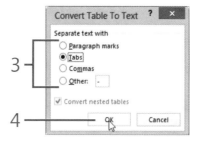

Setting tab atops in table cells

In a table that includes a column of numbers or currency, it's useful to set a decimal tab stop so that the numbers align properly.

Set a tab stop in a table

1 If the tab type shown in the box at the left end of the ruler isn't what you want, click the box one or more times until the desired tab type appears.

The box shows the decimal tab type as an upside-down T with a dot at its right side.

2 Select one or more table columns or a block of cells.

3 Click the ruler at the desired location within one of the selected columns.

Word automatically inserts a tab stop at the same relative position in each of the other selected columns; you don't have to set their tab stops separately.

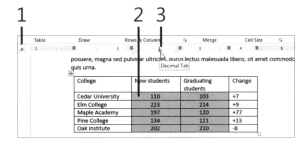

 TIP To insert a tab character in a table, you must press Ctrl+Tab. Pressing Tab by itself while in a table simply moves the insertion point to the next cell; it does not insert a tab character.

TIP If you set a decimal tab stop in a table, you don't need to insert a tab character to make the numbers line up.

Adding and deleting rows and columns

Instead of choosing the number of rows and columns when you create a table, you can start small and add to the table as needed. It's common, and very easy, to add a new row to the bottom of the table. Word 2013 makes it easier than ever to add rows and columns between existing ones, or to delete unneeded ones.

Add rows at the bottom of a table

1 Click the rightmost cell of the last row (or from any cell in the table, press the Tab key, to move the cursor from cell to cell until you arrive there).

2 Press the Tab key.

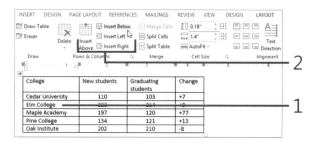

Add rows or columns anywhere in a table

1 Click in a row or column next to where you want the new row or column to appear.

2 On the Layout tab under Table Tools, in the Rows & Columns group, click one of the four Insert buttons.

> ✓ **TIP** In Word 2013, when you move the cursor above a column or to the left of a row, a plus sign (+) in a circle appears. Click the plus sign to add a column or row at that point.

Delete rows or columns

1 Click in the row or column that you want to delete.

2 On the Layout tab under Table Tools, in the Rows & Columns group, click Delete and then click Delete Rows or Delete Columns.

> ✓ **TIP** To add or delete more than one row or column at a time, first select the desired rows or columns.

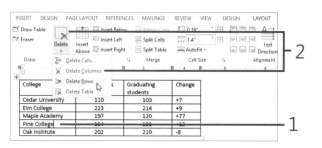

Resizing rows and columns

When you insert a table in a document, it automatically stretches from the left margin to the right margin, and the columns are all the same width. Each row starts at the height needed for one line of text, expanding automatically as you add more text to any of its cells.

If the items in your table range in width, you can resize the columns to make better use of the space. When you're using a table for positioning objects on the page, you might also want to resize the rows to set a minimum height.

In a typical situation, you have a wide column for a name or description, followed by several narrower columns for numbers or other bits of information. You can easily make all the narrower columns the same width.

Drag row and column borders

1 On the View tab, in the Show group, select the Ruler check box (if it hasn't already been selected).

2 Click in any cell of a table column, or select one or more whole columns that you want to resize.

3 Drag the marker on the horizontal ruler above the column's right border to increase or decrease the column's width.

4 Drag the marker on the vertical ruler to the left of the row's bottom border to increase or decrease the row's height.

> ⚠️ **CAUTION** If you select an entire cell and drag its vertical border, only that cell's width changes, rather than the width of the entire column. If that isn't what you intended, click Undo on the Quick Access Toolbar and try again.

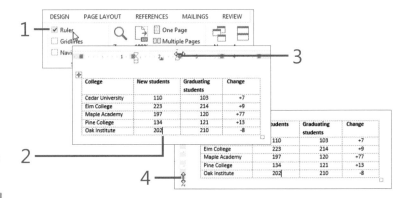

Make columns of equal widths

1 Select the columns whose widths you want to make equal.

2 On the Layout tab under Table Tools, in the Cell Size group, click Distribute Columns.

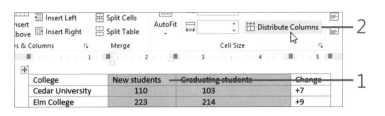

> ✓ **TIP** To distribute a group of rows so that they have the same height, select the rows, and then in the Cell Size group, click Distribute Rows.

Setting table alignment

If you resize a table so that it's narrower than the text column in which it is anchored, you can align the entire table to the left, center, or right with respect to the page margins.

Choose a table alignment

1 Click in the table.

2 On the Layout tab under Table Tools, in the Table group, click Properties.

The Table Properties dialog box opens.

3 Click Left, Center, or Right.

4 Click OK.

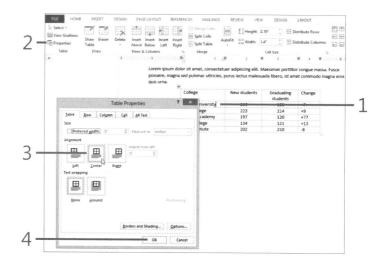

Setting table text wrapping

When you first insert a table, it forces the text before and after it to be separate paragraphs, and text can't flow around it. But, if you drag the table to a different position, the text wrapping setting will automatically change to Around. This means that if the table is narrow enough, text will run beside it.

Wrap text around a table

1 Click in the table.

2 Drag the Move box to reposition the table.

Lorem ipsum dolor sit amet, consectetuer adipiscing elit. Maecenas porttitor congue massa. Fusce posuere, magna sed pulvinar ultricies, purus lectus malesuada libero, sit amet commodo magna eros quis urna.

College	New students	Graduating students	Change
Cedar University	110	103	+7
Elm College	223	214	+9
Maple Academy	197	120	+77
Pine College	134	121	+13
Oak Institute	202	210	-8

Lorem ipsum dolor sit amet, consectetuer adipiscing elit. Maecenas porttitor congue massa. Fusce posuere, magna sed pulvina ultricies, purus lectus malesuada libero, sit amet commodo magna eros quis urna.

College	New students	Graduating students	Change
Cedar University	110	103	+7
Elm College	223	214	+9
Maple Academy	197	120	+77
Pine College	134	121	+13
Oak Institute	202	210	-8

TRY THIS Although dragging a table sets the text wrapping to Around, there isn't any similar way to remove the text wrapping. Instead, you need to click Properties on the Layout tab under Table Tools and then click None.

TRY THIS To get finer control of the table's position, on the Layout tab under Table Tools, click Properties, click Positioning, and then adjust the measurements.

Merging and splitting cells

Tables often need column heads that span more than one column of data. Likewise, cells in neighboring rows might need to be combined. Word 2013 makes it possible for you to select two or more cells and combine them into a single cell. You can go the other way, too: you can select a cell and split it into two or more cells within the same space. With these two tools, you can create almost any arrangement that you can imagine.

Merge cells

1 Select two or more adjacent cells. They can be side by side, above and below, or any rectangular block.

2 On the Layout tab under Table Tools, in the Merge group, click Merge Cells.

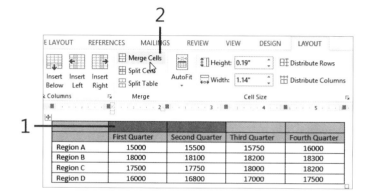

Split cells apart

1 Select the cell or cells that you want to split.

2 On the Layout tab under Table Tools, in the Merge group, click Split Cells.

The Split Cells dialog box opens.

3 Set the number of rows and columns that you want to create from the selected cells.

4 Click OK.

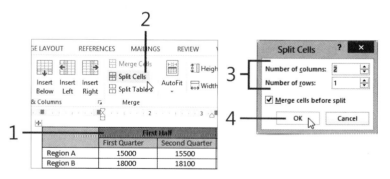

> ✓ **TIP** If the Merge Cells Before Split check box is selected, all the highlighted cells are merged into one cell, which is then split into the numbers of rows and columns you set. If the check box is cleared, each original cell is converted to the requested numbers of rows and columns.

> ✓ **TIP** If a single cell contains several paragraphs of text before you split the cell into multiple columns, the paragraphs will be separated into the resulting cells.

Setting cell alignment and direction

When a table cell is larger than the text it contains, you can decide whether you want the text aligned left, centered, or right, and whether it aligns at the top, center, or bottom of the row height. These settings can be especially useful for tables that have multiple levels of column headings.

The text within a cell can be rotated 90 degrees in either direction. This is great for column headings that would otherwise be much wider than the data below them.

Align text in cells

1 Select the cell or cells that you want to align.

2 On the Layout tab under Table Tools, in the Alignment group, click one of the nine small icons that represent the various alignments.

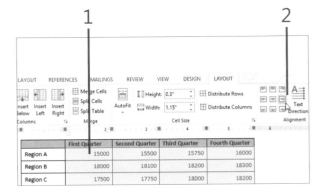

Change text direction

1 Select the cell or cells whose direction you want to change.

2 On the Layout tab under Table Tools, in the Alignment group, click Text Direction once or twice.

The first click causes the text to read top to bottom; the second causes it to read bottom to top. A third returns the text to its normal direction.

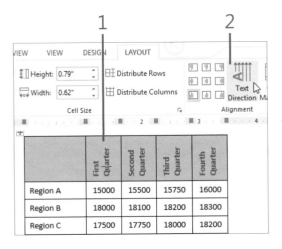

Repeating header rows

If a table contains many rows, or its rows contain long text, the table might flow onto another page. When that happens, you probably want the column headers to be repeated at the top of the page so that your readers don't have to flip the pages back and forth to identify the information.

Make header rows repeat

1 Select one or more rows of column headers at the top of the table.

2 On the Layout tab under Table Tools, in the Data group, click Repeat Header Rows.

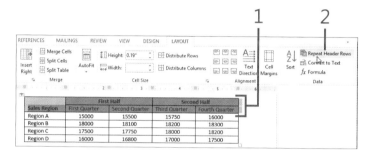

Using table styles for uniform appearance

If you're writing a document that has lots of tables, it can be hard to keep them all manually formatted the same way, using the same fonts, sizes, borders, shading, and so forth. That's where table styles are useful. Word 2013 supplies a large assortment of styles from which to choose. You can modify a built-in style or create your own and add it to the table style gallery. Then, you can apply the same table style to each table to maintain a uniform look throughout your document.

The fonts and colors used by the built-in table styles are determined by the *theme* that's currently applied to the document. If you change to a different theme, the formatting of all the tables will change at once. When you create your own table style, it's a good idea to choose its fonts and colors from the theme offerings, as well.

Apply a built-in table style

1 Click in a table.

2 On the Design tab under Table Tools, in the Table Style Options group, check or clear any of the options.

The options affect the appearance of the styles in the Table Styles group. (*Banded* rows and columns use alternating shading colors to make the data easier to read.)

3 In the Table Styles group, click a thumbnail picture.

To see more thumbnails, use the scroll arrows at the right side of the gallery.

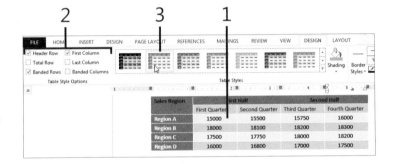

Create a table style

1 Click in a table.

2 At the right side of the Table Styles gallery, click the More arrow.

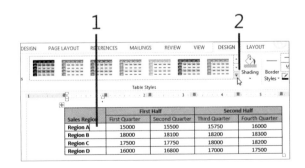

3 Click the New Table Style option.

The Create New Style From Formatting dialog box opens.

4 Enter a name for the new style.

5 If one of the built-in table styles is close to the format you want, open the Style Based On drop-down list and click that style's name. Otherwise, base your style on Table Normal.

6 Under Formatting, leave the Apply Formatting To drop-down list set to Whole Table and select each formatting item that you want to apply to the whole table.

7 Change the Apply Formatting To drop-down list to Header Row.

8 Select each formatting item that applies to just the header row, if that is different from the rest of the table.

9 If necessary, change the selection in the Apply Formatting To drop-down list to the other available parts of the table and set the formatting as needed.

10 When the style definition is complete, click OK.

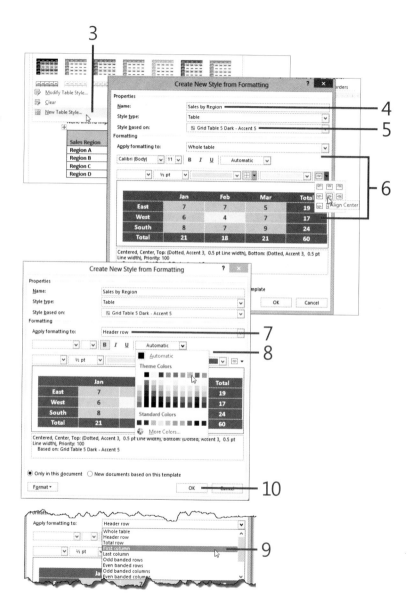

Inserting text boxes

You can use a text box to call attention to a quote from the document or to display some instructions for the document's use. You can also use a text box as a way to position a specific piece of text, such as the address block on a printed newsletter.

Insert a built-in text box

1 On the Insert tab, in the Text group, click Text Box.

2 Click one of the thumbnail pictures in the gallery.

3 Type or paste into the text box, replacing the sample text.

4 If the text box isn't in the right position, drag it to where you want it.

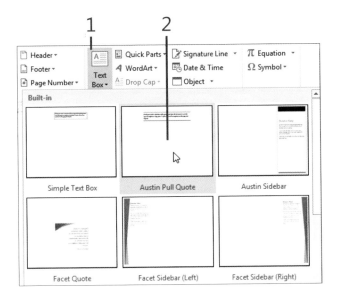

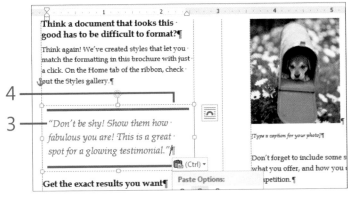

 TIP When you paste into the text box, the text might be formatted like the source instead of looking like the sample text. To correct this, click the Paste Options icon and choose Merge Formatting.

 TIP Use the green alignment guides to line up the text box with the margins or with the top of a paragraph.

Draw a text box and add text

1 On the Insert tab, in the Text group, click Text Box.

2 At the bottom of the gallery, click Draw Text Box.

3 Use the special cursor to drag a rectangle to the size and location you want.

4 Click the Layout Options icon.

5 Click the desired text wrapping for the text box.

6 Click inside the text box.

7 Type or paste text and format it as you like.

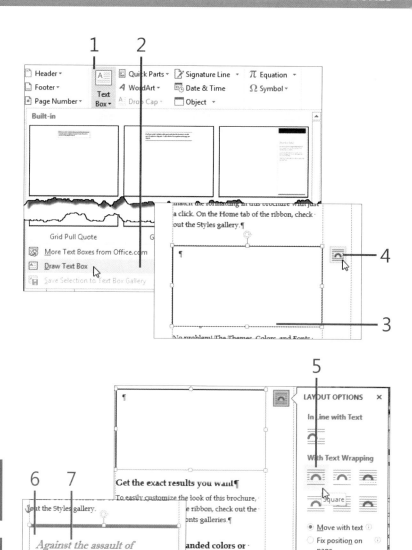

TIP Text inside a text box can be rotated 90 degrees in either direction. On the Drawing Tools Format tab, click Text Direction and choose the desired option.

TIP You can insert a picture into a text box, but the picture's text wrapping can't be changed from In Line With Text to any of the other values.

Linking a chain of text boxes

In newsletters and magazines, it's common to start several articles on the first page and continue each story on an inside page. How do you do that in Word 2013? Pretty simple, actually; put the beginning of each story into a text box and then link that to another text box on the continuation page. The text that doesn't fit in the first box will automatically flow to its linked continuation.

Link a text box to another text box

1 Draw a text box for the beginning of the story.

2 Move the cursor to the continuation page and draw a text box for the remainder of the text.

3 Click inside the first text box.

4 On the Drawing Tools Format tab, click Create Link in the Text group.

5 Use the special cursor to click in the second text box.

6 Type or paste text in the first text box.

When the text becomes too long to fit in the box, it will overflow into the second box.

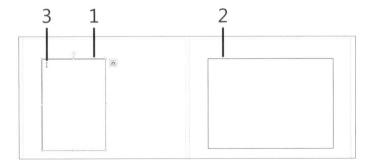

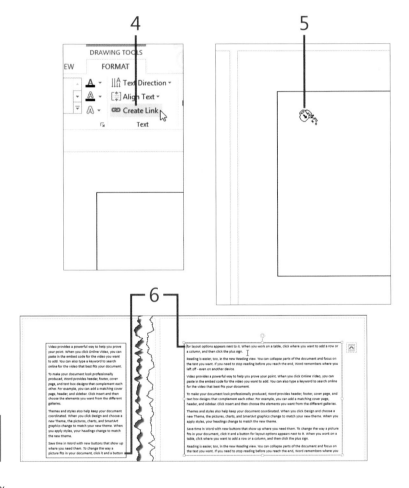

 TIP You can link the second box to a third box, and so on. You can connect up to a maximum of 32 text boxes in any one chain.

Managing data in documents

8

One of the great strengths of Microsoft Word 2013 is its ability to create a template for documents such as form letters and invoices, in which much of the content is constant and you just need to fill in the parts that change. Some of the variable parts can be generated automatically.

The tools that Word provides for working with data and for repeating information in documents include fields, hyperlinks, cross-references, and content controls. Another tool, the mail merge feature, is described beginning at "Starting a mail merge" on page 334.

In this section:

- Using the Field dialog box
- Inserting fields from the keyboard
- Toggling field codes and updating fields
- Controlling field formatting by using switches
- Inserting page and date fields by using shortcuts
- Using bookmarks
- Inserting hyperlinks
- Repeating information by using cross-references
- Inserting content controls
- Grouping content controls for a form
- Using document properties
- Sorting a list

Using the Field dialog box

Fields in Word 2013 are placeholders for values that might change from one time or place to another. Common examples of fields include page numbers, dates, file names, and totals of table columns. Some complicated features, such as a table of contents or an index, are built by single fields that collect information from throughout your document.

Each field is stored in your document as a field *code*, a sort of formula that tells Word what to display. Usually what you see is the field's *result*, the value that Word creates by evaluating the field code. Some kinds of fields evaluate automatically, but most fields must be updated explicitly. Several types of fields don't display any result, but they supply data for other fields (for example, an XE field supplies an entry for an Index field).

There are several ways to insert fields into a document. Some commands on the ribbon or on the Quick Access Toolbar, such as the Page Number button and the gallery items on the Table Of Contents button, create fields at the cursor location. Another method, which handles many more types of fields, uses the Field dialog box.

Insert a field by using the dialog box

1 On the Insert tab, in the Text group, click Quick Parts and then click Field.

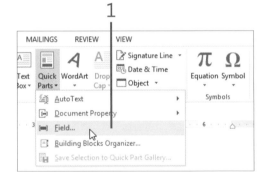

SEE ALSO For more information about switches in field codes, see "Controlling field formatting by using switches" on page 205.

2 In the Field dialog box, if you know the name of the field that you want to insert, click it in the Field Names list. To display in the list only the field names associated with a specific type of information, first select an item in the Categories drop-down list.

3 Some types of fields, when selected in the Field Names list, display additional text boxes or lists under the Field Properties heading. Type or select the properties that you want to use in the current field.

4 Some types of fields also display items under the Field Options heading. Type or select the options that you want to use in the current field.

5 By default, the Preserve Formatting During Updates check box is selected for most fields. This places the MergeFormat switch in the field code so that any direct formatting of the field's result before an update is retained after the field is updated. If you don't want this switch included, clear the check box.

6 If you want to see and perhaps edit the field code that will be generated by the dialog box, click the Field Codes button.

7 Click OK.

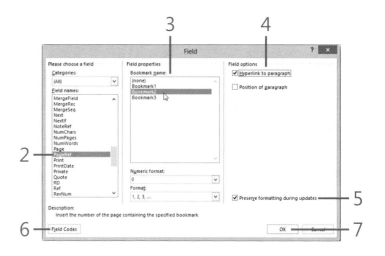

> ![checkmark] **TIP** For descriptions of what the fields do as well as their properties and options, click the Help icon (the question mark) on the title bar of the Field dialog box or press F1 to open the topic titled Field Codes In Word. Then, click the name of the field to read about the parts of its code, which correspond to the items in the Field dialog box.

> ![arrow] **TRY THIS** To change a field (for example, to change the date format), right-click the field result and then, on the shortcut menu that appears, click Edit Field. The Field dialog box opens with the field's current information in place.

Inserting fields from the keyboard

The field codes of some very useful fields are short and easy to remember, so it's quicker to type the field code than to use the Field dialog box, which requires multiple clicks. Among these fields are the Page, Date, CreateDate, and DocProperty fields.

A field code consists of a keyword (the name of the field) and, depending on which field it is, some data such as a formula

or a file name. The field code can include optional switches, which are abbreviations that instruct the code how to modify the field's result—for instance, formatting numbers or dates, or changing the capitalization of text. The entire field code is enclosed in a pair of field markers, which appear as bold curly braces ({ }).

Insert a field from the keyboard

1 Click in your document where you want the field result to appear.

2 Press Ctrl+F9 to insert a pair of field markers.

3 Type the field code between the markers, including any text and switches that are needed to produce the code result that you want.

4 Right-click the field code and then, on the shortcut menu that appears, click Update Field (shortcut, F9) to evaluate the field and show its result.

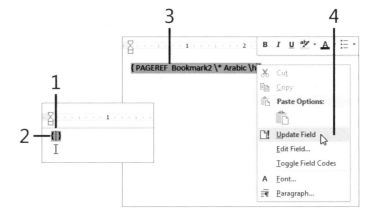

Toggling field codes and updating fields

Ordinarily, Word 2013 shows you only field results. If you need to display the field codes—to edit them or just to find out what produced the results—you can toggle the display back and forth for all the fields in the document. If you want to toggle just one field at a time, or just those in a selected part of the text, you can do that, as well.

Show and hide field codes

1 Open a document that contains some fields.

2 Press Alt+F9 to display all the field codes.

3 Press Alt+F9 again to redisplay all the field results.

4 Select a single field or a part of the document that contains several fields.

5 Right-click the selection, and then in the shortcut menu that appears, click Toggle Field Codes (shortcut, Shift+F9) to display the field codes of only the fields within the selected text.

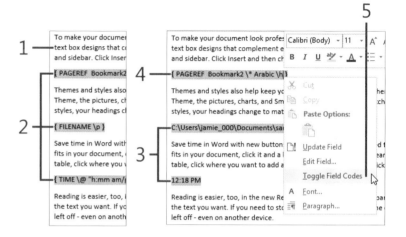

Update fields

1 Click in a document. On the Insert tab, in the Text group, click Date & Time and select a time format that includes the seconds. Select the Update Automatically check box and click OK.

2 To see the field result change, right-click the time field and then, on the shortcut menu that appears, click Update Field (shortcut, F9).

3 In a document with several fields, select the entire body text by pressing Ctrl+A. Right-click the selected text and then, on the shortcut menu that appears, click Update Field to update all the fields at once.

4 In a document that also has fields in the header or footer or in text boxes, click the File tab to display the Backstage view. Then, click the Print tab (shortcut, Ctrl+P) to display the Print page and Print Preview, which forces all of the fields to update. Click the circled arrow icon or press the Esc key to return to the document.

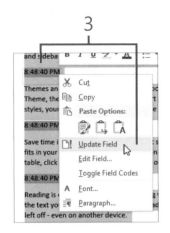

Controlling field formatting by using switches

You can control the appearance of fields that produce numbers, dates, or text as their field results by using optional switches that modify the result in the way that you specify.

In a field that produces a numeric result, you can insert a *numeric picture* switch that consists of the characters \# followed by a quoted expression that describes the desired format. In that expression, the following characters have special meanings:

- The character 0 (zero) indicates a required digit in the result, which appears as a zero if no other digit would be there. For example, the field { = 2 + 3 \# "$00.0" } displays the result $05.0.

- The character # indicates a required digit, in the same way as the character 0, except that it displays a space if no digit would be there. For example, the field { = 2 + 3 \# "$#0.0" } displays the result $ 5.0.

- If you include two or three format expressions separated by semicolons, the first expression is used if the result is a positive number, the second one is used if the result is a negative number, and the third one is used if the result is zero. For example, a field in the bottom cell of a table's column might be { =SUM(ABOVE) \# "$0.00;- $0.00;NA" }. If the total of the numbers in the column is positive, the field displays it with a dollar sign and two decimal places; if the total is negative, the field displays it with a minus sign; and if the total is zero, the field displays the characters NA.

In a field that produces a date as the result, you can insert a *date-time picture* switch that consists of the characters \@ followed by a quoted expression that describes the desired format.

In addition to the following special characters, you can include other text, punctuation, and spaces in the expression:

- Uppercase *M* for the month. One *M* displays the month as a one or two-digit number, but *MM* displays all months with two digits including a leading zero, if needed. The three-character *MMM* displays the month as a three-letter abbreviation, and the four-character *MMMM* spells out the month's name in full.

- Uppercase or lowercase *d* for the day. One *d* displays the day of the month as a one or two-digit number, but *dd* displays all days with two digits including a leading zero, if needed. The three-character *ddd* displays the day of the week as a three-letter abbreviation, and the four-character *dddd* spells out the day of the week in full.

- Uppercase or lowercase *y* for the year. One *y* or the two-character *yy* displays the last two digits of the year; the four-character *yyyy* displays the four-digit year. The three-character *yyy* displays an error message.

- Uppercase *H* for the hour based on the 24-hour clock. One *H* displays the hour without a leading zero, and the two-digit *HH* displays the hour with a leading zero, if needed.

- Lowercase *h* acts like uppercase *H* except that it displays the hour based on the 12-hour clock. Use this character with the AM/PM expression.

- Lowercase *m* for the minute. One m displays the minute without a leading zero; the two-digit *mm* displays the minute with a leading zero, if needed.

- Uppercase or lowercase *s* for the second. One *s* displays the second without a leading zero; the two-digit *ss* displays the second with a leading zero, if needed.

- Uppercase or lowercase *am/pm* for the morning or afternoon on the 12-hour clock. This expression always displays uppercase AM or PM unless you also include the * Lower switch in the same field code.

In a field that produces a text result, you can control the capitalization and formatting with a *format* switch that consists of the characters * followed by a keyword that specifies the change in appearance.

- *** Caps**   Capitalizes the first letter of each word in the result.

- *** FirstCap**   Capitalizes the first letter of the first word in the result.

- *** Upper**   Capitalizes all letters in the result.

- *** Lower**   Makes all letters in the result lowercase.

- *** CharFormat**   Applies the formatting (such as bold, italic, or a font name or size) of the first character of the field code to the entire field result.

- *** MergeFormat**   Applies the formatting of the field's previous result to the new result when the field is updated.

- *** alphabetic**   Displays a numeric result as the equivalent lowercase letter (*a* for 1, *b* for 2, and so forth). The * Alphabetic switch displays uppercase letters.

- *** roman**   Displays a numeric result as the equivalent lowercase Roman numeral. The * Roman switch displays an uppercase Roman numeral.

- *** ordinal**   Displays a numeric result as the number followed by *st*, *nd*, *rd*, or *th* as appropriate.

- *** OrdText**   Displays a numeric result as the ordinal number spelled out in full (for example, *twenty-third*).

- *** CardText**   Displays a numeric result as the cardinal number spelled out in full (for example, *twenty-three*).

- *** DollarText**   Displays a numeric result as the cardinal number, with the word *and* inserted in place of the decimal point and with the first two decimal places expressed as a fraction (for example, *twenty-three and 44/100*).

Format a numeric field

1 In a document that contains page numbers in the header, double-click the header area. Right-click the page number and then, on the shortcut menu that appears, click Toggle Field Codes.

2 At the end of the PAGE keyword in the field code, type *** CardText** and *** Caps**.

3 Right-click the field and then, on the shortcut menu that appears, click Update Field.

4 Double-click within the body of the document. Type the field code = **2.15 + 3.02 \# "00.00;(00.00)"**. Select the code and press Ctrl+F9 to insert the field markers.

5 Right-click the field. On the shortcut menu click Update Field.

6 Right-click the field. On the shortcut menu Toggle Field Codes. Change the + sign to a - sign and then update the field again.

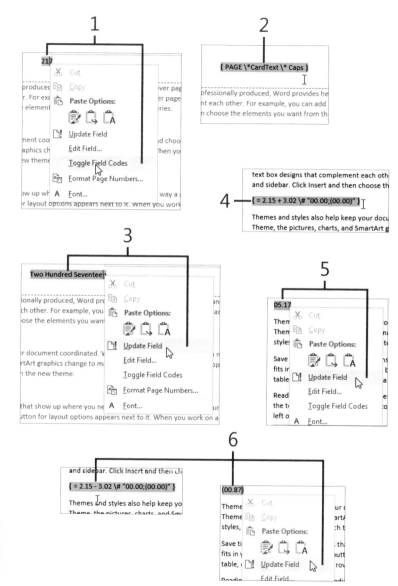

> **TRY THIS** In step 2, replace the * Caps switch with the * FirstCap switch or the * Upper switch to see the differences among the results.

Format a date field

1 On the Insert tab, in the Text group, click Date & Time.

2 In the Date And Time dialog box, in the Available Formats list, click one of the date formats. Select the Update Automatically check box and click OK.

3 Right-click the date and then, on the shortcut menu that appears, click Toggle Field Codes.

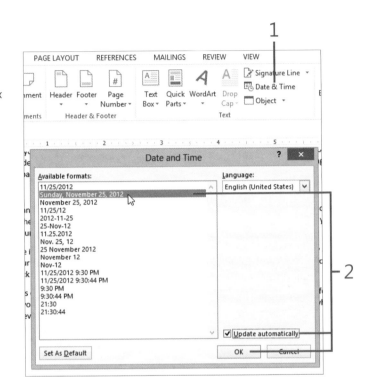

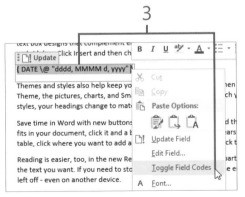

4 Inside the quote marks in the field code, type a time format such as **hh:mm am/pm**.

5 Right-click the field and then, on the shortcut menu that appears, click Update Field.

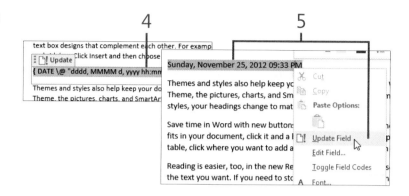

Format a text field

1 In a document, press Ctrl+F9 to insert a pair of field markers and type the field code **quote "sample text" * charformat * upper**.

2 Format the letter q with a different font and size, such as Arial Black at 14 points, that you want to apply to the entire field result.

3 Right-click the field and then, on the shortcut menu that appears, click Update Field.

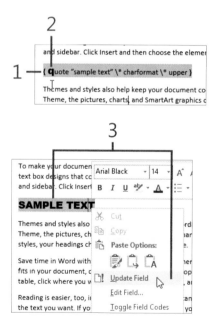

> ✓ **TIP** In a field code, the keyword and some of the formatting switches (such as CharFormat) are not case-sensitive. Date format expressions and some formatting switches (such as Roman) are case-sensitive.

Inserting Page and Date fields by using shortcuts

The Page and Date fields are used so frequently that Word includes default keyboard shortcuts for them.

Insert a Page field

1 Click in your document where you want the page number to appear.

2 Press Alt+Shift+P.

> ✓ **TIP**   Word automatically updates a page field that occurs in a header or footer, but page fields in the body of the document don't update unless you select them and update them manually or go to the Print Preview page of the Backstage.

Insert a Date field

1 Click in your document where you want the date to appear.

2 Press Alt+Shift+D.

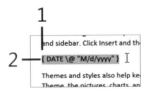

> ✓ **TIP**   The keyboard shortcut always inserts the short date format that you specify in the Region dialog box of Windows.

Using bookmarks

A bookmark in a Word 2013 document marks a specific place. This makes it possible for you to move the cursor to that spot or refer to it elsewhere in the document. The part of the text that you mark can be as little as the insertion point between two adjacent characters, or as large as the entire document.

When you mark one or more words or a picture with a bookmark, you can repeat that text or picture in other parts of the document by inserting Ref fields that contain the name of the bookmark. A bookmark can also serve as the location to which the cursor jumps when you click a hyperlink.

Insert a bookmark

1 Click in your document at the point where you want to insert the bookmark or select an area including text and/or pictures that you want surrounded by the bookmark.

2 On the Insert tab, in the Links group, click Bookmark.

3 In the Bookmark dialog box, in the Bookmark Name list box, type a name for the bookmark. You can use only letter, digit, and underscore characters. Other characters, including spaces, are not allowed.

4 Click the Add button.

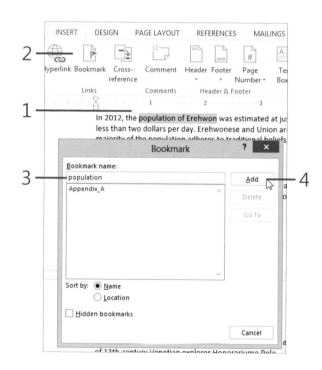

> **TIP** You can select an option to display bookmarks on the screen as gray brackets (see "Controlling what is displayed and printed" on page 429).

Inserting hyperlinks

You might often create documents that are intended to be read on computers rather than on paper. One advantage of online documents is that you can link to other places in your document, to other documents, and to websites. Your readers can click hyperlinks that you provide, which then takes them to instructions, original source material, or other information.

Link to a location within your document

1 Insert a heading or a bookmark at the place to which you want the hyperlink to go.

2 Move the cursor to the place in your document where you want the hyperlink to appear.

You can leave the cursor as a single point at which the hyperlink will be inserted or select one or more words or a picture that you want as the hyperlink.

3 On the Insert tab, in the Links group, click Hyperlink.

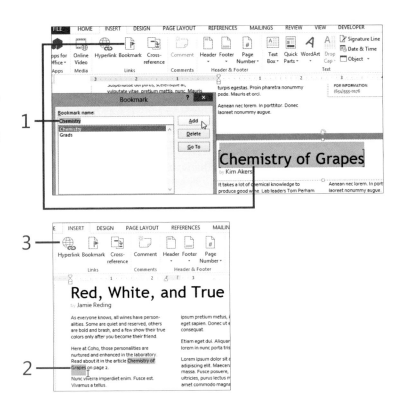

4 In the Insert Hyperlink dialog box, in the Link To section, click Place In This Document.

5 In the Select A Place In This Document list box, click the heading or bookmark that will be the destination of the hyperlink.

6 If you selected text in step 2, the text will appear in the Text To Display box, and you can edit that text if you want to. If you clicked in the document without selecting text, the text of the heading or bookmark will appear in that box and can be edited. If you selected a picture, the box will show <<Selection In Document>> and can't be edited.

7 If you want to define the text that appears when the mouse pointer hovers over the hyperlink, click the ScreenTip button, type the desired text, and then click OK.

8 Click OK.

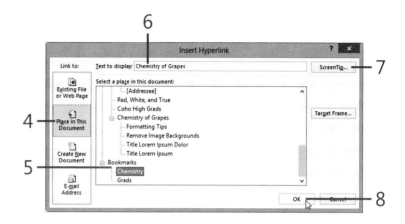

> **TIP** Word automatically formats the hyperlinks that you insert from the dialog box by applying the character style named Hyperlink. When you click a hyperlink, Word changes the formatting to the character style named FollowedHyperlink. These styles apply colors that are defined by the current theme.

> **TIP** If you open the AutoFormat As You Type page of the AutoCorrect Options dialog box and select the check box for Internet And Network Paths With Hyperlinks, Word automatically converts any address that you type in plain text into an active hyperlink. For more information about AutoFormat options, see "Setting AutoFormat options" on page 76.

Link to a different document or webpage

1 Move the cursor to the place in your document where you want the hyperlink to appear.

You can leave the cursor as a single point at which the hyperlink will be inserted, or select one or more words or a picture that will become the hyperlink.

2 On the Insert tab, in the Links group, click Hyperlink.

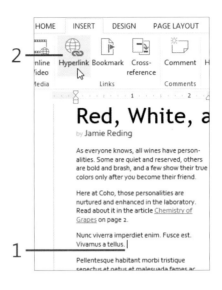

✅ TIP   When you link to a place in the same document, you can point to either a heading or a bookmark. When you link to a different document, only a bookmark can be a destination. If you want to link to headings in another document, you must first insert bookmarks at the headings.

3 In the Hyperlink dialog box, in the Link To section, click Existing File Or Web Page.

4 Click one of the three buttons in the column directly to the right of the Link To section to look for files in the current folder on your computer, webpages that you have visited, or files that you recently opened.

Click the file or webpage to which to link. If you don't see the item you want, you can click the Browse The Web button or the Browse For File button to open your default web browser or a File dialog box, respectively.

5 By default, the Text To Display text box contains the same text as the item you clicked in the list. If you want different text to appear in the document, edit or replace the text in the Text To Display box.

6 If you want to define the text that appears when the mouse pointer hovers over the hyperlink, click ScreenTip, type the desired text, and then click OK.

7 If you selected a Word file in step 4, and if that file contains bookmarks, you can set any of those bookmarks as the destination of the hyperlink. Click the Bookmark button, click the desired bookmark, and then click OK.

8 Click OK.

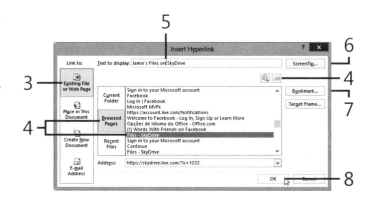

TRY THIS To change the display, the address, or the ScreenTip of an existing hyperlink, right-click the hyperlink and then, on the shortcut menu that appears, click Edit Hyperlink. In the Edit Hyperlink dialog box, make the desired changes and click OK.

TIP If you know that a webpage contains an anchor element (a named location), you can insert a hyperlink to the anchor. In the Insert Hyperlink dialog box, in the Address text box, at the end of the URL for the webpage, type the # symbol followed by the name of the anchor.

Repeating information by using cross-references

In a long document such as a report, you might need to refer to text, headings, captions, and other items elsewhere in the document. In Word 2013, you can insert cross-reference fields that repeat the item itself, or that display the page number of the item. If the item is a numbered heading or list paragraph, the cross-reference can display the numbering associated with the item. The cross-reference can also act as a hyperlink.

If the referenced item changes (for example, if the text is edited or the item moves to a different page or is renumbered), its cross-reference can easily be updated to reflect the new information.

Insert a cross-reference

1 On the Insert tab, in the Links group, click Cross-Reference.

2 In the Cross-Reference dialog box, in the Reference Type list box, click the type of item to which to refer.

The choices include numbered items, headings, bookmarks, foot-notes, endnotes, equations, figures, and tables.

3 In the For Which Bookmark list box, the specific item in the list box that will be referenced.

4 In the Insert Reference To list box, select how you want the refer-ence to appear.

For example, you can display the entire text of the reference or just its page number or list number. You can also include the word "above" or "below" in the reference.

5 The Insert As Hyperlink check box is selected by default; clear the check box if you don't want the reference to behave as a hyperlink.

6 Click the Insert button.

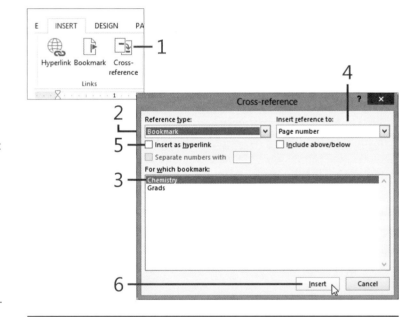

 TIP Cross-references to equations, figures, and tables are actually references to captions applied to those items.

TIP If you put a cross-reference to the page number of an item into the document's header or footer, it updates automati-cally when the item moves to a different page. None of the other cross-references are updated unless you select them and update them manually or go to the Print page of the Backstage view.

Inserting content controls

Content controls are great for setting up templates for letters, forms, and other documents that contain some static (unchanging) text as well as places to enter data specific to the subject of the document. Word 2013 offers eight kinds of content controls for various types of data.

Select and insert a content control type

1 By default, the Developer tab on the ribbon, which contains all the commands related to content controls, is hidden. To display the Developer tab, right-click the ribbon and then, on the shortcut menu that appears, click Customize The Ribbon, which opens the Word Options dialog box. In the list on the right side, select the check box adjacent to Developer and then click OK.

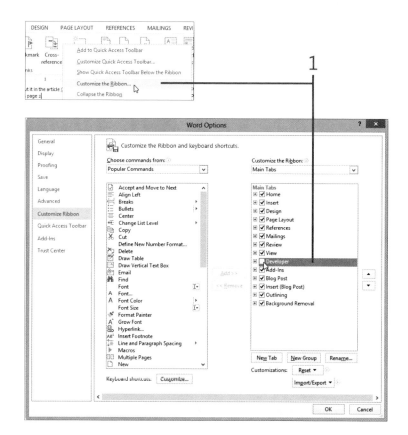

2 Click in your document where you want to insert a content control.

3 Click the Developer tab.

4 In the Controls group, click the button to insert the type of content control that you want. Your choices include the following:

- **Rich Text**   Accepts text with styles or direct formatting, pictures, videos, tables, other content controls, and so forth.

- **Plain Text**   Accepts only text. If you apply a style or direct formatting, it affects all the text in the content control. By default, the control can contain only one paragraph, but you can select an option in the Properties dialog box to allow multiple paragraphs.

- **Picture**   Accepts pictures from your computer, from Office.com clip art, or from the Internet.

- **Building Block Gallery**   Enables the user to choose from a gallery of building blocks. You specify the gallery that the control displays by selecting an entry in the Properties dialog box.

- **Check Box**   Displays a check box that the user can select or clear by clicking it or pressing the Spacebar.

- **Combo Box**   Displays a control in which you can type text or select from a drop-down list of entries.

- **Drop-Down List**   Displays a control in which you can select from a drop-down list of entries.

- **Date Picker**   Displays a control in which you can type a date or choose one from a drop-down calendar.

- **Repeating Section**   Accepts plain or formatted text, pictures, tables, other content controls, and so forth. When you click the plus-sign icon to the right of the Repeating Section content control, another copy of the control's contents appears below the existing copy. Any content controls inside the new copy show their placeholder text.

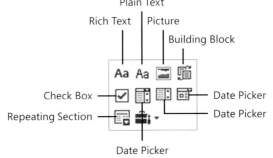

Change the placeholder text for a content control

1 On the Developer tab, in the Controls group, click Design Mode.

2 Edit the placeholder text of the content controls in the document.

3 Click Design Mode again to turn it off.

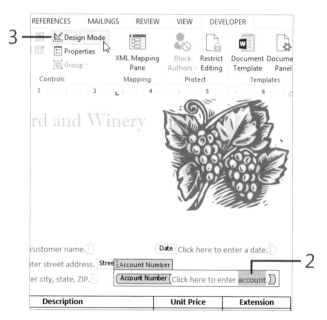

SEE ALSO For more information about managing content controls, including an add-in that simplifies using content controls to repeat data in multiple places in a document, see *gregmaxey. mvps.org/word_tip_pages/cc_var_bm_doc_prop_tools_addin.html*.

Set the properties for a content control

1 Click in the content control that you want to modify.

2 On the Developer tab, in the Controls group, click Properties.

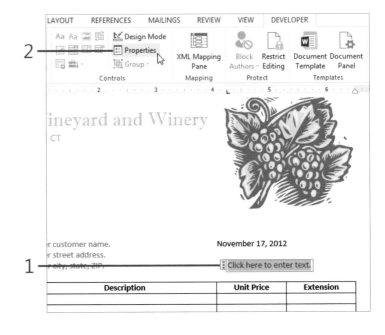

TIP The plus-sign icon of a Repeating Section content control adds the new copy below the existing copy. If you prefer to display the new copy above the existing copy, right-click the existing copy and then, on the shortcut menu that appears, click Insert Item Before.

3 In the Content Control Properties dialog box, type a name in the Title box.

This name will appear in the tab at the upper-left corner of the content control when you click in the control. You can use this to indicate the type of information that should be typed into the control.

4 If the content control will be used with a macro, you might type some text in the Tag text box so that the macro can identify that particular content control. If you leave the Tag text box empty, Word copies the text from the Title text box into the Tag text box.

5 By default, the content control displays a bounding box or outline. If you prefer to display start and end tags, or nothing but the control's contents, change the value in the Show As text box.

6 If you want to apply a color other than black to the outline around the content control, click the Color button and then click a color in the gallery that opens.

7 If you want all text typed into the content control to be formatted with a specific style, select the Use A Style check box and then select the style's name in the Style drop-down list.

8 If you want to remove the content control when you enter text or make a selection in the control (leaving only the contents as an ordinary part of the document), select the Remove Content Control When Contents Are Edited check box.

9 In the Locking section, select the Content Control Cannot Be Deleted check box to prevent accidental deletion of the whole control. Select the Contents Cannot Be Edited check box to prevent any change to the contents (which is useful mainly in forms that use macros).

10 The Properties dialog boxes for some of the content control types contain additional properties. For example, you can create entries in the list of a combo box content control or a list box content control, or select the date format used by a date picker content control.

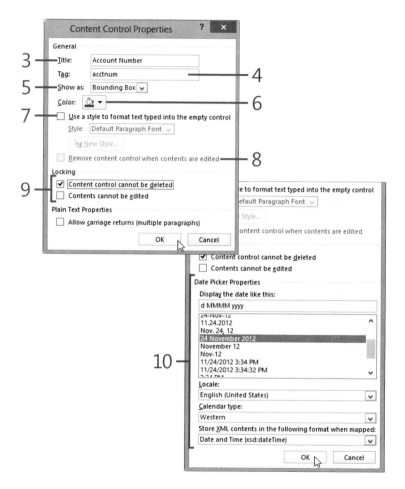

> ✓ **TIP** The Style drop-down list in the Content Control Properties dialog box shows only the character styles and linked styles that are currently visible in the Styles pane (shortcut, Ctrl+Alt+Shift+S). If you choose a linked style for the content control, only the style's character formatting is applied.

Grouping content controls for a form

When you create a template for a form document, you provide places for users to enter their data, but you don't want to allow editing of the static text surrounding those places. Word 2013 lets you prevent unwanted editing in a simple way.

Insert a group content control

1 Select a part of your document that contains both content controls and surrounding text. If you want to select all of the content controls and surrounding text in the body of the document, on the Home tab, in the Editing group, click Select and then click Select All (shortcut, Ctrl+A).

2 On the Developer tab, in the Controls group, click Group. In the drop-down list that appears, click Group.

3 Try to type or change the formatting outside the content controls. Observe that the attempt has no effect, but the status bar at the bottom of the Word window shows the message "This modification is not allowed because the selection is locked."

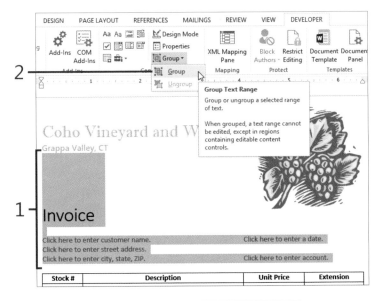

> ✓ **TIP** To remove the grouping, click in the grouped area and then, on the Developer tab, in the Controls group, click Group. In the drop-down list that appears, click Ungroup.

Using document properties

Every Microsoft Office 2013 document includes a set of fifteen *document properties*. These properties can hold information about the document. That information can be used in File Explorer to search for documents related to specific subjects. You can insert a content control anywhere in your document to display the value of one of the document properties. If you insert several content controls for the same document property, changing the value in any one of the controls automatically changes the display in the other controls.

If you want to handle data for which there is no built-in property, you can insert a content control for one of the properties that you aren't using, and then change the name displayed by the content control.

Insert a document property content control

1 Click in your document where you want the value of the document property to display.

2 On the Insert tab, in the Text group, click Quick Parts. In the drop-down list that appears, point to Document Property, and then click the name of the document property that you want to insert.

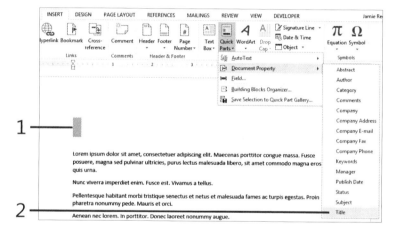

3 If you want to change the name displayed in the tag in the upper-left corner of the content control, on the Developer tab, in the Controls group, click Properties, edit the text in the Title box, and then click OK.

4 If you want to change the placeholder text to describe the data to enter in the content control, on the Developer tab, in the Controls group, click Design Mode and edit the text of the placeholder. Then, click Design Mode again to turn it off.

5 To repeat the same data elsewhere in the document, click the tag in the upper-left corner of the content control and copy the selection to the clipboard. Then, move to the location where the value should be repeated and paste a copy of the content control from the clipboard.

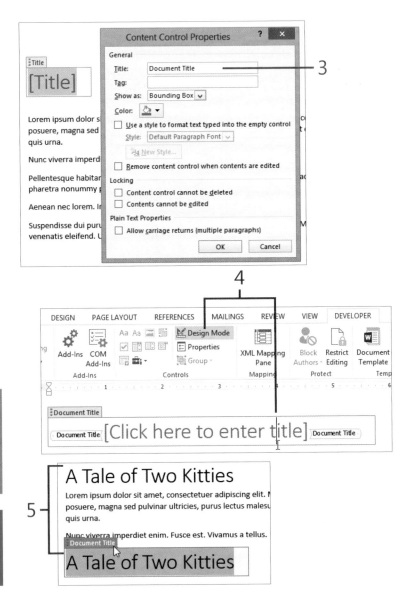

⚠ **CAUTION** Although you can change the name and placeholder text displayed by the content control, it's still attached to the original document property. If you insert another content control for the same property from the Document Properties list but you don't edit the name shown by the new control, the value it displays will be the same as the values in the modified content controls.

✓ **TIP** Some, but not all, of the fifteen document properties can be seen and edited on the Info page of the Backstage view. You can see a few of the properties when you select the document in the File Explorer, even when the document is closed.

Sorting a list

You might type or paste a list of names, book titles, or other information in a document, and then need to sort that list by a different order. Consider, for example, a list of people's names with the given name followed by the family name. You might want the list to be alphabetized by the family names, but without changing the way the names appear. To do this, you need to specify to Word 2013 what part of each name is the family name by using a unique character to separate the given name from the family name.

Names of people and places are notorious for not following rules. You can encounter family names that consist of two or three words. No computer program can decide accurately which of the names is the family name. Perhaps one is a middle name, for example. It usually takes examination by a human to prepare a list of names that can be sorted properly.

Prepare a list of names for sorting

1 Open the document containing the original list. On the Home tab, in the Paragraph group, click the Show/Hide ¶ button.

2 In each name, if the given name consists of two or more words, replace the space characters between them with nonbreaking spaces (select the space and press Ctrl+Shift+space). Similarly, if the family name consists of two or more words, replace the space characters between them with nonbreaking spaces. Leave only one space character in each name, separating the given name from the family name.

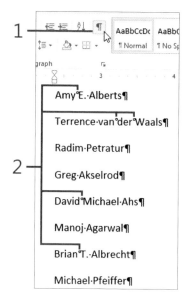

> **→ TRY THIS** After you prepare the list, you can easily convert it to a table, with the given names in one column and the family names in another column. On the Insert tab, click Table and then, at the bottom of the gallery that appears, click Convert Text To Table. In the Convert Text To Table dialog box, under the label Separate Text At, click the Other option button, type a space in the box to its right, and then click OK.

Sort the selected text

1 Select the list text.

2 On the Home tab, in the Paragraph group, click Sort.

3 In the Sort Text dialog box, click the Options button.

4 In the Sort Options dialog box, click the Other option, delete everything that appears in the text box to its right, and then type a single space character in the box. Click OK.

5 In the drop-down list of the Sort By text box, click Word 2 and then click OK.

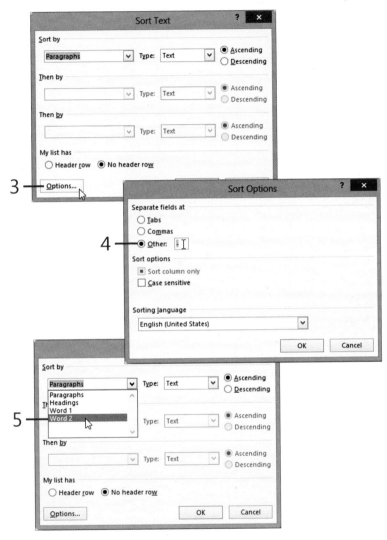

 TIP If the list is the only text in the document, you don't need to select it first in order to sort it.

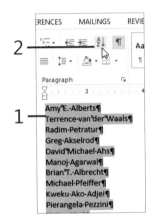 **TIP** If the list is in a table, you'll find another Sort button in the Data group on the Table Tools | Layout contextual tab. It works the same way as the one on the Home tab, except that the Sort By list offers only the table's columns as options, and it sorts only the table that contains the cursor.

Formatting reports and formal documents

9

Reports, scholarly papers, and other formal documents often have unique requirements, such as footnotes, a table of contents, an index, and a bibliography. Even in shorter documents, you might want headers and footers that change from one page to the next, or a watermark to identify a document as an unfinished draft.

In Microsoft Word 2013, each of these requirements is met by a specialized tool. The simplest form of each feature can be inserted in your document with just a few clicks. However, Word's capabilities go far beyond the simple versions. Tables of contents and indexes can be constructed for specific parts of the document. Watermarks can be made with custom text or with any available picture. A bibliography and citations are automatically formatted to conform to any one of an array of standards.

In this section:

- Making different headers
- Unlinking a header
- Extracting text for a header or footer from body text
- Inserting a watermark
- Adding footnotes and endnotes
- Making a table of contents
- Modifying table of contents styles
- Using multiple tables of contents
- Indexing a document
- Using multiple indexes
- Making tables of tables and tables of figures
- Creating a bibliography

Making a different first page header or different odd and even pages header

Each section of a Word 2013 document has three headers and three footers. There is one header and one footer for odd-numbered pages, another header and footer for even-numbered pages, and another header and footer for the first page of the section. In each section, you can choose which headers and footers to show and which to hide.

By default, even-page and first-page headers and footers are hidden, and the *main* header and footer appear on all pages. When you select the Different Odd & Even Pages option, the main header and footer become the odd-page header and footer.

You don't have to put any text or other content in any of the headers or footers. When you do put content in one, it's stored in the document even while that header or footer is hidden. If you later show the appropriate header or footer or when the document grows larger than a single page, the existing content will reappear.

Although the following tasks focus on headers, the procedures are the same when you're working with footers.

Create the main header

1 On the Home tab, in the Paragraph group, click Show/Hide ¶ (shortcut, Ctrl+Shift+8).

2 On the Insert tab, in the Header & Footer group, click Header. Near the bottom of the gallery that opens, click Edit Header.

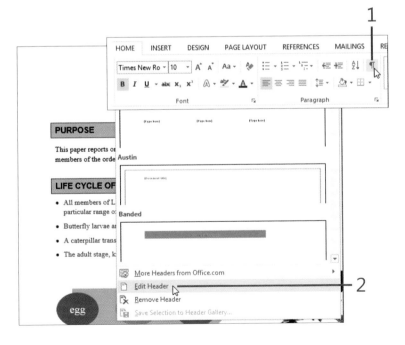

3 Enter text in the header area. Alternatively, on the Header & Footer Tools | Design contextual tab, in the Header & Footer group, click Header and click a building block in the gallery.

Observe the Header tag attached to the dashed line at the bottom of the header area, which indicates that this is the main header.

4 On the Header & Footer Tools | Design contextual tab, in the Close group, click Close Header And Footer.

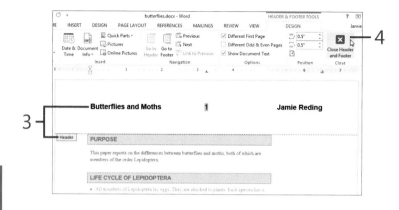

✓ **TIP** To open the header or footer area quickly, double-click in the area. To close the header or footer area, double-click in the main text area.

✓ **TIP** In Word 2013, a new addition to the Header & Footer Tools | Design contextual tab is the Document Info button in the Insert group. Although the items in the button's gallery are also available on the Insert tab, it's convenient to find them here. The File Name and File Path items that insert fields for those properties are especially useful.

Turn on different headers

1 Open a one-page document and click at the end of the text. On the Page Layout tab, in the Page Setup group, click Breaks and then click Page (shortcut, Ctrl+Enter) twice to insert two manual page breaks. Then, click in the text on the first page.

2 On the Insert tab, in the Header & Footer group, click Header. Near the bottom of the gallery that opens, click Edit Header.

Observe the Header tag attached to the dashed line at the bottom of the header area, which indicates that this is the main header.

3 In the header area, type the text **Main Header**.

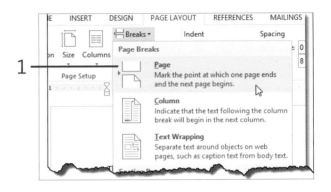

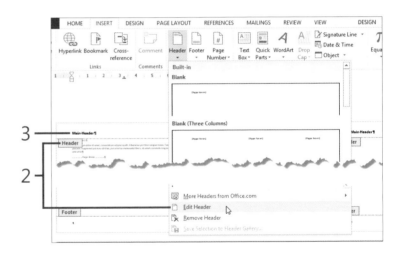

→ TRY THIS On the Header & Footer Tools | Design contextual tab, in the Options group, clear the check box for the Different First Page option. Observe that the header on the first page becomes an odd-page header containing the text Main Header. Reselect the check box for the Different First Page option and verify that the first-page header again displays the text First Page Header. This demonstrates how hiding a header doesn't delete it from the document.

4 On the Header & Footer Tools | Design contextual tab, in the Options group, select the check box for the Different First Page option.

Observe that the tag of the header area on the first page changes to First Page Header, but the tag on the header area on the second and later pages still shows Header.

5 In the header area on the first page, type the text **First Page Header**.

6 On the Header & Footer Tools | Design contextual tab, in the Navigation group, click Next to move from the first-page header to the main header. Verify that the main header starting on the second page still contains the text Main Header.

7 On the Header & Footer Tools | Design contextual tab, in the Options group, select the check box for the Different Odd & Even Pages option.

Observe that the tag of the header area on the second page changes to Even Page Header, and the tag on the third page changes to Odd Page Header.

8 In the header area on the second page, type the text **Even Page Header**.

9 On the Header & Footer Tools | Design contextual tab, in the Navigation group, click Next to move from the even-page header to the odd-page header (which was the main header until you activated the even-page header). Verify that the odd-page header on the third page still contains the text Main Header.

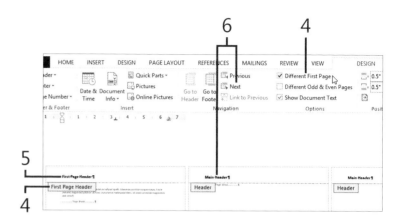

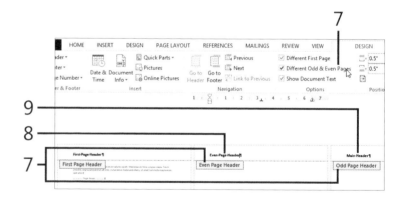

✓ **TIP** Save this document for use in "Unlink a header" on page 232.

Unlinking a header

In Word 2013, when you create a new section by inserting a section break, by default each of the headers and footers in that section repeats the content of the same type of header or footer in the preceding section. On the Header & Footer Tools | Design contextual tab, the connection between the current section and the preceding section is represented by the Link To Previous button, which is in the Navigation section.

When you want a header or footer in one section to differ from the same type of header or footer in the preceding section, you must position the cursor in the header or footer of the later section and click the Link To Previous button to turn it off.

The linkage operates separately for each type of header and footer. That is, the even-page header of a section links to the even-page header of the preceding section, independent of whether the even-page footer (or any of the other headers or footers) is linked.

Although this task discusses headers, the procedures are the same for footers.

Unlink a header

1 Open the document that you used in "Turn on different headers" on page 230.

2 Click at the end of the third page. On the Page Layout tab, in the Page Setup group, click Breaks and then click Odd Page.

   The first page of the new section 2 is numbered as page 5 because the Odd Page section break forces the document to skip over page 4.

3 On the Page Layout tab, in the Page Setup group, click Breaks and then click Page (shortcut, Ctrl+Enter) twice to insert two manual page breaks at the end of the text.

   There are now six pages numbered 1, 2, 3, 5, 6, and 7. Observe that the same first-page header appears on pages 1 and 5, the same even-page header appears on pages 2 and 6, and the same odd-page (or main) header appears on pages 3 and 7.

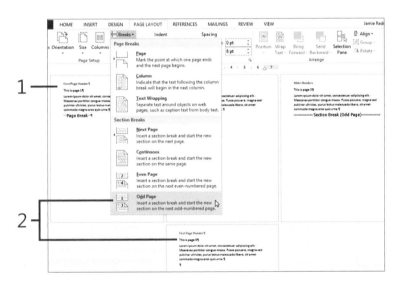

4 Double-click in the even-page header on page 6.

5 Edit the text of the header on page 6 to **Even Page Header in Section 1**.

Observe that the text in the header on page 2 contains the same text as the header on page 6, because the headers in section 1 and section 2 are linked.

6 Double-click in the even-page header on page 6. On the Header & Footer Tools | Design contextual tab, in the Navigation group, click the Link To Previous button to turn it off.

7 Edit the text of the header on page 6 to **Even Page Header in Section 2**.

Observe that the text in the header on page 2 does not change, because the headers in section 1 and section 2 are no longer linked.

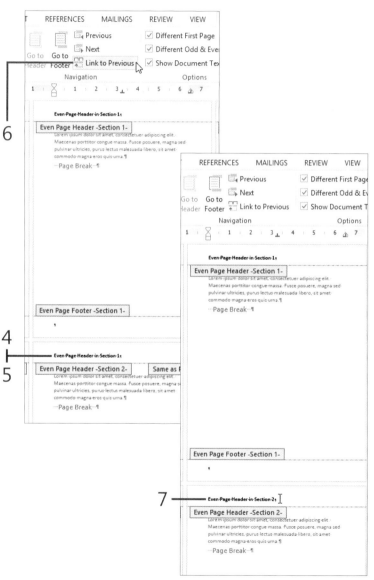

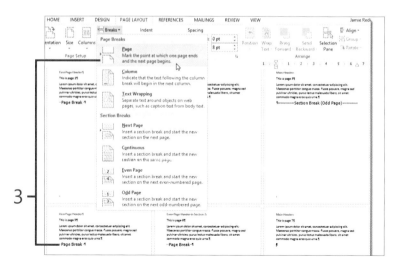

Extracting text for a header or footer from body text

You don't always need to start a new section to make a header or footer show different information from one page to the next. Instead, you might be able to display the most recent text that's formatted with a specific style—such as a heading style—in the body of the document. That is the purpose of the StyleRef field.

As an example, you might write a report in which each chapter begins with its title, formatted with the Heading 1 style. You can put a field in the document's header, using the code **{ StyleRef "Heading 1" }**. On each page, that field repeats the title of the current chapter.

The successful use of the StyleRef field depends on applying the specified style only to the text that you want to repeat in the header, not to anything else. If you need to use the built-in style for several different kinds of information, create a new style for use with the StyleRef field. Your custom style can even have the same formatting as the built-in style; only its name must be unique.

You might want to repeat only part of a paragraph from the document's body. For that purpose, you must use a character style instead of a paragraph style or a linked style. Although a linked style can be applied to just part of a paragraph, a StyleRef field won't recognize that text.

Create and apply a custom style

1 Select the first text in your document that you want to repeat in the header or footer. Apply any character formatting that you want that text to have.

2 On the Home tab, in the Styles group, click the More button. Near the bottom in the gallery that opens, click Create A Style.

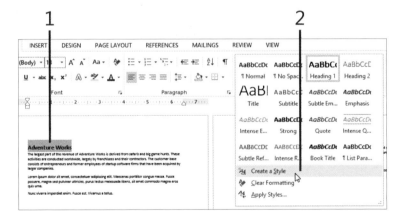

 SEE ALSO For more information about defining custom styles, see "Creating and modifying styles" on page 94.

3 In the Create New Style From Formatting dialog box, in the Name text box, type a unique name for the custom style.

It's best to choose a name that describes the purpose of the style, such as **Chapter Title**.

4 By default, the Create A Style command creates a linked style. If you expect to apply the custom style only to complete paragraphs, click OK and continue at step 6. Otherwise, click the Modify button and continue at step 5.

5 Click the Style Type box and click Character in the drop-down list. If you want the style to be saved in the template for use in other documents, click the option for New Documents Based On This Template and then click OK.

6 Select each occurrence of text in the document that should be used in the header and apply the custom style to those selections.

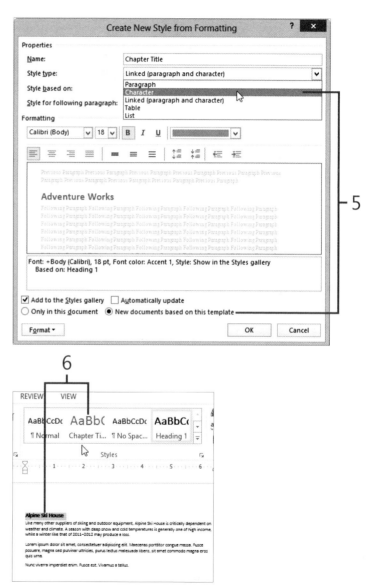

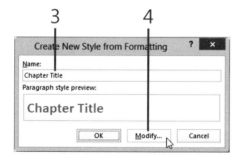

Insert a StyleRef Field

1 Double-click in the header area to open it and position the cursor where you want the extracted text to appear.

2 On the Header & Footer Tools | Design contextual tab, in the Insert group, click Quick Parts. In the drop-down list that appears, click Field.

3 In the Field dialog box, in the Field Names list box, click StyleRef.

4 In the Style Name list box, click the name of your custom style.

5 Click OK.

6 Format the result of the StyleRef field by applying a style or direct formatting to it.

7 Double-click in the body of the document to close the header area.

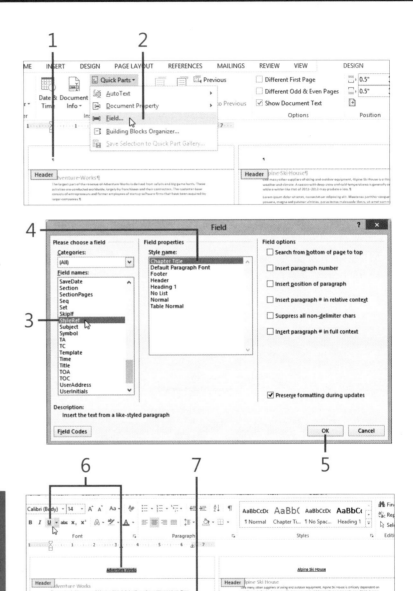

TIP The StyleRef field's result does not repeat most formatting from the text in the document, so you have to apply to the field any formatting that you want in the header. The only kind of formatting in the text that affects the StyleRef field's result is the Hidden attribute—text that is Hidden doesn't appear in the field result at all.

Inserting a watermark

Typically, a watermark is ghosted or faded text or an image that appears in the background of each page of a document. It serves as a subtle reminder to readers about something of significance or that perhaps the document requires special treatment. For example, a document might use a watermark to alert readers that its content is confidential or that it's a preliminary draft.

In Word 2013, you can use any of the built-in watermarks, such as DRAFT or SAMPLE, or you can create a watermark containing your own text or a picture.

Add a built-in watermark

1. On the Design tab, in the Page Background group, click Watermark.

2. Click the item in the Watermark gallery that you want to use as a watermark.

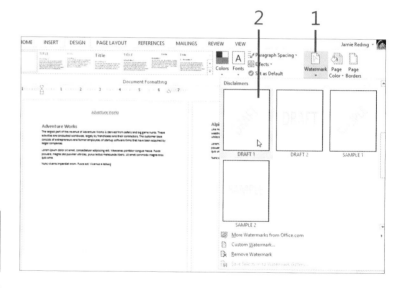

> **TIP** If there is already a watermark anywhere in the document, it will be automatically removed when you choose another watermark.

> **TRY THIS** A watermark in Word 2013 is actually a WordArt object or a picture that's inserted in the header area and then positioned in the middle of the page. As with all other items in the header, you can make the watermark in each section of the document different by first turning off the Link To Previous button on the Header & Footer Tools | Design contextual tab. However, you might first have to copy an existing watermark so that you can paste it back into place after you insert a new watermark into another section.

Add a custom text watermark

1 On the Design tab, in the Page Background group, click Watermark.

2 Near the bottom of the Watermark gallery that opens, click Custom Watermark.

3 In the Printed Watermark dialog box, click Text Watermark.

4 To use a different language for one of the built-in watermarks, click the Language box and choose a language from the drop-down list.

   As you select a different language, the built-in watermarks are automatically translated.

5 In the Text box, select an entry from the drop-down list or type your own text.

6 Select the font, size, color, and layout that you want.

7 Click OK.

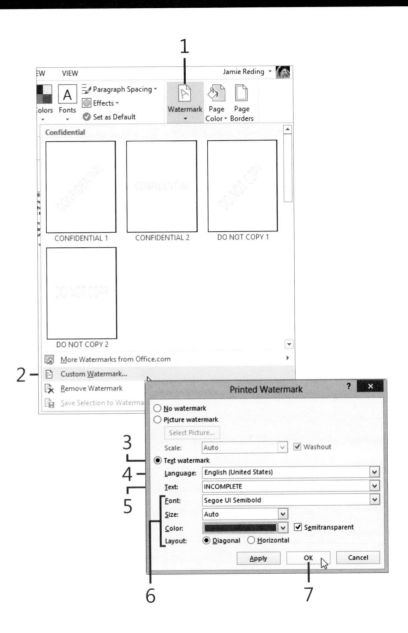

Add a custom picture watermark

1 On the Design tab, in the Page Background group, click Watermark.

2 Near the bottom of the Watermark gallery, click Custom Watermark.

3 In the Printed Watermark dialog box, click Picture Watermark.

4 Click the Select Picture button.

5 In the Insert Pictures dialog box, select a picture from your computer or from your SkyDrive storage, or search for clip art or a picture from the Internet.

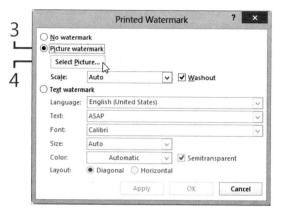

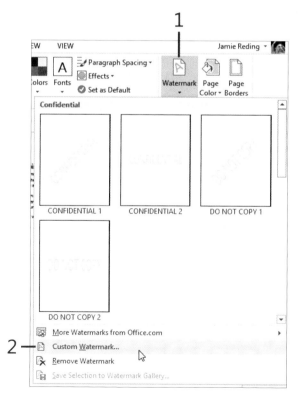

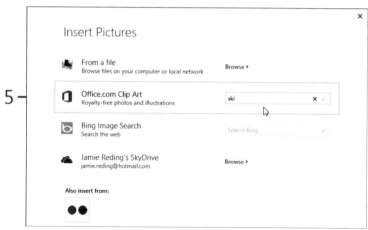

SEE ALSO For more information about inserting a picture, see "Inserting a picture from your computer" on page 274 and "Inserting an online picture" on page 276.

6 Back in the Printed Watermark dialog box, type a value in the Scale box or click an item in its drop-down list to specify the size of the picture.

7 By default, the Washout check box is selected, which fades the picture to make the foreground text in the document readable. If it fades the watermark too much, clear the Washout check box.

8 Click OK.

CAUTION Print a page of the document to verify the size and transparency of the watermark before you start a large print run. If you selected a built-in text watermark and alternating letters don't print, open the Printed Watermark dialog box and clear the check box for the Semitransparent option.

TRY THIS A watermark in Word 2013 is actually a WordArt object or a picture that's inserted in the header area and then positioned in the middle of the page. You can open the header pane and click the object to select it. If it's text, use the commands on the WordArt Tools contextual tab to change its shape, size, color, and so forth. If it's a picture, use the commands on the Picture Tools contextual tab to change its brightness, contrast, color, and other formatting.

Adding footnotes and endnotes

Footnotes and endnotes typically convey additional information about statements in the body of a document, or they describe the sources of quoted material. You typically see footnotes and endnotes being used in scholarly papers, business reports, and nonfiction books where there's a need for thorough information.

A footnote appears at the bottom of a page, whereas all endnotes are gathered at the end of the document or at the end of each section of the document. You can include both footnotes and endnotes in the same document. If you want, you can convert all the footnotes in a document to endnotes, or vice versa.

Each footnote or endnote is automatically numbered. The number, called a *reference mark*, appears as a superscript in the body of the document; the same number appears at the beginning of the footnote or endnote text as an identifier. If you insert both kinds of notes in the same document, Word 2013 creates separate number sequences for the footnotes and for the endnotes. The reference mark is a hyperlink to the location of the corresponding note, and the number in the footnote or endnote text is a hyperlink to the corresponding reference mark.

Add a footnote or endnote

1 Click in your document's text where you want to insert the reference mark for a footnote or endnote.

2 On the References tab, in the Footnotes group, click Insert Footnote or Insert Endnote.

Word inserts the next number in the footnote or endnote sequence as the new reference mark and inserts the same number at the bottom of the page or at the end of the document. The cursor appears after the footnote or endnote number, ready for you to insert your text.

3 Type or paste the text that you want in the footnote. When you finish typing the note, double-click the note's number to return to the location of the reference mark.

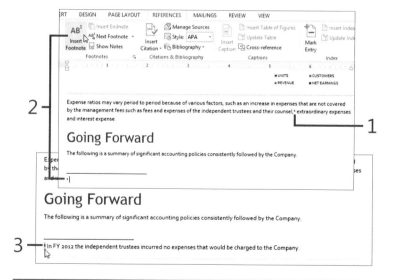

> ✓ **TIP** Footnotes and endnotes in Draft, Outline, or Web Layout view are usually hidden. On the References tab, in the Footnotes group, click Show Notes to open a Footnote pane or an Endnote pane at the bottom of the window.

> ✓ **TIP** If you insert or delete a footnote or endnote before the last existing note of that type, all the later notes in the sequence are automatically renumbered.

Change the format of footnotes and endnotes

1 On the References tab, in the Footnotes group, click the dialog box launcher (the small arrow in the lower-right corner of the group).

2 In the Footnote And Endnote dialog box, in the Location section, click either Footnotes or Endnotes, depending on which type of note you want to modify.

For footnotes, choose whether to position the footnote text at the bottom of the page or immediately below the last text on the page.

For endnotes, choose whether to collect all the endnotes at the end of the document or at the end of each section of the document.

3 If you selected Footnotes in step 2, you can click the Columns box. In the drop-down list that appears, choose whether to arrange the footnotes in the same number of columns as the text of the section, or in a specific number of columns, independent of the section layout.

4 Click the Number Format list box to select an Arabic or Roman numeral sequence, a letter sequence, or a symbol sequence.

Alternatively, type a symbol in the Custom Mark text box, or click the Symbol button to select any symbol in any available font. This choice disables the Number Format list box.

5 If you want the sequence to start at a number or letter different from the default, change the value in the Start At list box.

6 Click the Numbering list box and choose whether the numbering of footnotes or endnotes continues throughout the document, or restarts on each page or at the beginning of each section.

7 If the document contains section breaks, you can click the Apply Changes To list box and choose whether the changes in the dialog box affect the whole document or just the section containing the cursor.

8 Click Insert.

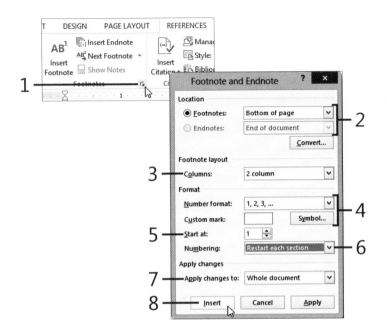

TIP If you need to convert all the footnotes in the document into endnotes, or vice versa, click the Convert button and choose the action that you want to perform.

TRY THIS If you need to refer to the same footnote or endnote in more than one location, insert the first occurrence of the note normally. Next, insert one or more cross-references to the note's reference mark in the other locations. Then, apply the Footnote Reference character style to each cross-reference. The cross-references must be updated manually if additions or deletions in the sequence cause the note's number to change. For more information about inserting cross-references, see "Repeating information by using cross-references" on page 216.

Generating a table of contents

A table of contents is one of the most important elements by which readers find information in your documents. Word 2013 easily creates a table that lists all the headings in the document and their page numbers. The entries in the list are hyperlinks to the headings in the text. This means that if the document is open in the Word program it's easy to jump directly to a topic of interest.

Before you insert a table of contents, it's a good idea to examine the headings in your document to be sure that all the paragraphs have the correct heading styles. The Navigation pane is an excellent tool for that task.

A table of contents usually contains the text that has been formatted by using the built-in heading styles in a document. However, Word gives you the option of including additional text that will be displayed only in the table of contents, but not in the document body. You enter this text in the field codes of hidden fields by using the keyword TC. For example, if each chapter title is just a Heading 1 that contains only the chapter number (just 1, 2, 3, and so on), that could be confusing in a table of contents. To make the table of contents more user-friendly, you can enter text such as "Chapter One" in a TC field, which you can then choose to include in the table of contents.

Check the headings

1 Open a document that contains text and headings formatted by using the various built-in heading styles.

2 On the View tab, in the Show group, select the Navigation Pane check box (if it isn't already selected).

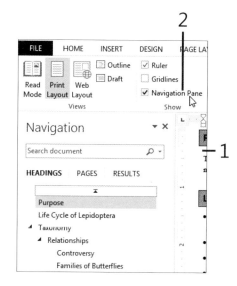

3 Toward the top of the Navigation pane, ensure that the Headings tab is selected. Then, verify that the Navigation pane displays all the headings that you want in the table of contents, that they form the correct outline, and that the Navigation pane doesn't display any text that should be excluded.

4 If you want to include a paragraph that doesn't appear in the Navigation pane, or one that has the wrong heading style, click in that paragraph and apply the correct heading style.

If you don't want a paragraph that appears in the Navigation pane to be included in the table of contents, apply a style that is not included in the table of contents (for example, Normal or Body Text).

> ⚠ **CAUTION** On the References tab, in the Table of Contents group, clicking the Add Text button opens a gallery containing the entries Do Not Show In Table Of Contents, Level 1, Level 2, and Level 3. These commands act differently depending on the style currently applied to the paragraph at the cursor.
>
> If the current style is Normal or one of the built-in heading styles from Heading 1 to Heading 9, the Level 1, Level 2, and Level 3 commands apply the styles Heading 1, Heading 2, and Heading 3, respectively, and the Do Not Show In Table Of Contents command applies the Normal style. If the current style is any style other than Normal or the nine built-in heading styles, the commands change the paragraph's outline level without changing the paragraph's style.
>
> This variable behavior can easily lead to confusion, so you should avoid the Add Text button. Instead, apply the correct paragraph styles from the gallery on the Home tab or from the Styles pane.

 SEE ALSO For more information about applying styles, see "Formatting with styles" on page 90.

Insert a table of contents

1 Click at the location in the document where you want the table of contents to start.

2 On the References tab, in the Table Of Contents group, click Table Of Contents.

3 In the Table Of Contents gallery that opens, click Automatic Table 1 or Automatic Table 2. These building blocks insert a table of contents inside a content control, which means that they can easily be updated or replaced.

The two automatic tables are the same except for the wording of the title above the table. The Manual Table building block doesn't use any text from the body of the document and cannot be updated automatically, so it's appropriate only for documents that have no heading paragraphs.

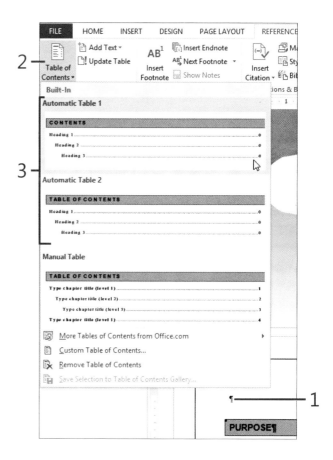

> **TIP** The Custom Table Of Contents command near the bottom of the Table Of Contents gallery inserts the same kind of table as the automatic building blocks, but it doesn't include the content control or the title above the table.

Use TC fields for special entries

1 Click at the location in your document corresponding to the desired position of the new entry in the table of contents.

2 On the Insert tab, in the Text group, click Quick Parts. In the drop-down list that appears, click Field.

3 In the Please Choose A Field section, in the Field Names list box, click TC.

4 In the Text Entry text box, type or paste the text that you want to insert in the table of contents.

5 In the section labeled Field Options, click in the text box to the right of the Outline Level label and type the number of the outline level (equivalent to the built-in heading style number) at which the entry will appear in the table of contents.

6 Click OK.

Repeat steps 1 through 6 for each entry that you want to insert in the table of contents.

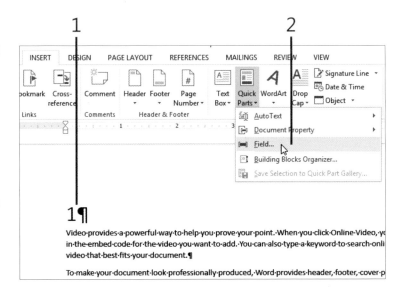

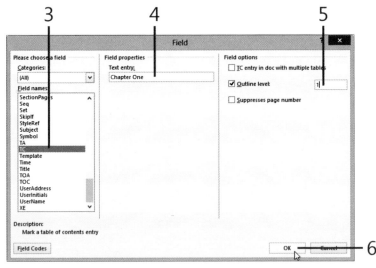

> ✓ **TIP** Each TC field is automatically formatted as Hidden text. If you need to edit the text in a TC field, on the Home tab, in the Paragraph group, click the Show/Hide ¶ button to display Hidden text and all other nonprinting characters.

7 Click to the left of the first character of the table of contents.

8 On the References tab, in the Table of Contents group, click Table of Contents. Near the bottom of the gallery that opens, click Custom Table Of Contents.

9 In the Table Of Contents dialog box, click the Options button.

10 In the Table Of Contents Options dialog box, select the Table Entry Fields check box and click OK.

The Table Entry Fields option configures the table of contents to include the text from any TC fields that exist in the document.

11 In the Table Of Contents dialog box, click OK.

12 In the message pop-up box that asks whether to replace the selected table of contents, click Yes.

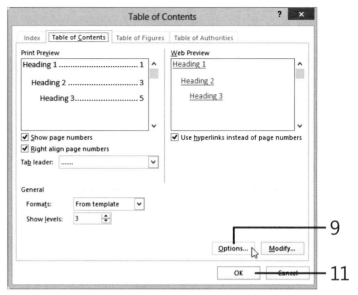

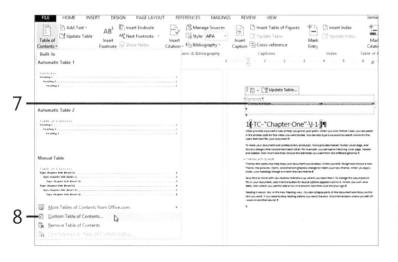

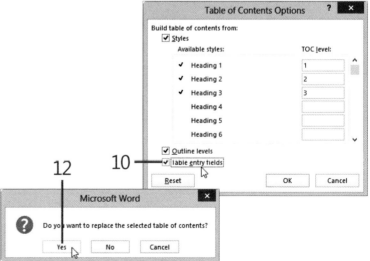

Updating a table of contents

Whenever you add or remove text or graphics, change page dimensions, or do anything else that affects the layout of your document, the page numbers or the items in the table of contents might need to change. Word 2013 gives you the choice to update the page numbers only, or to update the entire table, if entries must be added or removed.

Update page numbers only or the entire table of contents

1 Click inside the content control that contains the table of contents, but not on any of the hyperlinked entries.

2 When the content control's tag appears at the upper-left corner, click Update Table.

3 In the Update Table Of Contents dialog box, click the option that you want and then click OK.

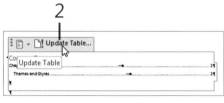

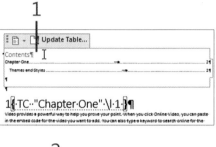

Modifying table of contents styles

Although a table of contents in Word 2013 repeats the text of headings in the document, it doesn't use the formatting of the heading styles. Instead, it applies separate styles named TOC 1 through TOC 9 to the nine possible outline levels. Any direct character formatting (such as bold or italic) that is applied to the headings is repeated in the table of contents entries.

The default TOC styles are very plain—just the Normal style with a little additional left indent in each successive outline level. For a better appearance, you might want to choose one of several other built-in sets of styles or modify the styles to your own preferences. For example, none of the built-in styles specify a hanging indent for entries that are long enough to extend to a second line. You might want to add this type of indent to the style definitions.

Change the formatting of the table entries

1 Click to the left of the first character of the table of contents.

2 On the References tab, in the Table of Contents group, click Table of Contents. Near the bottom of the gallery that opens, click Custom Table Of Contents.

3 In the Table Of Contents dialog box, click the Formats box and select each of the items in its list box while you look at the previews to find one that is suitable. Each item corresponds to a different set of definitions for the TOC 1 through TOC 9 styles.

4 In the Tab Leader list box, select the type of leader line to connect the text of an entry in the table of contents to its page number. The default leader depends on the setting in the Formats box.

5 In the Show Levels list box, enter the number of outline levels that you want to display in the table of contents. The default value shows heading levels 1 through 3.

6 Click OK.

7 If none of the built-in sets of styles are exactly right, you can modify the TOC styles directly. On the Home tab, in the Styles group, click the dialog launcher (shortcut, Ctrl+Alt+Shift+S) to open the Styles pane.

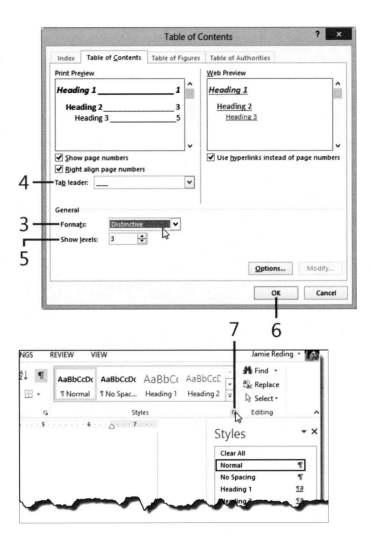

8 If the styles TOC 1 through TOC 9 are not displayed in the Styles pane, click the Options link at the bottom of the pane. Then, in the Style Pane Options dialog box, click the Select Styles To Show box, select All Styles, and then click OK.

9 Right-click any of the TOC styles that need adjustment and then click Modify. Change the definition of the style as described in "Modify an existing style by using a dialog box" on page 95.

SEE ALSO For more information about modifying the appearance of tables of contents, see *wordfaqs.mvps.org/ TOCTips.htm#Appearance*.

Using multiple tables of contents

For a large document with many chapters, you might need a separate table of contents in each chapter plus a comprehensive table of contents at the beginning of the document. In Word 2013, you can insert a bookmark in the document to enclose each chapter. Then, in the field code of the table of contents for a chapter, you can add a \b switch plus the name of the bookmark. That table of contents will display only the headings from within the specified bookmark.

Mark part of the document for a table of contents

1 Select the part of the document for which you want to create a partial table of contents.

2 On the Insert tab, in the Links group, click Bookmark.

3 In the Bookmark dialog box, in the Bookmark Name list box, type a name for the bookmark.

You can use only letters, digits, and underscores in the name. Other characters, including spaces, are not allowed.

4 Click the Add button.

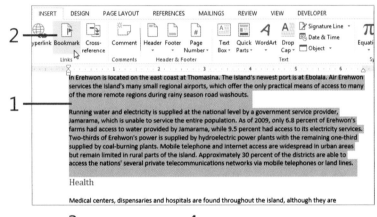

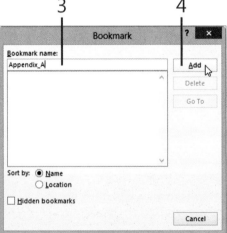

SEE ALSO For more information about selecting large amounts of text, see "Selecting text" on page 42. For more information about inserting a bookmark, see "Insert a bookmark" on page 211.

Make a table of contents for part of the document

1 Click in the document at the location where the partial table of contents should start.

2 On the References tab, in the Table Of Contents group, click Table Of Contents.

3 Near the bottom of the Table Of Contents gallery that opens, click the Custom Table Of Contents command.

4 In the Table Of Contents dialog box, select the desired format, tab leader, number of levels, and then click OK.

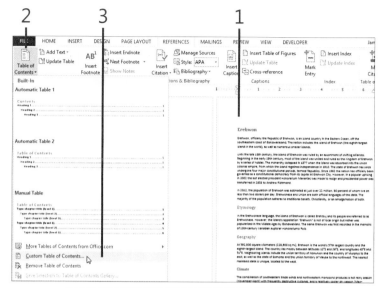

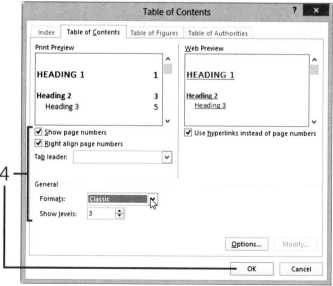

> ⚠ **CAUTION** If any other tables of contents already exist in the document, selecting any of the Automatic entries in the gallery will *replace* the first existing table of contents without any prompt. Only the Custom Table Of Contents command enables you to keep the existing tables and add a new one.

> 🔍 **SEE ALSO** For more information about defining the format of a table of contents, see "Modifying table of contents styles" on page 249.

5 If a message pop-up box appears, asking whether to replace the selected table of contents, click No.

6 At the left end of the first line, right-click the table of contents. On the shortcut menu that appears, click Toggle Field Codes.

7 Edit the field code to add the switch **\b** followed by the name of the bookmark that surrounds the desired part of the document.

For example, if the bookmark's name is Appendix_A, the completed table of contents field code should be similar to **{ TOC \o "1-3" \h \z \u \b Appendix_A }**.

8 Right-click in the field code and then, on the shortcut menu that appears, click Update Field (shortcut, F9).

9 In the Update Table Of Contents dialog box, click the Update Entire Table option and then click OK.

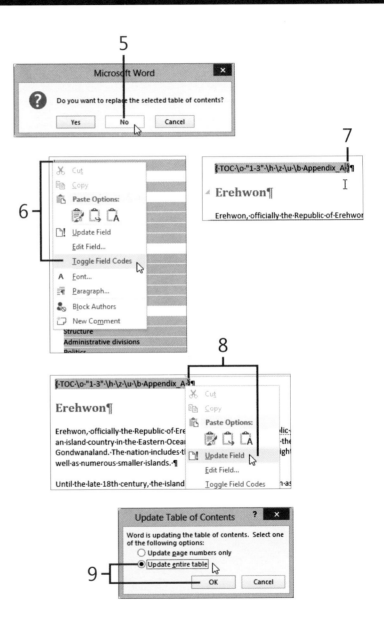

Indexing a document

In a long nonfiction document, especially one that will be printed on paper, it's vital to include an index so that readers can locate names, concepts, procedures, or other important topics. Word 2013 provides several tools that aid in compiling an index.

You index a document in two stages. In the first stage, you insert fields by using the keyword XE to mark the locations of entries that will be collected in the index. In these XE fields, you can repeat text from the document, or you can enter synonyms or any other words that are related to or in some way descriptive of the text you're indexing. Index entries can be constructed with a main phrase followed by a subentry.

The second stage consists of inserting the index itself, which is a field with the keyword INDEX. You can choose options that change the formatting of the index, such as the number of columns to display or how to separate the page numbers from the entry text.

Mark index entries

1   Click in your document at the location where you want to insert an index entry.

   If you want the entry to consist of the text in that location, select the text. If you intend to enter some word or phrase that doesn't specifically appear in the text, just click without selecting anything.

2   On the References tab, in the Index group, click Mark Entry.

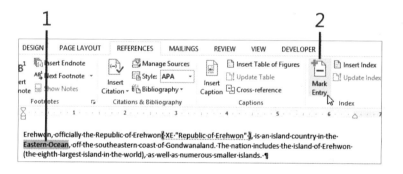

<table>
<tr><td>CAUTION</td><td>The index entries are case-sensitive. For example, if you mark both reading and Reading as entries, the index will display them separately rather than combining them. This might be intentional or a mistake. The final index requires a careful review for problems like this.</td></tr>
</table>

TIP   All XE fields are automatically formatted as Hidden text. If you want to see or edit the XE fields, on the Home tab, in the Paragraph group, click the Show/Hide ¶ button.

3 If you selected text in step 1, it appears in the Main Entry text box of the Mark Index Entry dialog box. If that is the desired index entry, click the Mark button to insert an XE field. To insert an XE field on each page on which the selected text occurs, click Mark All. Otherwise, continue at step 4.

4 If there is no text in the Main Entry text box, or if you want to change the entry, add or edit the text in the Main Entry box and the Subentry box, as appropriate.

For example, if the text you selected in the document is **Abraham Lincoln**, but you want the main entry to appear as **Lincoln** with the subentry **Abraham**, delete or cut **Abraham** from the Main Entry box and type or paste it into the Subentry box.

5 If the current entry should not have a page number, but instead should refer to another entry in the index, click the Cross-Reference option and type the desired text in the text box to its right.

6 If the current entry refers to a range of pages that are marked with a bookmark, click the Page Range option and then select the bookmark's name in the Bookmark box.

7 If the entry's page number should be bold or italic or both, select the desired check boxes in the Page Number Format section.

8 Click the Mark button or the Mark All button.

9 To continue marking entries, click in the document at the next location.

The Mark Index Entry dialog box remains open, and its Main Entry box updates to the new selection when you click in the dialog box again.

10 When you want to dismiss the Mark Index Entry dialog box, click Cancel.

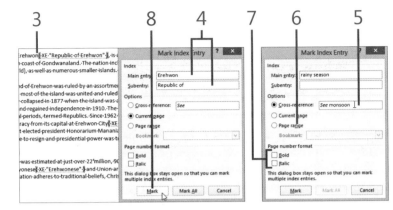

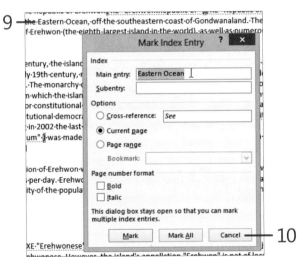

Insert an index

1 Click in your document at the location where you want the index to start.

2 On the References tab, in the Index group, click the Insert Index button.

3 In the Index dialog box, click the Formats box. Select each of the items in the Formats list in turn while you look at the Print Preview box. When you see the format that you prefer, leave that list item selected.

4 If you want to place the page numbers at the right margin of each column, select the check box for Right Align Page Numbers. Then, in the Tab Leader list box, select a tab leader style or (none).

5 If your index uses subentries, click the Indented option to start each subentry on a new line, or click the Run-In option to place all the subentries of the same main entry into a single paragraph.

6 In the Columns list box, enter the number of columns in which the index should be arranged.

7 In the Language list box, select the language that determines the sort order of the index. Languages that use the caret (^), tilde (~), and other accent characters have specific sorting rules.

8 Click OK.

9 If you add, edit, or delete XE fields, click in the index. Then, on the References tab, in the Index group, click Update Index.

> ✓ **TIP** Before you update the index, on the Home tab click Show/Hide ¶ to turn it off. Otherwise, the visible XE fields might change the pagination of the document by so much that the page numbers in the index are incorrect.

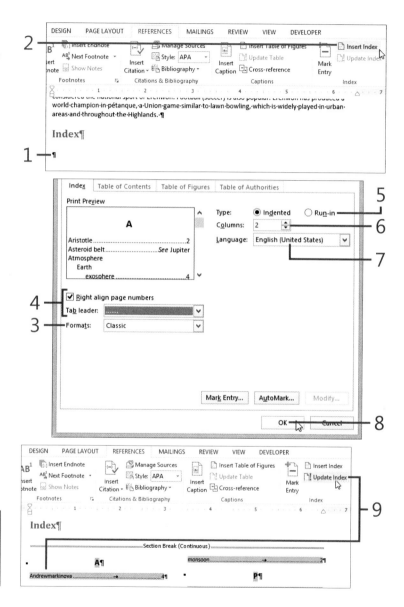

Using multiple indexes

The field code of an Index field can include switches that create different types of indexes. Two of these switches are quite useful in certain circumstances.

In one scenario, you might separate the document into chapters or other parts, and enclose each part in a bookmark. Then, you can insert an Index field and edit its field code to include a \b switch and the name of the bookmark enclosing the desired

part. That index will contain only the entries from the specified part.

In another scenario, you might want an index just for the names of people mentioned in the document, and another index for all other kinds of entries. To do this, edit the field code of each XE field to include an \f switch and a one-letter identifier. Then, insert the same \f switch and identifier into the corresponding Index field.

Make indexes for different parts of a document

1 Select the part of the document for which you want to create a partial index.

2 On the Insert tab, in the Links group, click Bookmark.

3 In the Bookmark dialog box, in the Bookmark Name list box, type a name for the bookmark.

You can use only letters, digits, and underscores in the name. Other characters, including spaces, are not allowed.

4 Click the Add button.

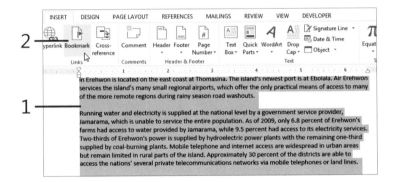

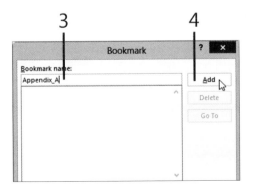

> **SEE ALSO** For more information about selecting large amounts of text, see "Selecting text" on page 42. For more information about inserting a bookmark, see "Insert a bookmark" on page 211.

5 Click in the document at the location where the partial index should start.

6 On the References tab, in the Index group, click Insert Index.

7 Select the options to create the appearance that you want for the index, as described in "Insert an index" on page 257.

8 If a message pop-up box appears, asking whether to replace the selected index, click No.

9 Right-click in the index. On the shortcut menu that opens, click Toggle Field Codes.

10 Edit the field code to add the switch **\b**, followed by the name of the bookmark that surrounds the desired part of the document.

For example, if the bookmark's name is Appendix_A, the completed Index field code should be similar to **{ INDEX \h "A" \c "2" \b Appendix_A }**.

11 On the References tab, in the Index group, click Update Index.

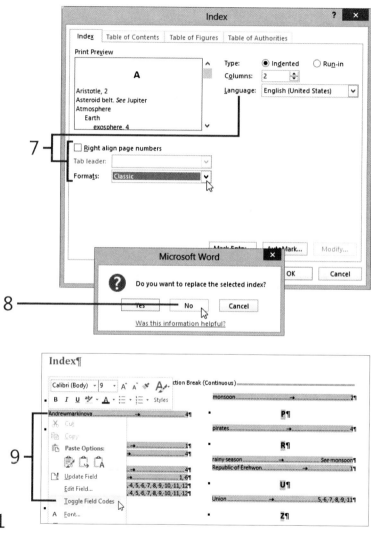

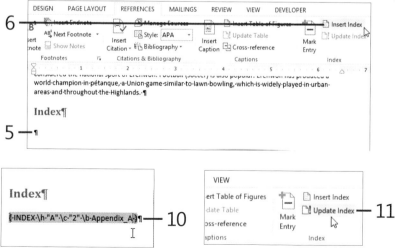

Make indexes for different kinds of entries

1 On the Home tab, in the Paragraph group, click Show/Hide ¶ to display the hidden XE fields.

2 Edit each XE field to add an **\f** switch and a one-letter identifier for the type of entry.

For example, you might insert **\f n** into entries for names, and **\f o** into entries for other topics.

The letters you use as identifiers are arbitrary. The only requirement is that each entry of the same type must have the same letter. Uppercase and lowercase of the same identifier are treated as the same entry type.

3 Click in the document at the location where the special index should start.

4 On the References tab, in the Index group, click Insert Index.

Upon·its·emergence·in·the·early·17th·century,·the·highland·kingdom·of·Imelda·was·initially·a·minor·power·relative·to·the·larger·coastal·kingdoms·and·grew·even·weaker·in·the·early·18th·century·when·King·Andrewmarkinova{·XE·"Andrewmarkinova"·\f·n·}·divided·it·among·his·four·sons.·Following·a·century·of·warring·and·famine,·Imelda·was·reunited·in·1793·by·King·Andrewpointylmelda{·XE·"Andrewpointylmelda"·\f·n·}·(1777–1800).·From·his·capital·of·Erehwon·City{·XE·"Erehwon·City"·\f·o·},·this·king·rapidly·expanded·his·rule·over·neighboring·principalities.·His·ambition·to·bring·the·entire·island·under·his·control·was·largely·achieved·by·his·son·and·successor,·King·Ramalama{·XE·"Ramalama"·\f·n·}·(1798–1822),·who·was·recognized·by·the·Burtish·government·as·King·of·Erehwon.·Ramalama·concluded·a·treaty·in·1817·with·the·Burtish·governor·of·Murphys·to·abolish·the·slave·trade·in·return·for·Burtish·military·and·financial·assistance.·Artisan·missionary·envoys·from·the·Missionary·Society·began·arriving·in·1818·and·included·such·key·figures·as·James·Cameron{·XE·"Cameron:James"·\f·n·},·David·Jones{·XE·"Jones:David"·\f·n·}·and·David·Griffiths{·XE·"Griffiths:David"·\f·n·},·who·established·schools,·transcribed·the·Erehwonese{·XE·"Erehwonese"·\f·o·}·language·using·the·Roman·alphabet,·translated·the·Bible,·and·introduced·a·variety·of·new·technologies·to·the·island.¶

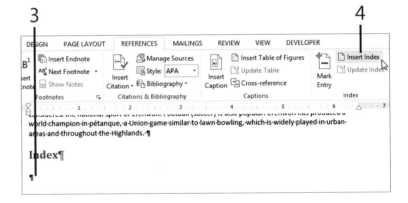

...considered·the·national·sport·of·Erehwon.·Football·(soccer)·is·also·popular.·Erehwon·has·produced·a·world·champion·in·pétanque,·a·Union·game·similar·to·lawn·bowling,·which·is·widely·played·in·urban·areas·and·throughout·the·Highlands.·¶

Index¶

5 In the Index dialog box, select the options to create the appearance that you want for the index, as described in "Insert an index" on page 257.

6 If a message pop-up box appears, asking whether to replace the selected index, click No.

7 Right-click in the index. On the shortcut menu that appears, click Toggle Field Codes.

8 Edit the field code to add the switch **\f**, followed by the identifier that you used for this type of entry in step 2.

For example, if the identifier for names is **n**, the completed Index field code should be similar to **{ INDEX \h "A" \c "2" \f n }**.

9 On the References tab, in the Index group, click Update Index.

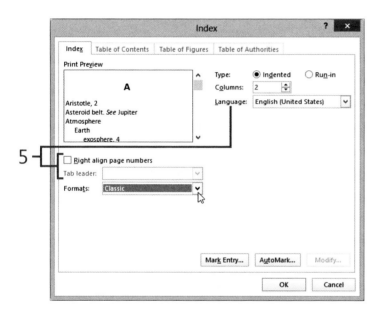

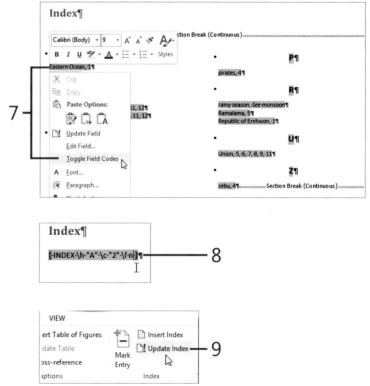

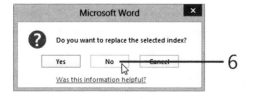

Making tables of tables and tables of figures

Some documents are heavily illustrated or use many tables, and readers often find it useful to have a table of figures or a table of tables, or both. Word 2013 has tools specifically designed for creating tables of those kinds.

To create tables of figures or tables of tables, you must insert *captions* to identify each of the items that should be included.

Insert captions

1 Click in a table, or select a picture or a chart.

2 On the References tab, in the Captions group, click Insert Caption.

3 In the Caption dialog box, click the Label list box and select the type of the current item.

4 Click the Position list box and select the placement of the caption.

5 Click the Caption text box and type a description of the current item, if desired.

6 Click OK.

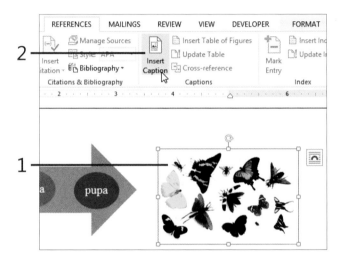

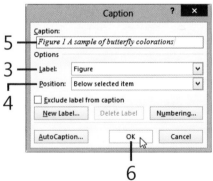

Insert a table of tables or figures

1 Click in the document at the location where the table of tables or figures should start.

2 On the References tab, in the Captions group, click Insert Table Of Figures.

3 In the Table Of Figures dialog box, click the Caption Label list box and select the type of item to be listed by the current table.

4 Click the Formats list box and select the appearance you want.

5 If you want to place the page numbers at the right margin of each column, select the check box for Right Align Page Numbers. Then, in the Tab Leader list box, select a tab leader style or (none).

6 Click OK.

7 If there is already a table of the same type in the document, Word displays a message pop-up box that asks whether to replace the selected table of figures. If you intend to change the existing table, click Yes; otherwise, click No.

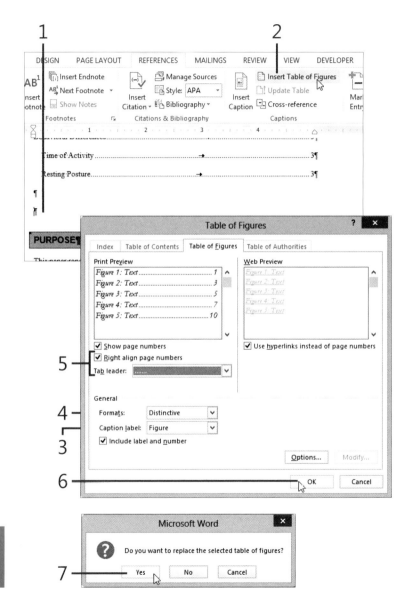

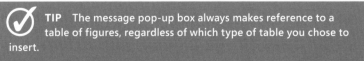

TIP The message pop-up box always makes reference to a table of figures, regardless of which type of table you chose to insert.

Creating a bibliography

When you write a paper for a school course or for publication in a journal, one of the most tedious and error-prone parts of the work is keeping track of the sources and properly formatting the citations and the bibliography. Word 2013 supplies tools that help with those tasks.

As you write your paper, insert each citation directly in the text and enter the information about its source. Word 2013 stores that information, so you can easily use it later to cite the same source again. If you don't have all the information to complete the citation, you can create a placeholder and fill it in later.

You can insert a bibliography in your document at any time after you insert at least one citation, or you can wait until the end of the project. The bibliography can be updated at any time to include added or modified citations. There are many different styles of citation and bibliography, but most schools and publishers accept one of a handful of standard styles. Word 2013 can automatically format information to conform to the styles in *Publication Manual of the American Psychological Association* 6th edition (APA), *The Chicago Manual of Style* 15th edition (Chicago), *MLA Handbook for Writers of Research Papers* 7th edition (MLA), and *Manual for Writers of Research Papers, Theses, and Dissertations* 6th edition (Turabian), among other styles.

Choose a citation style

1   On the References tab, in the Citations & Bibliography group, click the down-arrow next to the Style box. In the drop-down list that appears, click the name of the style that you want to use.

The citation style you select is one of the factors in determining which pieces of information are requested when you add a new source. However, you can select a different citation style later; Word will automatically change the formatting applied to the citations and the bibliography.

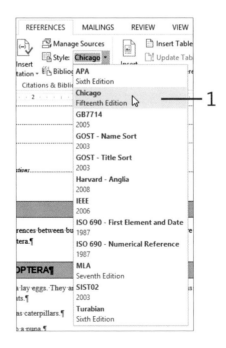

Add a source

1 Click in the text at the end of the sentence or passage that needs a citation.

2 On the References tab, in the Citations & Bibliography group, click Insert Citation. In the drop-down list that appears, click Add New Source.

3 In the Create Source dialog box, click the Type Of Source list box and select the form of the source material.

The fields displayed in the bottom part of the Create Source dialog box will change to those required for the selected source type and the current citation style.

4 Type or paste the information about the source and then click OK.

The citation appears at the insertion point in the document, in the format appropriate for the current citation style.

5 After you add a source, Word adds it to the gallery on the Insert Citation button. You can insert a citation for the same source elsewhere in the document by selecting it from the gallery.

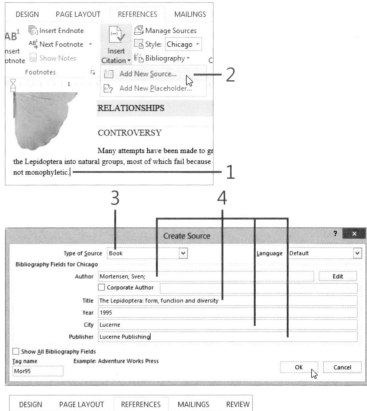

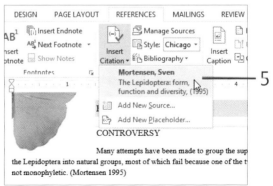

> ✓ **TIP** If a source has multiple authors, click the Edit button to open a dialog box in which you can enter and reorder the authors' names.

Add a placeholder

1 If you don't have all the information to complete the citation, on the References tab, in the Citations & Bibliography group, click Insert Citation. In the drop-down list that appears, click Add New Placeholder.

2 In the Placeholder Name dialog box, type a name for the placeholder and click OK.

The placeholder's name appears at the insertion point in the document.

> ✓ **TIP** A placeholder name can contain letters, digits, and underscores. Other characters, including spaces, are not allowed.

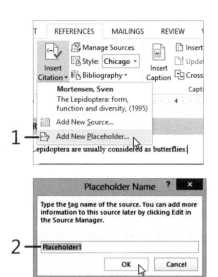

Manage sources

1 On the References tab, in the Citations & Bibliography group, click Manage Sources.

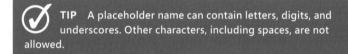

2 In the Source Manager dialog box, the Master List list box displays all the sources you've created on your computer, in all the documents that contain citations, except for any sources that you previously deleted. The Current List list box displays the sources that are cited in the open document, uncited sources that are available in the Insert Citation gallery, and any placeholders in the document.

After you click an entry in the Master List or the Current List, you can do one of the following:

- Click the Copy button to copy the selected source to the opposite list.

- Click the Delete button to remove the selected source from the list.

- Click the Edit button to change information in the selected source.

The preview at the bottom of the Source Manager dialog box shows the format of the selected source as a citation and as a bibliography entry in the current citation style.

3 If you want to create a new source without adding a citation in the text of the document, click the New button. Complete the entries in the Create Source dialog box and click OK. The citation is added to both lists in the Source Manager dialog box.

4 If you want to sort the lists in the Source Manager dialog box differently, click the Sort box and select the field by which to sort.

5 Click the Close button.

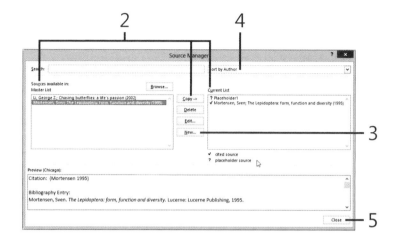

TRY THIS   The Master List is stored in a file named *Sources.xml*. In the Source Manager dialog box, click the Browse button to display the Open Source List dialog box. You can right-click the *Sources. xml* file and click Copy (shortcut, Ctrl+C). Then, select a different folder or network location and paste the file as a backup copy, or to transfer the file to another computer.

Insert a bibliography

1 Click in your document at the location where the bibliography should start.

2 On the References tab, in the Citations & Bibliography group, click Bibliography. In the gallery that opens, click one of the entries, or at the bottom of the gallery, click Insert Bibliography.

All of the entries in the gallery are the same except for their titles. They enclose the entire bibliography in a content control, which enables updating the bibliography with a click on the control's tag. The Insert Bibliography item inserts a bibliography without a title or a content control.

3 If you plan to submit the document to a different publication, you might need to change the citation style to another standard. On the References tab, in the Citations & Bibliography group, click the Style box and select the new style. Word 2013 automatically reformats all of the citations and the bibliography to match the new style.

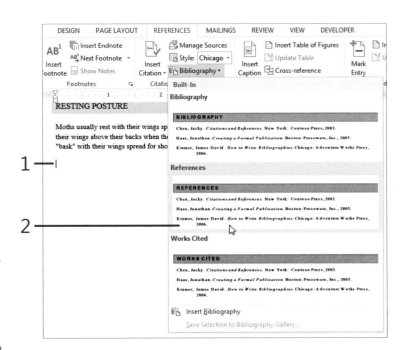

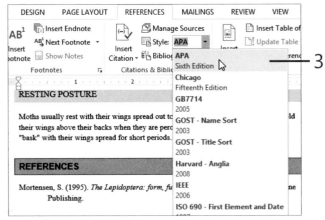

> **! CAUTION** The bibliography you insert contains all of the sources in the Current List list box of the Manage Sources dialog box, including any uncited sources but excluding any placeholders. It's a good idea to review the Current List to ensure that all of its entries are selected to indicate that they have citations in the document, and none of them have question marks, indicating that they are placeholders.

> **✓ TIP** If you use the APA 6th edition citation style and you insert multiple citations from the same author, the citations incorrectly include the publication title. To correct this, click the citation, click the down-arrow at the right end of the content control, and then click Edit Citation. In the Edit Citation dialog box, in the section labeled Suppress, select the Title check box and click OK.

Making pictures work for you

10

There are few things that you can place in your Microsoft Word 2013 documents that capture a reader's interest as much as an illustration. Photographs might show a family occasion, a house for sale, or a scene that sets a mood. A screenshot could demonstrate an application's display or an interesting website. Graphs and charts can help your readers to visualize data. Or, you could include an online video of assembly instructions or a concert performance.

When you add a picture to a document, it's important to consider how it is positioned with respect to the text. Word supports several layout options with which you can control how text flows around your graphic. You also have many tools available to modify the appearance of a picture, whether to correct problems or to add interesting texture or color effects.

In this section:

- Choosing illustration types
- Inserting a picture from your computer
- Inserting an online picture
- Inserting online video
- Inserting a screenshot
- Positioning pictures on the page
- Resizing or cropping a picture
- Replacing a picture
- Changing the appearance of a picture
- Removing the background from a picture
- Applying special effects
- Setting a transparent color

Choosing illustration types

Word 2013 helps you to illustrate your documents with photographs, drawings, screenshots, charts, and diagrams. You can insert graphics files from your computer or your online storage, or search the Internet for just the right image. Word 2013 introduces the ability to include online video clips that your readers can launch from within your documents. With so many possibilities, it's important to know which command is appropriate for a particular type of illustration. The commands that you can use to place graphics in your document are gathered on the ribbon, on the Insert tab. There, you'll find everything you need in the Illustrations group and the Media group.

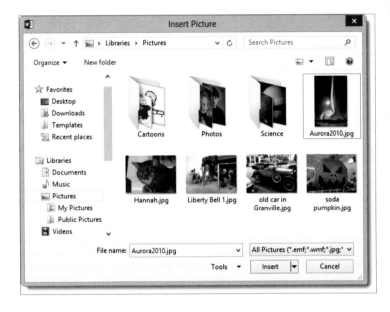

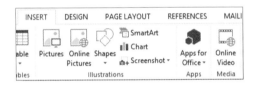

If you have a photograph, a drawing, or another kind of graphic file stored on your computer, use the Pictures command to open the Insert Picture dialog box. There, you can use the Search box to find files, and you can open the Preview pane to verify that you have the correct files.

When you need a graphic file from your SkyDrive storage or your Flickr account, or if you want to search the clip art on Office.com or the images available on the Internet, use the Online Pictures tool. Clip art includes both drawings and photographs that cover a wide range of topics. The Bing Image Search can retrieve from the web almost any image you can think of.

The Shapes gallery offers boxes, arrows, circles, and many other tools for drawing diagrams and for annotating other kinds of pictures. You can place shapes directly on the page, or first insert a drawing canvas to group several pictures and shapes into one object.

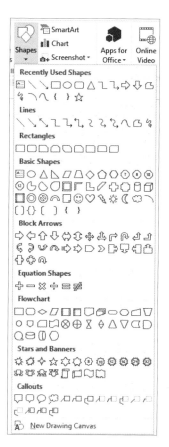

Using the Screenshot tool, you can take a picture of a window or a region of your computer screen and immediately insert it into your Word document. One screenshot or a series of captures can help you to explain how a program works, or to report an error message.

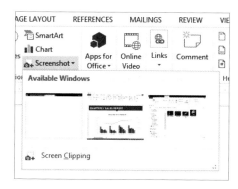

The SmartArt feature helps you to create well-designed diagrams that combine shapes and text to clarify abstract concepts. You can use the Themes feature to coordinate the colors and effects in all of the SmartArt in your document.

With the Chart tool, you can turn your numeric and time-related data into visually interesting charts and graphs. And, you can use the analytical features of Microsoft Excel to show the relevance of the data to your readers.

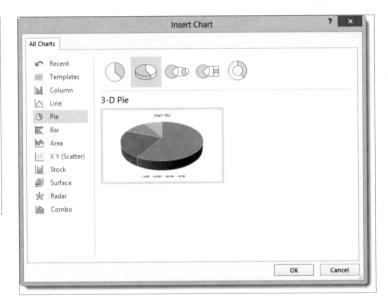

Increasingly, Word documents are distributed and read electronically rather than on paper. In Word 2013, you can find videos on the Internet or on your own website and insert links to them directly into your documents.

Inserting a picture from your computer

On your work computer, you might store the company logo, pictures of products, engineering drawings, and so on. Your home computer might contain hundreds of digital pictures of family, friends, vacations, and more. You can insert any of these files into your Word 2013 documents to illustrate and enliven your message.

Choose a picture file on disk

1 Click at the location in the document where you want the picture to appear.

2 On the Insert tab, in the Illustrations group, click Pictures.

3 In the Insert Picture dialog box, if the picture that you want is visible in the first folder that appears, click the picture's icon so that its name appears in the File Name box and then continue at step 5.

4 If you want a picture from another folder, use the folder display on the left side of the dialog box to navigate to that location or use the Search box in the upper-right corner of the dialog box to find the desired picture. Then, click the picture's icon so that its name appears in the File Name box.

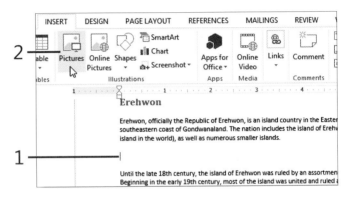

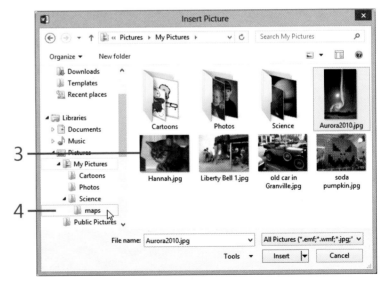

5 Click the down-arrow on the Insert button and do one of the following:

- Click Insert to store a copy of the picture file in your Word document.

- Click Link To File to insert only a link that connects the Word document to the picture file. This keeps your document file as small as possible. If you edit the picture file, you can then update the Word document to show the revised picture. However, if you share the document with others, they'll see an error message indicating a broken link instead of the picture.

- Click Insert And Link to store a copy of the picture file in your Word document and link it to the original picture file. This method lets you update modified pictures like the Link To File method, but you can share the file with others without breaking any links to the original.

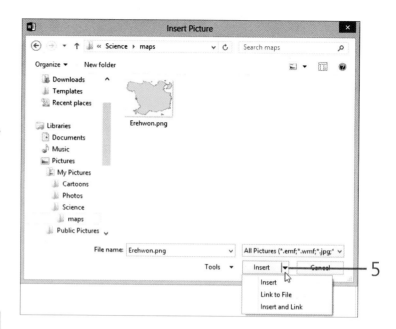

TIP Word 2013 can insert files saved in the following formats: .emf, .emz, .wmf, .wmz, .jpg, .jpeg, .jfif, .jpe, .png, .bmp, .dib, .rle, .gif, .pcz, .tif, .tiff, .wpg, .cgm, .eps, .pct, .pict, and .cdr. To filter the display of files in the Insert Picture dialog box to a specific format (and make it easier to find the file you want), click the drop-down list to the right of the File Name box and select that format.

TRY THIS If your document contains pictures that were inserted by using the Link To File option or the Insert And Link option, you can edit those links. To do this, first click the File tab to display the Backstage view and then click the Info tab. On the right side of the Info page, in the Related Documents section, click Edit Links To Files. (Your document must be saved at least once to make this link appear.) In the Links dialog box, you can change the source file of a linked picture or break the link and store a copy of the file in the document.

Inserting an online picture

Sometimes, you want to illustrate an idea or to decorate your document, but you don't have a suitable picture on your computer. You can probably find just what you need by searching either the collection of photographs and clip art on Office.

com or the millions of images that exist on the Internet. Both of these options are available through the Online Pictures tool in Word 2013. The same dialog box includes a link to browse your SkyDrive storage and your Flickr account, if you have one.

Find a picture or clip art

1 Click at the location in the document where you want the picture to appear.

2 On the Insert tab, in the Illustrations group, click Online Pictures.

3 In the Insert Pictures dialog box, click the Search Office.com box or the Search Bing box to look for clip art or images from those web resources, respectively.

4 Type or paste a word or phrase to describe the subject of your search. Press the Enter key or click the magnifying-glass icon in the search box.

5 Click the thumbnail of an image you like and then click the Insert button to copy the selected file into your document.

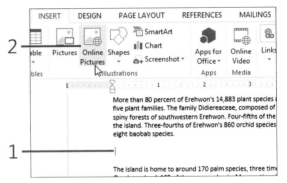

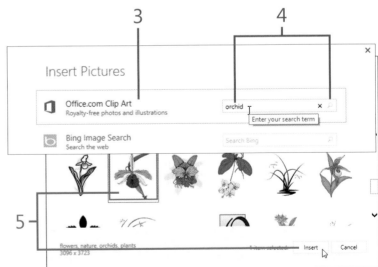

> **TIP** If you're working with a keyboard and mouse and you want to select more than one image simultaneously, hold the Ctrl key while you click additional images. If you're using a touchscreen device, tap the first image and then tap and hold that image while you tap additional images.

Get a picture from SkyDrive or Flickr

1 Click at the location in the document where you want the picture to
   appear.

2 On the Insert tab, in the Illustrations group, click Online Pictures.

3 In the Insert Pictures dialog box, in the section for your SkyDrive
   storage, click the Browse link or click the See More link for Flickr.

4 Click the thumbnail of an image and then click the Insert button to
   copy the selected file into your document.

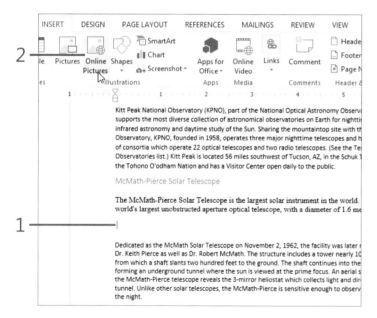

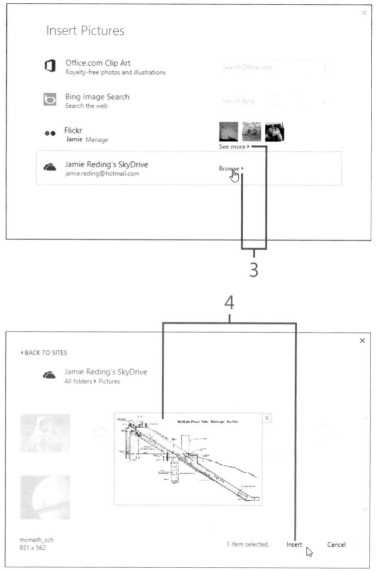

Inserting online video

If you produce educational or training documents, sales presentations, or other material that would benefit from including video clips, Word 2013 can help you to quickly find and insert video into your text.

Find a video clip

1 Click at the location in the document where you want the video to appear.

2 On the Insert tab, in the Media group, click Online Video.

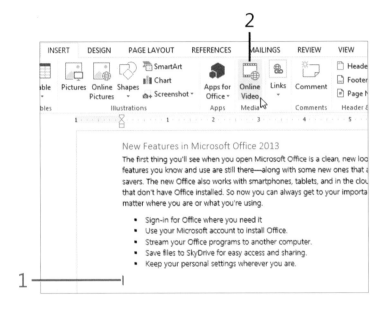

3 In the Insert Video dialog box, click the Search Bing text box or the Search YouTube text box and enter a word or phrase that describes the video for which you're searching on the web or specifically from YouTube.com, respectively.

Alternatively, you can insert a video from another website if it makes available an embed code (an HTML expression that gives the video's address and other information). To do that, copy the embed code from the webpage and paste it into the embed text box.

4 If you entered text in the Search Bing text box or the Search You-Tube text box, press the Enter key or click the magnifying-glass icon in the search box.

If you entered an embed code, click the right-arrow button in the embed code box to insert the video into your document.

5 In the results of a Bing search or a YouTube search, click the thumb-nail of a video and then click the Insert button to insert the selected video into your document.

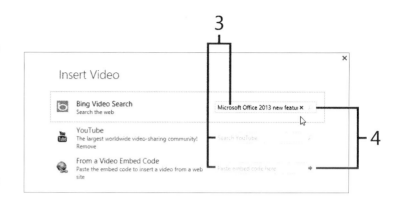

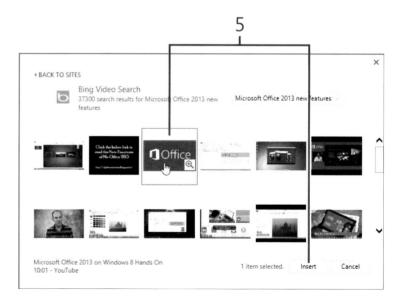

Inserting a screenshot

Perhaps you write instructions for how to use apps—maybe even for a book like this one—or you might want to capture a series of webpages or a video game's high score. In Word 2013 you can use the screenshot tool to take a picture of the entire window that is currently displayed on your computer screen or just a small part of it.

Copy an entire window

1 Open both Word 2013 and the app window that you want to capture.

2 Click at the location in the Word document where you want the screenshot to appear.

3 On the Insert tab, in the Illustrations group, click Screenshot and click the thumbnail of the window to capture.

4 A screenshot of the selected window appears in the Word document at the insertion point. You can use the sizing and rotation handles to change the appearance of the screenshot, or change its text wrapping or formatting, as you can for any inserted picture.

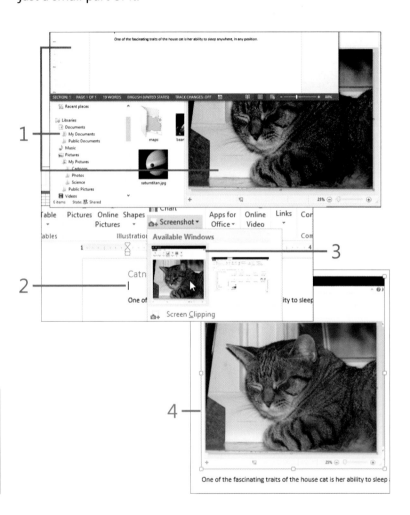

> **TIP** You can't use the Screenshot tool to capture the Word window into which the screenshot will be inserted. If you need a screenshot of the Word window, open another copy of the document and take a screenshot of it. Alternatively, if you have a keyboard, press Alt+Print Screen to place a screenshot of the current window on the clipboard and then paste it into your document.

Select part of the screen

1 Open both Word 2013 and the app window that you want to capture. Then, click in the Word document at the location where you want the screenshot to appear.

2 On the Insert tab, in the Illustrations group, click Screenshot. At the bottom of the gallery that opens, click Screen Clipping.

The Word window automatically minimizes, the entire screen dims, and the cursor changes to a cross-hair.

3 Drag the cross-hair cursor to establish a rectangle around the part of the screen that you want to capture. When the rectangle is correctly positioned and at the size you want, release the mouse button. The captured rectangle appears in the Word document at the insertion point.

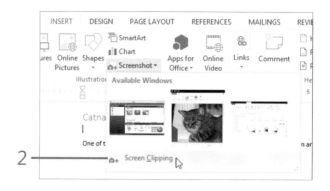

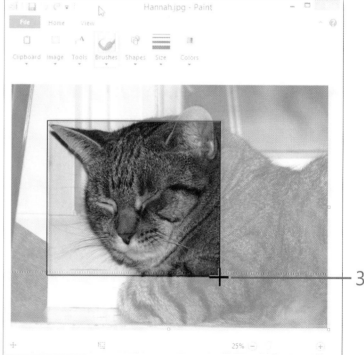

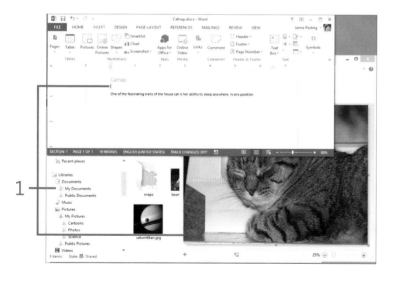

Positioning pictures on the page

When you insert a picture or any other graphic object into a Word 2013 document, you can choose how it affects the text around it. There are seven basic possibilities, which collectively are called *layout options*.

In many cases, you want the picture to behave as if it's a single large character, either within a line of text or in a paragraph by itself. The position of the picture on the page is determined by how much text occurs in the document before the picture's location. If you insert or delete text, the picture might move. This option is called *in line with text*.

The other six layout options involve making the text *wrap* (or flow) around or through the picture—that is, you can drag the picture to any position on the page, and the text adjusts accordingly. These layout options differ in how the text goes around or through the picture.

A new feature in Word 2013 called *alignment guides* helps you to position floating graphics so that their edges align with the margins, with the horizontal or vertical center of the page, or with paragraphs of text.

Choose the layout option

1 In a Word document that contains a picture, click a picture to select it.

2 At the upper-right corner of the picture, click the Layout Options icon.

3 In the Layout Options gallery, click the icon corresponding to the layout option that you want.

4 If you selected one of the icons in the With Text Wrapping section of the gallery, click either the Move With Text option or the Fix Position On Page option.

> **TIP** When you select a picture, the Picture Tools | Format contextual tab appears on the ribbon. In the Arrange group, click the Wrap Text button, which includes the items in the Layout Options gallery plus the Set As Default Layout item. When you click Set As Default Layout, pictures that you insert later will initially have the same layout option as you specified for the current picture.

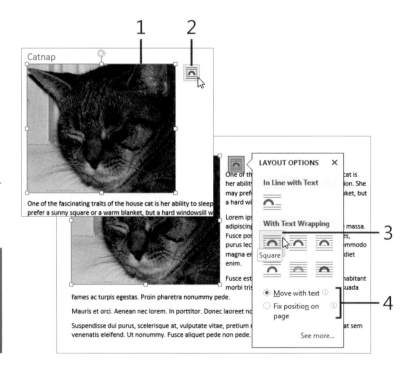

✓ **TIP** When you select a layout option with text wrapping, the picture has an *anchor*. This is the place in the text to which the picture is attached. The picture's position on the page can be specified with respect to the page margins or with respect to the anchor location. If editing the text causes the anchor to move to a different page, the picture will also move to that page. You can set an option so that an anchor icon appears in the margin at the anchor location when the picture is selected (see "Controlling what is displayed and printed" on page 429).

Align pictures and text

1 Click a picture to select it. If it's currently placed in line with text, set its layout option to one of the text wrapping types.

2 Drag the picture to a new position.

Observe the green alignment guides that appear as the edges of the picture touch any of the four page margins, or as the center of the picture aligns with the horizontal or vertical center of the page, or as the top edge of the picture aligns with the top line of a text paragraph.

🔍 **SEE ALSO** For more information about the default layout option for inserting or pasting pictures, see "Change options related to pictures" on page 437.

✓ **TIP** If a picture's layout option is set to Behind Text, it might be difficult to select the picture instead of the text. On the Home tab, in the Editing group, click Select and then click Select Object to activate a cursor that ignores the text. Alternatively, click the Selection Pane command on the same drop-down list. In the Selection pane, you can select individual graphic items, including those that overlap one another.

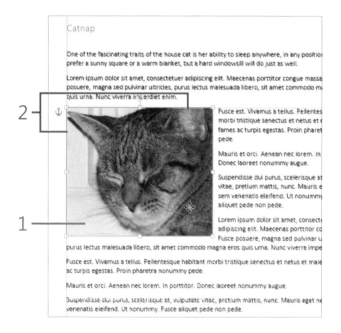

Resizing a picture

When you insert a picture in a document, initially it might be too large or too small for what you need. In Word 2013, you can adjust the picture's size visually to fit properly within the text, or you can specify a measurement.

When you select a picture in your document, eight small white squares called *sizing handles* appear at each of the picture's corners and at the center of each side. You can drag any of the sizing handles toward the center of the picture to make the picture smaller, or away from the center to enlarge it. The sizing handles at the corners adjust both the height and the width of the picture to keep them in the same proportion (called the *aspect ratio*), but the sizing handles at the centers of the sides affect only the height or the width.

Drag the sizing handles

1 Click a picture in the document to select it.

2 Drag any of the picture's sizing handles and observe the effect on the size or aspect ratio of the picture.

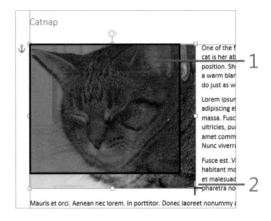

TRY THIS You will see a circular arrow icon attached to one of the sizing handles. This is the *rotation handle*. Drag it clockwise or counterclockwise about the center of the illustration to rotate the picture.

Set the size numerically on the ribbon

1 Click a picture in the document to select it.

2 On the Picture Tools | Format contextual tab, in the Size group, type the desired measurements in the Shape Height box or the Shape Width box.

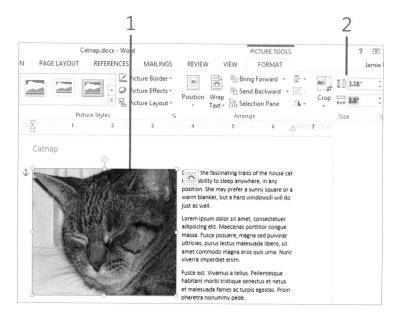

Cropping a picture

After you insert a picture in your document, you might decide that you want to show only part of the picture. You can use the Crop tool in Word 2013 to remove the unwanted parts.

In another situation, you might want to use a particular shape to crop a picture, rather than a simple rectangle. You might want to use a cloud or an arrow. Using the Crop tool, you can choose any of the items from the Insert Shapes gallery as the outline of the picture.

Remove unwanted parts of a picture

1 Click a picture in the document to select it.

2 On the Picture Tools | Format contextual tab, in the Size group, click the top part of the Crop button.

3 Drag any of the corner or side cropping markers toward the center of the picture.

The parts that will be removed are shaded.

4 Click in the document outside the picture to exit the Crop tool. If necessary, drag the picture to reposition it with respect to the text.

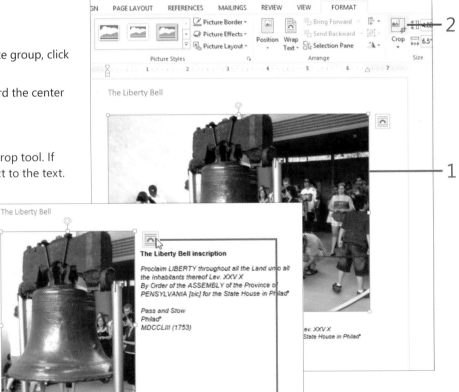

Crop to a shape

1 Click a picture in the document to select it.

2 On the Picture Tools | Format contextual tab, in the Size group, click the down-arrow on the bottom part of the Crop button. In the drop-down list that appears, click Crop To Shape.

3 In the Crop To Shape gallery, click the desired item.

4 If necessary, drag the picture to reposition it with respect to the text.

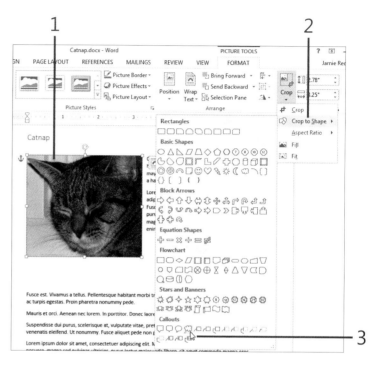

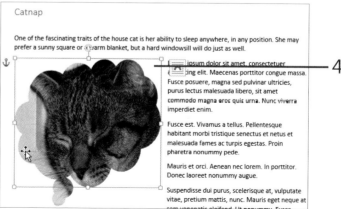

> ✓ **TIP** The shape you select automatically adopts the full height and width of the picture that you crop. You can't move the shape with respect to the contents of the picture. To get the best result, first crop the picture to make a rectangle or square that has approximately the same proportions as the shape you plan to use for cropping.

Replacing a picture

If you find a better illustration for your document than a picture you've already inserted, you can easily insert that new graphic. The new illustration will assume the same size and alignment specifications as the one that's already in place. Alternatively, you can search the clip art at Office.com or search the Internet for a replacement picture.

Choose a different picture

1 Click a picture in the document to select it.

2 On the Picture Tools | Format contextual tab, in the Adjust group, click Change Picture.

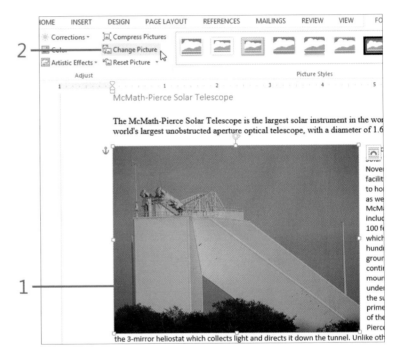

3 In the Insert Pictures dialog box, use one of the commands to select the new picture from your computer, from your SkyDrive account, from Office.com, or from the Internet.

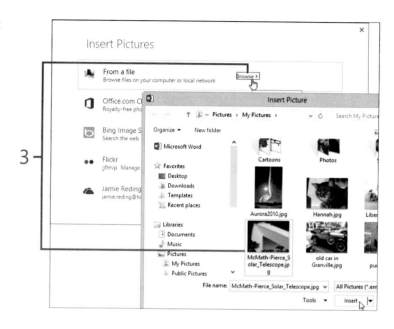

SEE ALSO For more information about searching and selecting in the Insert Pictures dialog box, see "Inserting a picture from your computer" on page 274 and "Inserting an online picture" on page 276.

Changing the appearance of a picture

Word 2013 offers tools for changing the general color appearance of a picture. You can use those tools to correct a picture so that it looks more natural, or you can completely alter the colors to create a special effect. For example, you can start with a full-color photograph and change it into a sepia-tone picture that appears to be 100 years old.

Correct the color balance

1 Click a picture in the document to select it.

2 On the Picture Tools | Format contextual tab, in the Adjust group, click the Corrections button.

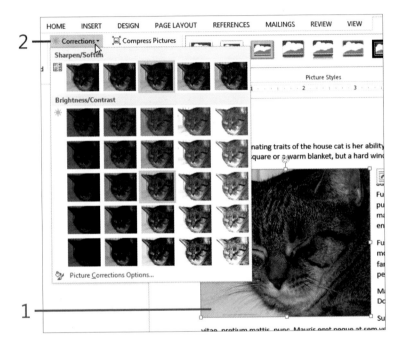

3 In the gallery that opens, point to the thumbnails in the Sharpen/Soften section or in the Brightness/Contrast section. Observe the live preview of the picture in the document. When you see the appearance that you want, click the thumbnail to apply that setting.

4 On the Picture Tools | Format contextual tab, in the Adjust group, click the Color button.

5 In the gallery that opens, point to the thumbnails in the Color Saturation section or in the Color Tone section. Observe the live preview of the picture in the document. When you see the appearance that you want, click the thumbnail to apply that setting.

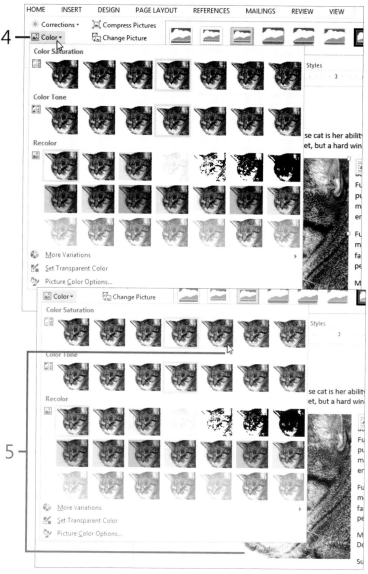

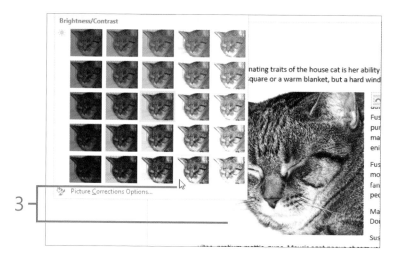

Recolor the picture

1 Click a picture in the document to select it.

2 On the Picture Tools | Format contextual tab, in the Adjust group, click the Color button.

3 In the gallery that opens, point to the thumbnails in the Recolor section. Observe the live preview of the picture in the document. When you see the appearance that you want, click the thumbnail to apply that setting.

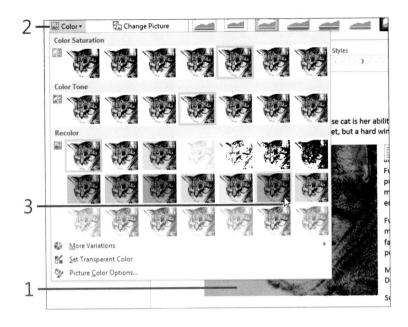

Removing the background from a picture

Sometimes you can make a picture more interesting by removing a drab or confusing background, leaving only the subject. Depending on the effect that you want to achieve, you can then apply other effects such as a shadow or a three-dimensional thickness to the image.

Remove the background

1 Click a picture in the document to select it.

2 On the Picture Tools | Format contextual tab, in the Adjust group, click the Remove Background button.

3 Drag the handles on the tool's lines so that the rectangle encloses the part of the picture that you want to keep and excludes most of the areas that you want to remove.

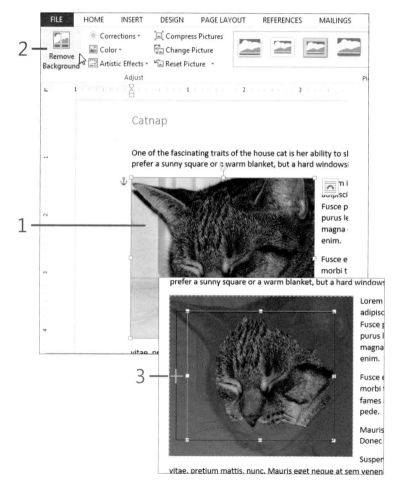

4 On the Background Removal contextual tab, in the Refine group, do one or both of the following:

- If some parts of the subject were incorrectly removed, click Mark Areas To Keep and then click one or more areas that you want to remain in the picture.

- If some parts of the background were incorrectly kept, click Mark Areas To Remove and then click one or more areas that you want to remove.

If you mark an area and then change your mind, click Delete Mark and then click that area.

5 When you have included the entire subject and excluded all of the background, on the Background Removal contextual tab, in the Close group, click Keep Changes.

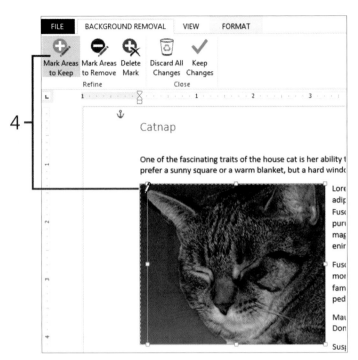

TIP Background removal works best with pictures or clip art in which the background is a single color that doesn't appear anywhere else in the picture. Sometimes you'll click an area to keep, and that will cause some other area to be removed, or other problems might occur. If you find that you have trouble getting the effect you want, in the Close group, you can click Discard All Changes and start again.

TRY THIS After you remove a picture's background, click the Layout Options button next to the picture and select the Tight text wrapping. Then, drag the picture into the middle of some paragraphs of text and observe how the text repositions as the picture moves.

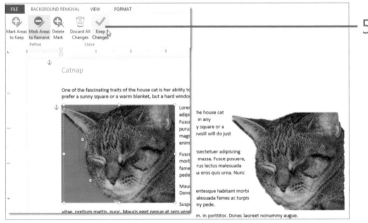

Applying special effects

Word 2013 includes a selection of artistic effects ranging from simple blurring to simulations of pencil or paint strokes as well as textures such as cement or plastic. You can apply these effects, together with other alterations such as color changes, shadows, or reflections, to create attention-grabbing illustrations.

Choose an artistic effect

1 Click a picture in the document to select it.

2 On the Picture Tools | Format contextual tab, in the Adjust group, click Artistic Effects.

3 In the gallery that opens, point to the thumbnails. Observe the live preview of the picture in the document. When you see the appearance that you want, click the thumbnail to apply that setting.

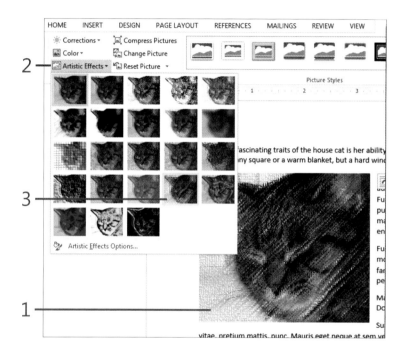

Setting a transparent color

If you insert a picture that contains large areas of a single color such as opaque white, you can use the Set Transparent Color tool to make that color transparent. Any text or another graphic that is behind the picture will show through the transparent areas.

Select a color to make it transparent

1 Click a picture in the document to select it.

2 On the Picture Tools | Format contextual tab, in the Adjust group, click Color. Near the bottom of the gallery that opens, click Set Transparent Color.

3 Click the background of the picture.

> **TIP** Only one color in the picture can be transparent at any one time. If you use the Set Transparent Color tool to select another color, the transparency of the first color will be canceled.

> **TRY THIS** After you make a color transparent, click the Layout Options button next to the picture and select the Through text wrapping. Then, click and drag the picture into the middle of some paragraphs of text, and observe how the text repositions as the picture moves. The Tight text wrapping configures the text to appear close to the outside of the picture's subject, but Through text wrapping makes it possible for text to occupy transparent areas in the middle of the picture, as well.

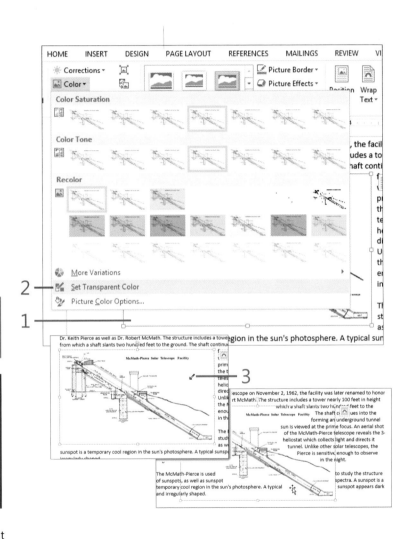

Adding your own artwork

11

In this section:

- Inserting a shape
- Changing the appearance of a shape
- Building charts to display data
- Creating SmartArt diagrams
- Adding WordArt effects

For many of your documents, the pictures you already have and those that you can find on the Internet are all you need to illustrate your text. Some documents, though, need unique drawings. They might involve data specific to your company or some research that you have done, or maybe you just want to show your artistic talent.

Microsoft Word 2013 provides you with a wide range of tools for creating new artwork. The Shapes gallery includes basic lines and geometric shapes as well as arrows, flowchart symbols, and callout balloons. You can use the Chart tool to present numeric data and time series in many variations. With the SmartArt feature, you can create organization charts, process diagrams, and various kinds of lists. The WordArt feature helps you to turn text into artwork by adding fills, shadows, three-dimensional effects, and other formatting.

Whenever you select a graphic object (a shape, a chart, a SmartArt graphic, or WordArt) in your document, the ribbon displays a contextual tab that presents specific tools for working with that type of object. Each type of object is also accompanied by one or more buttons on its right side, which you can click to open panes containing formatting controls.

Inserting a shape

You can use the Shapes button gallery to draw almost anything you can think of, from simple lines and arrows to clouds, scrolls, and complicated geometric shapes. Most of the shapes can contain text, and you can add shading or a picture to a shape's interior.

In Word 2013, a text box is a special kind of shape object. The Draw Text Box command appears on the Insert tab, both at the bottom of the Text Box button gallery and in the Basic Shapes section of the Shapes button gallery. Unlike other shape objects, a text box can be linked to another text box so that text will flow from one text box to the other.

Draw a shape

1 Click in your document at the location where you want to insert a shape.

2 On the Insert tab, in the Illustrations group, click Shapes.

3 Click the object in the Shapes button gallery that appears closest to the object you intend to draw. Each kind of shape can be stretched or squeezed both horizontally and vertically after you insert it. For example, the oval tool can make a circle, and the rectangle tool can make a square.

Conveniently, if you have used any of the tools before, they might appear in the Recently Used Shapes section of the gallery.

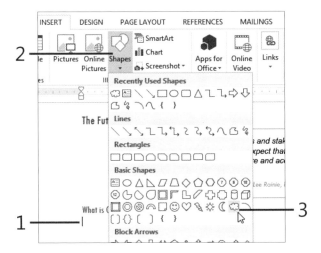

SEE ALSO For more information about text boxes, see "Inserting text boxes" on page 196.

4 Drag the special cursor to draw the shape.

If the shape is a single line or arrow, drag the cursor from the starting point to the end. Otherwise, drag the cursor diagonally from one corner of the shape to the opposite corner. The shape expands until you release the mouse button (or, on a touch-enabled device, until you lift your finger).

If you want a line or arrow to be restricted to multiples of 45 degrees, hold the Shift key while you drag the cursor. For other shapes, hold the Shift key while you drag the cursor to keep the shape's height and width equal, as for a circle or a square.

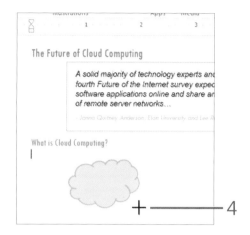

TRY THIS To draw a smooth curve by using the Curve tool, click and release at the start of the curve, click at the middle of the curve, and then double-click at the end of the curve. To draw a shape that includes both straight lines and curves by using the Freeform tool, click at the start and end of each straight edge or drag the cursor to draw a curved edge. Using the Scribble tool, drag the cursor as if you're drawing with a pencil.

Changing the appearance of a shape

The formatting of a shape includes its fill (the interior color or picture), its outline (the color and thickness of the line around the interior), and any effects applied to it (such as a shadow or reflection). When you insert a shape into your document, initially it has a default format. If you prefer a different appearance, you'll have to apply the formatting that you want.

You might place text inside a shape, or group two or more shapes into a single object. You can even add, delete, or move a shape's corners, or change a straight edge into a smooth curve.

Change a shape's outline and fill

1 Click a shape in your document to select it.

2 On the Drawing Tools | Format contextual tab, in the Shape Styles group, click the thumbnail in the Shape Styles gallery that is closest to the appearance that you want.

3 On the Drawing Tools | Format contextual tab, in the Shape Styles group, click the Shape Fill button. In the gallery that opens below it, click a theme color or a standard color, or click No Fill to render the interior of the shape transparent.

If you prefer, you can choose to fill the shape with a picture, a gradient, or a built-in texture.

4 On the Drawing Tools | Format contextual tab, in the Shape Styles group, click Shape Outline. In the gallery that opens, click a theme color or a standard color, or click No Outline. If you want to change the thickness of the outline or make it a dashed line, click Weight or Dashes and click an entry in the list.

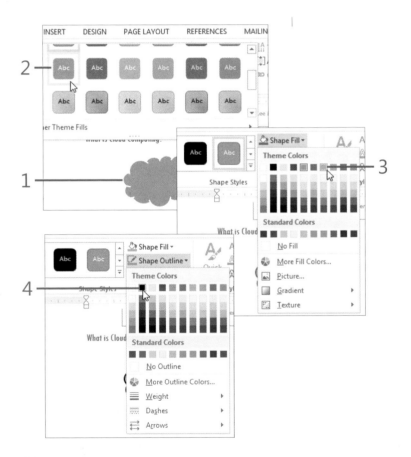

5 If you want to add effects such as a shadow, a reflection, glowing or softened edges, or three-dimensional (3-D) appearance, on the Drawing Tools | Format contextual tab, in the Shape Styles group, click Shape Effects. Click the name of an effect and then click a thumbnail in the list.

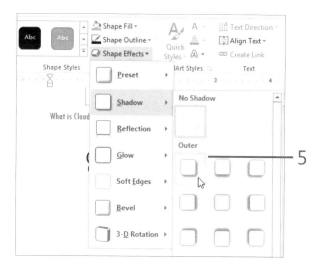

Add text to a shape

1 Click a shape in your document to select it.

2 Right-click the shape. On the shortcut menu that appears, click Add Text.

3 Type the text at the insertion point inside the shape.

4 If you want to rotate the text or change its alignment, on the Drawing Tools | Format contextual tab, in the Text group, click Text Direction or Align Text and then click an item in the list.

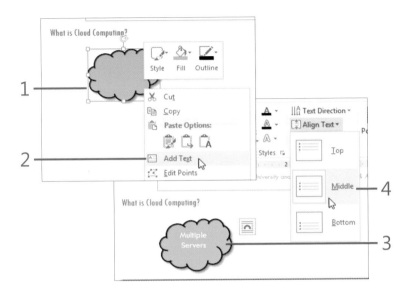

Group multiple shapes

1 Select two or more shapes (which must be on the same page of the document) that you want to combine into a single object.

If you're selecting just a few shapes, press and hold the Ctrl key while you click each of the shapes in turn. If you need to select many shapes, or shapes that overlap each other, on the Home tab, in the Editing group, click Select and then click Select Objects. Then, drag a rectangle on the page to surround all the shapes that you want to select.

2 On the Drawing Tools | Format contextual tab, in the Arrange group, click Group and then click the Group command.

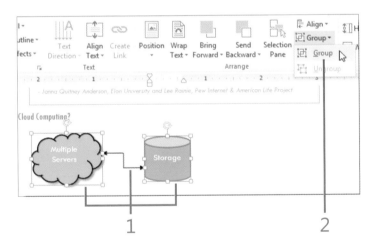

Edit points in a shape

1   Click a shape in your document to select it.

2   On the Drawing Tools | Format contextual tab, in the Insert Shapes group, click Edit Shape and then click Edit Points.

3   You can drag any of the black squares (*points*) on the shape's outline to change the shape. You can drag the white squares (*handles*) attached to the point to change the curvature of the outline.

You can click at any place on the outline to add a new point. You can right-click a point and then click an option on the shortcut menu that opens, which include deleting the point, opening the path at that point, or changing the path at that point to a smooth curve, a straight line, or a corner.

When you have made the needed changes, click outside the shape or press the Esc key to exit the shape editing mode.

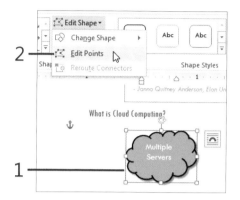

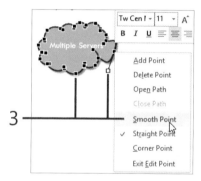

Building charts to display data

One of the best ways to help your readers understand numerical or time-related data is to include a chart or graph. Data visualization can make it clear where there are peaks and valleys much more easily than will combing through a table of numbers.

Word 2013 includes a chart feature, based on the capabilities of Microsoft Excel 2013, with which you can create impressive visualizations. The chart that's visible in your document is associated with a data sheet, which remains hidden unless you choose to edit the data. You can type numbers into the chart's

data sheet, or you can copy data from a Word table or from an Excel worksheet and then paste the table into the chart's data sheet. If you're working with a large amount of data, you can create the chart in Excel, copy that chart, and then paste it into your Word document.

The same chart feature is also included in Microsoft PowerPoint 2013. You can copy a chart from Word and paste it onto a slide in PowerPoint, or vice versa. The data associated with the chart and all of the chart's formatting are copied between the programs, and the chart remains fully editable.

Insert a chart

1 Click in your document at the location where you want to insert a chart.

2 On the Insert tab, in the Illustrations group, click Chart.

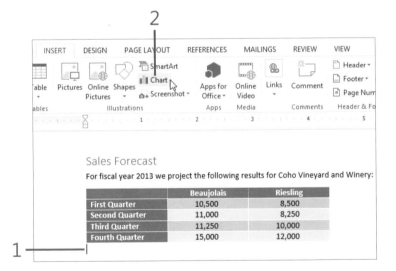

3 In the list on the left side of the Insert Chart dialog box, click the kind of chart that you want to create. Then, in the panel across the top of the dialog box, click the thumbnail that shows the variation you want.

4 In the chart's data sheet, type the numeric data and any column and row headings that you want to include in the chart.

If you already have the data in a Word table or in an Excel worksheet, select the table or the portion of the worksheet and copy the data to the clipboard. Then, click in the upper-left cell (A1) of the data sheet of the chart in your Word document, and press Ctrl+V to paste the contents of the clipboard into the data sheet.

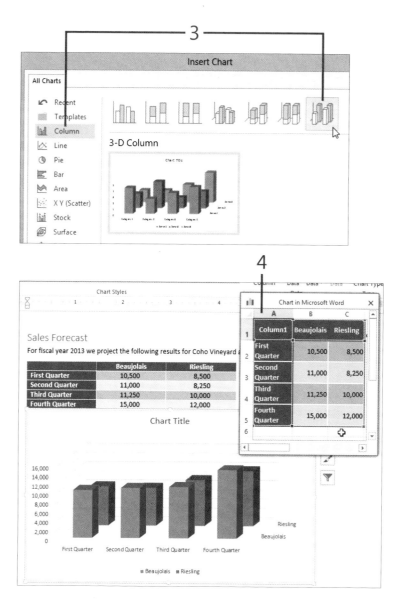

TRY THIS Click the Chart Tools | Design contextual tab. In the Data group, click the down-arrow on the Edit Data button. Then, either click Edit Data to open the chart's data sheet in Word or click Edit Data in Excel 2013 to open a worksheet containing the chart's data. Modify the data as needed and then close the data sheet or worksheet to see the revised chart.

Change a chart's appearance

1 Click a chart in your Word document.

2 If you want to change the chart's text wrapping, click the Layout Options button to the right of the chart. Then, in the Layout Options gallery that opens, click the desired option.

3 If you want to add or remove items in the chart, such as the title, the legend, or the gridlines, click the Chart Element button. Then, in the Chart Elements pane that opens, select or clear the check boxes as needed.

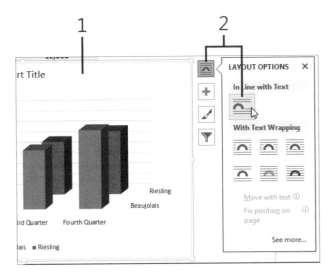

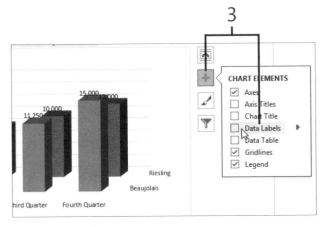

4 If you want to apply an interesting chart style or change the colors of the chart's elements, click the Chart Styles button. Then, in the Styles And Colors gallery that opens, click the desired style.

5 If you want to prevent some of the data from appearing in the chart without removing it from the data sheet, click the Chart Filters button and then select or clear any of the check boxes next to the data items. Then, click the Apply button at the bottom of the pane.

6 If you want to change the formatting of a specific part of the chart, first click that part. On the Chart Tools | Format contextual tab, in the Current Selection group, click Format Selection. In the Format pane that opens, change the formatting items as needed.

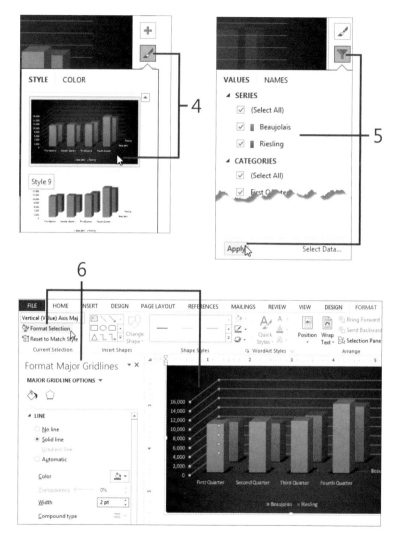

TIP The formatting tools provided by the buttons at the side of the chart are also available on the Chart Tools tabs. Because the buttons are close to the chart, they're more convenient than the ribbon tabs.

Creating SmartArt diagrams

If you're creating an organization chart, documenting a process, or describing the relationships of ideas, the SmartArt feature in Word 2013 can help you to produce a diagram that is both informative and attractive.

The Choose A SmartArt Graphic dialog box offers a broad assortment of shapes and arrangements, and the preview pane includes suggestions of uses for each selection. After you insert the starting diagram in the document, you can add more shapes, rearrange them, and enter text and pictures to complete the picture.

The fonts, colors, and effects used in SmartArt diagrams come from the theme applied to your document. By selecting another theme, you can instantly change the look of all the SmartArt along with the text and headings of the document.

Insert a diagram

1　Click in your document at the location where you want to insert a chart.

2　On the Insert tab, in the Illustrations group, click SmartArt.

3　In the panel on the left side of the Choose A SmartArt Graphic dialog box, you can click one of the entries to show only a small group of layouts in the center panel. If you prefer to display the entire list of layouts in the center panel, at the top of the left panel, you can click All .

4　In the panel in the center of the Choose A SmartArt Graphic dialog box, click one of the layouts to display its preview in the right panel.

Each layout's preview includes a description of the kinds of information for which that layout is best suited. Some layouts consist of just shapes and text, and other layouts can also include pictures.

5　When you have selected the layout that you want, click OK.

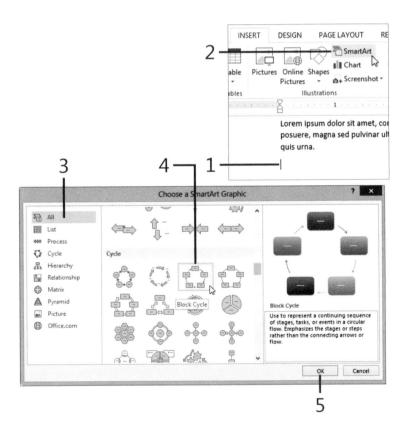

Format a diagram

1 Click a SmartArt diagram in your document to select it.

2 On the SmartArt Tools | Design contextual tab, in the SmartArt Styles group, click the thumbnail in the SmartArt Styles gallery that is closest to the appearance you want.

3 If you want to change which theme colors are used in the SmartArt diagram, on the SmartArt Tools | Design contextual tab, in the SmartArt Styles group, click Change Colors. Click the thumbnail in the gallery that displays the theme colors you want.

> **→ TRY THIS** To change the formatting of one shape in the SmartArt diagram, click that shape. On the SmartArt Tools | Format contextual tab, in the Shape Styles group, use the tools to choose a style, change the shape's fill and/or outline, or apply a shape effect. For more information about changing the formatting of a shape, see "Changing the appearance of a shape" on page 300.

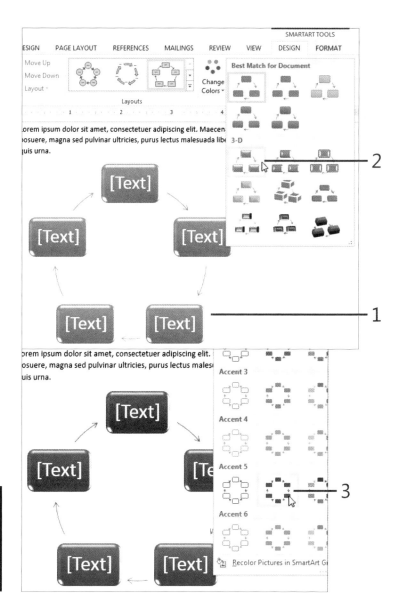

Change a diagram's type or data

1 Click a SmartArt diagram in your document to select it.

2 If you decide to change the layout of the SmartArt diagram, on the SmartArt Tools | Design contextual tab, in the Layouts group, point to the thumbnails in the Layouts gallery while you watch the live preview in the diagram. When you see the appearance that you want, click the thumbnail to apply the layout to the diagram.

3 On the Design tab under the SmartArt Tools contextual tab, in the Create Graphic group, click the Text Pane button.

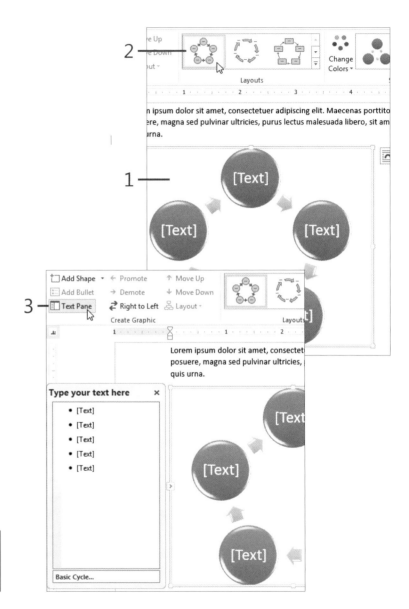

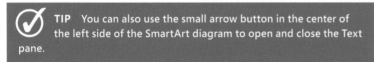

TIP You can also use the small arrow button in the center of the left side of the SmartArt diagram to open and close the Text pane.

4 Click each of the placeholders in turn and enter the text that you want to display in the SmartArt diagram.

If the text you type is too long to fit in the shape at the current size, the font size of the text is automatically reduced in all the shapes in the current SmartArt diagram, not just the one for which the text is too long.

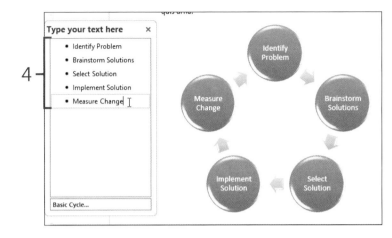

4 –

TRY THIS If you need to add more items to the diagram, on the SmartArt Tools | Design tab contextual tab, in the Create Graphic group, click Add Shape. If you need more second-level items within a shape, click in the shape and then, in the Create Graphic group, click Add Bullet.

Adding WordArt effects

In Word 2013, you can convert any text into eye-catching artwork. The Text Effects tool in the Font group on the Home tab offers options for adding effects such as outlines, shadows, reflections, and glows to plain text and headings. The WordArt feature includes all of these options and adds the ability to create three-dimensional rotation, edge beveling, and warped shapes.

Insert WordArt

1 Click in your document at the location where you want to insert a WordArt object.

2 On the Insert tab, in the Text group, click the WordArt button. In the WordArt gallery that opens, click the thumbnail that is closest to the appearance you want.

3 Replace the *Your Text Here* placeholder text with the text that you want to display.

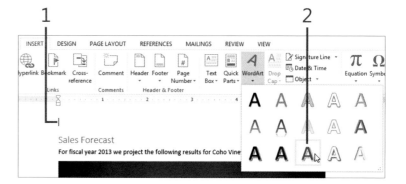

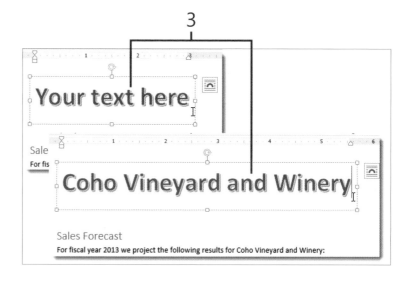

Format WordArt

1 Click a WordArt object in your document to select it.

2 If you want to change the font or the font size of the WordArt text, first select the text. Right-click the text and use the tools on the mini toolbar (or in the font group on the Home tab) to make the changes.

3 If you want to change the colors in the WordArt's letters, first select the text. On the Drawing Tools contextual tab, in the WordArt Styles group, click Text Fill or Text Outline and then, in the galleries that open, click the colors that you want.

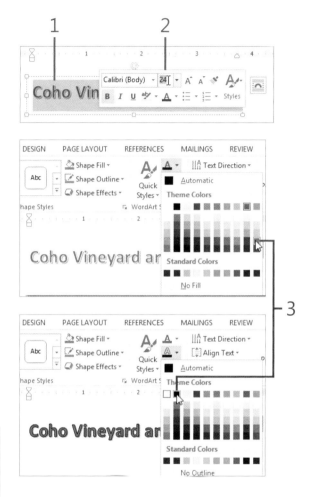

TIP Dragging the handles on the sides and corners of the box around the WordArt object doesn't change the font size, but it does affect the wrapping of text around the object. Resizing the box can also be useful for changing the number of lines that the WordArt occupies.

SEE ALSO For more information about formatting the fill and outline, see "Change a shape's outline and fill" on page 300.

4 If you want to add a three-dimensional effect, on the Drawing Tools | Format contextual tab, in the WordArt Styles group, click Text Effects and then click 3-D Rotation. In the gallery that opens, point to the thumbnails while you watch the live preview in the WordArt object. When you see the appearance that you want, click the thumbnail to apply the rotation to the object.

5 If you want to warp the WordArt text into a circle, an arch, or other shapes, on the Drawing Tools | Format contextual tab, in the WordArt Styles group, click Text Effects and then click Transform. In the gallery that opens, point to the thumbnails while you watch the live preview in the WordArt object. When you see the appearance that you want, click the thumbnail to apply the transformation to the object.

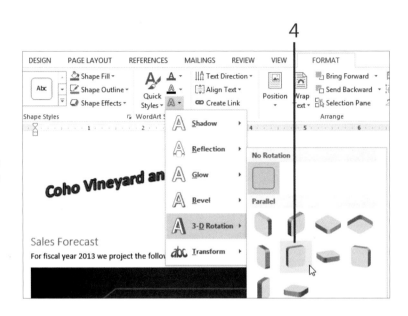

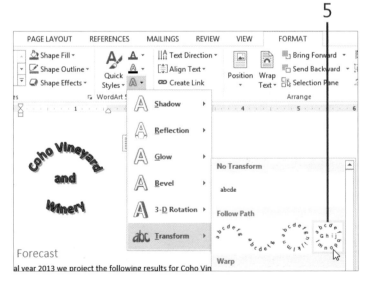

TRY THIS If the amount of rotation isn't quite what you want, or if you'd like to experiment with additional formatting, click 3-D Rotation Options at the bottom of the 3-D Rotation gallery to open the Format Picture pane. Use the controls in the 3-D Format and 3-D Rotation sections of the pane to adjust the formatting.

TIP To use a transformation that consists of two or three lines of text, first insert manual line breaks (Shift+Enter) in the text of the WordArt object to form the separate lines.

Mailing paper
or pixels

12

One of the most common uses of Microsoft Word 2013 is the creation of documents that are to be sent to other people. The documents might be printed on paper and mailed in an envelope, or they might be attached to an email message. They can be generated one at a time or built in large numbers from information in a worksheet or a database.

The mail merge feature in Word 2013 has many more uses than just mailing letters. Any task that involves a standard format that you want to populate with many pieces of information is a candidate for a merge. Think of name labels for a meeting, certificates for completing a course, a catalog of items for sale, or a voter registration list—any of these could be created with an appropriate mail merge.

In this section:

- Printing a single envelope
- Printing multiple copies of an envelope
- Changing envelope address formatting
- Creating mailing labels and business cards
- Sending a document by email
- Starting a mail merge
- Choosing the recipients
- Adding merge fields
- Adding information with rules
- Finishing the merge

Printing a single envelope

If you're addressing a letter, a greeting card, or other one-time item, you might want to print the envelope but not save it for future use. Word 2013 includes predefined layouts for many common envelope sizes, and you can define a custom size if necessary.

Address an envelope and print

1 If you're addressing a letter that contains the recipient's address, open the letter document. Otherwise, open any document (such as the default blank document).

If you create an envelope while the cursor is in a letter document, and if the document starts with up to four single-line paragraphs that are left-aligned, those paragraphs will automatically appear as the delivery address in the Envelope dialog box. If you want to determine which paragraphs will appear in the Envelope dialog box, select those paragraphs in the letter document before you launch the dialog box.

2 On the Mailings tab, in the Create group, click Envelopes.

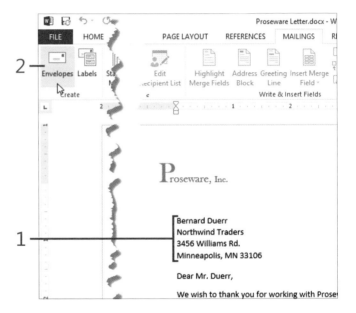

3 In the Envelopes And Labels dialog box, if the Delivery Address box is empty, or if the text is incomplete or incorrect, add or edit the text as needed.

4 If the Return Address box is empty, or if the text is incomplete or incorrect, add or edit the text as needed. If you don't want a return address to print on the envelope, select the Omit check box.

5 If the envelope size shown in the Preview thumbnail is incorrect, or if the orientation shown in the Feed thumbnail is incorrect, see "Change envelope size and print options" on page 318.

6 Click the Print button.

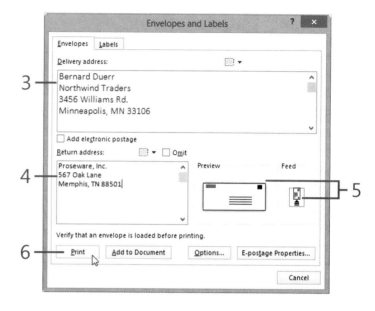

TRY THIS If you have an address book in Microsoft Outlook and it contains information for the envelope's recipient, you can click the Address Book icon above the Delivery Address box and select the recipient's name. The mailing address will be transferred from the address book entry to the Delivery Address box. You can also use the Address Book icon above the Return Address box to enter a return address from your address book.

TIP To use the electronic postage option, you must first install an electronic postage program and subscribe to a service.

Change envelope size and print options

1 On the Mailings tab, in the Create group, click Envelopes.

2 If you want to change the size of the envelope or the feed orientation, click the Options button.

3 On the Envelope Options tab in the Envelope Options dialog box, click the Envelope Size box and click the desired size in the drop-down list.

If none of the listed sizes match the envelope that you want to print, click Custom Size at the bottom of the list and enter the correct measurements.

4 If you want to change the font formatting of the delivery address, in the Delivery Address section in the Envelope Options dialog box, click the Font button, select the formatting in the Envelope Address dialog box, and then click OK. If you want to change the distance of the delivery address from the left and top edges of the envelope, in the From Left and From Top boxes enter the desired measurements.

If you want to change the same settings for the return address, use the Font button and the From Left and From Top boxes in the Return Address section of the Envelope Options dialog box.

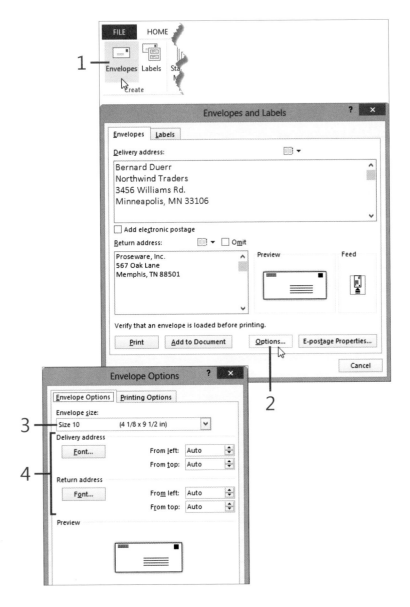

5 If you want to change the feed orientation, on the Printing Options tab, click the icon that matches the direction of your printer's envelope feed and the position of the envelope in the feed tray. If necessary, select whether the envelopes are placed in the feed tray with the printing side up or down, and which tray contains envelopes.

6 Click OK.

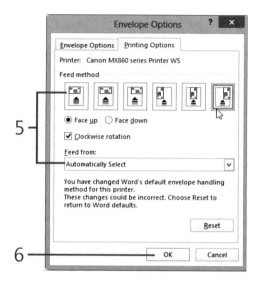

SEE ALSO   For more information about changing the formatting of the delivery address, see "Add direct formatting to one address" on page 323 and "Modify the Envelope Address style" on page 324.

Printing multiple copies of an envelope

You might need to print several copies of the same envelope at one time, for instance as self-addressed envelopes to include with items to be returned to you. The Print button in the Envelopes And Labels dialog box can print only one copy at a time, so you need a different approach.

In Word 2013, you can add the envelope to the current document and save it as part of the document's file. The envelope appears as page 0 in a new Section 1 at the beginning of the document, formatted with the page size and margins appropriate for the envelope. Then, you can use the Print command in the Backstage view, which offers a setting for the number of copies to print.

Add an envelope to a document

1 If you're addressing a letter that contains the recipient's address, open the letter document. Otherwise, open any document (such as the default blank document).

2 On the Mailings tab, in the Create group, click Envelopes.

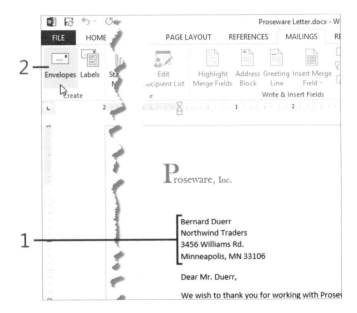

3 If the Delivery Address text box is empty, or if the text is incomplete or incorrect, edit the text as needed.

4 If the Return Address text box is empty, or if the text is incomplete or incorrect, edit the text as needed. If you don't want a return address to print on the envelope, select the Omit check box.

5 If the envelope size shown in the Preview thumbnail is incorrect, or if the orientation shown in the Feed thumbnail is incorrect, see "Change envelope size and print options" on page 318.

6 Click the Add To Document button.

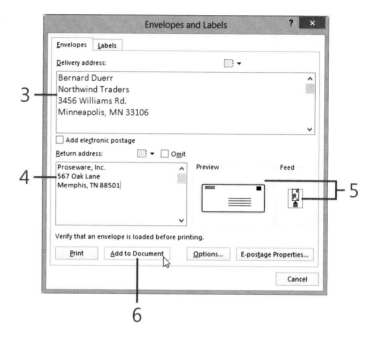

Print the envelope

1 Click in the envelope page in the document, and then click File to display the Backstage view.

2 Click the Print tab.

3 In the Settings section, click the first box and click Print Current Page.

4 If the selected printer is not the one on which you want to print the envelope, click the Printer box and select the correct printer.

5 Click the Copies box and enter the desired number of copies of the envelope.

6 Click the Print button.

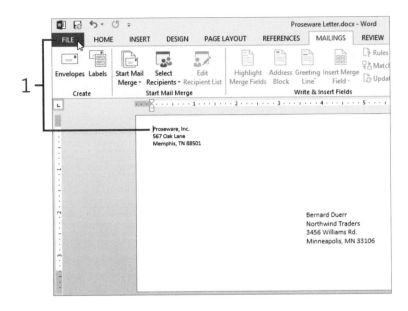

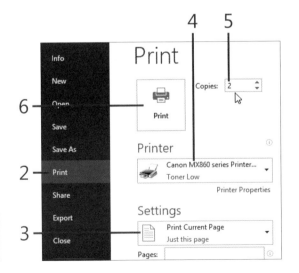

 TIP If you save the document that includes the envelope, you can print the envelope again at any time.

Changing envelope address formatting

If you want to change the formatting of the address on an envelope that you'll print only once, you can apply direct character formatting to it. If you want to change the formatting for all future envelopes, you'll save time and effort by modifying the address styles in the Normal.dotm template.

Add direct formatting to one address

1 Open the document for which you want to create an envelope.

2 On the Mailings tab, in the Create group, click Envelopes.

3 If the Delivery Address text box in the Envelopes And Labels dialog box is empty, or if the text is incomplete or incorrect, add or edit the text as needed.

4 Select the part of the address for which you want to change the formatting.

5 Right-click the selected text and then, on the shortcut menu that appears, click Font.

6 In the Font dialog box, change the font name, font size, bold, italic, color, or other formats as desired, and then click OK.

7 Click the Print button.

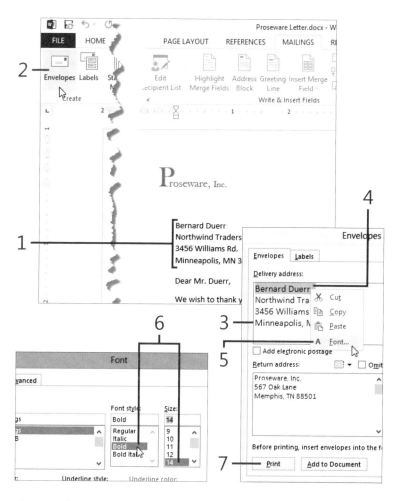

Modify the Envelope Address style

1 On the Home tab, in the Styles group, click the dialog box launcher (shortcut, Ctrl+Alt+Shift+S).

2 In the Styles pane, if the Envelope Address style and the Envelope Return styles are listed, continue with step 4. If the two styles are not listed, click the Options link at the bottom of the pane and continue with step 3.

3 In the Style Pane Options dialog box, click the Select Styles To Show list box, select All Styles, and then click OK.

4 In the Styles pane, right-click the name of the Envelope Address style and then, on the shortcut menu that appears, click Modify.

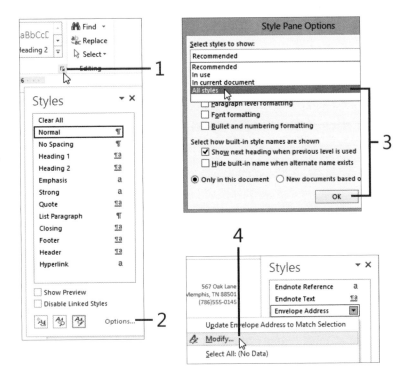

5 In the Modify Style dialog box, click the New Documents Based On This Template option. Then, select the font and paragraph formatting you want for the delivery address in all new envelopes. For more information about changing the definition of a style, see "Modify an existing style by using a dialog box" on page 95.

6 The definition of the Envelope Address style includes a borderless frame with a fixed size that positions the text on the envelope page. If the frame is too small to hold your typical addresses, at the bottom of the Modify Style dialog box, click the Format button and then, on the shortcut menu that appears, click Frame. In the Frame dialog box, change the Width and Height list boxes from Exactly to Auto.

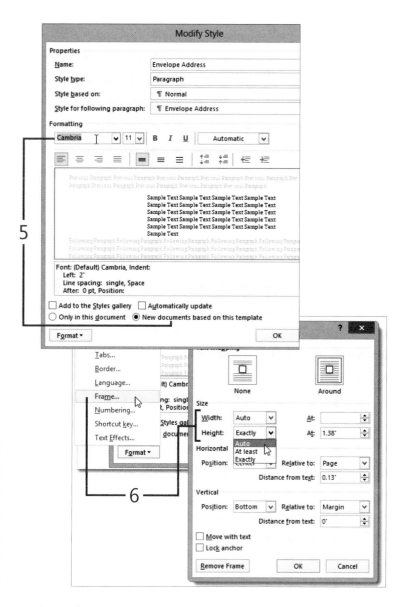

✓ **TIP** You can repeat steps 4 and 5 to modify the Envelope Return style to change the formatting of the return address in all new envelopes. The Envelope Return style does not include a frame.

🔍 **SEE ALSO** For more information about modifying the Envelope Address and Envelope Return styles, see *www.gmayor. com/changing_envelope_layout.htm* and *www.gmayor.com/alternative_return_addresses.htm*.

Creating mailing labels and business cards

Printed labels are useful for such things as mailing packages, creating personalized book plates, and labeling the wires plugged into the back of your computer. Stationers sell label paper in hundreds of sizes, colors, and shapes.

You can print business cards on perforated card paper, which is available from the same sources that sell label sheets. Word

2013 uses the same feature to create both labels and business cards—the only difference is your selection of the format to use.

If you don't want to create your own design, you can download label templates from Office.com and other online sources. For information about downloading templates, see "Get templates from Office.com" on page 159.

Print one label or a full page of labels

1 If you're creating a mailing label for a letter that contains the recipient's address, open the letter document. Otherwise, open any document (such as the default blank document).

2 On the Mailings tab, in the Create group, click Labels.

3 In the Envelopes And Labels dialog box, if the Address box is empty, or if the text is incomplete or incorrect, add or edit the text as needed.

4 If the product name and number shown in the Label section of the dialog box match the label paper in the printer, skip to step 9. Otherwise, at the bottom of the dialog box, click the Options button and continue at step 5.

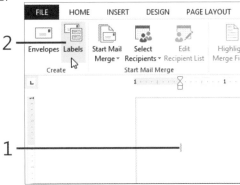

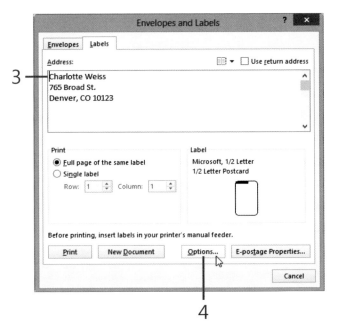

5 Click the option button that describes the type of printer attached to your computer. (Laser printers and most inkjet printers are page printers; dot-matrix printers are usually continuous-feed printers.) If the printer has more than one input tray, select the one that contains the label paper.

6 If the Label Vendors list box doesn't display the manufacturer of the label paper that you're using, click the box and select the correct vendor.

7 If the item selected in the Product Number list box doesn't match the label paper's description, select the correct item.

8 Click OK.

9 In the Print section of the Envelopes And Labels dialog box, click either the Full Page Of The Same Label option or the Single Label option, as needed.

If you select Single Label, you can specify the row and column in which to print the address. This is useful if you're printing on a sheet of label paper that is already partially used.

10 Click the Print button.

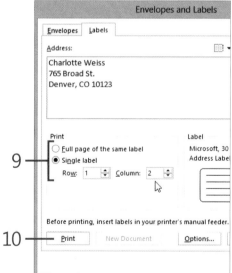

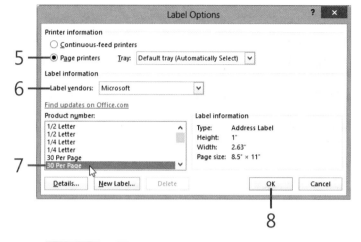

> ✓ **TIP** The entries in the Product Number list box are in alphabetical order, not numeric order. That is, all the entries that begin with the digit 1 precede the first entry that begins with the digit 2, regardless of how many digits are in each number.

Print a page of business cards

1 On the Mailings tab, in the Create group, click Labels.

2 In the Envelopes And Labels dialog box, if text appears in the Address box, delete it.

3 If the product name and number shown in the Label section of the dialog box match the card stock in the printer, skip to step 8. Otherwise, click the Options button and continue at step 4.

4 Click the option button that describes the type of printer attached to your computer. (Laser printers and most inkjet printers are page printers; dot-matrix printers are usually continuous-feed printers.) If the printer has more than one input tray, select the one that contains the card stock.

5 If the Label Vendors list box doesn't describe the manufacturer of the card stock that you're using, click the box and select the correct vendor.

6 If the item selected in the Product Number list box doesn't match the description of the card stock, select the correct item.

7 Click OK.

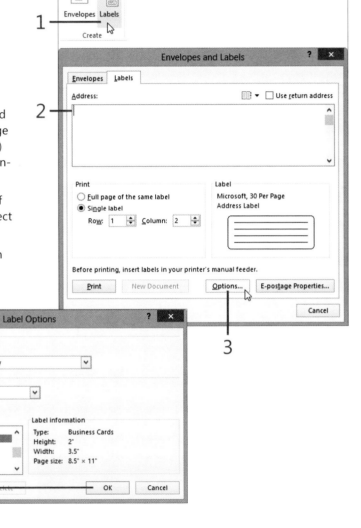

8 In the Envelopes And Labels dialog box, click the option button for Full Page Of The Same Label, and then click New Document.

9 The new document contains a table in which each cell's height and width match those of the cards in the selected card stock. The table's borders are set not to print. If you don't see the table cells, on the Table Tools | Layout contextual tab, in the Table group, click View Gridlines.

10 In the upper-left cell of the table, insert the text and graphics that you want on your business card.

11 Select the entire upper-left cell of the table and copy it to the clipboard (shortcut, Ctrl+C).

It's helpful to display nonprinting characters by clicking the Show/Hide ¶ button in the Paragraph group on the Home tab. This way, you can see and select everything in the cell, including the cell marker (¤).

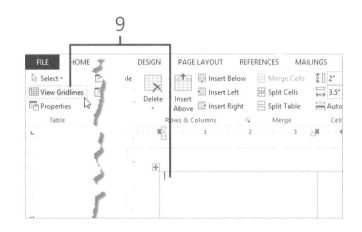

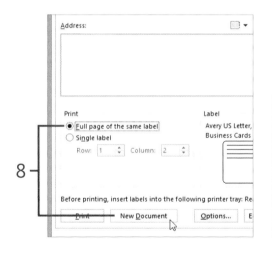

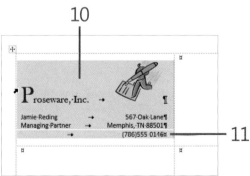

12 Click the table handle in the left margin to select the entire table. Then, paste the contents of the clipboard (shortcut, Ctrl+V).

13 Click the File tab to display the Backstage view. Click the Print tab and then click the Print button.

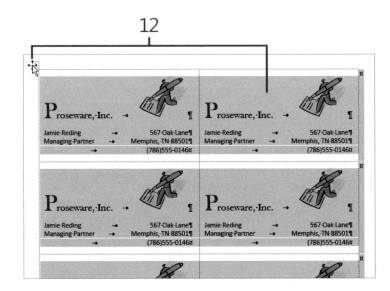

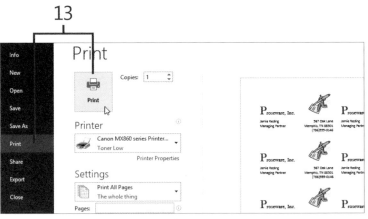

Print a page of different labels

1 In the procedure "Print one label or a full page of labels" on page 326, perform steps 1 through 8. In the Envelopes And Labels dialog box, click the option button for Full Page Of The Same Label and then click New Document. Continue with step 2 below.

2 In the table cell that corresponds to each label, type or paste the information for that label.

3 Click the File tab to display the Backstage view, click the Print tab, and then click the Print button.

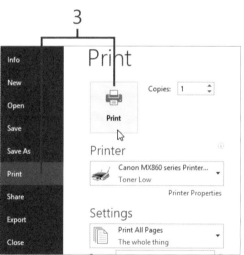

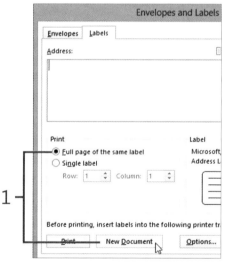

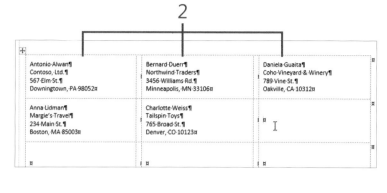

🔍 **SEE ALSO** If you already have the information for the labels stored in a Word table, a Microsoft Excel worksheet, a Microsoft Access database, or an Outlook contact list, a mail merge is an alternative way to print mailing labels. For information about using a mail merge, see "Starting a mail merge" on page 334.

Sending a document by email

You can share your documents with other Word users in several ways, and one of those ways is to send a copy of a document file by email. If you have an email program on your computer, you can send an open Word 2013 document as an attachment to a message directly from the Backstage view. You can send the document as an editable Word file, a PDF file, or an XPS file.

Send a document as an attachment

1 Open a document that you want to send to another person.

2 Click File to display the Backstage view and then click the Share tab.

3 Click Email.

4 To send the document as an editable Word file, click Send As Attachment. If you prefer to send a PDF file or an XPS file, instead, click Send As PDF or Send As XPS.

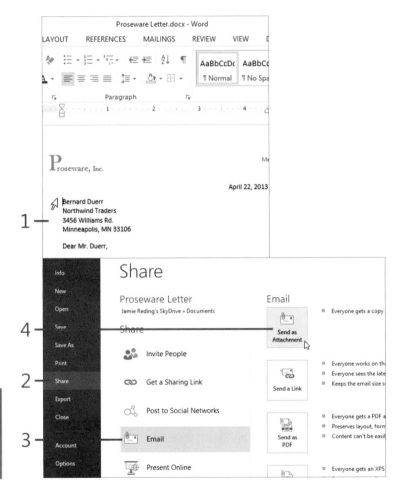

> **TIP** The entries in the middle pane for Get A Sharing Link and Post To Social Networks appear only if the document file is stored on SkyDrive or a SharePoint server. In the pane on the right, the Send A Link button is available only if the document file is stored on SkyDrive or a SharePoint server.

5 In the email program's window, type the recipient's address, the subject, and the body of the message, and then click the Send button.

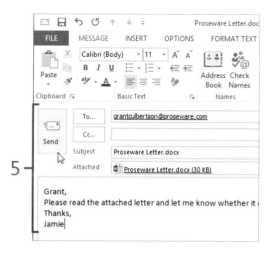

5—

 SEE ALSO For more information about sharing documents in Word 2013, see "Sharing with SkyDrive" on page 370.

Starting a mail merge

In Word 2013, a mail merge starts with a *main document*, which contains the formatting that you want in the final output. It might also contain text that you want to appear in each output document. You insert *merge fields* in the main document to reserve places for the *variable data*. You select a document or a database as the *data source* for the merge, and you can select which of the *recipients* listed in the data source will be used to create output. If you want, you can preview the output. Finally, you can send the output to a file, to the printer, or to an email program.

The mail merge feature in Word 2013 is quite flexible; you can use any of several kinds of data sources, you can sort and select the names or other items that you want to include, and you can create the output in several formats. However, this flexibility comes at the cost of some complexity. Completing a mail merge requires a sequence of steps, as described on the following pages.

The commands on the Mailings tab use the term *recipients* to refer to the names of people in a mailing list. You can also use Word's mail merge feature to work with other kinds of lists, such as product catalogs, in which case the term recipients refers to the items in the list.

Create the main document

1   Click File to display the Backstage view. Click the New tab and then click Blank Document or a custom template.

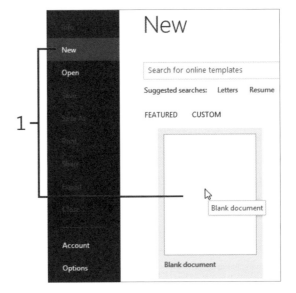

2 If you want to create a letter or an email message to send to multiple addresses, use the new document to write the body of the letter or message (that is, everything that will be the same in all of the letters).

If you're creating labels, envelopes, or a directory merge (called a *catalog* merge in some earlier versions of Word), leave the document blank.

3 When the main document is complete, on the Quick Access Toolbar, click the Save button. Then, while the document remains open, continue at "Select the merge type," which follows this task.

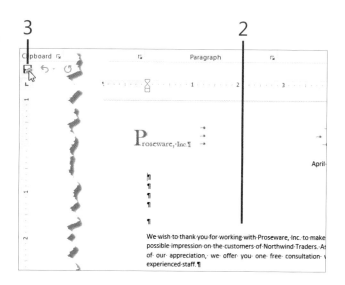

Select the merge type

1 On the Mailings tab, in the Start Mail Merge group, click Start Mail Merge. On the drop-down list that appears, click one of the following commands:

- **Letters** Creates an output document containing a separate section for each recipient, with each section starting on a new page

- **E-Mail Messages** Creates an email message to each recipient

- **Envelopes** Creates an output document containing an envelope for each recipient

- **Labels** Creates an output document containing labels, with one label for each recipient

- **Directory** Creates an output document in which each recipient's data starts a new paragraph

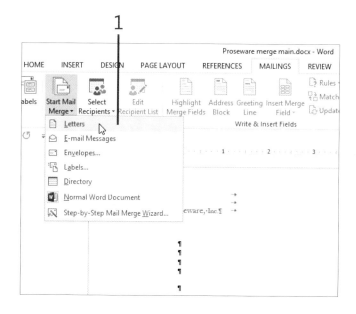

2 If you clicked Labels in step 1, the Label Options dialog box opens automatically. Select the printer tray, label vendor, and product number, and then click OK. While the document remains open, continue at "Choosing the recipients" on page 337.

3 If you clicked Envelopes in step 1, the Envelope Options dialog box opens automatically. Select the envelope size, choose the printing options, and then click OK. While the document remains open, continue at "Choosing the recipients."

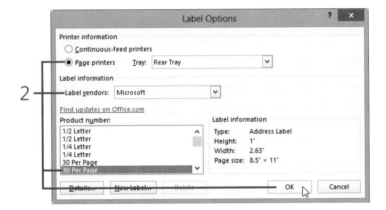

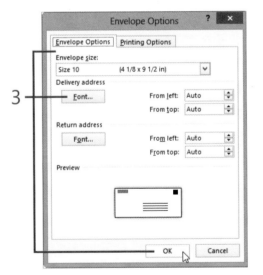

TIP   If you prefer the software to guide you through the same procedures described in this book, click the Step-By-Step Mail Merge Wizard command at the bottom of the Start Mail Merge gallery. The wizard leads you through each step.

Choosing the recipients

When you create a mail merge in Word 2013, you must choose the information that Word puts into the output document. The information could be stored in one of a number of places—as a table in a Word document, in an Excel worksheet, in an Access or Microsoft SQL Server database, or in an Outlook contact list.

After you select the file or other source of the data, Word provides tools with which you can refine the list of recipients or other records, to sort them on one or more fields, and to edit the list entries if necessary.

Select a data source

1 On the Mailings tab, in the Start Mail Merge group, click Select Recipients. On the menu that appears, click one of the following commands:

- **Type A New List**   Opens the New Address List dialog box, in which you can type entries for a list and then save them as a database (.mdb) file

- **Use An Existing List**   Opens the Select Data Source dialog box, in which you can select an existing file (a Word or plain text document, an Excel worksheet, or an Access or SQL Server database) containing the entries

- **Choose From Outlook Contacts**   Opens the Select Contacts dialog box, in which you can select which contact folder to use, if your Office edition includes Outlook

2 If you clicked Type A New List in step 1, in the New Address List dialog box, type the names, addresses, and other information. To add each entry after the first one, click New Entry. When the list is complete, click OK and continue at step 3.

> ✓ **TIP**   Click the Customize Columns button to add, remove, rename, or reorder columns in the New Address List dialog box. To sort the entries on any column, click the header of that column.

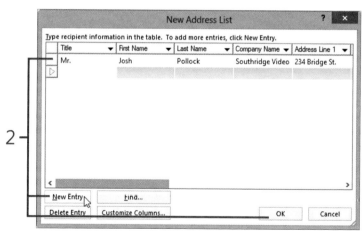

3 In the Save Address List dialog box that automatically opens, enter a file name and click Save. Then, continue at "Edit the list of recipients" on page 339.

4 If you clicked Use An Existing List in step 1, the Select Data Source dialog box initially displays the contents of the My Data Sources folder in your user profile. If the data source that you want to use is a Word or plain text document, an Excel worksheet, or an Access (.mdb or .accdb) database, navigate to the correct folder and select the file containing the data. Then, click Open and continue at "Edit the list of recipients."

5 If you clicked Choose From Outlook Contacts in step 1, click the contact folder that contains the data that you want to use and click OK. Then, continue at "Edit the list of recipients."

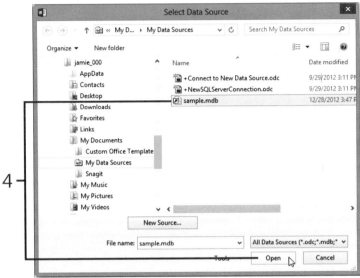

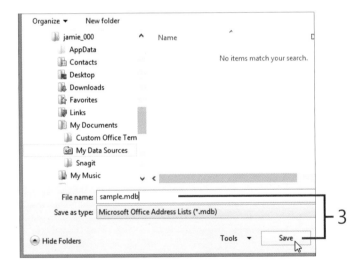

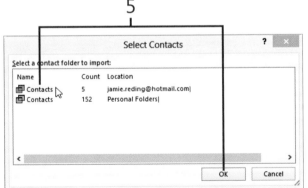

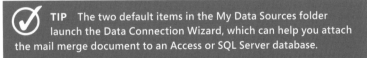

TIP The two default items in the My Data Sources folder launch the Data Connection Wizard, which can help you attach the mail merge document to an Access or SQL Server database.

Edit the list of recipients

1 If you chose an Outlook contacts folder as your data source, the Mail Merge Recipients dialog box opens automatically. Otherwise, on the Mailings tab, in the Start Mail Merge group, click Edit Recipient List to open the Mail Merge Recipients dialog box.

2 Clear the check boxes next to entries that you do not want to include in the mail merge; select the check boxes for those that you do want to include.

   Selecting or clearing the check box in the header row of the list causes all of the entries to become selected or cleared, respectively. If you want to keep only a few entries selected, first clear the entire list and then select those that you want.

3 If you want to add or delete entries in the list of recipients, click the name of the source file in the Data Source box and click Edit. The Edit Data Source dialog box that appears is the same as the New Address List dialog box shown in step 2 of "Select a data source" on page 337.

   If the data source is an Outlook contact list, the Edit button does not become available. To edit entries in a contact list, you must use Outlook's contact editor.

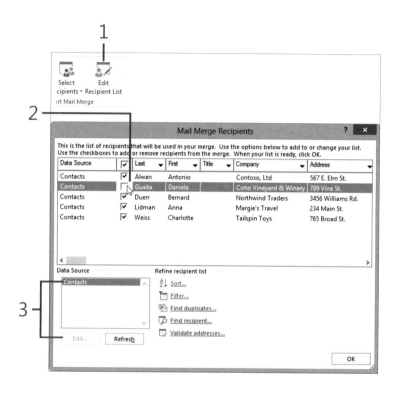

4 The order in which the merge's results appear is determined by the order of the entries in the list of recipients. If you want to sort the list of recipients on a single column, click that column's header. To sort on two or three columns, click the Sort link in the Refine Recipient List section to open the Filter And Sort dialog box. On the Sort tab, in each drop-down list, select the name of the column on which to sort, and whether to sort it in ascending or descending order.

For example, you can sort the recipients by state, then by last name, and finally by first name. In the merge's results, someone named Smith who lives in Arizona would be listed before someone named Jones who lives in Wyoming.

5 If you want to include in the merge only the entries that satisfy certain criteria, click the Filter link in the Refine Recipient List section to open the Filter And Sort dialog box. On the Filter tab, select the name of a column in the Field drop-down list, select a condition in the Comparison drop-down list, and if necessary enter a value in the Compare To list box. You can continue adding criteria, connected by *And* or *Or*, as needed to specify the set of recipients to include.

For example, to limit the list of recipients to those whose last names start with the letter M, select the criteria **Last | Greater than or equal to | M | And | Last | Less than | N**.

6 When the list of recipients is complete and correctly sorted, click OK.

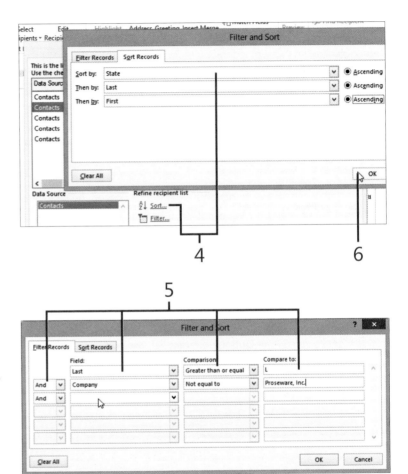

Adding merge fields

For a mail merge to place values from the data source into the output, you must insert one or more merge fields into the main document. During the merge, each merge field is replaced by the corresponding value in the data source for the current recipient. For example, suppose a recipient's record in the data source contains the values First_Name = John and Last_Name = Clarkson. In the main document for a letter merge, a line might contain the merge fields «First_Name» «Last_Name». When

the record is processed during the merge, those fields will be replaced with the text John Clarkson.

You can insert copies of the same merge field into the main document in multiple places. For example, the merge field «First_Name» could be used in the address, in the greeting line, and in the body of the letter.

Insert merge fields in the document

1 Click in the main document at the location where you want information from the data source to be inserted during the merge.

2 On the Mailings tab, in the Write & Insert Fields group, click the drop-down arrow on the Insert Merge Field button and then, in the list that appears, click the name of a column from the data source. Repeat steps 1 and 2 until the main document contains all the necessary merge fields.

If you selected a label merge, insert merge fields and other text only in the upper-left cell of the table in the main document. During this step, the other cells contain only a «Next Record» merge field. The other cells will be filled in step 4 of this procedure.

If you place another merge field on the same line as the first merge field, type a space, text, or punctuation between them as necessary. Otherwise, there won't be any separation between the values in the output. If you want the next merge field to appear on the next line, press Enter at the end of the first line.

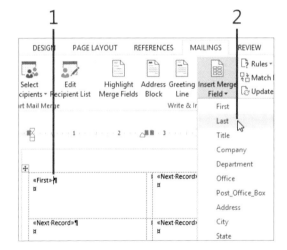

3 If you want, apply character formatting to some of the merge fields in the main document, either directly or by using a character style.

You can right-click a merge field in the main document and click Toggle Field Codes to display the complete field code. Then, you can insert formatting switches to control the appearance of the results in the output. For information about inserting formatting switches, see "Controlling field formatting by using switches" on page 205.

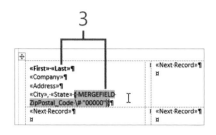

4 If you selected a label merge, on the Mailings tab, in the Write & Insert Fields group, click Update Labels. This copies the merge fields and text that you entered in the upper-left cell of the table into all the other cells.

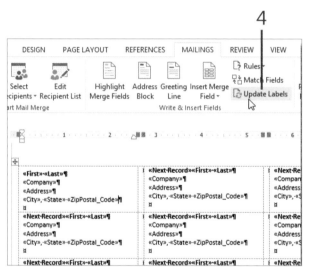

> → **TRY THIS** On the Mailings tab, in the Write & Insert Fields group, click either Address Block or Greeting Line to insert special merge fields. These merge fields combine data from several columns of the recipient's record. When you insert one of these fields, Word displays a dialog box in which you can select options for the formatting of the output. If you use either of these merge fields, be sure to preview the results for every recipient and correct any unexpected output.

> ⚠ **CAUTION** If the style applied to the merge fields includes paragraph formatting with extra space before or after the paragraphs, the lines might be spaced too widely. This particularly affects label and envelope merges, in which addresses with more than three or four lines might not fit. If necessary, apply another style such as No Spacing to the main document.

Adding information with rules

The entries in the Insert Merge Field gallery represent only the columns that are present in the data source. In addition, you can use the fields in Word 2013 to perform comparisons and

calculations during a mail merge, so you can display additional information, depending on the data in the data source.

Modify the merge with rules

1   Insert a SET field if you want to store an unchanging number or text that can be used to perform comparisons or calculations for all of the recipients in a merge. On the Mailings tab, in the Write & Insert Fields group, click Rules and then, on the list that appears, click Set Bookmark. Continue at step 2.

2   In the Insert Word Field: Set dialog box, type a bookmark name in the Bookmark list box, type the number or text in the Value text box, and then click OK.

The bookmark is located inside the SET field, which doesn't display any result in the document. However, the bookmark can be referenced in other fields elsewhere in the document, such as a REF field that will display the value, or a formula field that will use the value in a calculation.

3   Insert an ASK field if you want to store a number or text that might be different for each recipient. On the Mailings tab, in the Write & Insert Fields group, click Rules and then, on the list that appears, click Ask. Continue at step 4.

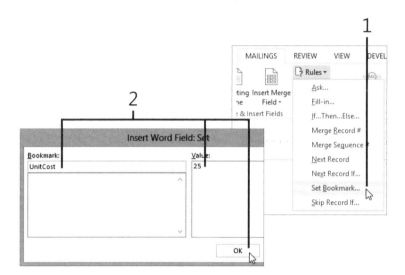

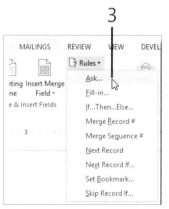

4 In the Insert Word Field: Ask dialog box, type a bookmark name in the Bookmark box, type a question in the Prompt box, type a default value if desired, and then click OK.

During the merge, the prompt will be displayed for each recipient, and the value you enter will overwrite any previous value in the bookmark. If you want to use the same value for all of the recipients during the current merge, select the Ask Once check box.

The bookmark is located inside the ASK field, which doesn't display any result in the document. However, the bookmark can be referenced in other fields elsewhere in the document, such as a REF field that will display the value, or a formula field that will use the value in a calculation.

5 If you want to display a number or text that might be different for each recipient, insert a FILLIN field. On the Mailings tab, in the Write & Insert Fields group, click Rules and then, on the list that appears, click Fill-in. Continue at step 6.

6 In the Insert Word Field: Fill-in dialog box, type a question in the Prompt text box, type a default value if desired, and then click OK.

The FILLIN field is similar to the ASK field, except that the FILLIN field displays its value in the document and doesn't store its value in a bookmark.

7 Insert an IF...THEN...ELSE field where you need to display different results in the document, depending on the value of a merge field or other field. If you want to base the decision on a bookmark value (such as one in a SET field or an ASK field), continue at step 9.

On the Mailings tab, in the Write & Insert Fields group, click Rules and then, on the list that appears, click If...Then...Else. Continue at step 8.

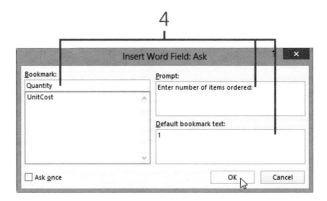

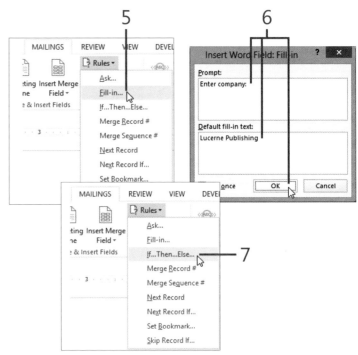

8 In the Insert Word Field: If dialog box, select a merge field in the Field Name list box, select a condition in the Comparison box and, if necessary, enter a value in the Compare To list box. In the Insert This Text box, enter the result that the field will display if the comparison is true. In the Otherwise Insert This Text box, enter the result that the field will display if the comparison is false. Click OK.

9 If you want to base the decision on a bookmark value (such as one in a SET field or an ASK field), click the Insert tab. In the Text group, click Quick Parts and then click Field. Continue at step 10.

10 In the Field dialog box, in the Field Name list box, click If. Then, click the Options button.

In the Field Options dialog, click the desired bookmark name and then click Add To Field. Click at the end of the expression in the Field Codes box and type the rest of the code.

For example, suppose the selected bookmark is Quantity, and you want the result to display *copy* if Quantity is 1 or *copies* if Quantity is greater than 1. The completed code for this field is **IF Quantity = 1 "copy" "copies"**.

Click OK in the Field Options dialog box and then click OK in the Field dialog box.

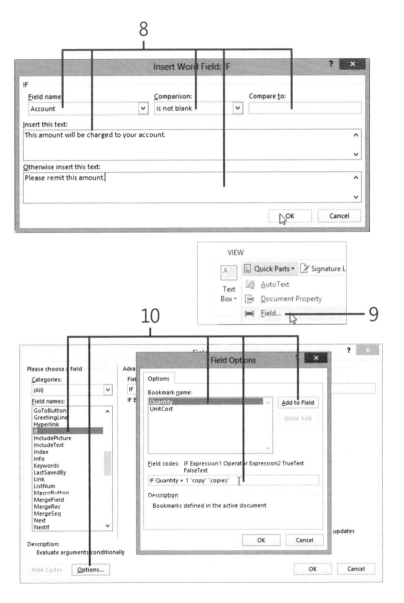

Finishing the merge

When the main document contains all of the merge fields, other fields, text, and graphics needed to prepare the output, it's time to perform the final steps. Because of the length and complexity of the setup, you should first examine a preview to ensure that everything is in place. When you're confident of the correctness of the document and the sorting and filtering of the data source, you can run the final merge.

Merge to special outputs

1   On the Mailings tab, in the Preview Results group, click Preview Results. If you selected a label merge, the preview shows the pages of labels. For any other kind of merge, the preview shows the output for only one recipient at a time. You can use the arrow buttons in the Preview Results group to display previews of the rest of the output.

If unwanted information appears in any of the previews or information is missing, click Preview Results to turn it off. Then, edit the main document or the records in the data source to correct the problem and repeat the preview.

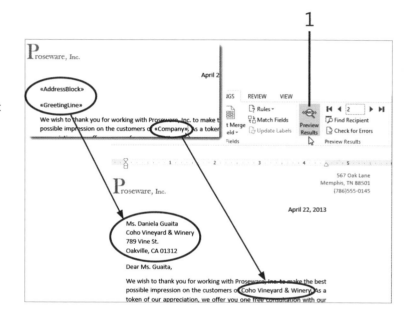

> ✓ **TIP**   If you preview a label merge and only the first recipient's label appears, you have skipped the step of clicking the Update Labels button (step 4 in "Insert merge fields in the document" on page 342).

2 On the Mailings tab, in the Finish group, click Finish & Merge and then, in the list that appears, click one of the following:

- **Edit Individual Documents** Merges the data from the data source into the merge fields to create a new document. You can edit this document, save it for later use, or print it like any other document.

- **Print Documents** Merges the data from the data source into the merge fields and sends the result to the printer. The Print dialog box appears so that you can set the printer properties, the number of copies, and other options. Click OK to print.

- **Send Email Messages** Merges the data from the data source into the merge fields and sends the result to the default email program. The Merge To Email dialog box appears so that you can enter the subject line and select the merge field that contains the email address. Click OK to send.

3 When the merge runs successfully, save the main document so that it can be used again.

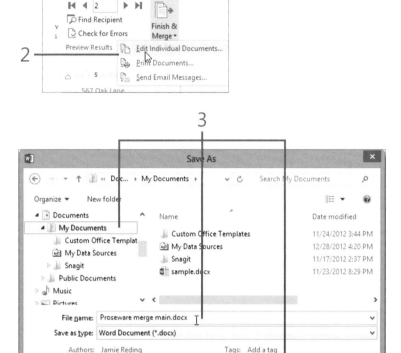

> 🔍 **SEE ALSO** For more information about mail merges, see *www.gmayor.com/merge_labels_with_word_2007.htm*. **The descriptions presented there also apply to Word 2013.**

Reviewing documents

13

When you prepare a document with input from many coworkers, you might use any of several methods. In one style, each person works alone on one or a few sections. Then somebody puts all the pieces together, smooths out differences in formatting and writing style, and publishes the result. Another method involves writing a draft, passing it around for review and comments, and editing the document to resolve any questions.

The Comments and Track Changes features provided by Microsoft Word 2013 are ideal for multiple rounds of reviews, and the new Simple Markup view makes even heavily revised documents more readable.

In another scenario, perhaps your workflow results in several copies of the same document from different reviewers, with or without change tracking. The Compare and Combine features can pull together those multiple versions into a single document so that you can see all the changes at once.

In this section:

- Adding comments
- Showing and hiding comments
- Tracking changes
- Showing and hiding tracked changes
- Setting options for tracked changes
- Accepting and rejecting changes
- Comparing reviewed versions
- Merging reviewed versions

Adding comments

If you send your document out for review, you or the other Word users can insert comments that don't become part of the text. In Word 2013, you can also reply to a comment as you might in an email conversation. When you've settled the issue raised by a comment, you can delete the comment or you can mark the comment as completed. The completed comment and its replies remain in the document as a record of the issue's resolution.

Insert a comment

1 On the Review tab, in the Comments group, click New Comment.

2 Type your comment under your name in the Comments balloon.

TIP To remove a comment, click it, and then on the Review tab, in the Comments group, click Delete.

TIP If you use a tablet or a drawing pad, you can click Ink Comment and handwrite or draw your comment.

TRY THIS If your Office 2013 installation includes Microsoft OneNote, you can type notes in OneNote about your Word document. OneNote automatically links the note to the current location your document. To make a note in OneNote, select the Review tab in Word and click Linked Notes.

Reply to a comment

1 Click the reply icon at the right side of the Comment balloon.

2 Type your reply in the Comment balloon under your name.

3 To mark a comment as completed, right-click the Comment balloon and click Mark Comment Done.

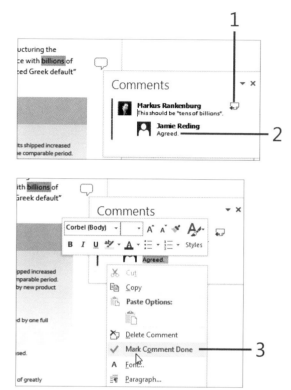

TRY THIS When you're reviewing your own documents, you might want to show some of your comments with a different color as a way of separating comments into categories. You can do this by slightly changing your user name in Word. On the Review tab, in the lower-right corner of the Tracking group, click the dialog box launcher (the small arrow). In the Track Changes Options dialog box, click Change User Name. In the User Name box, add a digit or other text to your user name. Select the Always Use These Values Regardless Of Sign In To Office check box and then click OK. Add a new comment or reply to an existing comment. (Don't forget to change back to your real user name after adding your comments.)

Showing and hiding comments

When you're reading and responding to comments, you'll want to see all of them. When you're reading the document for other purposes, though, the lines and balloons can be distracting.

Word 2013 has a new Simple Markup view that hides the clutter and shows just an icon in the margin to indicate the presence of a comment.

View all markup

1 On the Review tab, at the top of the Tracking group, click the drop-down list and select All Markup, if it isn't already selected.

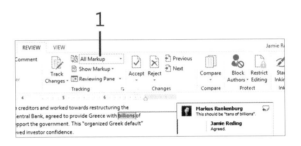

View simple markup

1 On the Review tab, at the top of the Tracking group, click the drop-down list and select Simple Markup, if it isn't already selected. Click any Comment balloon to see its complete comment.

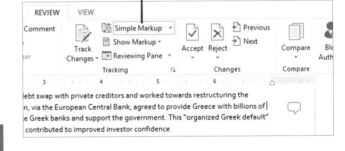

> ✓ **TIP** When All Markup is selected, the comments appear in Outline or Draft view as tags in the text. You can position the cursor on a tag to see the comment or, on the Review tab, click Reviewing Pane.

> ✓ **TIP** To control what items are shown in balloons, on the Review tab, in the Tracking group, click Show Markup, point to Balloons, and then choose a setting from the menu.

Tracking changes

Whether you work on a document alone or with others, it's often important to keep a record of what's been changed, who made the changes, and when the changes were made. In Word 2013, the Track Changes feature handles those details.

Turn on Track Changes

1 On the Review tab, in the Tracking group, click Track Changes, if it isn't already selected.

2 Click the drop-down list at the top of the Tracking group and select All Markup, if it isn't already selected.

3 Edit or reformat the text.

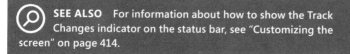

TIP In Outline or Draft view, you can position the cursor on a change to see its information or, on the Review tab, click Reviewing Pane.

CAUTION The built-in keyboard shortcut to switch Track Changes on and off is Ctrl+Shift+E. If you suddenly start seeing red text in a document while you're editing, you might have pressed that combination by mistake.

SEE ALSO For information about how to show the Track Changes indicator on the status bar, see "Customizing the screen" on page 414.

Showing and hiding tracked changes

When you're revising a document, you'll want to show the details for tracked changes to decide which ones to keep or reject. Conversely, when you just want to read a document without distraction, you can use the new Simple Markup view to hide the lines and balloons, leaving just an unobtrusive change bar in the margin.

Whichever markup view you select, you can list all the changes and comments in the Reviewing Pane. Double-clicking an entry in that pane moves the cursor to the location in the document so that you can navigate quickly through the changes.

View all markup or simple markup

1 On the Review tab, at the top of the Tracking group, click the drop-down list and select All Markup, if it isn't already selected.

2 At the top of the Tracking group, click the drop-down list and select Simple Markup. Click any change bar to return to All Markup view.

> ✓ **TIP** When many reviewers have added changes to the document, you can show the changes from only one or a selected few of them. On the Review tab, in the Tracking group, click Show Markup, point to Specific People, and then clear the check boxes next to the names of reviewers whose changes you want to hide.

> ⚠ **CAUTION** When tracked changes and comments are hidden, they're still stored in the document and can be seen by anyone who receives a copy of the document. In some cases, that can be extremely embarrassing! Before you send out final copies of your document, use the procedures in "Accepting and rejecting changes" on page 358 to remove all changes and comments.

Display the Reviewing pane

1 On the Review tab, in the Tracking group, click Reviewing Pane.

2 Double-click an item in the Revisions list.

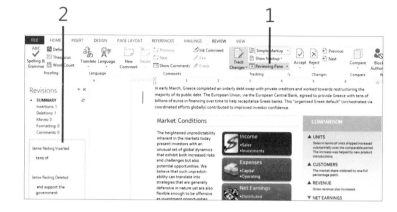

→ **TRY THIS** Click the arrow next to Reviewing Pane to open the drop-down list and choose Reviewing Pane Horizontal. You can also drag the edges of the pane to resize it, or drag the pane's title to make the pane "float" over the document.

Setting options for Track Changes

The Track Changes feature works well with the default settings, but it also offers a lot of flexibility for different ways of working with reviewed documents. You can turn on tracking in your document and lock it so that the reviewers are required to record all of their changes. You can determine how changes and comments are displayed, and easily change those settings at will.

Lock tracking

1 On the Review tab, in the Tracking group, click the bottom half of Track Changes and click Lock Tracking.

The Lock Tracking dialog box opens.

2 Enter a password in the top text box. Enter the password again in the second box.

If you don't want to protect Lock Tracking with a password, leave both boxes blank.

3 Click OK.

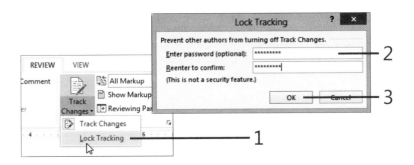

Set common options and advanced options

1 On the Review tab, in the lower-right corner of the Tracking group, click the dialog box launcher.

The Track Changes Options dialog box opens.

2 Select or clear the check boxes for the kinds of changes that you want to display.

3 Click Advanced Options to change other settings, or click OK to return to the document.

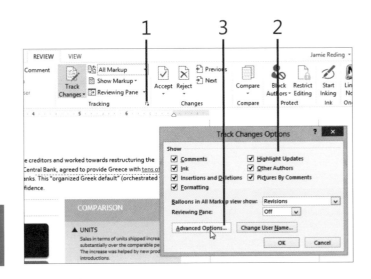

> **✓ TIP** Most of the items in the Track Changes Options dialog box also appear on the Show Markup menu. The Advanced Options, however, are accessible only through the dialog box.

4 In the Markup section of the Advanced Track Changes Options dialog box, select the color and formatting you want to use for insertions and deletions, the location of the change lines, and the color of the shading applied to commented text.

You can choose the same color for all reviewers, or you can let Word choose a different color for each reviewer.

5 In the Moves, Table Cell Highlighting, and Formatting sections, choose the way you want those types of changes to appear. If you prefer not to track Moves and Formatting at all, clear their check boxes.

6 In the Balloons section, set the width of the column in which balloons are shown, the margin at which you want balloons to appear, and whether you want a line leading from each balloon to its corresponding change in the document.

For a document in portrait orientation, you can instruct Word to print in landscape orientation to avoid compressing the text column.

7 Click OK.

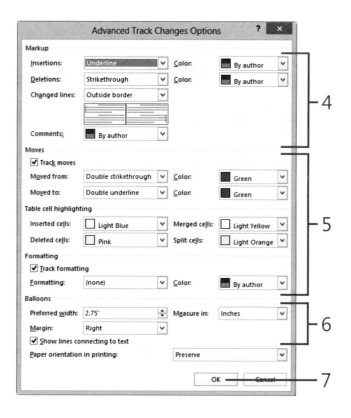

TIP Whether you set a specific color for changes by all reviewers or select By Author, that setting applies only on your computer. Other reviewers who open the document will see colors according to their settings. You can't be sure that a particular color will be assigned to a specific reviewer on other computers.

Accepting and rejecting changes

If a document contains tracked changes, all the information about each change will stay in the document until you accept or reject the change. Setting the markup view or the options so that you can't see the changes only hides them—it doesn't remove them. Anyone else who opens the document can easily show the changes again. That isn't necessarily a good thing.

For example, you might not want a client to see that you copied part of a report for another client and just changed the names. To protect yourself against such possibly embarrassing situations, you must review the changes and accept or reject them before you send your documents to others.

Accept or reject changes

1 Open a document that has been reviewed. If it's a Read-Only document, save it with a different name or in a different folder.

2 On the Review tab, in the Tracking group, ensure that Track Changes is not selected. If it is selected, click Track Changes to turn it off.

3 At the top of the Tracking group, click the drop-down list and select All Markup, if it isn't already selected.

4 Click Next or Previous in the Changes group to locate a change, or click a change in the text or in a balloon. Select Accept to make the change permanent, or Reject to remove the change. Continue clicking Accept or Reject until you've handled all the changes in the document.

5 Instead of working through the changes one at a time, you can click the bottom half of Accept or Reject and choose one of the other actions from the menu.

The Accept All Changes and Reject All Changes actions affect all the changes in the document at once. If you first use the Show Markup menu to hide some types of changes, the Accept All Changes Shown and Reject All Changes Shown actions affect only the changes that haven't been hidden.

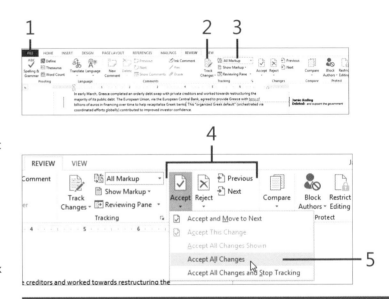

SEE ALSO For information about comparing two versions of the same document and marking the differences between them, see "Comparing reviewed versions" on page 359.

SEE ALSO For information about ensuring that the document doesn't contain any revisions or comments, see "Using the Document Inspector" on page 392.

Comparing reviewed versions

If you receive a reviewed copy of your document but the reviewer didn't have Track Changes turned on, you can have Word 2013 mark the changes for you. All you need is the original document, the reviewed copy, and the Compare feature.

Set up a comparison

1 On the Review tab, in the Compare group, click Compare and choose Compare in the gallery.

The Compare Documents dialog box opens in its collapsed view.

2 Specify the original document by clicking the down-arrow and selecting it from the list of recently used documents, or you can select the folder icon to browse for another file. In the same way, specify the revised document.

3 If both versions of the document contain markup from the same reviewer, you can keep the two sets separated by entering a different name or other text in the Label Changes With text box.

4 If the dialog box is not expanded, click More.

5 Leave the check boxes selected in the Comparison settings section for only the types of changes that you want to have marked in the result of the comparison.

6 Choose whether the comparison will be made character by character or word by word. Also choose where the changes will be shown. You can choose for the changes to appear in one or the other of the documents being compared, or in a new third document.

7 Click OK.

> **TIP** You can use the Compare feature to create "legal blacklining" in contracts; this way, each party can see what revisions were made.

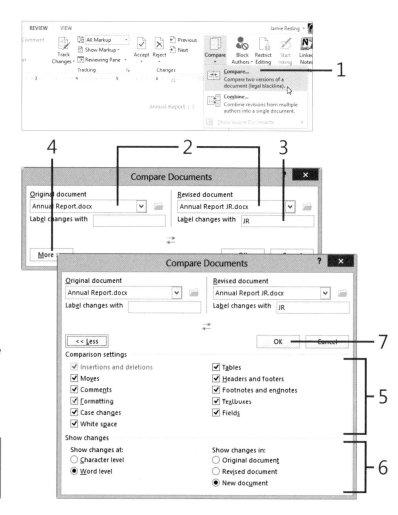

View the results of comparing documents

1 Examine the compared document (the one containing tracked changes) in the large pane. The two source documents are in smaller panes.

2 On the Review tab, in the Tracking group, click Reviewing Pane to show or hide the pane.

3 Save the compared document with the marked changes as a separate file.

4 Scroll through the compared document, accepting or rejecting the changes as you would for any document that has tracked changes. As you scroll the compared document, the source documents scroll to the same position so that you can see where the changes originated.

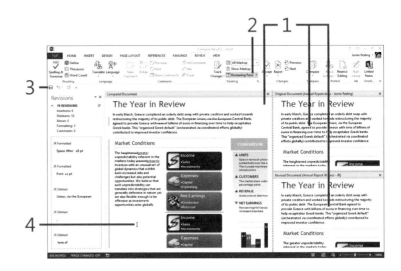

TIP To hide one or both of the source documents, click Compare, point to Show Source Documents, and then select which source documents you want to see.

Merging reviewed versions

If you've sent your document to several reviewers who edited it separately, but with Track Changes turned on, you can use the Combine feature to merge the versions into one document with marked changes. You can then use the merged document to prepare a final version.

Merge reviews

1 On the Review tab, in the Compare group, click Compare and choose Combine in the gallery.

2 Specify the first document containing review changes by clicking the down-arrow and selecting from the list of recently used documents, or you can select the folder icon to browse for another file. In the same way, specify the second document containing changes.

3 In each Label Unmarked Changes With text box, type a name or other text to identify the source of the changes in the corresponding version of the document.

4 If the dialog box isn't expanded, click More.

5 Leave the check boxes selected in the Comparison settings section for only the types of changes that you want to have marked in the result of the combination.

6 Choose whether the combination will be made character by character or word by word. Also, choose where the changes will be shown. You can choose for the changes to appear in one or the other of the documents being combined, or in a new third document.

7 Click OK and save the combined document.

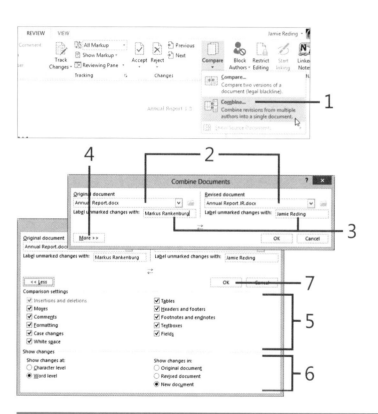

> ✅ **TIP** You can combine only two documents at a time. If you have several reviewed versions to combine, first combine two of them and then combine the result with a third reviewed version, and so on.

> ✅ **TIP** When you combine documents, the result can contain formatting changes from only one of them. If Word detects formatting changes in either source document, a dialog box gives you a choice of which set of formatting changes to keep in the result.

Sharing and coauthoring in Word

14

An increasingly important way of working in Microsoft Word documents is collaboration or simultaneous coauthoring. Unlike older versions of the program, Word 2013 makes it possible for multiple users to open the same document file and edit at the same time. You and your coauthors can see one another's changes, make and reply to comments, and discuss what you're doing in real time.

A companion to the desktop version of Word 2013, Microsoft Word Web App, runs in a web browser. With Word Web App, you can read and edit documents from any computer—even one on which Microsoft Office is not installed. When you're on the go with a laptop, or using a public workstation, you can see your documents and participate in coauthoring sessions.

In this section:

- Exploring Word Web App
- Sharing with SkyDrive
- Working with coauthors
- Talking to your coauthors
- Blogging with Word
- Presenting a document online

Exploring Word Web App

Word Web App is an online companion to Word 2013. Using nothing more than a web browser, you can read and edit documents that are stored on SkyDrive or on a SharePoint server. It costs nothing to use—all you need is your free Microsoft Account—and it works on desktops, tablets, and smartphones. You can use Word Web App on almost any computer that has an Internet connection, with or without a locally installed copy.

In the Reading view of Word Web App, you can add and reply to comments, find words and phrases, and share the document with other users by sending them a link. You can also save the document as a PDF file, which you can view and print in your web browser.

In the Editing view of Word Web App, you can add text, pictures, tables, and hyperlinks. You can also change the text formatting and modify the page layout.

Word Web App has fewer features than the Word program that you install on your computer. Thus, editing in Word Web App is best suited for quick changes such as making corrections, rather than heavy-duty document creation. If you need more capabilities, you can open the document in Word 2013 on your computer, directly from Word Web App.

Open or create a document in Word Web App

1 Use your web browser to log on to SkyDrive or a SharePoint server and then access the appropriate folder. If you want to create a new document, skip to step 4.

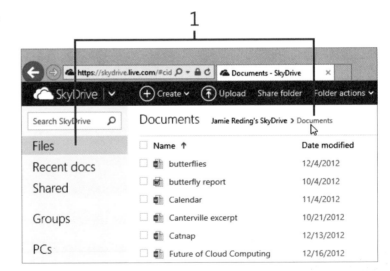

2 If an existing document file that you want to edit is not already stored in the folder, upload the file from your computer. Otherwise, continue at step 3.

In SkyDrive, click Upload. In the Choose File To Upload dialog box that opens, select the file on your computer and then click Open.

3 Click the name of the document file that you want to edit.

Word Web App displays the document in Reading view.

4 If you want to create a new document in SkyDrive, click Create and then click Word Document.

5 In the New Microsoft Word Document dialog box, enter a name for the document file and click Create.

Word Web App displays the new document in Editing view.

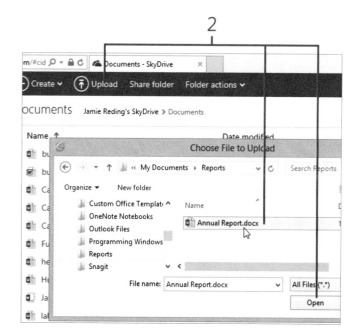

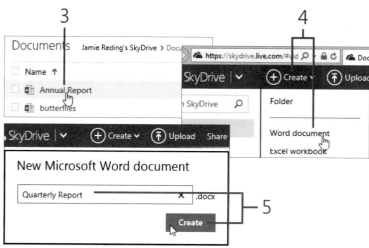

> **TIP** If you don't yet have a Microsoft Account, click File to display the Backstage view, click the Account tab, and then click Sign Up. Follow the instructions to set up your free account. You can also get a Microsoft Account by using a web browser. Simply go to *skydrive.live.com* and click the Sign Up Now link.

Read in Word Web App

1 If the document in Word Web App is displayed in Editing view, click the View tab and then, in the Document Views group, click Reading View.

The Reading View displays the document as it appears in Print Layout view in Word 2013.

2 If you want to add a comment, click the Comments tab. In the Comments pane, click New Comment and type your comment.

3 The presence of a comment is indicated by a balloon in the right margin. Click the balloon to see the text of the comment.

4 To reply to an existing comment, click the reply icon and type your response.

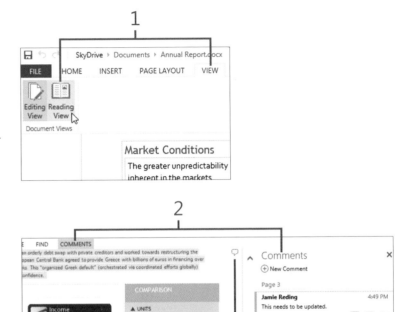

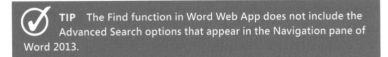

TIP The Find function in Word Web App does not include the Advanced Search options that appear in the Navigation pane of Word 2013.

5 To search for text, click the Find tab. In the Find pane, enter a word or phrase in the search box. Click the magnifier icon or press Enter. Then, click the thumbnail of any of the matches to move the document view to that occurrence in the text.

6 To make a document that you own available to other users, click the Share tab. The display lists the user(s) with whom the document is already shared. You can click the Share With More People button to invite others by sending email, posting a link on a social networking service such as Facebook or LinkedIn, or generating a link that you can send or post elsewhere.

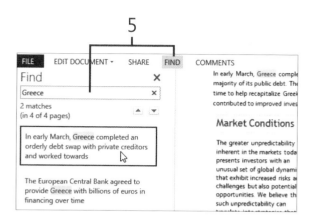

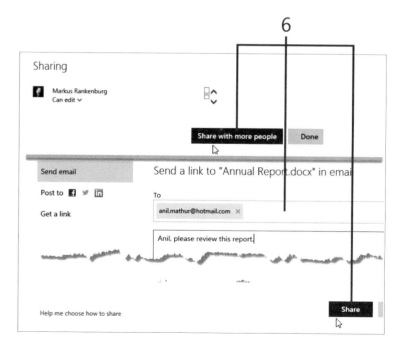

 SEE ALSO For more information about sharing documents with other users, see "Share files in SkyDrive" on page 370.

Edit in Word Web App

1 If the document in Word Web App is displayed in Reading view, click the Edit Document tab and then, in the list that appears, click Edit In Word Web App.

2 You can add, delete, modify, and format the text in the document. In addition, you can apply styles, but you can't modify styles or create new styles.

3 You can insert a table, a picture from your computer, clip art from Office.com, or a hyperlink to a webpage (but not to another location in the document).

1

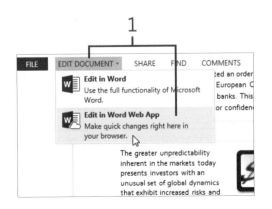

2

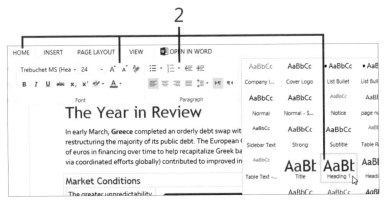

3

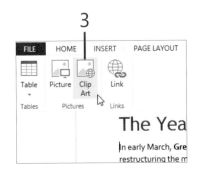

 TIP   The Editing view doesn't show page breaks. To see where pages break, switch to Reading view.

Switch to Word on your computer

1 Click File to display the Backstage view.

2 If the document was in Reading mode, click the Edit tab. If the document was in Editing mode, click the Info tab. Then, click Edit In Word.

3 If a warning message appears, but you know that the file is safe, click Yes. Word 2013 opens and the document is downloaded and displayed.

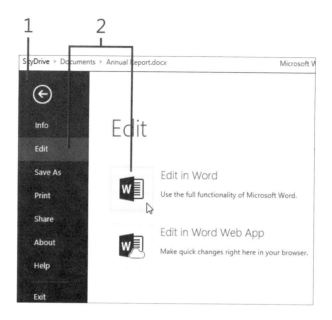

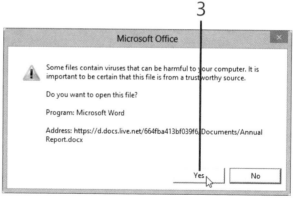

TIP In addition to the Edit page of the Backstage view, there are other ways to open the document in Word 2013. In the Reading view, you can click the Edit Document tab and click Edit In Word. In the Editing view, you can click the Open In Word tab.

SEE ALSO For more information about using Word Web App on touch-enabled devices, *see blogs.office.com/b/officewe-bapps/archive/2012/08/20/bringing-touch-editing-to-office-web-apps-on-windows-8-and-ios-tablets.aspx.* For more information about differences between Word Web App and Word 2013, *see office. microsoft.com/en-us/web-apps-help/differences-between-using-a-doc-ument-in-the-browser-and-in-word-HA102748596.aspx.*

Sharing with SkyDrive

SkyDrive (*skydrive.live.com*) is a free file storage and sharing service offered by Microsoft. You can use it to back up important files, you can access your files from any computer, and you can let other users download specific documents or edit them in a browser with Word Web App. To use SkyDrive, all you need is a Microsoft Account.

On the Account page of the Backstage view, in any Office 2013 program, you can connect your SkyDrive storage to Office. Your SkyDrive folders will be offered in the Open and Save As pages along with the folders on your computer.

You can use Microsoft SharePoint Workspace, which is included in Office 2013 Professional Plus, to connect to a SharePoint server and use the SharePoint folders and libraries as if they were on local drives. In addition to facilitating coauthoring of documents, SharePoint offers the ability to manage multiple versions of documents, to set permissions for viewing and editing files, and to add property values that make searching easier. If you need to use SharePoint Workspace, you will need instructions from your system administrator.

Share files in SkyDrive

1 To share an entire folder of documents, in Details view, select the check box next to that folder (or the check box in the folder's tile in tile view) and click Share. Continue at step 3.

2 To share only one file in a folder, open that folder. Select the check box next to the file that you want to share (or the check box in the file's tile and click Share. Continue at step 3.

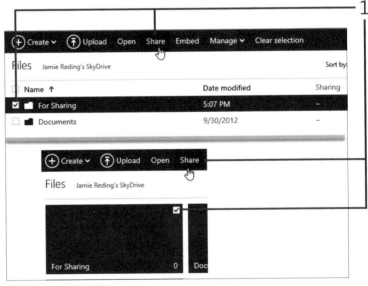

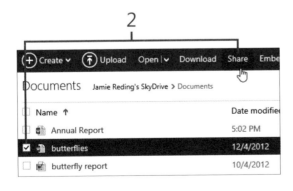

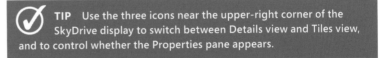

TIP Use the three icons near the upper-right corner of the SkyDrive display to switch between Details view and Tiles view, and to control whether the Properties pane appears.

3 In the Send A Link pane, to send a link to a shared folder or file by email to another user, enter an email address. You can add a description and choose options for the sharing permissions. Click Share to send the email.

4 To post a link on a social network that you've connected to your Microsoft Account, such as Facebook, LinkedIn, or Twitter, click Post To and then, in the Post On A Social Network pane, select the check box next to the desired service. Click Post to post the link.

5 To display a direct link that you can copy and then paste on a webpage or other location, click Get A Link and then, in the Get A Link To pane, click Create or Make Public under the desired permission type. Press Ctrl+C to copy the link to the clipboard. Click Done to dismiss the pane.

TIP When a Microsoft Account is connected to Office on your computer, you can use the Share tab of the Backstage view to save to SkyDrive and send invitations to other users directly from Word 2013.

TIP When a long address appears in the Get A Link pane, you can click Shorten to create a shorter alias that leads to the real address.

Working with coauthors

When you share a document on SkyDrive or a SharePoint server with other users, any or all of those people can edit the document simultaneously by using Word 2010, Word 2013, Word for Mac 2011, or Word Web App. A coauthoring session can be much more interactive than the traditional edit-and-review cycle that was required when only one person at a time could open the document.

Word notifies you when others are editing the same document. The program locks each paragraph in which one of the coauthors is actively making changes, but you can continue to edit anywhere else in the document.

View the list of active authors

1 When you open a shared document and a coauthor begins to edit the same document—and again when a coauthor stops editing—an alert appears briefly to let you know who is working with you.

2 To see a list of the active coauthors, in the status bar, click the Number Of Authors Editing indicator.

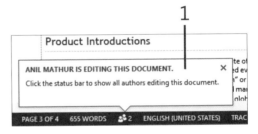

> **TIP** In Word 2013 on the desktop, the alert appears in the lower-left portion of the window, above the Number Of Authors Editing indicator. In Word Web App, the alert appears in the upper-right portion of the window, below the ribbon.

View changes made by other authors

1 Edit the file as you normally would. When you make a change in a paragraph, a dashed line appears next to that paragraph to show what text you have locked. Paragraphs being edited by others are marked with a solid line.

2 Save the document frequently to send your changes to SkyDrive so that the coauthors can see them and to synchronize your copy with the changes made by the coauthors. When you save the document, any paragraphs that you edited become unlocked.

Changes made by others are highlighted with pale-green shading.

TIP To temporarily prevent any coauthors from editing part of the document while you work on it in Word 2013, select the text to protect and then, on the Review tab, in the Protect group, click Block Authors. To release the text, click Block Authors again and then save the document. The Block Authors command is not available in Word Web App.

TIP Coauthors using Word Web App can see an indicator in the status bar when the Tracked Changes feature is turned on, and any changes they make will be tracked, but they can't turn Tracked Changes off or on.

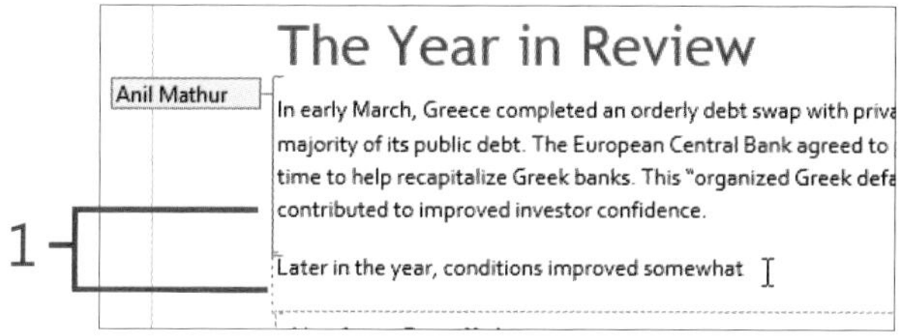

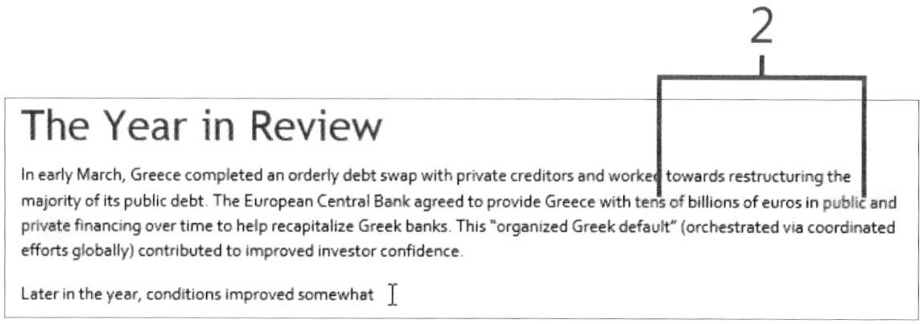

Talking to your coauthors

When you're working together with another person during a coauthoring session, you can see one another's changes and comments in the document. However, you might need to discuss those changes or plan for additional work. With Word 2013, you can contact an active coauthor by email, instant messaging, or phone with just a few clicks. This eliminates the need to open another program and manually locate the coauthor's address.

Contact a coauthor

1 Click the indicator on the status bar and click the coauthor's name.

2 Click an icon to choose the contact method.

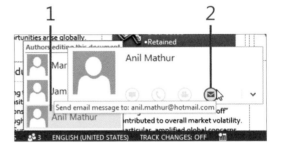

Blogging with Word

You can publish a *blog* (a contraction of the rarely heard term *web log*) as a record of a work project, as a personal diary, or as a commentary on life or literature. A number of sites on the Internet offer hosting and tools for publishing and maintaining blogs. Usually, they make it possible for your readers to leave comments, to which you can reply.

Word 2013 supplies a blog post template, and a dedicated Blog Post ribbon tab contains commands to help you publish and manage your posts.

Set up a blog account

1 If you have access to a Microsoft SharePoint Server site, apply to the site manager for a blog account. Otherwise, if you don't have an account on a blog provider such as WordPress (*www.wordpress.com*) or Blogger (*www.blogger.com*), visit the home page of the site you prefer and sign up for an account.

2 Click File to display the Backstage view. Then, click the New tab and click the Blog Post template's thumbnail.

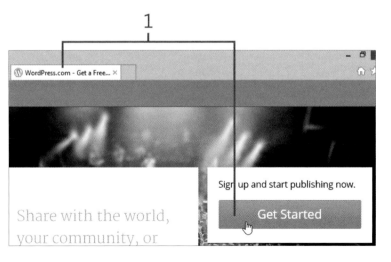

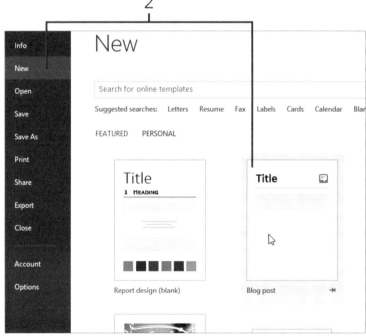

3 Click Create.

4 In the Register A Blog Account dialog box, click Register Now.

5 In the New Blog Account dialog box, click the Blog list box and select the name of your blog provider. Then, click Next.

6 Type the user name and password for your blog account, and any other information required by the blog provider.

7 By default, pictures that you include in your blog posts will be uploaded to the blog provider's site. If you prefer to store the picture files on another server, click Picture Options. In the Picture Options dialog box, change the setting and then click OK in each dialog box.

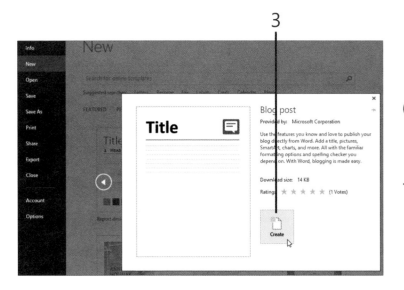

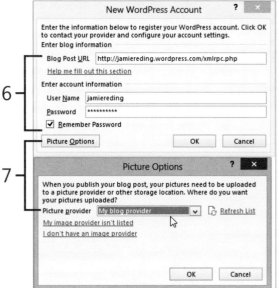

Post a blog entry

1 Click the [Enter Post Title Here] heading and type the title that you want for this blog post. You can apply styles from the Styles gallery on the Blog Post tab or apply direct formatting.

2 Click the paragraph below the post title and type the body of your post. Use styles and formatting as you would in any other Word document.

3 On the Insert tab, you can click the commands to insert tables, pictures, clip art, hyperlinks, and other special items.

4 If you want to separate your posts into categories, on the Blog Post tab, in the Blog group, click Insert Category. Then, click the Category list box below the post title and type a new category name or select one from the drop-down list.

5 When the blog post is complete, on the Blog Post tab, in the Blog group, click Publish.

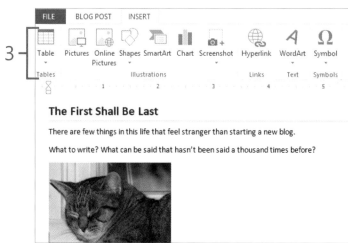

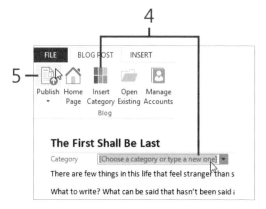

TIP To send the post to the blog provider but not make it publically available, you can click the drop-down arrow on the Publish button and then, in the list that appears, click Publish As Draft. After making any needed changes, click Publish to finalize the draft.

TIP If you need to change a post after you have published it, on the Blog Post tab, in the Blog group, click Open Existing and select the post title of the entry that you want to edit.

Presenting a document online

A new feature in Office 2013 is the ability to use a document as the display in an online presentation. You can invite people to attend the presentation by sending email or by posting a link to the presentation on a webpage or social networking site. The attendees will see your document in Word Web App in their web browsers.

Post or send invitations

1 Open the document that you want to present and then click File to display the Backstage view.

2 Click the Share tab and then click Present Online. Then, click the Present Online button.

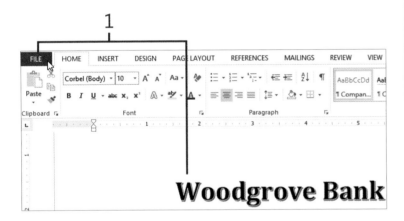

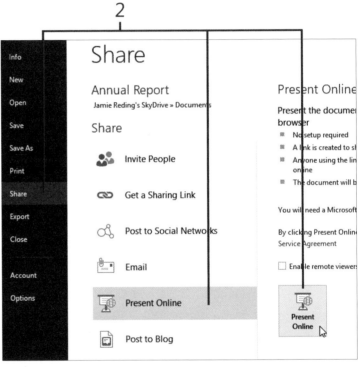

TIP   If you want to allow the attendees to download your document, select the Enable Remote Viewers To Download The Document check box. Otherwise, they will be able to print the document to a PDF file, but they won't be able to download it as an editable Word document.

3 Word 2013 uploads your document to the presentation service and then displays a link to the server. Click the Send In Email option to start a message in your default email program, enter the email addresses of the people whom you want to invite to the presentation, and then send the message.

Alternatively, you can click Copy Link and then paste the link on a webpage or a social network such as Twitter.

Start the presentation

1 When attendees click the link to the presentation, your document opens in Word Web App in their web browsers.

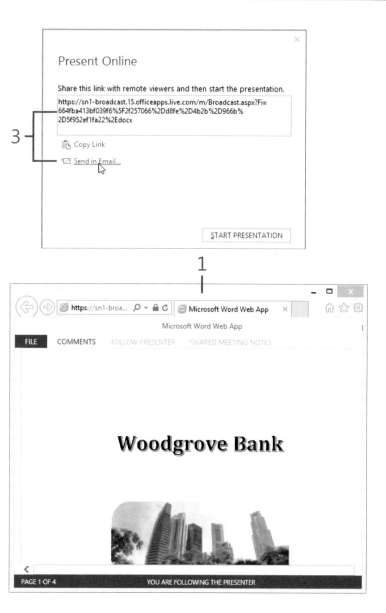

2 Click the Start Presentation button.

As you scroll through the document, the copies in the attendees' browsers will scroll correspondingly.

3 If you need to make changes in the document during the presentation, on the Present Online tab, in the Present Online group, click Edit. When the changes are complete, click the Resume button in the Online Presentation Paused banner.

4 When the session is completed, on the Present Online tab, in the Present Online group, click End Online Presentation. In the prompt, click End Online Presentation.

The attendees see a black screen that displays the message "The presentation has ended".

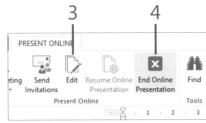

> ✓ **TIP** One type of change that you can make is to add comments by clicking the Review tab and clicking New Comment. The attendees see a comment balloon in the right margin of the document, which they can click to read the contents in the Comments pane.

> ⚠ **CAUTION** Some email programs insert a line break in the middle of the very long URL of the presentation, so clicking the link doesn't work. If this happens, instruct the attendees to copy the entire URL and paste it into the address box of their browsers.

> ✓ **TIP** The presentation service doesn't offer audio, and it doesn't notify you when attendees join or leave the session. It's important to set up an audio conferencing session to accompany the Word presentation. An alternative is to use Microsoft Lync for your presentations.

Ensuring privacy and security

15

Microsoft Office 2013 includes many measures that are intended to protect your computer and your data from viruses and other malicious attacks. It also helps you to protect your personal and confidential information from being revealed by accident. Most of these protections operate silently, and their default settings are nearly always appropriate; there are relatively few adjustments that you can or should make.

There are many ways that personal information in a Microsoft Word document can be temporarily hidden from view, so there is a risk that another user could discover it without your knowledge. An important safeguard is the Document Inspector. The Inspector will inform you whether the document contains occurrences of personal or confidential information, and you can opt to remove any that it finds.

You can control whether other users can edit a document at all. You can also permit others to edit only certain parts of a document. In this section, you'll learn about several ways to restrict editing, protect documents against unauthorized changes, and mark documents as final versions.

In this section:

- Viewing the Word 2013 Trust Center
- Changing which files open in Protected View
- Adding trusted locations and trusted publishers
- Setting privacy options
- Using the Document Inspector
- Protecting a document by using a password
- Restricting editing and formatting
- Marking a document as read-only or final
- Adding a digital signature

Viewing the Word 2013 Trust Center

Each Office 2013 application includes a Trust Center in its Options dialog box. The Trust Center gathers many of the settings that control privacy and protection against security threats. Most of the default settings in the Trust Center are appropriate and should not be changed except in special circumstances.

Open the Trust Center settings page

1 Click File to display the Backstage view and then click the Options tab.

2 In the Word Options dialog box, click the Trust Center tab and then click Trust Center Settings.

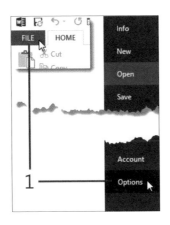

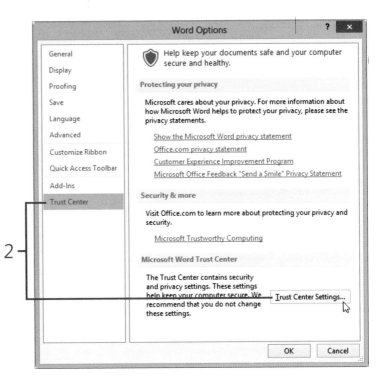

Changing which files open in Protected View

Files that you download from sites on the Internet and from other potentially unsafe locations can contain viruses or other kinds of malware. To help protect your computer, Word 2013 normally opens files from potentially unsafe locations in *Protected View*. Protected View is a read-only mode in which most editing functions are disabled, and the document is displayed in Read Mode. In Protected View, you can inspect a document's contents while reducing the risk of damage. If you know the document is safe, you can exit Protected View and edit it as you would normally.

Protected View can be annoying, particularly if you're always careful not to open suspicious files and don't need this view

to check each file. For example, documents that you create on SkyDrive and later download to your desktop are considered to come from the Internet, and thus they open in Protected View. Documents that you receive as attachments to email messages also open in Protected View. Under some circumstances, documents from older versions of Word might open in Protected View or might not be allowed to open at all. In all of these situations, you can change the settings in Word to allow the documents to open normally when you know that the files are safe. You can still use Protected View to open documents about which you're unsure.

Exit Protected View

1 If the yellow Protected View message bar appears when you open a document, and you know the document is safe, click the Enable Editing button on the message bar.

If you aren't sure about the document's safety, or if you don't need to edit it, you can leave the document in Protected View until you close it.

 TIP The wording of the Protected View message depends on which of several rules caused Protected View to occur.

2 If the red Protected View message bar appears when you open a document, the document did not pass a validation process that Office applies to every file you open. This can occur if the file is damaged by a hardware or software problem or it was modified for a malicious purpose. If the file is suspicious or unknown, the best action is to close the document and delete it from your computer. If you know the document's creator, request another copy of the file.

If you decide to try to edit the document despite the warning, click File to display the Info tab of the Backstage view, and then click Edit Anyway.

2

❌ PROTECTED VIEW   Office has detected a problem with this file. Editing it may harm your computer. Click for more details.

> ✅ **TIP**   If you click Edit Anyway to open a damaged document, the document might still fail to open. The behavior depends on the type of damage the file has suffered.

Change the Protected View settings

1 Open the Trust Center as described in "Open the Trust Center settings page" on page 382.

2 In the Trust Center dialog box, in the panel on the left, click the Protected View tab.

3 If you open document files that you download from the Internet (including SkyDrive) only when you know that they're safe, clear the check box for Enable Protected View For Files Originating From The Internet.

4 If you open document files that you receive as email attachments only when you know that they're safe, clear the check box for Enable Protected View For Outlook Attachments.

5 Click OK.

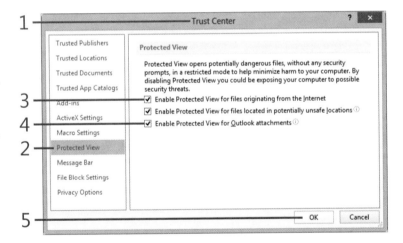

> ✅ **TIP**   It's a good idea to keep the check box selected for Enable Protected View For Files Located In Potentially Unsafe Locations. These locations include folders, such as the Temporary Internet Files folder, from which you can't be sure of a file's history.

> ✅ **TIP**   When you click the Enable Editing button on the message bar to allow editing of a document, that document automatically becomes trusted. When you open the same document in the future, it won't open in Protected View.

Change the File Block settings

1 If the Protected View message bar appears when you open a document created by an older version of Word, and if the message mentions your File Block settings, you can change the settings to allow editing of that type of document. Open the Trust Center as described in "Open the Trust Center settings page" on page 382.

2 In the Trust Center dialog box, in the panel on the left, click the File Block Settings tab.

3 In the Open column, clear the check box for the type of file that you want to open. If you want to enable saving of changes to the file in the same format, also clear the check box in the Save column, if any.

4 Select one of the following option buttons:

- **Do Not Open Selected File Types** If you try to open a file of a type that has been selected in the Open column (one that displays a check mark), a message box appears and the document does not open.

- **Open Selected File Types In Protected View** If you open a file of a type that has been selected in the Open column, the file opens in Protected View, but the Enable Editing button on the message bar is not available.

- **Open Selected File Types In Protected View And Allow Editing** If you open a file of a type that has been selected in the Open column, the file opens in Protected View and the Enable Editing button on the message bar is available.

5 Click OK.

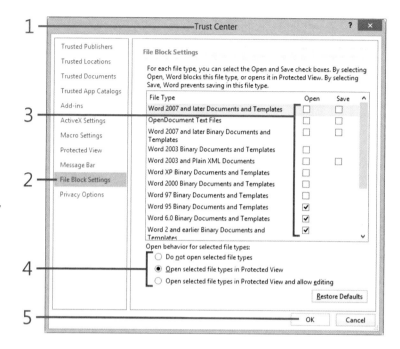

 TIP If the Protected View message bar displays a red shield instead of a yellow shield, the File Block settings cannot allow editing of the document.

 SEE ALSO For more information about File Block settings, see *office.microsoft.com/en-us/word-help/what-is-file-block-HA010355927.aspx*.

Enable Protected View for specific files

1 If you disabled Protected View for one or more types of files, you can enable it when you open a file that might not be safe. Click File to display the Backstage view and then click the Open tab. Select the location, such as your computer or SkyDrive, and click Browse.

2 In the Open dialog box, go to the folder that contains the document that you want to open and click the file's icon to select it.

3 Click the drop-down arrow on the Open button. On the shortcut menu that appears, click Open In Protected View.

4 The document opens in Protected View.

Don't click the Enable Editing button unless you can determine that the document is safe.

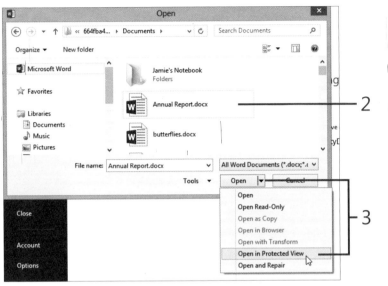

Adding trusted locations and trusted publishers

Some documents and templates might have active content (macros, ActiveX controls, data connections, and so forth). Although this content is often very useful, it can also be used for malicious purposes. When you open a document with active content or start a new document based on a template with active content, the default behavior of Word is to disable the active content and notify you on the message bar.

If you know the source of the active content and trust its safety, you can avoid this inconvenience. One way to do that is to store the file in a folder that is designated as a *trusted location*. Any file that you put in a trusted location can be opened without being checked by the Trust Center security feature.

Another way to avoid disabling active content is to designate a particular source as a *trusted publisher*. When a software developer creates a macro, ActiveX control, or other active content, the developer can apply a digital signature to the code. That signature contains information about the developer's identity, the certificate authority (usually a company such as VeriSign, Inc.) that issued the certificate used to create the digital signature, and the signature's expiration date. If the signature is valid, you can designate that developer as a trusted publisher, and all active content signed with the same certificate will be enabled.

Trust a file location

1 Open the Trust Center as described in "Open the Trust Center settings page" on page 382.

2 In the Trust Center dialog box, in the panel on the left, click the Trusted Locations tab.

3 If you plan to trust a location on a network drive, select the check box for Allow Trusted Locations On My Network.

4 Click the Add New Location button.

> ⚠ **CAUTION** It is generally recommended that you not trust network locations, and especially public folders, because of the security risk that they represent.

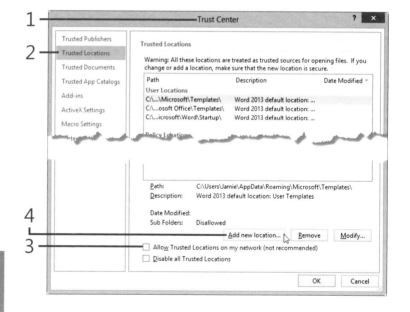

5 In the Microsoft Office Trusted Location dialog box, click in the Path box and type the full path to the desired folder, or click the Browse button, locate the folder, and then click OK.

6 If you want to trust all subfolders of the location, select the Subfolders Of This Location Are Also Trusted check box. If desired, enter a description that will appear in the Trusted Locations dialog box.

7 Click OK in each dialog box.

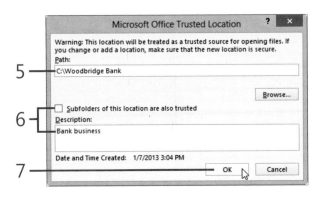

Trust a publisher

1 Open a document that has disabled active content from the publisher.

2 Click the File tab to display the Backstage view.

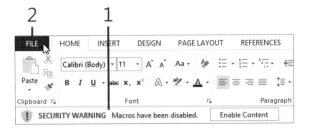

3 On the Info tab of the Backstage view, click the Enable Content button.

4 On the menu that appears, click Advanced Options.

5 In the Microsoft Office Security Options dialog box, click the Trust All Documents From This Publisher option and then click OK.

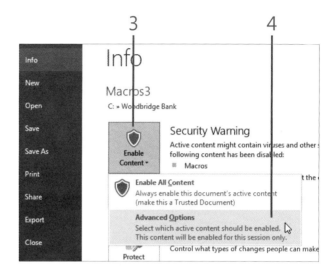

TIP If the option button for Trust All Documents From This Publisher doesn't appear, the publisher's certificate might be invalid or the digital signature might be missing.

Setting privacy options

Word 2013 uses the Internet to communicate with Microsoft and other locations for assorted purposes. When you download a template, insert online pictures or videos, or use the Research pane or the online translator, Word must use your Internet connection. You can enable or disable these and other functions that use the Internet.

There are several options designed to help you prevent the accidental inclusion of personal or confidential information in documents that you might send to other computers.

Control how Word uses the Internet

1   Open the Trust Center as described in "Open the Trust Center settings page" on page 382.

2   In the Trust Center dialog box, in the panel on the left, click the Privacy Options tab.

3   Select or clear the check boxes in the Privacy Options section of the dialog box as desired.

It is generally safe to leave all of these check boxes selected. However, to minimize network traffic, you might want to clear most of them. You should not clear the option for Allow Office To Connect To The Internet, because doing so disables the Online Pictures, Online Video, and Apps For Office commands on the Insert tab. It also prevents the display of templates from Office.com on the New tab of the Backstage view.

4   Click OK.

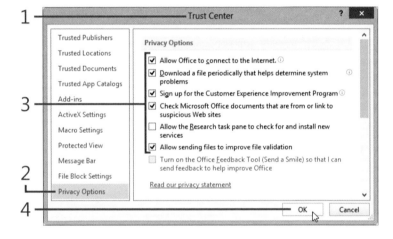

> **TIP**   The Customer Experience Improvement Program collects anonymous data about which features of Office you use. That information is part of the input used by Microsoft to design the next version. Participating in the program is one way you can vote for your most-used features.

Change privacy settings for documents

1 Open the Trust Center as described in "Open the Trust Center settings page" on page 382.

2 In the Trust Center dialog box, in the panel on the left, click the Privacy Options tab.

3 In the Document-Specific Settings section, select or clear the check boxes as desired.

The option Warn Before Printing, Saving Or Sending A File That Contains Tracked Changes Or Comments is intended to remind you that personal or confidential information might be in the document, especially when you can't see the information because of the markup setting or because there are no changes or comments on the current page.

If you clear the check box for Store Random Numbers To Improve Combine Accuracy, you won't be able to edit the document simultaneously with coauthors.

Selecting the Make Hidden Markup Visible When Opening Or Saving check box also helps to prevent the release of sensitive information.

4 Click OK.

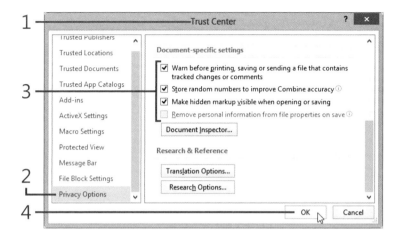

> ✓ **TIP** An alternative to launching the Document Inspector from the Backstage view (described in "Inspect a document" on page 392) is to click the Document Inspector button in the Privacy Options dialog box.

> ✓ **TIP** The Remove Personal Information From File Properties On Save check box is available only if the document came from Word 2003 or earlier and the equivalent option was selected in that version.

Using the Document Inspector

Before you send a document to another user or share it in a public folder, you should use the Document Inspector to find and remove any personal or confidential information that should not be disclosed.

Sensitive data might be in comments or tracked changes, which you might not notice if the document is set to show Simple Markup or No Markup. Names, dates, and other information might be found in document properties, in text under headings that are collapsed, or in text that is formatted as hidden. The Document Inspector can search for these locations and more. If the Document Inspector finds these types of locations, it offers to remove them. In some cases—for example, text under collapsed headings—the removal of all the locations would be wrong. Instead, you should examine the document and remove only sensitive information.

Inspect a document

1 Click File to display the Info tab of the Backstage view.

2 Click the Check For Issues button and then, on the menu that appears, click Inspect Document.

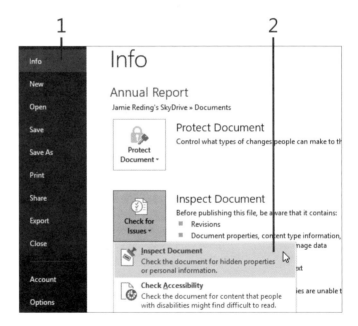

3 In the Document Inspector dialog box, clear the check box for any type of content for which you don't want the Document Inspector to search, and then click Inspect.

4 When the inspection is complete and the Document Inspector dialog box reappears, click the Remove All button next to any type of content that you want to remove from the document.

5 To verify that the document has been cleaned, click the Reinspect button. Otherwise, click Close.

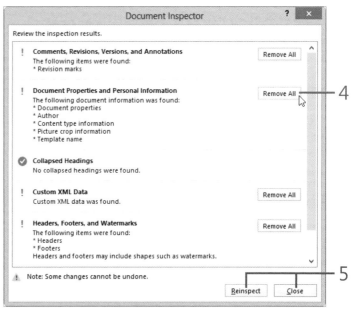

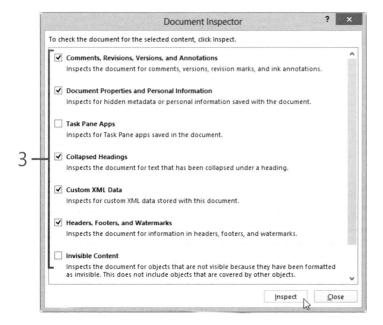

TIP If you remove Document Properties And Personal Information, but you don't remove Comments, Revisions, Versions, And Annotations, the names attached to all tracked changes and comments are replaced by *Author*, and the dates and times of the changes and comments are removed.

Protecting a document by using a password

You might have some documents that should never be opened by unauthorized people. To protect such documents from prying eyes, you can save them in an encrypted form that can't be opened without a password. Or, perhaps you want to create a document that anyone can open and read, but you need to restrict those people from making any changes unless they know a password. With Word 2013, you can assign passwords of either or both types.

When someone tries to open an encrypted document, Word requests the password. If the text the person enters is incorrect, Word will not open the document. If you try to read the document file outside of Word, it just appears to be gibberish.

If someone tries to open a document that requires a password to modify it, but he doesn't have that password, the document opens as read-only. In that case, editing is allowed but the document cannot be saved in the original file; the user would need to save the document to a new, separate file.

Set a password to open or edit

1 Open an existing document or create a new document that you want to password protect.

2 Click File to open the Backstage view and then click the Save As tab. Select a location (such as Computer or SkyDrive) and select or browse to the folder in which to save the file.

If this is the first time an unnamed document is being saved, the Save command automatically opens the Save As tab of the Backstage view.

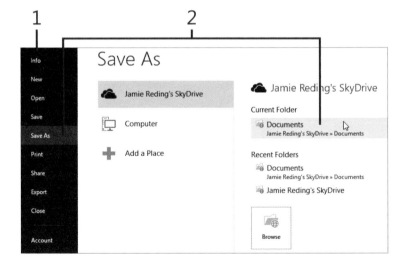

3 At the bottom of the Save As dialog box, click Tools and then, on the menu that appears, click General Options.

4 In the General Options dialog box, click in the Password To Open text box and type the desired password for opening the document.

5 Click in the Password To Modify text box and type the desired password for modifying the document.

6 Click OK.

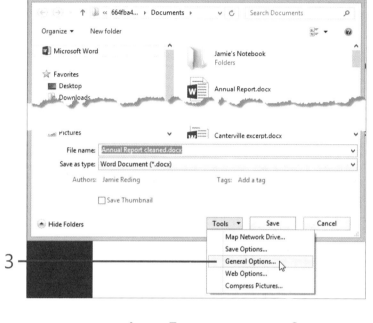

3 —

4 5 6

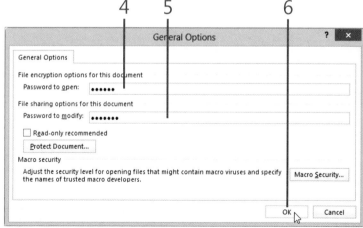

⚠ **CAUTION** If you apply a password for opening the document, the file is encrypted as it is saved on the drive. If you forget the password, the document cannot be reopened.

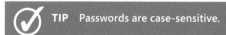 **TIP** Passwords are case-sensitive.

7 Type the password for opening the document a second time as confirmation and then click OK.

8 Type the password for modifying the document a second time as confirmation and then click OK.

9 In the Save As dialog, verify or change the file name and file type, and click Save.

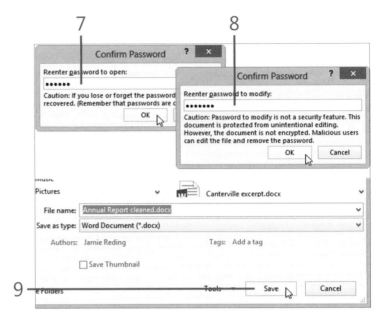

✓ **TIP** To remove passwords from a document, use the same procedure again, but delete the password entries in the General Options dialog box and leave the boxes blank.

→ **TRY THIS** You can also set a password for opening the document as follows: click File to display the Info tab of the Backstage view. Click the Protect Document button and then, in the drop-down list that appears, click Encrypt With Password. However, the Encrypt Document dialog box that you open by this procedure doesn't give you access to the password for editing the document.

Restricting editing and formatting

If your project requires collecting documents from coauthors to compile a larger document, it's helpful to ensure that everyone uses the same styles and that there is little or no direct formatting if the text. With Word 2013, you can specify a set of styles that are allowed and prevent any other formatting. This arrangement works best when you create this formatting restriction in a template and then distribute the template to the coauthors.

Word also supports several ways to restrict editing. You can ensure that all changes made in the document are tracked, you can allow changes only in specified areas of the document, or you can disable all changes except for comments.

Limit formatting to selected styles

1 On the Review tab, in the Protect group, click Restrict Editing.

2 In the Restrict Editing pane, select the Limit Formatting To A Selection Of Styles check box.

3 Click the Settings link.

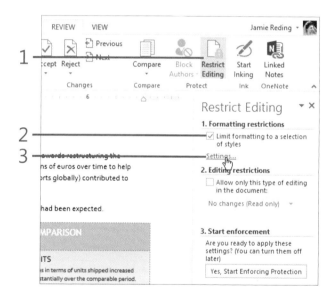

4 In the Formatting Restrictions dialog box, in the list of styles, select the check box next to any style that you want to allow to be used; clear the check boxes for the styles that you want to restrict. Use the All button or the None button to start with all styles allowed or with all styles disabled.

5 In the Formatting section of the dialog box, select any of the three check boxes, according to your preferences.

6 Click OK.

7 In the Restrict Editing pane, click the Yes, Start Enforcing Protection button.

8 If you want to require a password to turn off the formatting restrictions, in the Start Enforcing Protection dialog box, enter the password twice in the corresponding boxes. If you don't want a password, leave the boxes blank.

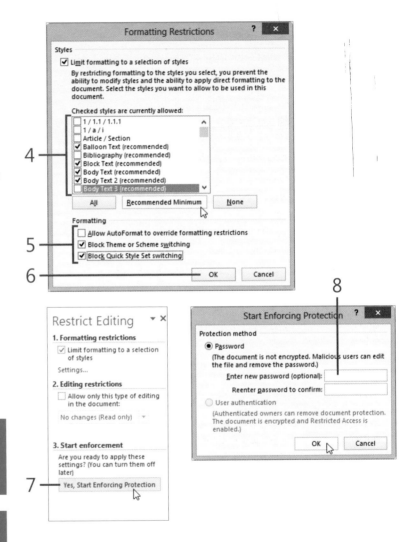

> ✓ **TIP** The set of styles selected by clicking the Recommended Minimum button is a good starting point, although you might want to change that list for your document. The Normal style isn't in the list, because it is always allowed.

> ✓ **TIP** When you apply formatting restrictions, all direct formatting is disabled. To be able to apply character formatting such as bold and italic, enable the corresponding character styles such as Strong and Emphasis.

Limit the type of editing

1 On the Review tab, in the Protect group, click Restrict Editing.

2 In the Restrict Editing pane, select the Allow Only This Type Of Editing In The Document check box.

3 Click the list box below the check box and select one of the following:

- **Tracked Changes** Behaves the same way as the Lock Tracking command described in "Lock tracking" on page 356

- **Comments** Disables all editing and formatting except adding, deleting, or replying to comments

- **Filling In Forms** Disables all editing and formatting except within legacy form fields

- **No Changes (Read Only)** Disables all editing and formatting

4 If you selected either Comments or No Changes (Read Only) in step 3, the Exceptions section appears in the Restrict Editing pane. Select one or more areas of the document (hold the Ctrl key while you select noncontiguous areas) and then select the Everyone check box.

You can specify individuals instead of Everyone by clicking the More Users link and entering their email addresses or domain names.

5 In the Restrict Editing pane, click the Yes, Start Enforcing Protection button. In the Start Enforcing Protection dialog box that opens, if you want to require a password to turn off the formatting restrictions, enter the password twice in the text boxes. If you don't want a password, leave the boxes blank.

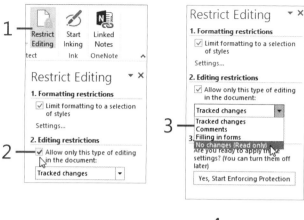

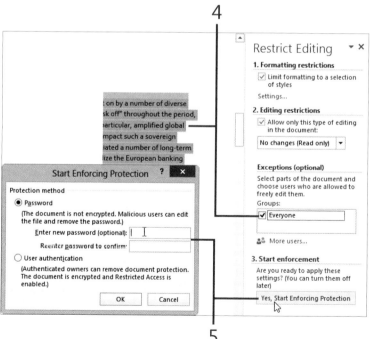

Marking a document as read-only or final

When you pass a document to other users, you might want to indicate that the document is in its final form, and that no changes should be made to it without authorization. Word 2013 offers two ways to specify this state.

When you make a document read-only recommended, anyone who opens the document first sees the message *The author would like you to open this as read-only unless you need to make changes. Open as read-only?* If the user clicks the Yes button,

the document opens in Read Mode. The user can switch to Print Layout view and edit the document. However, if any changes are made, the document can be saved only to a new, separate file with a different file name(or the same name, but to a different location).

When you mark a document as final, all changes are disabled and the document is also marked as read-only. The user must take specific action to enable editing and saving of the document.

Make a document read-only recommended

1 Click File to display the Backstage view and then click the Save As tab. Select a location (such as Computer or SkyDrive) and select or browse to the folder in which to save the file.

   If this is the first time an unnamed document is being saved, the Save command automatically opens the Save As tab of the Backstage view.

2 At the bottom of the Save As dialog box, click Tools and then, on the menu that appears, click General Options.

3 In the General Options dialog box, select the Read-Only Recommended check box and click OK.

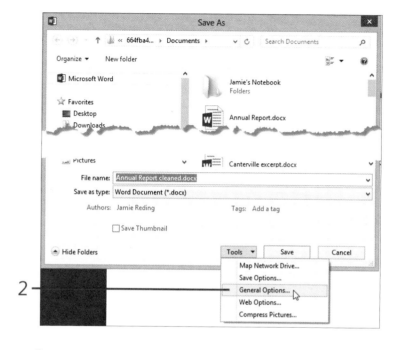

2 —

3

Mark a document as final

1 Click File to display the Info tab of the Backstage view.

2 Click Protect Document and then, on the menu that appears, click Mark As Final.

3 In the pop-up message box that appears, click OK.

4 The Marked As Final message bar appears below the ribbon whenever you open the document. If you need to edit the document, click the Edit Anyway button on the message bar. When you click that button, the Final marking and the Read-Only state are turned off.

1

2

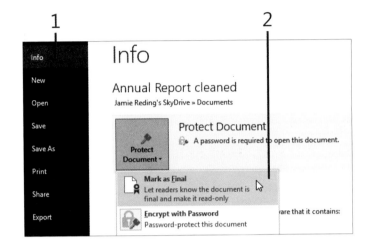

3

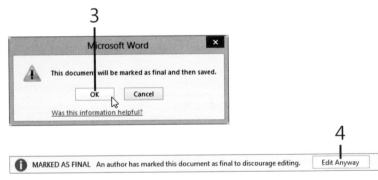

4

Adding a digital signature

When a document is signed with a digital signature, you can be sure that the document's contents have not been changed after it was signed. Any editing or tampering with the document will cause the digital signature to be removed or to be marked as invalid.

To add a digital signature, you must first have a *signing certificate*. You can obtain a signing certificate from a certificate authority such as VeriSign, Inc., or your organization might have a local certificate server that can supply one.

Add a digital signature to a document

1 Click File to display the Info tab of the Backstage view.

2 Click Protect Document and then, on the menu that appears, click Add A Digital Signature.

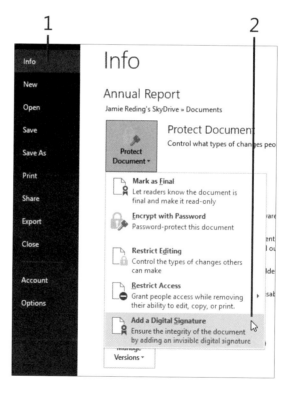

3 In the Sign dialog box, click the Commitment Type box and select one of the values.

4 If desired, type a description in the text box for Purpose For Signing This Document.

5 If desired, click the Details button and enter your title and address.

6 If the name in the Signing As section isn't the one for the certificate you want to use, click the Change button and select another certificate.

7 Click the Sign button.

	Sign	?	×

ⓘ See additional information about what you are signing...

You are about to add a digital signature to this document. This signature will not be visible within the content of this document.

Commitment Type:

3 —— Created this document ▼

Purpose for signing this document:

4 —— Security

5 —— To include information about the signer, click the details button.   Details...

6 —— Signing as: Woodbridge   Change...

7 —— Sign   Cancel

⚠ **CAUTION** Office 2013 includes a program named SelfCert.exe that can create certificates for signing your macro projects. Because these certificates aren't issued by a certificate authority and don't prove your identity, they are not usable for signing documents.

→ **TRY THIS** A digital signature added by this procedure isn't visible in the document. However, you can place a visible signature in the document, associated with a digital signature. On the Insert tab, in the Text group, click Signature Line. When the signature line appears in the document, right-click it and then, on the shortcut menu that appears, click Sign. In the Sign dialog box, type or ink your name, or choose a picture of your signature. At the bottom of the dialog box, select the certificate to use to create the digital signature.

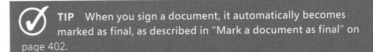

✓ **TIP** When you sign a document, it automatically becomes marked as final, as described in "Mark a document as final" on page 402.

Installing and using Apps for Office

16

In this section:

- Adding an app from the Office Store
- Using an app in a document

Microsoft Office 2013 includes a new feature called Apps for Office and SharePoint. An App for Office is a web-based program that appears within an Office application's window and interacts with your documents. Typically, an app recognizes text that you select in a document and displays information about it, which you can insert into the document or use in other ways.

Examples of Apps for Office include dictionaries and reference works, calculators, templates and forms, file format converters, and news. Apps for Office are available only online from the Microsoft Office Store. Many of them cost nothing to install and use; others are paid products. New Apps for Office are frequently added to the Office Store.

Because the app is stored on a server in the cloud, it's available to you anywhere that you can log on to your Microsoft Account.

Adding an app from the Office Store

You can add an App for Office to your Microsoft Account directly from within the Microsoft Word 2013 program, or you can visit the website for the Office Store.

Some Apps for Office can be used in Word 2013 and in other Office 2013 programs. However, many apps are specific to one Office program. You can click a link on the Office Store to narrow the display to only the apps that are compatible with Word.

Visit the Office Store

1 On the Insert tab, in the Apps group, click the Apps For Office button.

   The top half of the button immediately opens the Apps for Office dialog box. The drop-down arrow in the bottom half of the button opens a gallery of recently used apps (if any), and a See All command at the bottom of the gallery opens the Apps for Office dialog box.

2 In the Apps For Office dialog box, click the My Apps link to display the apps (if any) that are already associated with your Microsoft Account.

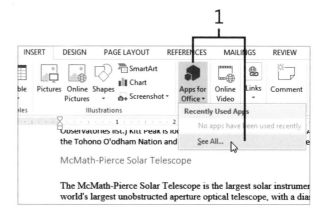

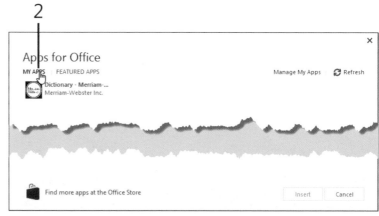

3 Click the Featured Apps link to display thumbnails of the apps that are current Editor's Picks. Scroll down to see thumbnails of apps that were most recently added to the Office Store.

4 In the Featured Apps display, click the More Apps link to open the Office Store website in your default browser.

5 In either the Apps For Office dialog box or the Office Store website, when you see a thumbnail for an app that seems interesting, click the thumbnail to view a page with a description, a list of requirements, and any reviews that users have submitted.

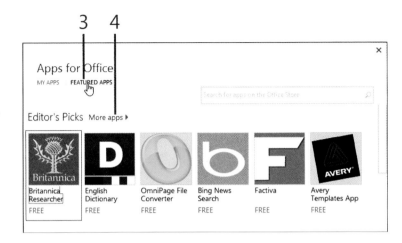

SEE ALSO To visit the Office Store website when an Office 2013 application isn't available, go to *office.microsoft.com/store*.

Adding an app from the Office Store: Visit the Office Store **407**

Install an App for Office

1 Go to the Office Store as described in "Visit the Office Store" on page 406. In the Office Store website, on the description page for an app that you want to install, click the Add button.

2 If you aren't already logged on to your Microsoft Account, enter your name and password.

3 On the confirmation page, click the Continue button.

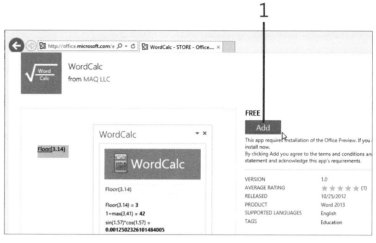

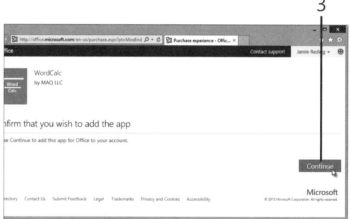

Manage Apps for Office

1 On the Insert tab, in the Apps group, click the top part of the Apps For Office button.

2 Click the Manage My Apps link.

3 If you aren't already logged on to your Microsoft Account, enter your name and password.

4 If you want to hide an app so that it isn't offered in the Office applications, in the Action column for that app, click the Hide link.

5 If you have hidden any apps and you want to make them visible again, click the Hidden link.

6 To make a hidden app visible, in the Action column, click the Retrieve link for that app.

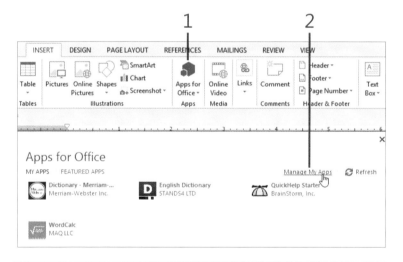

TIP After you retrieve a hidden app, if that app doesn't appear in the Apps For Office dialog box, in the upper-right corner of the dialog box, click the Refresh link.

Using an app in a document

In Word 2013, an App for Office opens a task pane that contains the text boxes, buttons, or other objects that you use to work with the app. Apps vary widely in the ways that they interact with your documents. Typically, though, they accept any text that you select in the document as their input, and they display some text in the task pane as a result. You might be able to click a button to make the task pane's result replace the selected text, or you might need to copy the result to the clipboard and paste it where you want it.

Activate an app

1 On the Insert tab, in the Apps group, click the drop-down arrow on the Apps For Office button.

2 If the app you want to activate appears in the drop-down list, click its name and continue at step 5.

3 At the bottom of the Apps For Office drop-down list, click the See All command. (Or, you can click the top part of the Apps For Office button.)

4 Click the icon or name of the app that you want to activate and then click the Insert button.

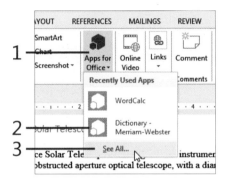

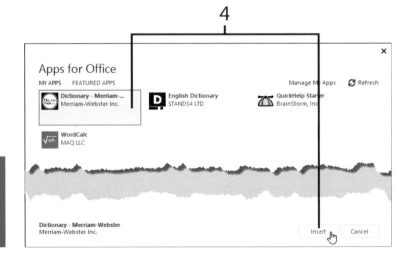

> **TIP** To drag the task pane into the document area or dock it to the other side of the Word window, hold your cursor over the task pane's title until it changes to a four-way arrow. You can then move the pane where you want. Also, while the task pane is undocked, you can drag its sides to resize it.

5 Select text in your document, or click a button or icon in the app's task pane, depending on the app's instructions.

6 To close the task pane, in its upper-right corner, click the X button.

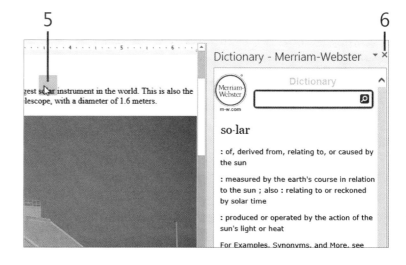

5

6

TIP There are other kinds of Apps for Office and SharePoint, called *content apps*, which display directly in a document rather than in a task pane. In Office 2013, content apps are supported only in Excel 2013 and in Excel Web App. There are also *mail apps*, which are supported only in Outlook 2013.

SEE ALSO For more information about Apps for Office, see *technet.microsoft.com/en-us/library/jj219429.aspx*.

Customizing Word 17

You can customize almost every part of Microsoft Word 2013 to match your preferences, no matter how unique your work requirement and methods might be. The tabs, groups, and tools on the ribbon; the buttons on the Quick Access Toolbar; and the default locations of document files can all be modified.

In addition, the Word Options dialog box contains settings that modify the way Word 2013 displays, prints, saves, and edits documents. You can control how your spelling and grammar are checked, and you can protect your documents against possible loss of data.

Styles are central to the way Word documents are formatted, and different types of documents need different groups of styles. By learning to use the Manage Styles dialog box, you can control which styles appear in the Styles pane and the Quick Style gallery on the Home tab. You can also determine the order in which they are sorted.

In this section:

- Customizing the screen
- Customizing the keyboard
- Customizing the Quick Access Toolbar
- Customizing the ribbon
- Setting general options
- Controlling what is displayed and printed
- Setting spelling and grammar options
- Changing the default file format for saving documents
- Working with advanced options
- Managing styles
- Recording macros

Customizing the screen

You can change the way Word 2013 displays many of its tools so that they suit the way you work. If you find that you're distracted by the ribbon and other items that appear by default, you can reduce the clutter to the minimum. Alternatively, if you prefer to reduce the number of clicks needed to work on documents, you can make all of the tools visible.

In addition to the options mentioned here, there are many display choices available in the Word Options dialog box (these are discussed in "Show or hide information on screen and on paper" on page 429).

Show or hide items on the status bar

1 Right-click the status bar to display the Customize Status Bar shortcut menu.

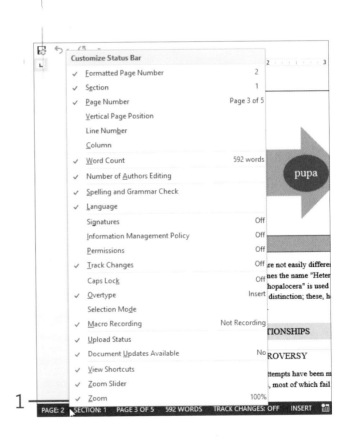

> **TIP** For many of the items on the Customize Status Bar shortcut menu, when you change their state, the corresponding text or icon either appears or disappears immediately. However, some icons—for example, Number Of Authors Editing and Selection Mode—will not appear even after they're enabled unless there is some information for them to show.

2 Click any item on the shortcut menu to add or clear the check mark to the left of the item.

3 Click anywhere outside the shortcut menu to dismiss it.

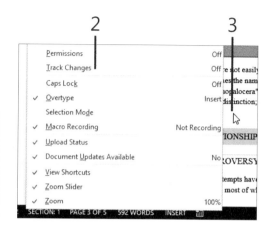

> ✓ **TIP** The Formatted Page Number item shows the number that would be displayed by a Page field on the current page. It is affected by the restarted numbering that you can apply in the Format Page Numbers dialog box. Conversely, the Page Number item shows the count of pages from the beginning of the document to the current page as well as the number of pages in the whole document.

Show or minimize the ribbon

1 Right-click anywhere on the ribbon and then, on the shortcut menu that appears, click Collapse The Ribbon.

2 When the ribbon is minimized, right-click any of the tabs and then, on the shortcut menu, click Collapse The Ribbon to clear the check mark to its left.

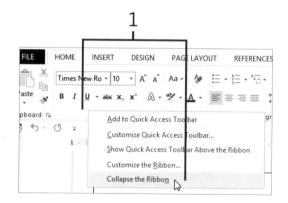

> ✓ **TIP** Other ways of showing and hiding the ribbon include clicking the up-arrow at the right end of the ribbon, pressing the keyboard shortcut Ctrl+F1, and double-clicking any tab.

> 🔍 **SEE ALSO** For information about auto-hiding the ribbon, see "Hide the ribbon" on page 15.

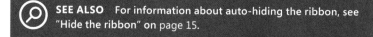
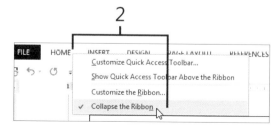

Show or hide white space

1 If the document isn't already in Print Layout view, on the View tab, in the Views group, click Print Layout. Hold the cursor over the space between the bottom of one page and the top of the next page so that the cursor changes to a pair of boxes containing arrows pointing toward one another.

2 Double-click to collapse the space between pages and to hide any header or footer.

3 Double-click the collapsed space between pages to restore the space and any header or footer.

Customizing the keyboard

Much of the work that you do in Word 2013 typically consists of typing text. When your hands are on the keyboard, it can be time-consuming and disruptive to reach for the mouse to select and format text, copy and paste, or do other tasks that involve buttons on the ribbon. By remembering a small set of keyboard shortcuts, you can greatly increase your efficiency.

There is a list of common built-in keyboard shortcuts in "Use keyboard shortcuts" on page 18, and many other commands

also have default keyboard shortcuts. When you find that you often use a command that doesn't have a keyboard shortcut, you can assign a shortcut of your own.

Keyboard shortcuts in Word aren't limited to commands. You can also assign keyboard shortcuts to macros, styles, fonts, building blocks, and symbols.

Assign a keyboard shortcut to a command

1 Click File to display the Backstage view and then click the Options tab. In the Word Options dialog box, in the left panel, click Customize Ribbon.

2 Toward the bottom of the dialog box, click the Customize button.

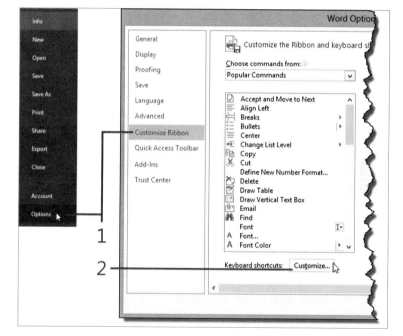

3 In the Customize Keyboard dialog box, if the open document is based on a custom template, and you want the new keyboard shortcut to apply only to documents based on that custom template, click the Save Changes In list box and select the template's name. Otherwise, leave Normal.dotm selected.

4 Click one of the following items in the Categories list:

- If the command to which you want to assign a keyboard shortcut is visible on one of the tabs of the ribbon, click the name of that tab.

- If the command to which you want to assign a keyboard shortcut is not visible on any of the tabs of the ribbon, or if you aren't sure which tab contains the command, click All Commands.

- If you want to assign a keyboard shortcut to a macro, a font, a building block, a style, or one of a small set of common symbols, click the corresponding item at the bottom of the list.

5 In the Commands list, click the command to which you want to assign a keyboard shortcut.

If you selected one of the items at the bottom of the Categories list in step 4, the label above the Commands list changes to the name of the category you selected.

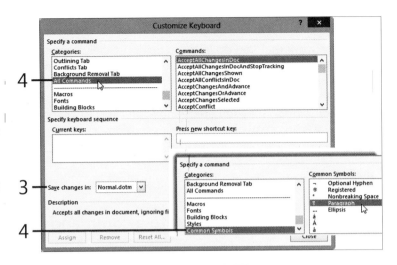

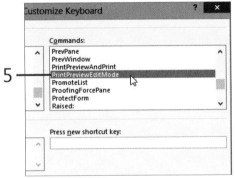

TIP If the keyboard shortcut that you press is already assigned to another command, the message *Currently assigned to: command name* (where *command name* is the actual command) appears below the Current Keys list box. If you want to leave the keyboard shortcut assigned to its original command, delete the contents of the Press New Shortcut Key text box and then press a different shortcut. Otherwise, the keyboard shortcut will be removed from the original command and assigned to the new command.

6 Click the Press New Shortcut Key text box and then press the key or group of keys that you want to use as the keyboard shortcut for the selected command.

7 Click Assign.

8 If the selected command has a keyboard shortcut that you no longer want, click that keyboard shortcut in the Current Keys list box and then click the Remove button.

9 While the Customize Keyboard dialog box remains open, you can assign more keyboard shortcuts. When you have assigned all the shortcuts that you want, click Close.

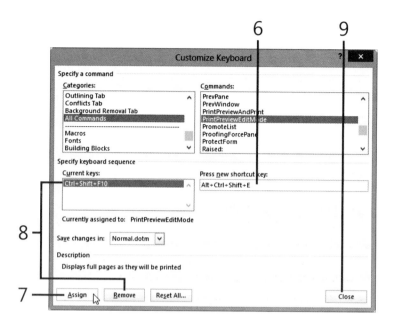

Assign a shortcut to a symbol

1 If the symbol to which you want to assign a keyboard shortcut is not one of those in the Common Symbols category, on the ribbon, click the Insert tab. Then, in the Symbols group, click Symbol. At the bottom of the drop-down gallery that appears, click More Symbols.

2 Click the Font list box and then click the name of the font that contains the symbol you want.

3 Click the symbol that you want.

4 Click Shortcut Key.

5 In the Customize Keyboard dialog box, place the cursor in the Press New Shortcut Key text box and then press the key or group of keys that you want to use as the keyboard shortcut for the selected symbol.

6 Click Assign and then click Close.

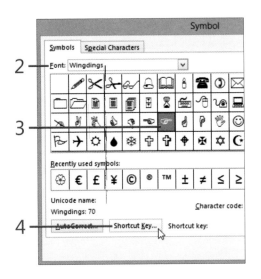

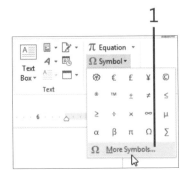

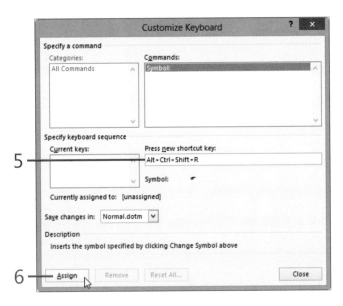

→ TRY THIS When you click a symbol in the Symbol dialog box, a label next to the Shortcut Key button shows the built-in keyboard shortcut (if any) for that symbol. For some symbols it is of the form **Alt+number**, which means that you hold the Alt key while typing the number on the numeric keypad (with Num Lock turned on). For other symbols it is of the form **number, Alt+X**, which means that you type the number as ordinary text in the document and then press Alt+X.

Customizing the Quick Access Toolbar

The Quick Access Toolbar is a place where you can put buttons for frequently used commands. This makes it easy for you to reach them no matter which tab is selected on the ribbon. It's very easy to add and remove buttons on the Quick Access Toolbar. You can add any command or group that appears on the ribbon and many more that don't appear there.

Although the Quick Access Toolbar initially sits in the title bar above the ribbon, you can move it below the ribbon. In that position the toolbar is closer to your document, and it can hold more buttons.

Add a ribbon item to the Quick Access Toolbar

1 On the ribbon, right-click the tool that you want to add to the Quick Access Toolbar.

2 On the shortcut menu that appears, click Add To Quick Access Toolbar.

If you clicked a thumbnail in a gallery on the ribbon, such as the Styles gallery on the Home tab, the shortcut menu shows Add Gallery To Quick Access Toolbar. Individual thumbnails can't be added to the Quick Access Toolbar.

3 To remove a tool from the Quick Access Toolbar, right-click the tool on the toolbar and then, on the shortcut menu, click Remove From Quick Access Toolbar.

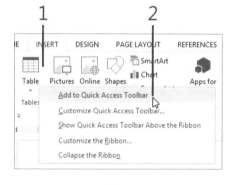

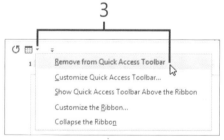

TIP You can click the drop-down arrow at the right end of the Quick Access Toolbar and select or clear the check mark next to any of the common commands to show or hide them on the toolbar. One of those commands is the Touch/Mouse Mode tool, which changes the spacing of the ribbon and toolbar buttons.

TRY THIS Right-click anywhere on the Quick Access Toolbar or on the ribbon and click Show Quick Access Toolbar Below The Ribbon. When the Quick Access Toolbar is below the ribbon, the item on the shortcut menu changes to Show Quick Access Toolbar Above The Ribbon.

Add other items to the Quick Access Toolbar

1 Right-click anywhere on the Quick Access Toolbar or on the ribbon. Then, on the shortcut menu that appears, click Customize Quick Access Toolbar.

2 In the Word Options dialog box, click the Choose Commands From list box and click a category of commands.

3 Click the name of a command that you want to add to the Quick Access Toolbar.

4 Click Add.

5 To change the order of the tools on the Quick Access Toolbar, click a command name in the list on the right and then click the up-arrow or down-arrow to move the command in the list.

6 If you added a macro to the Quick Access Toolbar, you can click Modify. Then, in the Modify Button dialog box, you can edit the display name that is shown in the button's tooltip and select an icon from the Symbol box. Tools other than macros cannot be modified.

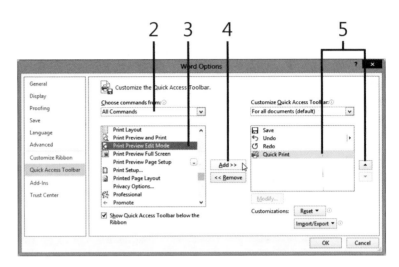

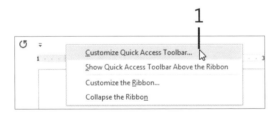

✓ TIP When the value in the Customize Quick Access Toolbar list box is *For all documents (default)*, your customizations will be stored in the Normal.dotm template. If you want to keep the customizations only in the current document, click the box and select the document's name. To store your customizations in a template other than Normal.dotm, use the Open command in the Backstage view to open that template and then select the template's name in the Customize Quick Access Toolbar list box.

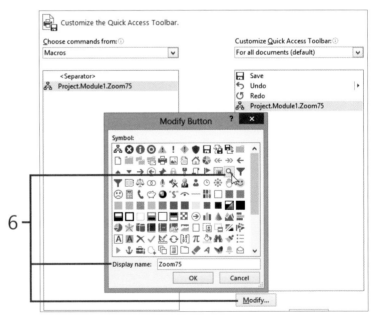

Creating a custom tab or group on the ribbon

As you work in Word 2013, you might find that the arrangement of tools on the ribbon tabs doesn't match your preferences. Instead of struggling to change your habits, you can change the ribbon. You can add new groups to the existing tabs, and you can create entirely new tabs, with just a few clicks.

You can't add or remove tools in the built-in groups. However, you can add a new custom group to an existing tab, and then put the tools of your choice into that group.

Insert a new custom tab

1 Right-click anywhere on the ribbon and then, on the shortcut menu that appears, click Customize The Ribbon.

2 In the Word Options dialog box, click New Tab to insert a new custom tab in the list box on the right. The new custom tab automatically contains one new custom group.

3 To change the order of the tabs, in the list box on the right, click a tab's name and then click the up-arrow or down-arrow to move the tab within the list.

4 Click OK.

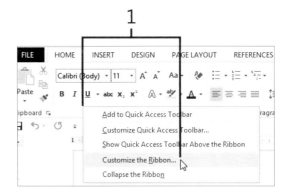

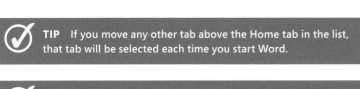

TIP If you move any other tab above the Home tab in the list, that tab will be selected each time you start Word.

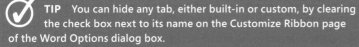

TIP You can hide any tab, either built-in or custom, by clearing the check box next to its name on the Customize Ribbon page of the Word Options dialog box.

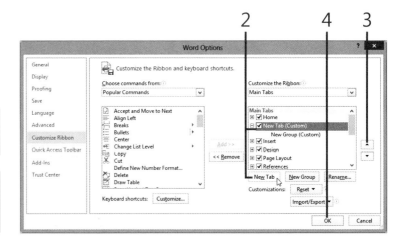

5 Click the new tab in the list, click the Rename button, and then, in the Rename dialog box, enter the name that you want the tab to display and click OK. Next, click the new group in the list, click the Rename button, and then, in the Rename dialog box, enter the name you want the group to display and click OK.

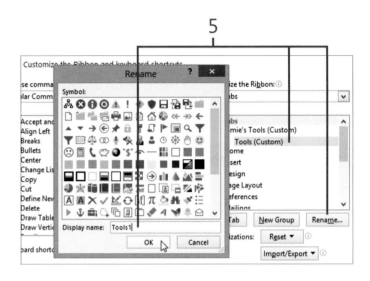

TRY THIS Click the Choose Commands From list box and select All Tabs. Click the plus sign next to a tab's name in the list box on the left and click the name of a built-in group. Then, click Add to copy the group to the tab that is selected in the list box on the right. For example, you could add a copy of the Envelopes And Labels group to the Insert tab.

Insert a new custom group

1 Right-click anywhere on the ribbon and then, on the shortcut menu that appears, click Customize The Ribbon.

2 In the Word Options dialog box, in the list box on the right, click the name of the tab to which you want to add a custom group.

3 Toward the bottom of the dialog box, click the New Group button.

4 Back in the list box, click the new group, click the Rename button, and then, in the Rename dialog box, enter the name that you want the group to display.

1

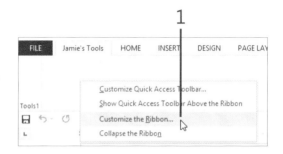

2

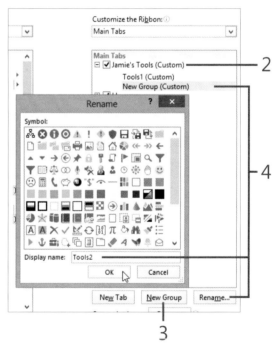

4

3

 TIP You can add custom groups to both built-in tabs and custom tabs.

Adding tools to a custom group

You can add any tools to a custom group that will make your work sessions more efficient. You can mix and match items from any of the built-in tabs, including the contextual tabs, and you can add commands that don't appear anywhere on the built-in tabs.

Add a tool to a group

1 Right-click anywhere on the ribbon and then, on the shortcut menu that appears, click Customize The Ribbon.

2 Click the Choose Commands From list box and select the category that contains the tool that you want to add. If you aren't sure which category contains the tool, click All Commands.

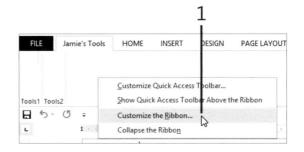

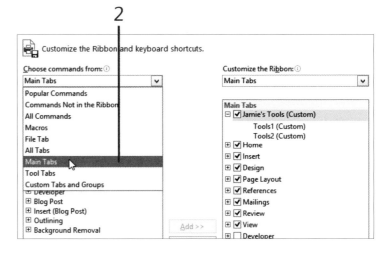

TIP The category named Tool Tabs encompasses the commands on the contextual tabs.

3 In the list box on the left, if the names of tabs appear, click the plus signs next to the tab and group that contain the tool you want to add, expanding the group so that the tool's name is visible.

4 Click the name of the tool.

5 In the list on the right, click the custom group to which you want to add the tool.

6 Click Add.

7 If you want to change the name or icon of the tool, you can click the Rename button. Then, you can edit the display name that is shown below the tool's button and select an icon from the Symbol box.

8 Click OK in each dialog box.

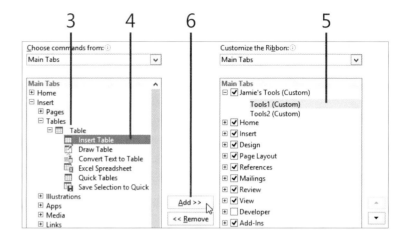

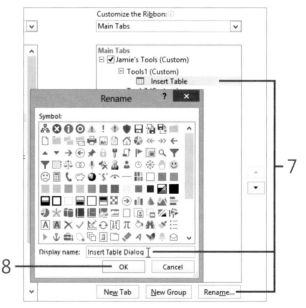

Setting general options

The General tab of the Word Options dialog box contains an assortment of configuration choices that you'll probably set shortly after you install Office 2013, and never change again.

Set options on the General tab

1 Click File to display the Backstage view and then click the Options tab. In the Word Options dialog box, in the left panel, click General.

2 Select all the check boxes in the User Interface Options section unless your computer isn't powerful enough to show live previews at full speed.

You might set the ScreenTip Style list box to Show Feature Descriptions In ScreenTips until you become familiar with most tools. Then, to avoid clutter on the screen, you can change it to Don't Show Feature Descriptions In ScreenTips.

3 Enter your user name and initials, if you didn't do so during installation of Office 2013. These values are used to identify your tracked changes and comments. If you use your copy of Word 2013 with multiple accounts, select the check box to use the same user name and initials with all accounts.

4 Select an Office Background (a design that appears in the right side of the title bar) and an Office Theme (the shading of the areas that surround the document surface). The values you choose affect all Office 2013 programs.

5 In the Start Up Options section, select the check boxes according to your preferences.

6 Click OK.

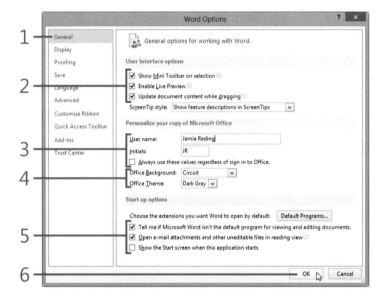

> **TIP** To see more information about an option that displays a circular icon with an *i* in the middle of it, hover the mouse pointer over that icon.

> **TIP** The Start screen is a part of the Backstage view that can appear when you start Word from its program icon. It includes a list of recently used documents and the template thumbnails from the New tab. If you clear the Show The Start Screen When This Application Starts check box, Word shows a new blank document immediately when it starts.

Controlling what is displayed and printed

The Display tab of the Word Options dialog box is where you can control some of the information that can be shown in and around your documents. It also contains some options that affect what appears when you print a document.

Show or hide information on screen and on paper

1 Click File to display the Backstage view and then click the Options tab. In the Word Options dialog box, in the left panel, click Display.

2 Select all the check boxes in the Page Display Options section.

3 In the Always Show These Formatting Marks On The Screen section, select the check boxes for Paragraph Marks and for Object Anchors. You can clear the other check boxes unless you want to see those marks at all times.

4 In the Printing Options section, select the check boxes for Print Drawings Created In Word, for Print Background Colors And Images, and for Update Fields Before Printing. You can clear the other check boxes, unless you want those items to print.

5 Click OK.

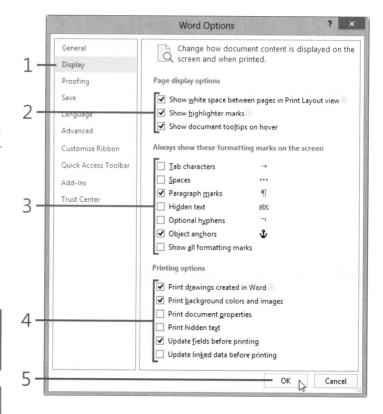

> ✓ **TIP** Changing the state of the Show All Formatting Marks check box is equivalent to clicking the Show/Hide ¶ button in the Paragraph group on the Home tab.

> ✓ **TIP** Changing the state of the Show White Spaces check box is equivalent to double-clicking the space between pages, as described in "Show or hide white space" on page 416. If you clear the Show Document Tooltips check box, tooltips won't appear when the mouse pointer hovers over hyperlinks, cross-references, or Table of Contents fields.

> 🔍 **SEE ALSO** For other options that affect what is displayed, see "Control screen and printing behavior" on page 439.

Setting spelling and grammar options

The Proofing page of the Word Options dialog box is where you can change the behavior of the spelling checker and the grammar checker. You can decide whether you want Word to notify you with red and blue squiggles whenever it detects a problem or whether you prefer to run a manual check at your convenience. You can determine which rules the grammar checker will apply, and you can add or remove custom dictionaries.

The Proofing page also contains the AutoCorrect Options button, which opens a separate dialog box. For a description of the AutoCorrect and AutoFormat options, see "Set AutoCorrect options" on page 73 and "Setting AutoFormat options" starting on page 76.

Change the behavior of the spelling checker

1   Click File to display the Backstage view and then click the Options tab. In the Word Options dialog box, in the left panel, click Proofing.

2   In the When Correcting Spelling In Microsoft Office Programs section, select the check boxes for at least the first four options. If you select the Suggest From Main Dictionary Only check box, the spelling checker won't use any custom dictionaries that you have configured.

3   Select or clear any of the check boxes in the When Correcting Spelling And Grammar In Word section according to your preferences.

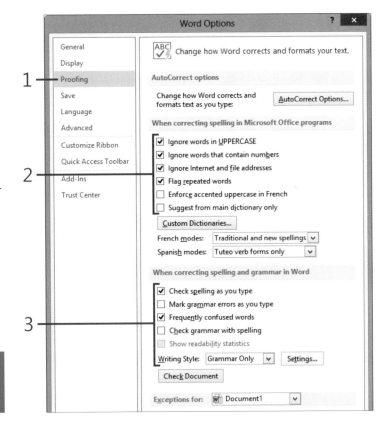

TIP   To make the Show Readability Statistics check box available, you must select the Check Grammar With Spelling check box.

4 If you want to choose which rules the grammar checker applies to your documents, click the Settings button and then, in the Grammar Settings dialog box, select or clear the check boxes.

5 Click OK.

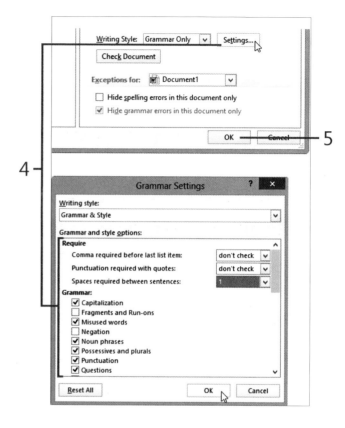

Add a custom dictionary

1 Click File to display the Backstage view and then click the Options tab. In the Word Options dialog box, in the left panel, click Proofing.

2 In the When Correcting Spelling In Microsoft Office Programs section, click Custom Dictionaries.

3 In the Custom Dictionaries dialog box, if you want to create a new custom dictionary, click New.

4 In the Create Custom Dictionary dialog box, enter a name for the dictionary file and click Save.

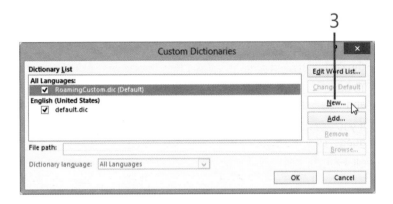

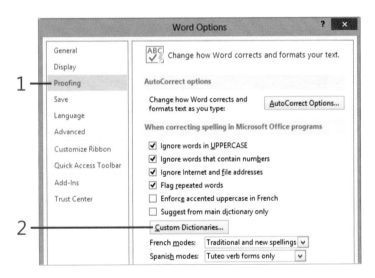

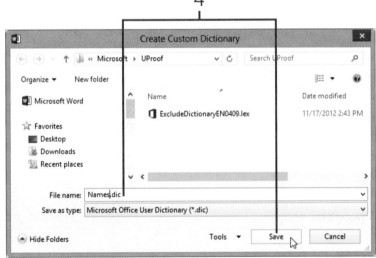

5 The new dictionary is initially in the All Languages section of the Custom Dictionaries dialog box. If you want this dictionary to be specific to one language, click the dictionary's name and then, in the Dictionary Language list box, select a language.

6 To add or remove words in a dictionary, click the dictionary's name and click Edit Word List.

7 If you want to change which dictionary is the default for a language, click the dictionary's name and click Change Default.

8 Click OK.

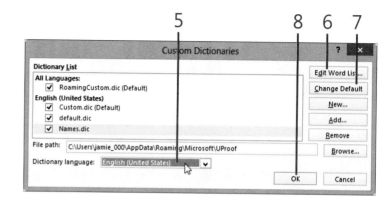

TIP The All Languages section and each of the individual languages have one dictionary that is designated as its default dictionary. When you right-click an unrecognized word in a document and click Add To Dictionary, that word is stored in the default dictionary for the proofing language applied to the word.

Changing the default file format for saving documents

When you save a document in Word 2013, you can choose one of the many available file formats by clicking the Save As Type list box in the Save As dialog box. If the format you choose most often is not Word Document (*.docx), you can choose another format as the default. For example, if many of the documents you write will be sent to users who might not have a version

of Word later than Word 2003, you can choose Word 97-2003 (*.doc) as the default format. Then, you'll need to change the Save As Type list box only when you want to save a document in some other file format.

Set a default file format

1 Click File to display the Backstage view and then click the Options tab. In the Word Options dialog box, in the left panel, click Save.

2 Click the Save Files In This Format list box and select the format you want to use as the default for saving new documents.

3 Click OK.

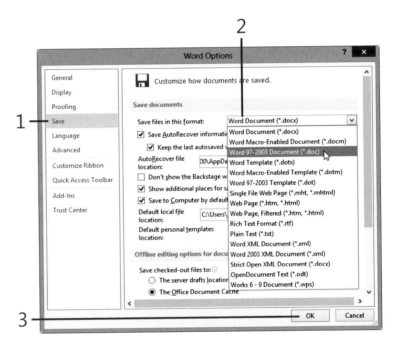

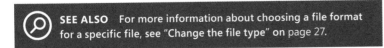
SEE ALSO For more information about choosing a file format for a specific file, see "Change the file type" on page 27.

Set default file locations

1 Click File to display the Backstage view and then click the Options tab. In the Word Options dialog box, in the left panel, click Save.

2 Click the AutoRecover File Location text box and enter the desired path, or click Browse to choose the folder.

3 Click the Default Local File Location text box and enter the desired path, or click Browse to choose the folder.

4 Click the Default Personal Templates Location text box and enter the desired path for the folder that opens when you create and save a new template.

5 Click OK.

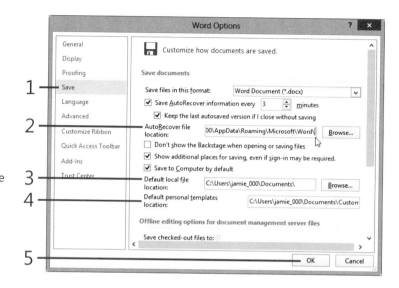

SEE ALSO For more information about AutoRecover options, see "Configure AutoRecover" on page 28. For more information about saving templates, see "Modify and save the template" on page 163.

TIP If you prefer to go directly to the Open and Save As dialog boxes instead of the Open or Save As tabs of the Backstage view, select the Don't Show The Backstage When Opening Or Saving Files check box.

TIP If you want the Save page of the Backstage view to default to Computer instead of your SkyDrive, select the Save To Computer By Default check box.

Working with advanced options

The Advanced page in the Word Options dialog box contains a large set of options that control the behavior of dozens of functions. It is divided into sections to help you navigate through the list.

Enable and disable editing features

1   Click File to display the Backstage view and then click the Options tab. In the Word Options dialog box, in the left panel, click Advanced.

2   In the Editing Options section and the Cut, Copy, And Paste section, select or clear the check boxes for the options according to your preferences. Set the more important or troublesome options as follows:

- Select the Typing Replaces Selected Text check box. If it's cleared, selected text is pushed aside when you type or paste.

- Select the Use Ctrl+Click To Follow Hyperlink check box. If it's cleared, it will be difficult to select a hyperlink in order to edit or format it.

- Clear the Enable Click And Type check box. If it's selected and you click in an area where there is no text, Word inserts empty paragraph marks and a tab character to create a paragraph at the place you clicked. You should avoid empty paragraph marks whenever possible. Instead, apply a style with a Space Above setting or insert a text box or floating table to achieve the desired text position.

- Select the Show AutoComplete Suggestions check box. Auto-Complete suggestions include those for dates and for AutoText entries that are stored in the Normal.dotm template.

- Set the list box for Insert/Paste Pictures As to the text wrapping that you use most often. When you need a text wrapping that's different from the default chosen in this option, click the Layout Options button next to the picture.

3   Click OK.

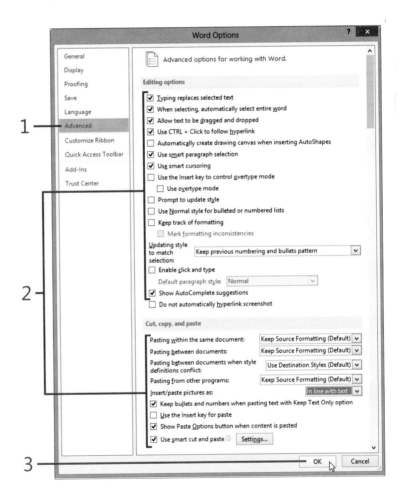

Change options related to pictures

1 Click File to display the Backstage view and then click the Options tab. In the Word Options dialog box, in the left panel, click Advanced.

2 In the Image Size And Quality section, select or clear the check boxes as follows:

- If you think you might need to restore cropped or modified images to their original state, clear the Discard Editing Data check box. Otherwise, selecting the check box will help to minimize the document file size.

- If you intend to print the document and need high-quality images, select the Do Not Compress Images In File check box. If you clear the check box and save the document, the images will be changed to the resolution shown in the Set Default Target Output box, which reduces the document file size but might degrade the image quality.

3 If your document contains charts, and you modify the formatting of the data points, select the Properties Follow Chart Data Point check mark.

4 In the Show Document Content section, select the check boxes for Show Background Colors And Images In Print Layout View and for Show Drawings And Text Boxes On Screen. Clear the Show Picture Placeholders check box.

5 Click OK.

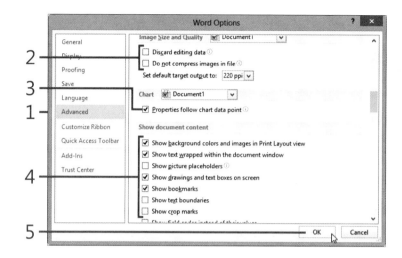

> **TIP** The option Show Background Colors And Images In Print Layout View affects only the screen, whereas the option on the Display page of the Word Options dialog box for Print Background Colors And Images affects only the printed copy.

Change options related to fields

1   Click File to display the Backstage view and then click the Options tab. In the Word Options dialog box, in the left panel, click Advanced.

2   In the Show Document Content section, clear the Show Field Codes Instead Of Their Values check box. Set the Field Shading list box according to your preference.

3   In the Print section, clear the Print Field Codes Instead Of Their Values check box.

4   Click OK.

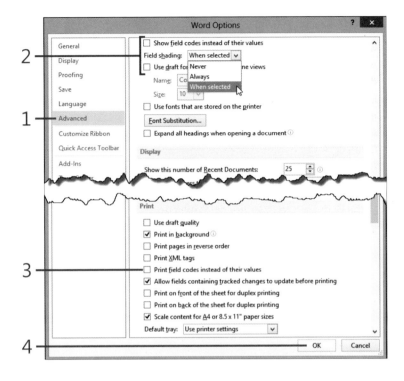

✓   **TIP**   If you create a complicated form that uses fields, it might be useful to select the Print Field Codes Instead Of Their Values check box and then print one copy of the document as a record of how the form was constructed. When printing is completed, clear the check box again.

Control screen and printing behavior

1 Click File to display the Backstage view and then click the Options tab. In the Word Options dialog box, in the left panel, click Advanced.

2 In the Show Document Content section, it's often useful to select the check boxes for Show Bookmarks and for Show Text Boundaries, at least temporarily. Select the Expand All Headings When Opening A Document check box.

3 In the Display section, set the first five options according to your preferences.

4 In the Print section, select or clear the check boxes as follows:

- Clear the Use Draft Quality check box unless you want to conserve ink or toner while printing a large draft document. It might be easier to set a similar option in the Printer Properties dialog box when preparing a specific print run.

- Select the Print In Background check box. This option makes it possible for you to get back to editing the document while printing is occurring. Otherwise, you have to wait until the document has been processed and passed to the Windows Spooler Service. Clearing the check box can be a useful step in troubleshooting printing problems.

- Select Print Pages In Reverse Order only if your printer delivers the pages so that you have to reorder them by hand. Most printers have a similar setting in the Printer Properties dialog box.

5 Click OK.

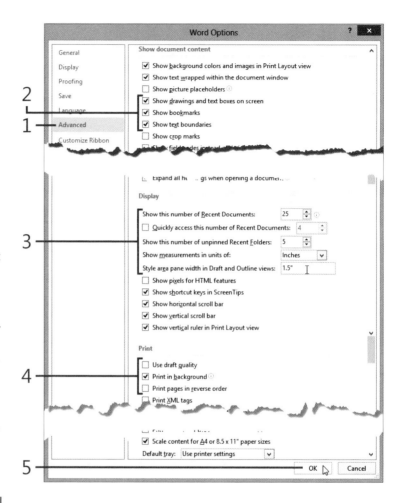

> **TIP** The option Quickly Access This Number Of Recent Documents places the names of recent documents at the bottom of the left panel on the Open page in the Backstage view. However, the recent documents also appear on the right side of the view, and you can pin frequently used documents to keep them at the top of the list.

Control opening and saving behavior

1 Click to display the Backstage view and then click the Options tab. In the Word Options dialog box, in the left panel, click Advanced.

2 In the Save section, select the check boxes for Prompt Before Saving Normal Template, Always Create Backup Copy, and Allow Background Saves.

3 In the General section, enter your address in the Mailing Address text box. This entry is used as the return address in the Envelopes And Labels dialog box.

4 Click OK.

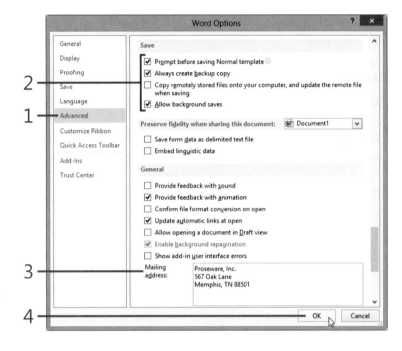

> ✓ **TIP** The prompt before saving the Normal Template can alert you when a change is about to be saved by mistake or when a macro has made an unexpected change.

> ✓ **TIP** The backup copy mentioned in the Always Create Backup Copy option is actually the most recently saved file (without any of the changes that have been made since then), renamed as Backup of *filename*.wbk (where *filename* is the actual name of the file) and stored in the same folder as the document. It might be useful if no other backup copy exists.

Set file locations

1 Click File to display the Backstage view and then click the Options tab. In the Word Options dialog box, in the left panel, click Advanced.

2 In the General section, click the File Locations button.

3 In the File Types list box, click one of the lines and click the Modify button.

4 If you want to change the folder that Word 2013 uses for the file type you selected, open the desired folder in the Modify Location dialog box and then click OK.

5 Repeat steps 3 and 4 for any other locations that you want to change and then click OK.

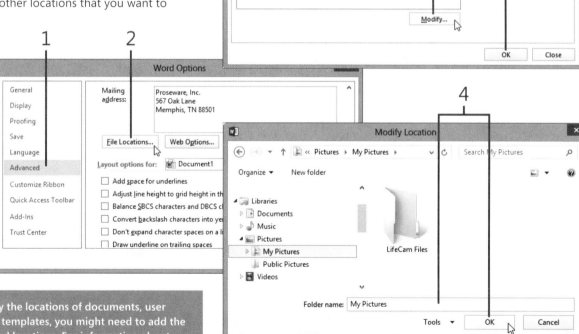

⚠️ **CAUTION** If you modify the locations of documents, user templates, or workgroup templates, you might need to add the new locations to the list of trusted locations. For information about trusted locations, see "Trust a file location" on page 387.

Managing styles

You can configure the Styles pane and the Quick Style gallery in Word 2013 to show just the set of styles that you prefer, in the order you want. The Manage Styles dialog box contains the tools you need to do this task.

For each style, you can specify whether its name is visible in the Styles pane or hidden when the Styles pane shows recommended styles. Also, for each style, you can specify a *priority number* that determines the order in which the style names are sorted. When the Styles pane is set to sort in the recommended order, the styles are displayed with the smallest priority numbers at the top of the list. The priority numbers also determine the order in which the styles appear in the Quick Style gallery.

Set the recommended order of styles

1 On the Home tab, in the Styles group, click the dialog box launcher to open the Styles pane (shortcut, Ctrl+Alt+Shift+S).

2 At the bottom of the Styles pane, click the Manage Styles button.

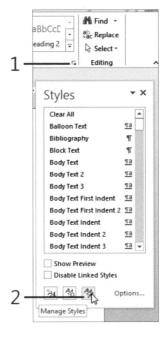

> **TIP** The Sort Order and Show Recommended Styles Only settings don't affect how styles are shown in the Styles pane. To change the display in the Styles pane, click the Options link at the bottom of the pane and change the settings in the Style Pane Options dialog box.

3 In the Manage Styles dialog box, click the Recommend tab.

4 Click the Sort Order list box and select the order in which you want the list of styles in the Manage Styles dialog box to be sorted. If you want the list box to contain only the recommended styles, select the check box for Show Recommended Styles Only.

5 Click the name of a style in the list box or hold the Ctrl key while clicking several names. Alternatively, click Select All or Select Built-In.

6 Click Move Up to subtract 1 from the priority number of each selected style, or click Move Down to add 1 to the priority number of each selected style. Alternatively, you can click Make Last to assign the last possible priority number to the selected styles, or you can click Assign Value and enter the priority number that you want.

7 Click one of the following to change which styles appear in the Styles pane when that pane is configured to display recommended styles:

- **Show** Always display the style

- **Hide Until Used** Display the style only when it has been applied to text in the document

- **Hide** Never display the style

8 To save your changes in the template on which the current document is based, click the option New Documents Based On This Template.

9 Click OK.

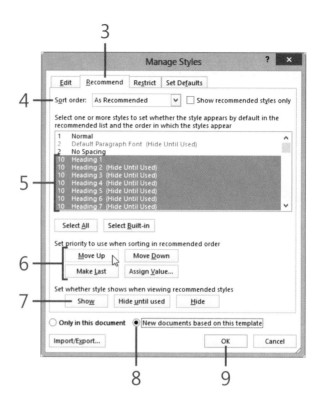

TIP The Restrict tab of the Manage Styles dialog box performs the same function as the Formatting Restrictions section of the Restrict Editing pane, described in "Limit formatting to selected styles" on page 397. The Manage Styles dialog box contains an option for New Documents Based On This Template, which makes it useful for defining restrictions for a template.

Recording macros

With Word 2013, you can automate series of actions that you perform frequently. For example, suppose that you receive a monthly report from which you need to copy a set of numbers and paste them into a table in a new document. You can record the entire sequence of actions as a macro and play it back each month with a single click.

Word's macros are written in Microsoft Visual Basic for Applications, which is a complete and powerful programming language. Although recorded macros are useful, macros created by knowledgeable programmers can greatly expand Word's capabilities by adding features and enhancing its interactions with the other Office programs.

Start and stop the macro recorder

1   On the View tab, in the Macros group, click the drop-down arrow in the bottom part of the Macros button, and then, on the menu that appears, click Record Macro. Alternatively, if the macro recording icon is displayed on the status bar, click that icon.

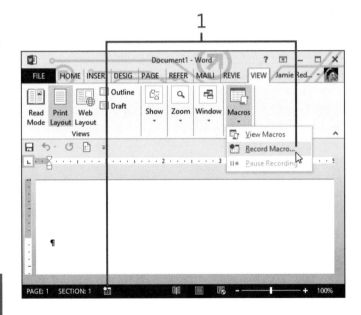

> **TIP**   During recording, the cursor changes to a drawing of an arrow attached to a cassette tape. The macro recording icon on the status bar, if it is visible, changes to a solid square.

> **TIP**   The macro recorder cannot record mouse movements in the document area, such as selecting text or dragging pictures. Only keystrokes—including text editing and formatting—and mouse clicks on command buttons are recorded.

2 In the Record Macro dialog box, in the Macro Name text box, enter a name that describes the purpose of the macro that you want to record.

You can use letters, numbers, and underscore characters in the name. Spaces and other characters are not allowed.

3 Click the Store Macro In list box and choose whether to store the macro in the Normal.dotm template, the current document, or the template on which the current document is based (if that is different from Normal.dotm).

4 If you want to store a description of the macro as a comment in the macro's code, type text in the Description text box.

5 If you want to create a button on the Quick Access Toolbar or to assign a keyboard shortcut to run the macro, click the corresponding button in the Assign Macro To section. Otherwise, click OK.

6 Perform all the actions that you want the macro to do, such as typing and formatting text, clicking commands, or inserting graphics or other objects.

7 On the View tab, in the Macros group, click the drop-down arrow in the bottom part of the Macros button, and then, on the menu that appears, click Stop Recording. Alternatively, if the macro recording icon is displayed on the status bar, click that icon.

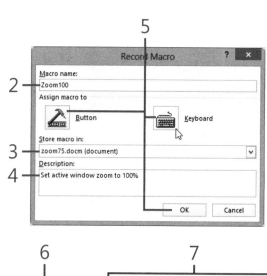

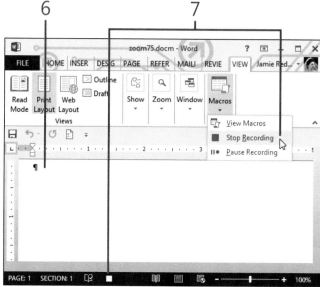

> ⚠️ **CAUTION** If you click one of the buttons in the Assign Macro To section, the macro recorder will start immediately after you close the Customize Quick Access Toolbar dialog box or the Customize Keyboard dialog box. Make all the necessary entries in the Record Macro dialog box before you click either button.

Play back a macro

1 On the View tab, in the Macros group, click the top part of the Macros button (shortcut, Alt+F8) to open the Macros dialog box.

2 In the Macro Name list box, select the name of the macro that you want to run.

3 Click the Run button.

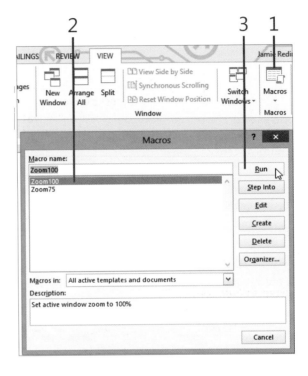

> **TIP** When you play back some recorded macros, they might not perform the actions that you executed during the recording session. This might be caused by running the macro when the document content differs from the document used to record the macro, or the macro recorder might have failed to record all of your actions. For information about modifying recorded macros to repair such problems, see *www.word.mvps.org/FAQs/MacrosVBA/ModifyRecordedMacro.htm*.

Index

Symbols

* (asterisk), wildcard searches, 57
@ (at sign), wildcard searches, 57
? (question mark), wildcard searches, 57

A

accepting document changes, 358
accounts, blog, 375
activating apps, 410
adding
    commands to the toolbar, 16
    comments, 350
    common misspellings to AutoCorrect, 72
    rows and columns, 187
    words to custom dictionaries, 69
addresses
    adding to envelopes, 316
    formatting on envelopes, 323
aligning
    floating objects, 282
    pictures and text, 283
alignment
    cells, 192
    guides, 282, 283
    paragraphs, 107
    tables, 189
anchor, for picture, 283
applying set styles, 177
apps
    from the Office Store, 406
    using in documents, 410
art borders, 153

artistic effects in pictures, 295
asterisk (*), wildcard searches, 57
at sign (@), wildcard searches, 57
attachments, email, 332
AutoCorrect
    adding common misspellings, 72
    using AutoCorrect entries as shortcuts, 74
AutoFormat
    manual AutoFormat, 78
    setting options for, 76
AutoRecover, 28
AutoText, 63

B

background for Office, 428
backgrounds, removing from pictures, 293
Backstage view
    about, 20
    printing, 34
    templates, 41
bibliographies, 264
Block Authors command, 373
blogging, 375
blue squiggles
    formatting, 69
    grammar, 68
bold, applying, 19
booklets, printing, 34
bookmarks
    mail merge, 343
    using, 211

borders
    applying around a page, 151
    dragging row and column borders, 188
    styles, 116
Borders and Shading dialog box, 118
breaks (line and page), 113
Building Block Gallery content control, 218
building blocks
    creating, 62
    inserting, 61
    organizing, 64
built-in footers, 138
built-in headers, 138
built-in page numbers, 138
built-in themes, 173
built-in watermarks, 237
bulleted list styles, 120
business cards, 326
business documents, 2

C

captions, inserting, 262
categories for blog posts, 377
cells
    alignment and direction, 192
    merging and splitting, 191
    setting tab stops in, 186
center-align shortcut, 19
changes
    accepting and rejecting document
        changes, 358
    tracking, 353
    viewing changes made by coauthors, 373

changing
    bulleted or numbered lists, 121
    character formatting, 103
    numbering values, 126
character formatting, changing, 103
character styles
    applying from the Styles gallery, 93
    defined, 90
characters
    allowed in path file names, 24
charts, building, 304
Chart tool, 272
Check Box content control, 218
citation style, 264
clipboard
    pasting contents, 19
    using, 45
closing documents, 19
cloud computing
    logging on to Office with Microsoft
        Account, 10
coauthors
    communicating with, 374
    working with, 372
collapsing headings, 59
color balance, pictures, 290
colors
    font, 104
    paragraph shading, 116
    themes, 173, 174
    transparent color in pictures, 296
columns
    adding and deleting, 187
    changing number of, 148
    multicolumn, 148
    resizing, 188
Combo Box content control, 218

commands
    adding and removing from the toolbar, 16
    assigning keyboard shortcuts to, 417
    shortcuts for undo and redo, 19
comments
    adding, 350
    replying to, 351
    showing and hiding, 352
comparing reviewed document versions, 359
configuration, AutoRecover, 28
content controls
    grouping for a form, 222
    inserting, 217
    inserting document property content
        controls, 223
contextual errors, 68
contextual tab, objects, 14
converting text to a table and back
        again, 184
copying
    Excel tables into Word, 183
    formatting to another location, 106
    items, 45
    selections, 19
    windows, 280
counting words, 82
cover pages, inserting, 154
cropping pictures, 286
cross-references, 216
Ctrl key (for discontinuous selection), 42
custom dictionaries, adding a word to, 69
custom templates, basing a new document
        on, 168
cutting
    items, 45
    selections, 19

D
data, changing in diagrams, 310
date fields
    formatting, 208
    inserting using shortcuts, 210
Date Picker content control, 218
defaults
    AutoCorrect, 72
    headers and footers, 228
    spacing in Normal style, 110
    views, 17
definitions, obtaining, 79
deleting rows and columns, 187
deselecting, 42
diagrams, SmartArt, 308
dialog boxes
    creating new styles with, 99
    modifying styles with, 95
dictionaries
    adding a word to custom dictionary, 69
    custom, 432
    definitions, 79
digital signatures
    adding, 403
    trusted locations and publishers, 387
discontinuous selection with Ctrl key, 42
display
    customizing, 414
    options, 429, 439
    resolution, 6
Document Inspector, 392
documents
    accepting and rejecting changes, 358
    adding comments to, 350
    adding envelopes to, 320
    apps, 410
    basing on a custom template, 168
    closing, 19

comparing reviewed versions, 359
digital signatures, 403
exporting to other file types, 26
getting information about, 23
headers, 228
linking to, 214
linking to locations within, 212
margins, 140
merging reviewed versions, 361
navigating, 50
opening, 19, 20, 29
passwords, 394
presenting online, 378
printing, 34
privacy settings, 391
properties, 223
read-only or final, 400
recovering, 28
saving, 19, 24
sending by email, 332
setting options for track changes, 356
sharing, 367, 370
showing and hiding
    comments, 352
    tracked changes, 354
starting
    a new document, 40
    Word with an existing document, 12
tracking changes, 353
Word Web App, 364
downloading
    proofing packages, 87
    templates, 159
dragging row and column borders, 188
drawing shapes, 298
Drop-Down List content control, 218

E

editing
    headers and footers, 139
    options, 436
    PDF documents, 22
    security, 397
    templates, 161
    in Word Web App, 368
effects
    themes, 174
    WordArt, 312
email, sending documents, 332
Encarta Dictionary, 79
endnotes
    adding, 241
    formatting, 242
end points in shapes, 303
entries (index), 255
envelopes
    address formatting, 323
    printing multiple copies, 320
    printing single envelopes, 316
    size and print options, 318
even and odd headers and footers, 171
examples
    creating new styles with, 98
    modifying styles with, 94
Excel
    copying table into Word, 183
    data source for mail merge, 337
expanding
    headings, 59
    objects, 31
exporting documents to other file types, 26
expressions, wildcard
    in find expressions, 56
    in replace expressions, 58
Extend Mode, F8 key, 43

F

F8 key (Extend Mode), 43
Field dialog box, 200
fields
    cross-reference fields, 216
    Field dialog box, 200
    formatting using switches, 205
    inserting from the keyboard, 202
    inserting page and date fields using
        shortcuts, 210
    mail merge, 341
    options, 438
    StyleRef fields, inserting, 236
    table of contents, 246
    toggling field codes and updating, 203
    XE fields, 255
figures, tables of, 262
File Block settings, 385
files
    default file format, 434
    default location, 435
    locations, 441
    path names, 24
    Protected View, 383
    SkyDrive, 370
    trusted locations, 387
file types, exporting documents to, 26
filling shapes, 300
final documents, 400
Find dialog, 52
finding
    templates, 159
    using wildcards, 56
Flickr, inserting pictures from, 277
folders, user templates, 157
fonts
    character formats, 94
    themes, 173, 174

footers
    extracting text for, 234
    inserting, 138
    odd and even, 171
    unlinking, 232
footnotes
    adding, 241
    formatting, 242
formatting
    changing character formatting, 103
    copying to another location, 106
    default file format, 434
    diagrams, 309
    envelope addresses, 323
    fields using switches, 205
    footnotes and endnotes, 242
    Format Painter, 106
    highlighting, 105
    replacing, 54
    revealing existing formatting styles, 132
    security, 397
    setting AutoFormat options, 76
    styles
        about, 90
        adding borders and shading, 116
        bulleted or numbered lists, 120
        changing character formatting, 103
        changing line and paragraph
            spacing, 110
        changing numbering values, 126
        changing paragraph alignment and
            indents, 107
        creating and modifying, 94
        kinds of, 90, 91
        line and page breaks, 113
        using multilevel numbered
            headings, 128
    table of contents, 249

text entries in the AutoCorrect list, 74
    WordArt, 313
forms, grouping content controls for, 222

G

galleries, selecting building blocks from, 61
General tab, 428
grammar
    correcting, 68
    options, 430
    setting proofing language, 86
    using the grammar pane, 70
grouping
    content controls for a form, 222
    shapes, 302
groups
    adding tools to, 426
    creating on the ribbon, 423

H

header rows, repeating, 193
headers
    changing, 228
    extracting text for, 234
    inserting, 138
    odd and even, 171
    portrait header on landscape pages, 145
    unlinking, 232
headings
    collapsing and expanding, 59
    list of, 50
    spanning across multiple columns, 149
    table of contents, 243
    using multilevel numbered headings, 128
Help system
    about, 36
    shortcut for, 19

hide and show codes, 203
hiding
    comments, 352
    ribbon, 15, 19
    tracked changes, 354
highlighting, 105
hyperlinks
    bookmarks, 211
    cross-references, 216
    inserting, 212
hyphenation
    automatic, 113
    preventing, 115

I

illustrations, about, 270
indents, 107
indexing
    about, 255
    multiple indexes, 258
Info page, 23
inserting
    art borders, 153
    bibliographies, 268
    blank pages at the end of a section, 136
    bookmarks, 211
    building blocks, 61
    built-in page numbers, 138
    charts, 304
    comments, 350
    content controls, 217
    cover pages, 154
    cross-references, 216
    diagrams, 308
    document property content controls, 223

fields
    from the keyboard, 202
    using the Field dialog box, 200
group content controls, 222
headers and footers, 138
hyperlinks, 212
indexes, 257
odd and even headers and footers, 171
online video, 278
page and date fields using shortcuts, 210
pictures, 284
    from online, 276
    from SkyDrive or Flickr, 277
    from your computer, 274
screenshots, 280
section breaks, 136
shapes, 298
StyleRef fields, 236
table captions, 262
table of contents, 245
table of tables or table of figures, 263
tables, 181
tab stops on the ruler, 180
text, 44
text boxes, 196
watermarks, 237
WordArt, 312
inspecting, documents, 392
installing, apps for Office, 408
Internet
    finding help on, 37
    security, 390
invitations, sending, 378
italics, applying, 19

J

justifying text, 107

K

keyboard
    customizing, 417
    inserting fields from, 202
    recording macros, 444
    selecting text, 43
    shortcuts
        about, 18
        assigning to a command, 417
        assigning to symbols, 420
keytips, using with keyboard shortcuts, 18

L

labels
    mailing, 326
    mail merge to, 335
landscape pages, portrait headers, 145
language
    setting proofing language, 86
    translations, 83
left-align, shortcut for, 19
line borders, 151
linebreaks, 113
line spacing, changing with styles, 110
linked styles, 90, 91
linking
    a chain of text boxes, 198
    to documents or webpages, 214
    to Excel worksheets, 183
    to locations within your document, 212
lists
    bulleted or numbered lists with styles, 120
    Drop-Down List content control, 218
    including unnumbered paragraphs in, 126
    multilevel list styles, 128
    sorting, 225

locations
    default file locations, 435
    files, 441
    trusted, 387
Lock Tracking, 356
logon, to Office with Microsoft Account, 10
lost documents, recovering, 28

M

macros, recording, 444
mailing labels, 326
mail merge
    adding fields, 341
    finishing, 346
    recipients, 337
    rules, 343
    starting, 334
main header, creating, 228
manual AutoFormat, 78
manual spell check, 70
margins
    choosing, 140
    mirror margins, 170
marking
    document for a table of contents, 252
    index entries, 255
    text for no proofing, 88
markup, viewing, 352, 354
merging
    cells, 191
    reviewed document versions, 361
Microsoft Accounts
    logging on to Office, 10
    Office Store apps, 406
    setting up, 6
    SkyDrive, 370
Microsoft Excel 2013, charts, 304

Microsoft Office
    logging on with Microsoft Account, 10
    Office clipboard, 48
Microsoft PowerPoint 2013, charts, 304
Microsoft SharePoint Workspace, 370
minimize, ribbon, 415
Mini Translator, 85
mirror margins, 170
modifying, styles, 94
mouse, selecting text, 42

N

names, preparing a list of for sorting, 225
Navigation pane
    about, 50
    organizing topics, 60
    search feature, 51
Normal.dotm, starting a new document, 40
Normal style
    default spacing, 110
    shortcut for applying, 19
Normal template, using, 156
numbers
    built-in page numbers, 138
    changing values, 126
    headings, using multilevel numbered
        headings, 128
    numbered lists, styles, 120
    Numbering Library, 125
numeric fields, formatting, 207
numeric picture switch, 205

O

objects
    contextual tab, 14
    expanding, 31
odd and even headers and footers, 171

Office Background, 428
Office clipboard, 48
Office.com, templates, 159
Office Store, apps, 406
OFFLINE, 36
online
    accounts, 32
    pictures, inserting, 276
    presentation of documents, 378
    video, inserting, 278
opening
    documents, 19, 20
    in Word Web App, 364
    options for, 440
    unsaved documents, 29
    Word Web App in Word, 369
options
    Advanced page, 436
    Display tab, 429
    General tab, 428
    spelling and grammar, 430
Organizer, Building Blocks, 64
orientation of pages, 144
outline of shapes, 300
Outline view
    about, 17
    organizing topics, 60
overtyping
    switching between insert and
        overtyping, 44
    text, 44

P

pages
    applying borders around, 151
    fields, inserting using shortcuts, 210
    inserting blank pages at the end of a
        section, 136

inserting cover pages, 154
numbers
    built-in, 138
    updating in the table of contents, 248
orientation of, 144
portrait headers on landscape pages, 145
positioning pictures on, 282
size of, 140
paragraphs
    breaks, 113
    changing alignment and indents, 107, 109
    changing spacing with styles, 110
    numbered lists, 126
    shortcuts for left-, right- and
        center-align, 19
    styles
        applying from Styles gallery, 92
        defined, 90
paragraph styles
    applying from the Styles gallery, 92
    defined, 90
passwords, documents, 394
pasting
    a table from Excel, 183
    clipboard contents, 19
    items, 46
    from Office clipboard, 48
    using Paste Special, 45, 46
PDF documents
    editing, 22
    saving, 26
    using, 11
pictures
    aligning, 283
    blog posts, 376
    changing the appearance of, 290
    content control, 218
    cropping, 286

inserting
from online, 276
from SkyDrive or Flickr, 277
from your computer, 274
options, 437
positioning on page, 282
recoloring, 292
removing backgrounds, 293
replacing, 288
resizing, 284
special effects, 293, 295
transparent color, 296
watermarks, 239
placeholders
bibliographies, 266
text, content controls, 219
Plain Text content control, 218
portrait headers, landscape pages, 145
positioning, pictures on the page, 282
posting
blog entries, 377
invitations, 378
presentations, 379
printing
business cards, 328
documents, 34
envelopes, 322
labels, 326, 331
multiple copies of an envelope, 320
options, 439
shortcut for, 19
single envelopes, 316
templates for two-sided printing, 170
Print Layout view
about, 10, 17
using, 17

proofing, changing the proofing language of
text, 86
properties
content controls, 220
documents, 23, 223
Protected View, 383
publishers, trusted, 387

Q

question mark (?), wildcard searches, 57
Quick Access Toolbar, 16
customizing, 421
Quick Style gallery, 442
Quick Tables building block gallery, 181

R

Reading view of Word Web App, 364
Read Mode
about, 10
optimization of, 17
using, 30
read-only documents, 400
recoloring, pictures, 292
recording, macros, 444
recovering, documents, 28
redo, shortcut for, 19
red squiggles, 68
rejecting, document changes, 358
removing
backgrounds from pictures, 293
commands from the toolbar, 16
unwanted parts of pictures, 286
repeating, header rows, 193
Repeating Section content control, 218
replacing
formatting, 54
pictures, 288
text, 54

using wildcards, 56
wildcards in replace expressions, 58
replying, to a comment, 351
resizing, rows and columns, 188
resolution, display, 6
restoring, using the Undo list, 49
revealing, existing formating, 132
reviewing
document versions and comparing, 359
merging reviewed document versions, 361
ribbon
about, 14
adding a ribbon item to the Quick Access
Toolbar, 421
buttons
adding borders and shading with, 116
formatting text with, 103
changing paragraph alignment and
indents, 107
hiding or showing, 19, 415
resizing pictures, 285
tabs and groups, 423
Rich Text content control, 218
right-align, shortcut for, 19
rotating
pictures, 284
text in table cells, 192
rows
adding and deleting, 187
repeating header rows, 193
resizing, 188
ruler
changing paragraph alignment and
indents, 107
tab stops, 180
rules, mail merge, 343

S

saving
  building blocks, 62
  documents, 19, 24
  options for, 440
  templates, 163
screen, customizing, 414
screenshots
  inserting, 280
  using, 271
ScreenTip Style list box, 428
search, Navigation Pane, 51
sections
  breaks, inserting, 136
  headers, 228
  inserting blank pages at the end of, 136
security
  digital signatures, 403
  Document Inspector, 392
  document passwords, 394
  editing and formatting, 397
  marking documents read-only or
    final, 400
  privacy settings, 390
  Trust Center, 382
  trusted locations and trusted
    publishers, 387
selecting
  objects behind text, 283
  text, 42
  text that has the same style, 102
selections
  copying, 19
  cutting, 19
shading
  Borders and Shading dialog box, 118
  styles, 116

shapes
  changing appearance of, 300
  cropping to, 287
  gallery, 271
  inserting, 298
SharePoint server
  opening documents from, 20
  SkyDrive, 370
sharing
  using SkyDrive, 370
  with Word Web App, 367
shortcuts
  assigning, 417
  inserting page and date fields using, 210
  obtaining synonyms, 80
  starting Word, 12
  using AutoCorrect entries as shortcuts, 74
show and hide codes, 203
Show/Hide button, revealing formatting, 132
showing
  comments, 352
  ribbon, 19
  tracked changes, 354
Simple Markup view
  showing and hiding comments, 352
  tracked changes, 10
SkyDrive
  inserting pictures from, 277
  opening documents from, 20
  sharing, 370
SmartArt, 272
  creating diagrams, 308
social networking, with SkyDrive, 371
sources, bibliographies, 265, 266
spacing, changing line and paragraph
  spacing, 110
special effects, pictures, 295

spelling
  adding common misspellings to
    AutoCorrect, 72
  correcting, 68
  manual spell check, 70
  marking text to ignore spelling, 71
  options, 430
  setting proofing language, 86
  using AutoCorrect entries as shortcuts, 74
splitting, cells, 191
squiggles underlining text, 68
starting the Word program, 12
status bar
  show or hide items, 414
  word count, 82
Style Inspector, 133
StyleRef fields
  headers and footers, 234
  inserting, 236
styles
  about, 90
  adding borders and shading, 116
  bulleted or numbered lists, 120
  changing
    character formatting, 103
    line and paragraph spacing, 110
    numbering values, 126
    paragraph alignment and indents, 107
  citations, 264
  creating and modifying, 94
  custom styles, 234
  envelope addresses, 324
  gallery
    applying character styles, 93
    applying paragraph styles, 92
  mail merge, 323
  options, 442
  revealing existing formatting, 132

security, 397
style sets, using, 173
Styles pane, 100
table of contents, 249
using multilevel numbered headings, 128
using table styles for uniform appearance, 194
switches, formatting fields using, 205
switching, views, 17
symbols, assigning keyboard shortcuts to, 420
synonyms, obtaining, 79

T

tab stops
    creating on the ribbon, 423
    inserting on the ruler, 180
    table cells, 186
table of contents
    generating, 243
    multiple table of contents, 252
    styles, 249
    updating, 248
tables
    adding and deleting rows and columns, 187
    alignment, 189
    cell alignment and direction, 192
    converting text to a table and back again, 184
    copying an Excel table into Word, 183
    inserting, 181
    merging and splitting cells, 191
    repeating header rows, 193
    resizing rows and columns, 188
    setting tab stops in table cells, 186
    tables of tables and tables of figures, 262
    text wrapping, 190

using table styles for uniform appearance, 194
table styles, 90, 91, 194
templates
    basing a new document on a custom template, 168
    blog posts, 375
    customizing, 161
    designing, 165
    finding and downloading, 159
    labels, 326
    modifying and saving, 163
    Normal template, 156
    saving changes, 64
    security, 397
    starting documents with, 40
    two-sided printing, 170
    user templates folder, 157
text
    adding to shapes, 302
    aligning, 283
    converting to a table and back again, 184
    direction in cells, 192
    entering text in a new blank document, 40
    extracting for headers and footers, 234
    fields, formatting, 209
    headers and footers, 228
    inserting and overtyping, 44
    marking to ignore spelling, 71, 88
    replacing, 54
    selecting, 42
    sorting selected list text, 226
    translations of selected text, 84
    watermarks, 238
text boxes
    as a shape object, 298
    inserting, 196
    linking a chain of text boxes, 198

text wrapping
    charts, 306
    pictures, 282
    tables, 190
themes
    using, 173
    using table styles for uniform appearance, 194
thesaurus, synonyms, 81
thumbnails, Navigation Pane, 50
toggling, field codes, 203
tools, adding to groups, 426
topics, organizing, 59
touchscreens, 7
tracking changes
    setting options for track changes, 356
    showing and hiding tracked changes, 354
    Simple Markup view, 10
    turning on track changes, 353
translations, 83
transparent color, pictures, 296
Trust Center, 382
trusted locations and trusted publishers, 387
two-sided printing, templates, 170

U

underline, applying, 19
undo
    shortcut for, 19
    using, 49
unlinking, headers and footers, 232
unsaved documents, recovering, 29
updating
    fields, 203
    table of contents, 248
user name and initials, 428
user templates folder, 157

V

versions
    comparing reviewed document
      versions, 359
    exporting to earlier Word file formats, 26
    merging reviewed document versions, 361
    previous versions of Word
      compatibility with Word 2012, 3, 21
    saving new versions of documents, 25
video, inserting online video, 278
viewing markup, 352, 354
views, switching, 17

W

watermarks, inserting, 237
Web Layout view, about, 17
webpages, linking to, 214
what's new, 10
white space, show or hide, 416
wildcards
    find and replace, 56
    replace expressions, 58
Windows 8, Word shortcut, 13
windows, copying, 280
WordArt, effects, 312
words, counting, 82
Word Web App, 11, 364
worksheets, links to Excel worksheets, 183
wrapping table text, 190

X

XPS (XML Paper Specification), support
    for, 26

About the author

Jay Freedman has worked as a textbook editor, technical writer, and software engineer. He has answered users' online questions about Microsoft Word for more than 15 years, and has been awarded as a Microsoft Most Valuable Professional every year since 2001.

What do you think of this book?

We want to hear from you!

To participate in a brief online survey, please visit:

microsoft.com/learning/booksurvey

Tell us how well this book meets your needs—what works effectively, and what we can do better. Your feedback will help us continually improve our books and learning resources for you.

Thank you in advance for your input!